COMPARATIVE PHILOLOGY
AND THE TEXT OF
THE OLD TESTAMENT

COMPARATIVE PHILOLOGY
AND THE TEXT OF
THE OLD TESTAMENT

BY

JAMES BARR

OXFORD
AT THE CLARENDON PRESS
1968

Oxford University Press, Ely House, London W. 1

GLASGOW NEW YORK TORONTO MELBOURNE WELLINGTON
CAPE TOWN SALISBURY IBADAN NAIROBI LUSAKA ADDIS ABABA
BOMBAY CALCUTTA MADRAS KARACHI LAHORE DACCA
KUALA LUMPUR HONG KONG TOKYO

PRINTED IN GREAT BRITAIN

PREFACE

THE research for this book has been done over a number of years, but the basic information was gathered in the excellent facilities of the Speer Library at Princeton Theological Seminary. I owe thanks to the staff of this library, and to Mr. Terence Fretheim, who as a graduate student and departmental assistant worked on the collection of data. My first attempt to present the problem in public was at the meeting of the Catholic Biblical Association of the United States in the summer of 1964. During 1965 my research was greatly assisted by the generosity of the John Simon Guggenheim Memorial Fund, which enabled me to travel in the Near East and study certain relevant linguistic problems. Among scholars who have assisted me with advice and criticism I am particularly indebted to the Revd. John A. Emerton, Reader in Semitic Philology at Oxford and now Regius Professor-elect of Hebrew at Cambridge. I owe much to the opinions of colleagues at Manchester, especially Mr. P. R. Weis, Dr. Meir Wallenstein, Dr. P. Wernberg-Møller, Dr. J. D. Latham, Dr. T. L. Fenton, and the late Mr. Arie Rubinstein. Mr. W. G. Lambert of Birmingham favoured me with an opinion on a point of Accadian. I have been greatly helped by the excellent secretarial assistance provided by Manchester University, in the persons of Mrs. Rowena Scaife and her assistants.

J. B.

The University
Manchester

CONTENTS

I

TEXTUAL TREATMENT AND
PHILOLOGICAL TREATMENT

THE Hebrew manuscript text of the Old Testament shows a high degree of uniformity. This characteristic constitutes a peculiarity of Old Testament textual criticism, and provides a considerable contrast with the situation found in many classical authors or in the New Testament.

This uniformity, indeed, should not be exaggerated. Large collections of variants were made by Kennicott and de Rossi. As all investigators have recognized, however, most of these variations are of a comparatively minor nature. While they undoubtedly merit attention and may form useful evidence for the history of the text, they are generally not such as to lead to, or provide the chief clues for, the resolution of the major difficulties which have been found in the reading of the Old Testament.

It is true that, with the discovery of the Qumran scrolls, access has at last been gained to a Hebrew text which shows in some places a substantial variation from the text previously known to us. This qualification also, however, is limited in its effect. Only a smallish portion of the Old Testament text has as yet been found at Qumran and in the associated discoveries. Apart from the book of Isaiah, the amount of text where real alternative controls have been made available is still small. Moreover, the Qumran texts, being unvocalized, do not provide exactly the same kind of information as the Massoretic text does. Again, many of the fragments, like the later manuscripts, vary very little from the Massoretic text; and it is widely agreed that the text-type which we call the Massoretic in a broad sense was already in existence in the Qumran period, or the latter part of it.

Therefore we are justified in reiterating that the Hebrew text of the Old Testament shows a striking uniformity in comparison with the text of some other types of ancient literature. For a very large proportion of the serious points of difficulty which the reader encounters, and where he might pause and wonder whether the

B

text is in order, the Hebrew manuscripts provide him with no series of substantial alternatives from which to select.

The reader of the Old Testament, indeed, is not dependent solely upon the Hebrew text of that literature. There are also the ancient translations, 'versions' as they are called in the technical convention, in Greek, Latin, Aramaic, and other languages. These translations were made at relatively early dates, in some cases before the Christian era. Thus the Massoretic manuscripts are antedated by several centuries by the origin of the versions, and even by some of the extant manuscripts of them. A version, once translated and in use, originated a line of transmission different from that of the Hebrew text. This difference does not always mean absolute separation; attempts were made to bring the Greek version into line with the Hebrew text as it was in the post-Christian era. But in general the versions enjoyed some considerable independence from the historical development of the Hebrew text. They have therefore always been highly valued in Old Testament studies, for they provide that choice between substantial alternatives which is so often lacking in the Hebrew text itself.

Nevertheless the scholar cannot use the ancient versions as if they were actual Hebrew texts. The translators may have misunderstood the original Hebrew, so that their version is not a good, but a very bad, guide to what the original text said. Finding a difficult passage in Hebrew, they may have just guessed at the sense. They may not have translated literally, but have given a rough paraphrase of what was said. They may be literal at one place but paraphrastic at another; and in some versions, like the LXX, the translating techniques differed from book to book, and even between sections of books.

For these and similar reasons, the very high importance which attaches to the ancient versions does not alter the fact that they are not Hebrew manuscripts. The effect they have upon our thinking is, in respect of directness and complexity, quite different from the effect of manuscript evidence in Hebrew. The attention we give to a reading in a version is usually proportionate to the degree of difficulty which we find in the Hebrew text itself. In general, therefore, the existence and the importance of the ancient versions do not really alter the peculiar aspect to which I have drawn attention, namely the relatively high uniformity of the Hebrew text in points of substantial effect on meaning.

This leads to an important distinction. The starting-point of a textual discussion is different where the texts are divergent and where the texts are uniform. If the text of a book varies, the normal starting-point for a textual discussion will be the fact that different readings exist. Given this fact, it obviously becomes important to discuss which reading may have been the original, or to classify the readings or assess them in some other way. This discussion has to take place because the texts vary; its necessity is not removed if several, or indeed if all, of the readings appear to lend a satisfactory sense within the context.

Where there is no substantial variation in the text, however, a textual discussion usually begins from a different starting-point, which we can name only vaguely as a 'difficulty'. The reader finds 'a difficulty' in the text which he is reading. He feels that it 'does not make sense'. The grammar is 'wrong', i.e. does not fit with usual patterns of usage. The use of words is anomalous. Or perhaps the text contradicts what is said elsewhere in the same literary work, so that it seems to 'spoil the effect' of the whole; or it may contradict something well known from altogether other sources. These are simple examples of what is a 'difficulty'.

Now so long as the reader is confident that the text is right, he has to resolve his difficulties through various linguistic and literary explanations: perhaps the grammar should be recognized as an anomaly; perhaps we have a case of poetic licence, an unusual meaning for a word, an ellipse of something usually expressed explicitly, a metaphor, or an allegory with a hidden meaning. Or, indeed, the reader may just give up, and decide that he does not know the meaning and cannot know it with the data he now possesses.

The more sophisticated reader, however, will know that texts may be wrongly transmitted; and, after trying the expedients mentioned above, or even before trying them, he may begin to suspect an error in the text. If there is no manuscript reading to support his conclusions, what he produces will be a conjectural emendation, which he will support by arguing that it makes much better sense.

Even a conjectural emendation, however, will point out some kind of relation between the reading conjectured and the text actually found. There may be some features in common; or it will be possible to show how the conjectured text, once misunderstood or miswritten, could naturally have led to the text actually found;

or some other such relation will be suggested. In other words, even conjectural emendations are seldom *purely* conjectural in nature; they normally take departure from, or have some logical link with, some aspect of the existing text.

I repeat, then, my generalization. With a non-uniform text we may find variant readings, and textual discussion begins from these variant readings, even if all of them 'make sense'. With a text of high uniformity, however, textual discussion will more frequently begin from the feeling that there is a 'difficulty'; the procedure will be more independent of the existence of variant readings, and conjectural emendation will take a larger place in the discussion.

This may be illustrated vividly from the difference between Old and New Testaments. In the latter it is quite common to find a variant which differs substantially in meaning and yet each of the readings 'makes sense'. It is quite uncommon to find that by the judgement of competent readers the passage does not 'make sense', to the degree that the extant texts must be despaired of and resort be made to a conjectural emendation found in none of them. Thus conjectural emendation has been used with considerable restraint in the New Testament. Metzger[1] tells us that

the apparatus of the twenty-fourth edition of Nestle's Greek New Testament includes from various sources about 200 conjectures, 90 of which are identified by the name of the scholar who first suggested them.

The average student, however, if we may hazard a guess, will find it hard to recall a single one of these conjectures, unless it be the addition at I Peter 3. 19 of the name 'Enoch' as the person who preached to the spirits in prison. Not only for the average student, but for the general current of New Testament scholarship, the procedure of conjecture is decidedly a marginal one, considerably more marginal than the recording of 200 examples would suggest. It is in fact extremely seldom that a scholar judges the text so desperately hopeless that a conjecture seems better than all the attested variants.

In the Old Testament our average experience is just the opposite. It is quite seldom that textual problems which are substantial in point of meaning arise because variant Hebrew readings exist. On the other hand it is quite normal experience to find that a reading is almost unanimously supported by Hebrew manuscripts but

---

[1] B. M. Metzger, *The Text of the New Testament*, p. 185.

that scholars turn to emendation to find a text which seems to be viable. The well-known example at Ps. 2. 11–12 reads materially alike in all Hebrew manuscripts:

עבדו את־יהוה ביראה וגילו ברעדה נשקו־בר . . .

This high unanimity of the manuscripts has been equalled, however, by the high degree to which scholars have preferred emendation. The text contains difficulties. If we take the AV and read:

'Serve the Lord with fear, and rejoice with trembling. Kiss the Son . . .'

the prima-facie difficulties are: (1) בר 'son' is not a Hebrew, but an Aramaic, word; (2) the sequence 'rejoice with trembling' seems to make poor sense. We need not here decide whether these considerations are final. Let us observe that in fact scholars have generally been inclined to favour such a rearrangement of the text as:

עבדו את־יהוה ביראה ברעדה נשקו ברגליו:

'Serve the Lord in fear; in trembling kiss his feet.'

This removes both difficulties. It implies that corruption took place by a fairly simple loss of sequence for a few letters, which explains the corruption fairly well. It involves no very drastic rewriting of letters in the text beyond this. Finally, it produces good conformity to known types of expression in Hebrew.

Thus the beginning of a textual discussion arises not primarily from the existence of variant readings but from the perception of difficulties in the Hebrew text. The solution just described does not even have direct support from any of the versions, though these differ from each other in their understanding of the text. The position is not materially changed, however, when active use is made of the versions.

Thus far I have tried to establish a characteristic of the situation where a relatively uniform text exists, and to show that this is so in the Old Testament. Now in this situation there are in principle two quite different and indeed opposed methods which can be used for the achievement of understanding. One I shall call textual and the other I shall call philological. The distinction is of central importance for this book.

(*i*) A textual treatment works on the hypothesis that an error has occurred in the *graphic* transmission. A scribe has misread some letters in the manuscript being copied, or has missed out some words and later added them in the wrong place, or inserted a marginal note as if it was part of the text. If variant readings exist, they probably imply such an error in the past; if there is no variation, but conjectural emendation is used, the same possibilities are implied as a hypothesis.

A philological treatment does not suggest a differing original text, corrupted by graphic error; rather, it elucidates the meaning of the existing text through the application of linguistic evidence hitherto ignored. It thus justifies the existence of the rare or anomalous words which had constituted the original difficulty, and by removing the difficulty it undercuts the foundations of the textual treatment. The principal evidence used in a philological treatment is the linguistic usage of the cognate languages, and with it the usage of other stages of the same language, Hebrew. For a difficult form in the existing text the scholar will consider words in cognate languages which might be related. This consideration, if successful, may suggest for the Hebrew form a meaning other than that which has normally been acknowledged, and this new-found meaning now removes the original difficulty.

Thus the philological treatment, compared with the textual, means a shift from problems of writing, of scripts, of scribes, to problems of meaning; it leads not to a text which has been copied wrongly, but to a meaning which has been obscured or interpreted wrongly. It does not rewrite the characters of the text but explains them in a new way.

The limited scope of the Old Testament provides a reason in favour of the philological approach. It is a comparatively small body of literature; there is little direct external evidence for the Hebrew of biblical times, and the post-biblical language has some striking differences. Not surprisingly the Old Testament contains many rare or unique expressions, which are difficult because they are unexampled elsewhere in Hebrew. Is it not then natural to turn to the large resources of the cognate languages, such as Arabic? These may suggest words which in their form could be cognate with a Hebrew form and which by their known meaning could suggest a suitable sense for it.

Isa. 44. 8 has the expression וְאַל־תִּרְהוּ. If the text is right, the verb is a *hapax legomenon*, so unexampled elsewhere that the dictionaries are uncertain what verb it is in the first place; some register it as יָרָה, others as רָהָה. Emendations have been suggested, such as that to תִּרְאוּ, from the familiar יָרֵא 'fear', and that to תִּרְהֲבוּ, which would mean 'be arrogant'. The Qumran reading תיראו, though almost identical with the former emendation, does not settle the matter, since it may have been caused by exactly the same motives which led modern scholars to suggest the emendation. The question remains: is there any reason to suppose that a form תִּרְהוּ may have existed?[1]

If there is suitable evidence in the cognate languages, then our form, though unique in the Bible, may yet in some sense be explained or justified. This is done in dictionaries which quote an Arabic verb *wariha*, said to mean 'be stupefied' or the like.[2] The argument tacitly runs as follows: if this word, known in Arabic, had a cognate in Hebrew, the latter would, in respect of form, come close to the form of the MT; moreover, in respect of meaning, the sense known for the Arabic word, or a sense relatable to it by a reasonably probable analogy, fits the contextual setting of the Hebrew word. This being so, the Hebrew text has been both justified and explained; an account has been given of the form of MT, and a meaning has been suggested which appears to fit the passage well. The resources for this solution are supplied by comparative philology.

Thus in principle the philological treatment, if right, cancels out textual treatment; the question is not one of exploring hypothetical scribal errors, but one of exploring the forms and meanings of words in cognate languages.

Having established the difference between the two types of treatment, one must go on to say that these are not distinct in the sense that one must consistently follow one and ignore the other. A competent worker must understand both, and, as we shall see, it is very common for practice to mingle the two.

At any one point, however, the distinctness between the two may be very marked. They move the scholar in exactly opposite directions. The textual approach leads towards the detection of a corruption in transmission and therefore, if the text is uniform,

[1] Cf. below, pp. 166, 188, 231 f.
[2] Freytag, iv. 459b; but does Freytag's entry really justify this sense?

towards a conjectural emendation, with or without support from the versions. The philological approach suggests the rightness of the text (for without it there is no basis for a search in the cognate languages) and leads on towards an exploration of resources, hitherto neglected, in the other Semitic languages. Formally speaking, the former should be registered in a critical apparatus to the text; the latter should mean a modification to the Hebrew lexicon. Thus, although the two methods are frequently mingled or their differences obscured in a number of ways, it is important to observe that at any one point they offer sharply distinct possibilities.

This is a reason for the writing of this book. For the textual criticism of the Old Testament adequate guidance already exists in the standard works of Würthwein and Roberts. But the whole weight of their work lies, and quite properly, on the textual kind of treatment, and the philological approach receives only the barest mention. Würthwein devotes about a page (pp. 78 f.) to it, mentioning one example (Hab. 3. 6 f.); he does not discuss the criteria or the ultimate implications of the method. The subject requires not only to be mentioned, but to be discussed in detail, with plentiful examples, and with consideration of the criteria by which it can be guided, of the further implications which it carries, and of the lines of new research which it appears to demand. In this book the existing studies of the textual approach will be complemented with a general survey of the philological approach and of the interaction between the two.

Modern textual criticism, even when it adopts an 'eclectic' policy in its decision about readings, does not work atomistically, but depends on a general survey of the history of the manuscript tradition and the modes by which alterations may occur. For philological treatments, however, such a general discussion has hitherto been lacking.

This is illustrated by the way in which the results of philological treatments have been made public. Very often this has been in the form of small and disparate notes, which are scattered throughout the technical journals and neglect to discuss the problem systematically. Even dictionaries and commentaries, which might be expected to gather together all that has been published in detailed notes, have frequently not done so in fact. Sometimes scholars proposing philological treatments seem to have paid little attention to the proposals of other scholars on the same passages.

If this breakdown in communication and discussion is a difficulty for the scholar, it is a very much more serious one for the student, who is much less able to judge for himself. He may be so much in awe of the linguistic erudition of suggestions that he hesitates to use his intellect critically upon them. This book is intended to provide him with the necessary critical equipment.

Moreover, the discrimination of students is often hindered rather than fostered by works devoted to the 'flood of light' (or some such cliché) shed upon the Old Testament by modern discovery. Such works often spend more time in admiring the advance of knowledge about the cognate languages than in examining the difficulties which attend the application of this knowledge. They give the impression that, so long as advance in the knowledge of Semitic languages is being made, one can somehow rest assured that the elucidation of Old Testament passages formerly obscure will follow. To suppose this, as we shall see, is to ignore some awkward problems.

The fact that many attempts at philological treatment are to be found only in scattered notes in the journals is one reason why this present work was undertaken in the first place. I found it necessary for my own information to gather these suggestions together; this I did simply by card-indexing. The mere existence of an index, however, was itself an invitation to survey the principles and problems involved. The juxtaposition of so many attempts could not fail to raise questions which might be missed so long as one looked at each suggestion individually.

For it should be observed that the number of philological treatments has become very large. The question I raise is not a marginal or an occasional one. In recent years interest in the philological approach has so expanded that a competence in it may possibly have become more important than the traditional training in the textual approach. The passages so treated number many hundreds, if not thousands, even if one discounts obviously incompetent or fantastic solutions. It is not uncommon for a scholar in a brief article to publish notes which claim to add to the Hebrew vocabulary a score of words not previously recognized. One article of 34 pages by Eitan has provided my index with over 40 suggested new words, most of them otherwise quite unrecognized, from the book of Isaiah alone.[1]

[1] The article is *HUCA* xii–xiii (1937–8) 55–88.

It remains for this introductory chapter to say something about the limitations which will be observed in this work.

Our subject is the application of philological means to elucidate Old Testament passages which would otherwise be regarded as obscure or corrupt. This book is not intended to be an introduction to comparative philology itself. Certain aspects of this discipline, however, call for special remark, and for this reason some discussion of Semitic comparative philology will be given. This discussion is not intended, however, to be a substitute for the actual study of comparative philology.

Again, this book will not discuss the problems involved in the wider study which might be called comparative literature. For example, there are relations between Babylonian and Hebrew creation stories. It is possible that this study of the larger literary complexes, their content, themes, and styles is the most fruitful way in which the Semitic background can be made to illustrate the Old Testament. Nevertheless this form of research will not be discussed here; we shall work not on the macrocosmic scale of the literary forms, but on the microcosmic scale of the lexical forms.

Moreover, within the study of lexical forms, there are a number of ways in which comparative data may be used. Sometimes comparative data may enrich with additional nuances our appreciation of a word the basic sense of which is already known. Examples of this, however, will not generally be discussed here. Again, sometimes a Hebrew word is quite familiar but comparative studies have been invoked in order to identify more exactly the referent to which the word is applied—for example, animal names like רְאֵם or נֶשֶׁר. This also will not be discussed in this book. In such cases, although an important service is rendered if the meaning of the word can be more closely identified, the word was not in the first place of such obscurity as to constitute for the reader a source of doubt about his text; he knows that רְאֵם is some sort of strong animal and נֶשֶׁר some kind of bird.

In general, then, this book concentrates mainly on the situation where the use of comparative study is most critical, because without it the reader would be likely to question his text. It does not attempt to give equal attention to all the various kinds of contribution that comparative philology can make.

Readers should observe that some of the words and meanings mentioned in this book have a somewhat hypothetical character.

This follows from the nature of the enterprise; we are discussing suggestions which have been put forward rather than facts which are certainly known. If I mention that an Arabic word with a certain meaning has been cited in the course of a scholarly suggestion, the reader should not conclude that I guarantee the accuracy of the information cited. I have not intentionally left unremarked, however, anything which seems to me to be misleading. Nor have I, except in special cases, used the asterisk which is conventional for hypothetical or reconstructed forms.

For my purpose it has not been particularly important to trace the scholar who first made a particular suggestion. Our question is of the logical status, rather than the historical priority, of philological treatments. I have not, therefore, made any great effort to discover the first author of a suggestion, especially since, as I have found, later workers often remained ignorant of earlier suggestions in any case. Conversely, a treatment cited may sometimes later have been abandoned by its author; but this makes no difference to its logical status. I have cited treatments, where possible, in modern sources of suitable form and accessibility.[1] I apologize in advance if I seem to have failed to give credit where it is due.

This book does not contain many philological treatments of my own suggestion. The positive need of the present time is not the production of larger numbers of such treatments, but the elucidation of the criteria by which they can be sifted and evaluated. The examples cited below are, I believe, a fair example of the contribution which philological study has made; but it may be more important that we use facts critically than that we store facts themselves, and more valuable that we should learn to appraise suggestions than that we should produce them. The thoughtful restudy of past scholarship is not criticism for the sake of criticism, but an attempt to elucidate the principles involved in the discovery of truth. In doing this, however, it is right that we express our gratitude and respect to those whose work is being used and restudied, and without whose pioneering zeal and daring the present evaluation could not have been attempted.

Various chapters of this book discuss different criteria, which

---

[1] Thus the idea that רבע at Num. 23. 10 means 'dust' (Index, nos. 294–5) can be found in a much earlier form in Jacob, *ZAW* xxii (1902) 111; but the circumstances of the modern treatments are lacking, even if the suggestion has the same result.

may be applicable to the various examples cited. For many examples I have not been able to give a final decision at the point where each is considered, because this would involve other criteria than the one at present under discussion and would thus immensely complicate the presentation. In order to avoid the impression that a decision is being evaded, however, I have sometimes offered a summary decision, even if I have not been able to state the grounds for it in full. In any case the logical structure of the argument does not lie in the rightness or wrongness of individual examples, each to be decided on its own merits, but in the elucidation of the criteria.

Earlier in this chapter attention was drawn to a difference between scholarship in the field of the Greek classics or of the New Testament and scholarship in the Old Testament field. To this another difference may be added. It is the relative prominence of languages other than the language in which the texts were written. The Old Testament is a relatively restricted amount of text for use as a sample for the language of the ancient Israelites. In classical or Hellenistic Greek the bulk of text available is very much greater. Interpretative discussion of specific points will usually appeal to evidence observable elsewhere in extant Greek literature; a scholar does not very often explain a word as one not elsewhere extant in Greek, the existence of which may, however, reasonably be postulated from a similar word in Sanskrit or Lithuanian or Gothic. Only on the margins of Greek textual scholarship are such explanations likely to occur, and the proportion of them is surely infinitesimal in relation to the whole. In Hebrew scholarship, however, such forms of explanation are quite normal. Probably no body of ancient literature has benefited (or suffered?) so much as the Old Testament from explanations based upon languages other than that in which it is written. The only exceptions are literatures which have had no form of continuous literary transmission from the ancient world into the modern, and which, being discovered only by modern archaeological research, have had to be deciphered anew wholly on the basis of comparative data. Ugaritic is the prime example. The decipherment and interpretation of the Ugaritic texts and others of the same kind are indeed a triumph of scholarship. But the growing emphasis on this kind of scholarship has affected our relationship to a language like Hebrew, in which we do have a transmission of meaning by tradition from the past to the present. The increasing prominence of *other* languages than Hebrew and the increasing dominance of *comparative* methods have had effects upon the study of the Old Testament which have not yet been fully investigated.

So far this subject has been considered with some generality. Only one or two examples have been given. Our next step will be to look in much greater detail at a number of examples, in order to consider the methods and the logic by which they operate, and to bring to light some of the questions which emerge from them.

II

SOME EXAMPLES IN GREATER DETAIL

THIS chapter will be devoted to the setting out of some examples of philological treatment of the Old Testament text. The examples have been chosen to illustrate the various kinds of problems which may arise and the various kinds of evidence which may be adduced. In these respects they form a representative cross-section of the suggestions which philological work has produced. Some of them are, in my opinion, very convincing, while some others are doubtful or improbable. At this stage, however, I have tried to hold back my own judgement, and simply to present the arguments implied in the treatment under review.

(1) כלם 'speak'

Judges 18. 7 has long been considered difficult. Five scouts of the Danites came to Laish. They found the people living quietly, with a sense of security; and then the text goes on:

$$\text{וְאֵין־מַכְלִים דָּבָר בָּאָרֶץ}$$

Moore translated 'there was no one to put them to shame (or, insult them) in anything'; but he pronounced this to be 'wholly irrelevant'.[1] Many scholars have emended the text to read:

$$\text{ואין מַחְסוֹר כָּל־דבר בארץ}$$

—a phrase the strength of which lies in the very similar locution a few verses later (18. 10). The meaning would then be: 'there was no lack of anything in the land'. Moore himself preferred to emend to מְכַלֵּא, giving the sense 'there is no one to restrain (us) from anything in the land'.

This discussion has thus far assumed for כלם the sense 'humiliate, insult, reproach' which is normal in Hebrew. If, however, the difficulty causes us to look for help in the cognate languages, we

---

[1] Moore, *Judges* (ICC), p. 392.

at once think of the very common Arabic verb *kallama* 'speak' and the noun *kalām* 'speech, word'.

This Arabic sense, when applied to the passage, gives what appears to be a good sense, 'no one uttering a word in the land'. This fits well with the quiet security of life at Laish. The removal of the difficulty thus abolishes the original ground for emendation. I do not know which scholar first proposed this interpretation; it is already known to Reider, who in 1954 uses the same evidence for another difficult passage.

The testimony of the ancient versions may be added. Moore stated baldly that 'the versions give no help'. But in Judges the LXX has two different versions. The B text has καταισχύνων, which confirms the MT מכלים by translating it with its usual sense 'make ashamed'. The A text, however, has καὶ μὴ δυναμένους λαλῆσαι ῥῆμα, and the λαλῆσαι 'to speak' appears at first sight to confirm the interpretation made from Arabic.[1] This is not argued, however, by Reider himself.

Reider applied this result to Mic. 2. 6. A prohibition, usually taken to mean 'do not preach', is followed by the words: לֹא יִסַּג כְּלִמּוֹת.

Reider not only finds here כלם 'speech'; he holds the entire phrase to be 'really an Arabism', corresponding to *nasaja l-kalām* 'he forged speech'. The sense is 'they shall not forge speeches', and is parallel to the earlier prohibition of preaching. Reider thus identifies also a verb נסג 'forge' in Hebrew. Previous scholarship had some considerable uncertainty about the meaning, and emendation has been tried.

We shall not decide whether Reider's suggestion is right; we note only some general characteristics of the method:

(a) The existence of a difficulty, with a previous resort to emendation.

(b) A dependence on the text, and, accordingly, a rejection of extensive emendation, as a starting-point for the philological treatment.

(c) A use of the ancient versions as a source which may show that a sense, now disclosed to us only through comparative philological methods, was already known in antiquity.

[1] Further examination, however, shows that the A text should not be interpreted in this way; it is not λαλῆσαι, but δυναμένους, that comes from מכלים. The form in the Hebrew, whether identical with MT or not, was taken as from יכל.

(2) טוֹב 'speech'

Anyone who knows any Hebrew knows the familiar word טוֹב 'good'. There are certain places where this word appears not to make very good sense. Hos. 14. 3 (EV 14. 2), a passage difficult also in other respects, seems to suggest that the repentant man should address God with the phrase קַח־טוֹב 'accept that which is good' (so RSV).

There seems to be something unsuitably condescending in the idea that repentant sinners should ask God to accept that which is good, and especially so in the teaching of Hosea. Moreover, the beginning of the same verse has the phrase קְחוּ עִמָּכֶם דְּבָרִים which would seem to address the repentant with the command 'take with you words' in their returning to the Lord.

It is thus no surprise that Gordis holds טוֹב here to mean 'speech'. He writes:

The biblical and rabbinic root דבב 'speak' (Cant. 7. 10), from which דִּבָּה 'report, evil report' (Gen. 37. 2, Num. 14. 37) is derived (cf. Accadian *dabābu* 'speak, charge'), apparently has a cognate טבב, טוֹב. Thus דבה is rendered as טִיבָא by Onqelos and as *ṭbḥwn* by Peshitta in Gen. 37. 2, and by טָאבָא by the Targum on Prov. 10. 18.

For these reasons, along with other aspects of the context into which we shall not enter, Gordis concludes that the meaning is 'accept our speech'. This interpretation appears to overcome certain of the difficulties of the context; and it furnishes a close parallelism between טוֹב and דברים, both of which mean 'speech' or 'words'.

Not only this; for Gordis goes on to cite other places, e.g. Neh. 6. 19:

גַּם טוֹבֹתָיו הָיוּ אֹמְרִים לְפָנַי וּדְבָרַי הָיוּ מוֹצִיאִים לוֹ :

He renders:

'His utterances they were wont to repeat to me, and my words they would bring to him.'

Here טוֹבֹתָיו is represented in the LXX (II Esdras 16. 19) by τοὺς λόγους αὐτοῦ: καὶ τοὺς λόγους αὐτοῦ ἦσαν λέγοντες πρός με καὶ λόγους μου ἦσαν ἐκφέροντες αὐτῷ.

Previous scholars (Geiger, Löw) had proposed an emendation to טָבָתָיו; this is favoured by Rudolph in his commentary,[1] and is

---

[1] *Esra und Nehemia* (1949), p. 137.

incorporated in KB.[1] It implies that the Aramaic word טבא or
טבה 'rumour, report' existed in the Hebrew of Nehemiah, and
this in itself is of course possible. The proposal of Gordis,
however, seems to suggest that the meaning 'speech' is present (a)
without any emendation and (b) without reliance on an Aramaic
loan-word in Hebrew.

A third case quoted by Gordis is Ps. 39. 3 (EV 39. 2), where
נֶאֱלַמְתִּי דוּמִיָּה הֶחֱשֵׁיתִי מִטּוֹב might then mean[2] 'I was dumb
and silent; I refrained from speech'.

To the three points of general interest raised by our previous
example the following further characteristics may now be added:

(d) Multiple exemplification of the same solution, once it has
first been found. There exists not only one case where טוב
'speech' is identified, but several; and these several, after the first
identification is made, appear to support and confirm one another.
Gordis indeed identified yet other instances at Job 34. 4 and
Hos. 3. 5, but he was less sure about them.

(e) The identification of a new homonym. In addition to the
familiar טוב 'good' there is another טוב 'speech' which is homonymous with it. This is not all, for wide recognition has been given
to yet another טוב 'perfume', related to the Arabic ṭīb with that
sense and identified at Isa. 39. 2, Jer. 6. 20, Cant. 7. 10 in senses
like 'the perfumed oil' (הַשֶּׁמֶן הַטּוֹב), 'the perfume stalks' (קְנֵה
הַטּוֹב), and 'the perfumed wine' (יֵין הַטּוֹב). Another טוב is a
place-name. For yet other homonyms which have been suggested,
see Index, nos. 147–8.

(3) יקח 'be impudent, shameless'

The story of Korah's rebellion begins in Num. 16. 1 with the
words וַיִּקַּח קֹרַח.

If this was the familiar verb לקח 'take' one would expect an
object. AV, following Ibn Ezra, supplies one, namely 'men', and
RSV follows this also. The 1962 Jewish American version translates 'betook himself', but in a note says the word is literally 'took'
and adds 'Heb. obscure'. Gray in the ICC (1912, p. 189) did not
try to make anything of it, being sure that part of the text had

---

[1] KB, p. 346a.
[2] There is a complication in Gordis's own treatment, for he takes דומיה also
to mean 'speech', though it is usually taken to mean 'silence'; I leave this aside
at present for simplicity's sake.

become entirely lost. *BH*³ offers us as a probable emendation the too facile וַיָּקָם 'and he rose up'.

The early versions present a varied picture. LXX says ἐλάλησε 'he spoke'; the Targum and Syriac say 'he split off, broke away' or the like (Tg. אתפליג); the Vulgate, which begins *ecce autem Core* followed by a list of Korah's assistants, has no verb at all (could *ecce* be from a transliteration?).

Eitan argued that this is a Hebrew word corresponding to Arabic *waqiḥa* 'be impudent, shameless'.

This might be supported by a piece of evidence which Eitan himself did not use, but which *BH*³ cites: the Hexaplaric note that ὁ ʽΕβραῖος has ὑπερηφανεύθη 'was insolent'.[1]

Two things should be noted about this interpretation which have not been exactly exemplified in the previous instances.

(*a*) If this explanation is correct, it is probable that the similarity of the (presumably uncommon) verb יקה to certain comparable parts of the familiar verb לקח 'take' was itself an actual cause which contributed to the loss of understanding of the meaning, and even of the existence, of the former. The familiar verb over-shadowed the less familiar until the philological treatment restored it to our sight. This in turn depends on the accident that the verb יקה is found only in the imperfect; a perfect form, which in the 1st singular would be *יָקַחְתִּי, would be much less liable to con-fusion with לקח.

(*b*) In many cases of this type the new identification will probably require a change of vocalization. Thus for a verb cognate with Arabic *waqiḥa* we would expect an imperfect qal form like יִיקַח or יִקַּח, without the daghesh which we find in the MT of Num. 16. 1 and which gives a form identical with that from לקח 'take'. Or, conversely, the mistaking of the form for one from the verb לקח 'take' carried with it the wrong pointing of the form.

Neither of these arguments is actually made by Eitan at this point; but they are very frequently implied in philological treat-ments.

Eitan finds another case of this verb at Job 15. 12, where the MT reads:

מַה־יִּקָּחֲךָ לִבֶּךָ וּמַה־יִּרְזְמוּן עֵינֶיךָ׃

---

[1] Cf. again below, p. 271.

Eitan's translation is:

'What does your heart dare, and why are your eyes lifted up?'

Concerning this interpretation some brief remarks may be made.
(a) One reason why a scholar may favour such an explanation as this is a doubt whether לקח 'take' can really be used, in the words of BDB, 'figuratively, of passion carrying one away'.[1]
(b) Though Eitan does not say so at this point, one might wonder whether his interpretation is not supported by the LXX:

τί ἐτόλμησεν ἡ καρδία σου,
ἢ τί ἐπήνεγκαν οἱ ὀφθαλμοί σου;

(c) Eitan uses a philological treatment for the first verb in the verse, but for the second he resorts to textual treatment by conjectural emendation, reading יְרוּמוּן from the verb רוּם 'be high'.

(4) ידע not meaning 'know'

The standard dictionaries GB, BDB, and KB recognize and register only one verb ידע, the familiar and extremely frequent one meaning 'know'. There are, however, a number of places where this does not appear to give satisfactory sense, and in some of these scholars have proposed other meanings supported by the existence of words in the cognate languages, especially Arabic. This example is of special interest because of two things: (a) the familiarity of the word ידע 'know', and (b) the large number of passages in which philological treatments have claimed to identify a different word. Several different such identifications, indeed, have been proposed.

(1) the most important of these is a sense 'make quiet, make submissive, subject to discipline or humiliation', which has been explored particularly by Winton Thomas. The clearest case perhaps is at Judges 8. 16, where Gideon obtained certain instruments and

וַיֹּדַע בָּהֶם אֵת אַנְשֵׁי סֻכּוֹת:

If the verb is related to Arabic wadaʻa, this might mean:

'With them (i.e. the instruments) he made submissive the men of Succoth.'

[1] BDB, p. 542b; the sense 'carry away' appears also in translations like AV RSV, and in the work of scholars like Dhorme (*Job*, p. 193).

The sense 'teach', represented by AV and RSV, is drawn of course from the usual יָדַע 'know'; but it is doubtful if this is used without an object stating what is 'known'. The favourite treatment has been by emendation to וַיָּדָשׁ, giving the sense 'and he threshed with them the men of Succoth'. The philological treatment removes both the anomaly and the need for emendation.

If this line of thought is sound, one can extend it to quite a large number of other passages. At some of these, while an understanding based on the sense 'know' for ידע may be more plausible than at Judges 8. 16, nevertheless the success of the other approach at this text may encourage one to try again the sense which was helpful there.

At Isa. 53. 3 the well-known יְדוּעַ חֹלִי may mean not 'acquainted with grief' or 'knowing sickness' (these do not, in the opinion of some scholars, explain why the passive participle is used; and this is the only case where the passive participle of ידע is used in such a context; Deut. 1. 13, 15 are not parallel). The meaning may be rather 'humbled, afflicted by sickness', which fits well with the context as a whole. At 53. 11, similarly, it may be argued that בדעתו means 'by his chastisement'; it is by his chastisement, rather than by his knowledge, that the servant brings justification to others.

At Qoh. 10. 20 we have the word מַדָּע. AV and RSV take this as 'thought', implying that the word belongs with the verb ידע 'know'.[1] The text reads:

גם במדעך מלך אל תקלל　ובחדרי משכבך אל תקלל עשיר:

Here the parallelism with the clear words 'in your bedchamber' has suggested that מדע means not 'thought' but 'repose' or even 'bedroom'. This sense, or one like it, indeed, can be reached by another route, which is tried by KB; it attaches it to ידע in its sexual sense. KB itself is uncertain of this explanation, which indeed seems unlikely; but it is sure that 'bedroom' rather than 'thought' is in general the right kind of meaning.[2] It prefers, however, the emendation בְּמַצָּעֶךָ, with the word מַצָּע 'couch' (from the root יצע), found also in Isa. 28. 20. The suggestion of the

---

[1] So, for example, BDB, p. 396a.

[2] KB, p. 497b. Semantically, it is one thing to say that 'know' can have a sexual sense, and quite another to suggest that a word like 'knowing-place' would thereupon be coined for a bedroom!

sense 'repose' related to Arabic *wada‘a* makes it unnecessary either
to emend or to appeal to the sexual sense of ידע 'know'.
Another example: Prov. 14. 33 reads in the MT

בְּלֵב נָבוֹן תָּנוּחַ חָכְמָה וּבְקֶרֶב כְּסִילִים תִּוָּדֵעַ׃

The RSV, to avoid declaring that wisdom is known in the heart
of fools, took the fairly drastic step of supplying the word 'not',
which, as its note ingenuously says, is lacking in the Hebrew, though
present in the Greek and Syriac. It is possible that this difficulty
would be overcome if the sense were as in the other examples just
cited, giving a rendering like:

> 'Wisdom rests in an understanding mind
> but in the heart of fools it is laid low.'

If this interpretation is right, it means that the 'not' of the Greek
and Syriac versions is not evidence of a superior text; rather, it
suggests that these ancient authorities were going through exactly
the same condition of puzzlement, resolved by guessing, which the
RSV translators suffered many centuries later.

These are by no means the only cases where senses such as 'make
submissive', 'humiliate' and 'chastise' have been found for ידע.
Without setting out the evidence, I shall mention also Prov. 10. 9,
Jer. 31. 19, Job. 20. 20, and the variant תדע at Sir. 7. 20.

Another impressive case is Judges 16. 9, where it is said of
Samson ולא נודע כחו. 'So his strength was not known', renders
the AV. But this is difficult, for his strength *was* known very well.
RSV gets over this by saying that 'the secret of' his strength was
not known. But one can also follow Winton Thomas and consider
'and his strength was not brought to submission', 'laid low',
which fits the context well.[1]

Thus perhaps about ten cases can be quoted where this treatment of passages with the verb ידע has been suggested.

(2) At least one prominent example has been treated as meaning
'take leave of, dismiss'. This is I Sam. 21. 3 (EV 21. 2):

וְאֶת־הַנְּעָרִים יוֹדַעְתִּי אֶל־מְקוֹם פְּלֹנִי אַלְמוֹנִי׃

If the verb were from ידע 'know', this would have to be

---

[1] In the end, however, my own opinion would be that the sense 'know' is more
probable, for the repeated asking of Delilah implies that *knowing* or *understanding*
the source or nature of Samson's strength is the real issue at stake; cf. the
repeated question במה כחך גדול (vv. 5, 6, 15, cf. 10, 13).

explained as 'I have caused to know, i.e. I have directed'; so BDB, but BDB itself prefers to emend to a form from the verb יעד 'appoint', and so also *BH³*. If it is from ידע 'know', this is the only case found of this theme, the poel.

Eitan says that this exceptional form has in Arabic a parallel which is quite usual; it is *wāda'a* (III theme, corresponding to Hebrew poel), and means 'say farewell, take leave of, abandon, leave'. Thus the sense of the sentence is 'I sent (or, dismissed) the young men to the place of so and so.' The verb ידע in its usual sense 'know' appears in the very same verse.

(3) Several cases have been interpreted as meaning 'care for, keep in mind'. Of these the most prominent is Exod. 2. 25:

$$\text{וירא אלהים את־בני ישראל וַיֵּדַע אלהים:}$$

It is peculiar to find ידע 'know' used absolutely without object in a context like this, and this has led to emendation. If the sense could be 'and God cared', evidenced from Arabic *wadi'a* in this sense, the difficulty might be removed. Winton Thomas argued that this is the meaning of *y-d-'* in ESA theophoric names, giving a sense such as 'cared for by Il' and the like.

If this is sound, then there is a case for seeing the same meaning in an example like Job 9. 21:

$$\text{תם־אני לא־אֵדַע נפשי אמאס חיי:}$$

which might be rendered:

'I am blameless; I care not for myself; I reject my own life.'

This example illustrates how the result achieved by a philological treatment may be so close to one achieved through the traditional understanding that only a narrow partition separates them; for 'I do not know about myself' (from traditional Hebrew ידע 'know') is not really distant semantically from 'I care not for myself'.

(4) At Hos. 7. 9 it has just been said that Ephraim is a cake, and then it is twice added והוא לא ידע. The more traditional understanding of this would be 'and he did not know'; but Hirschberg argues that the sense is rather 'and he did not wrap it up', quoting *wada'a* meaning to wrap up an article so as to preserve it. This interpretation, being connected with a very special metaphor, not surprisingly does not recur again, so far as I know.

(5) It has also been argued that, while the normal Hebrew form meaning 'sweat' is יֹזֻע, a dialect form יֹדֻע also exists. This explanation was tried by Noeldeke in some of the passages mentioned above, most prominently in Isa. 53. 11, where בדעתו is taken to give the sense 'by his sweat he shall justify', and also in Prov. 10. 9, 32, 14. 33. Dahood more recently has followed this line further.

Such, then, are some suggestions relating to the verb יֹדֻע. Still others could be added. For instance, the word מֹדֻע at Qoh. 10. 20, which we above saw interpreted as 'bedroom', has also been interpreted by Dahood as 'messenger'. More than one of these suggestions may be right, but they cannot all be right.

Thus once again we observe how homonyms are multiplied in many kinds of philological treatment. Even if we regard cases (4) and (5) as improbable, as I should be inclined to do, we have suggestions for three meanings which are, or seem to be, substantially distinct from the familiar sense 'know'.

It will doubtless occur to the reader at this point that these meanings might, if all the facts were known, be seen to be related in some way.[1] The implications of this will be fully discussed later.[2] For the present we observe only that the discovery of new meanings has, for our purpose, practically the same effect whether or not later research classifies the words as cases of homonymy ('different words' which are formally identical) or polysemy (different senses of 'the same word'). The distinction does not make great difference to the problems now in hand.

The complexity of the situation raised by multiple philological treatments is not lessened when we consider the next case, the suggestion of the existence of a verb דעה 'call'.

(5) דעה 'call'

The standard dictionaries do not recognize a verb דֻעֻה, though they do take it into account for the personal name אלדֻעֻה. Philological treatments, however, have identified such a verb, corresponding to the familiar Arabic da'ā 'call'. The Hebrew meaning is usually stated rather as 'ask, desire'.

If a verb דעה exists in Hebrew, it is not homonymous with

---

[1] e.g. M. D. Goldman, ABR iii (1953) 46, who argues that Hebrew יֹדֻע 'know' originally had the sense 'put' or 'lay down', and that the Israelite thus knew what was 'laid down' before him—a dubious enough argument, indeed.

[2] See below, pp. 142 ff.

יָדַע 'know' in the entirety of its paradigm; but in part of that paradigm, and especially so if we consider the vocalization to be uncertain, there will be a homonymy, or at least a homography within the unvocalized writing system. If the existence of a דעה 'ask, desire' has been concealed from us until now, this has been because its forms were classified as forms of יָדַע and its sense correspondingly confused with the sense 'know'.

The most impressive instance is Prov. 24. 14:

כֵּן דְּעֵה חָכְמָה לְנַפְשֶׁךָ׃

By the philological treatment, this might mean:

'So ask for (seek) wisdom for thy soul'

—a sense which fits well with the following clause 'if you find it'.

The sense 'know' is not very easy, and one may doubt whether RSV is successful with its 'Know that wisdom is such to your soul'. The difficulty of understanding the word as יָדַע 'know' is indicated by the crop of suggested emendations. The vocalization of the MT is anomalous for the imperative of יָדַע; hence the suggestion to vocalize as דְּעֶה and to suppose that some words have fallen out.[1]

Other passages may be mentioned briefly. Hos. 6. 3

וְנֵדְעָה נִרְדְּפָה לָדַעַת אֶת־יהוה

might mean

'let us desire, and pursue, the knowledge of God';

and Prov. 29. 7

יֹדֵעַ צַדִּיק דִּין דַּלִּים רָשָׁע לֹא־יָבִין דָּעַת

might mean:

'the righteous knows the right of the poor
the wicked does not understand (his) suit (claim)'.

These examples would then include in the same verse both the word דעה and the familiar יָדַע 'know'.

At Prov. 10. 32:

שִׂפְתֵי צַדִּיק יְדַעוּן רָצוֹן

one might understand as:

'the lips of the righteous desire (call for) what is acceptable',

perhaps vocalizing the verb as יְדַעוּן.

---

[1] The anomalous form is discussed by GK § 48 l; see Gemser, *Sprüche*, p. 89.

In addition there have been suggestions of a sense 'pull down, destroy' for דעה, cognate with Arabic *da'ā* III 'destroy' (of a wall). (Index, no. 98.)

In examples of this kind it is suggested that a word or words, knowable to us from the cognate languages, existed in biblical Hebrew, but became obscured, so that such traces as were left were interpreted as forms from the paradigms of other words. The next example illustrates a very different situation. The form is quite distinctive from any other known Hebrew word. Its very rarity has caused it to be taken as a corruption of some kind, until comparative philology succeeded in showing that there was reason to believe in the existence in Hebrew of the form found, and with a meaning which fits the text.

(6) להקה 'body of elders'

At I Sam. 19. 20 Saul sent messengers to apprehend David, and they found, as MT has it,

אֶת־לַהֲקַת הַנְּבִיאִים נִבְּאִים

with Samuel at their head. What is this word להקה? BDB pronounced it dubious. It has generally been held that the reference is to a 'band' or 'company', which fits the fact that many prophets of this time lived and worked in groups; so for example AV with its 'company', and RSV likewise. The question would then be: how did this sense come to be represented by this word?

There are two obvious ways. Firstly, it could be taken as an historical linguistic metathesis of the familiar stem קהל, in which case the text may be right but a very peculiar dialect feature is postulated, with vocalization also peculiarly altered. This approach is, rather doubtfully, favoured by BDB (p. 530a). Secondly, it could be a textual error. The original text was קְהִלַּת, and by some strange accident, which had nothing to do with dialects or phonology, this familiar word was changed by the scribes in the course of *written* transmission into the totally unfamiliar (and indeed nonsensical) להקת. This process is implied by those who emend to קהלת, as *BH*[3] advises.[1]

But a stem *l-h-q* is familiar to anyone with some knowledge of Ethiopic; it is known especially in the word *ləhiq* 'old man, elder'

---

[1] Cf. below, pp. 231 f., 267 n., 270 f.

and a solution along these lines has been propounded not only by
Driver (1928), Winton Thomas (1941), and Ullendorff (1956), but
even some centuries earlier by Ludolf in his dictionary of Ethiopic,
cited recently by Ullendorff. If this interpretation is right, the
word is probably a collective of feminine form and means something like 'group of elders' among the prophets (*senatus prophe-
tarum*, said Ludolf); and the word, though a *hapax legomenon* in
Hebrew, seems to be deserving of acceptance.

(7) בְּצִקְלֹן 'fresh vegetables'

II Kings 4. 42 relates that a certain man brought Elisha a variety
of presents, including כַּרְמֶל בְּצִקְלֹנוֹ. The word כרמל occurs
elsewhere, and most scholars take it to refer to ripe corn or produce.
The following בְּ has often, not unnaturally, been taken to be the
preposition 'in', and this has left a strange word צִקְלֹן (?) to be
interpreted as 'garment' or 'wallet' (BDB), 'sack' (RSV), or 'husk'
(AV). The reading בְּקִלְעָתוֹ, a fairly drastic emendation based on
the Arabic word *qala'a*, said to mean 'wallet' or 'bread-bag', is
preferred by BDB (p. 862b) and KB (p. 841b); this suggestion is
traced to Lagarde.

A Ugaritic text, however, shows Danel praying for the chance to
see *bṣql* growing in his dry land, and the word is repeated several
times.[1] Driver translates 'green corn'; he attributes the identification to Cassuto. If this text may be taken as guidance, and the suggestion seems a very probable one, we may assume that the letter
בְּ of the biblical text is not the preposition 'in', but rather part of
a Hebrew word, pointed perhaps בְּצִקְלֹון in the absolute state,
meaning 'fresh vegetables' or 'green plants' or, perhaps most likely,
in view of the termination /-on/ which is lacking in the Ugaritic
word, 'garden' or 'plot' where such plants are grown.

Thus the discovery of a text in a hitherto unknown language
serves in a remarkable way to sustain the reading of a Hebrew text
which had long been taken to be obscure or corrupt.

(8) נַשָּׁר 'herald'

The beginning of Hos. 8. 1 reads:

אֶל־חִכְּךָ שֹׁפָר כַּנֶּשֶׁר עַל־בֵּית יהוה

---

[1] The text is Aqhat I ii 13 ff.; Driver, *CML*, pp. 60, 164; Gordon, *UH*, p. 180,
lines 62 ff.

This extremely difficult passage has begotten numerous emendations and some artificial explanations. Taken literally as it stands, the text would seem to mean:

> 'To your palate the trumpet, like the eagle upon the house of the Lord . . .'

We may think that 'palate' here must mean gums or lips, so BDB, p. 335a; we may think that the bird is not an eagle but a vulture, though it is not clear what difference this will make to the present problem. AV supplied the words 'he shall come' before 'like an eagle', which makes good sense except that the words 'he shall come' are just not there. RSV says:

> 'Set the trumpet to your lips,
> for a vulture is over the house of the Lord';

and this is a fairly simple emendation, i.e. to read כִּי 'for' instead of the preposition כְּ 'like'. *BH*[3] doubtfully considers an emendation which would eliminate the difficult bird; it reads נֹצֵר, which would mean 'watchman over the house of the Lord' and would be addressed to the trumpet-blower.

A possible philological treatment has been proposed by Tur-Sinai. On the basis of an Arabic *naššār* meaning 'herald', who is thus the one who blows the trumpet, he reads a Hebrew נֹשֵׂר or נַשָּׂר (the former would be the more normal correspondence, if the word was of direct descent from proto-Semitic in both languages, but Tur-Sinai seems to prefer the latter). The passage would then mean:

> 'Set the trumpet to thy mouth, as a herald . . .'

This gives good sense, with no emendation except for the punctuation.

Tur-Sinai tries the same solution on another passage, Job 39. 25. In the description of a battle-scene, the war-horse hears something which in MT is:

$$\text{רַעַם שָׂרִים וּתְרוּעָה}$$

perhaps 'the thunder of officers and the war-cry'.

Finding this phrase puzzling, he reads it as

$$\text{רֵעַ נַשָּׂרִים וּתְרוּעָה}$$

'the noise and shouting of the heralds'.

In this case, however, an emendation of the consonantal text is required; moreover, it is doubtful whether the original difficulty was very great, or whether the new solution is very good. This may be another instance of a solution which, proposed with some reason for a really desperate text, goes on to generate similar solutions for passages for which a better explanation was already in existence.

(9) אדם 'pleasant, delightful'

קוּר 'dig, bore'

The reader will by now have realized that, if philological treatments are numerous, there may be a good number of words in the Old Testament of which he previously did not know. The consequent sense of surprise or dismay may be savoured by studying a more complex example, involving several words in a brief text.

At Prov. 12. 27 MT reads:

וְהוֹן־אָדָם יָקָר חָרוּץ

AV renders: 'but the substance of a diligent man is precious'.

This might indeed be the right sense; but it fails to indicate one essential point, namely that this sense cannot be obtained from the text with the word order as it now is. The usual treatment is to transpose two of the words, which can give us:

והון יקר אדם חרוץ

'A valuable treasure is a man who is diligent' (Gemser, p. 60).

Or, with a different transposition:

והון אדם חרוץ יקר

'The wealth of the diligent man is much' (Driver).

Or, with transposition plus the preposition ל:

והון יקר לאדם חרוץ

'The diligent man will get precious wealth' (BH³, and so RSV also).

A treatment, proposed by Eitan, is both textual and philological. He reads יָקָר as יָקוּר. This change of vocalization makes the form into part of the verb קוּר 'dig, bore', found at Isa. 37. 25 and more familiar from the noun מָקוֹר 'spring, source'. He then takes the word אָדָם to be not the familiar word for 'man', but an adjective meaning 'delightful', following a sense known from Ethiopic. Thus the phrase הוֹן אָדָם is equivalent to the אוֹצָר נֶחְמָד of Prov. 21. 20, and the sense of our verse is:

'The diligent (man) digs out a delightful treasure.'

The effect of this on the reader is considerable. He knows indeed that the sentence as it stands has its difficulties. But in his uncertainty there seems to be some firm ground in the two very familiar Hebrew words אדם 'man' and יקר 'precious'. Both of these certainties are now removed. Of four words in the sentence, two mean something quite other than what would at first occur to the Hebrew reader; and in one of these two the meaning now suggested is not evidenced from within Hebrew at all.

It is indeed possible to argue that a connexion between the senses 'man', 'red', and 'pleasurable' did exist in the historical development of the Semitic languages;[1] or one can point to places where that which is אָדֹם 'red' is in fact delightful or is so regarded. It is another thing to say that anything of this is the actual meaning of אָדָם in Hebrew.

(10) זמר 'protect' and עזי 'warrior'

Exod. 15. 2, MT עָזִּי וְזִמְרָת יָהּ, is familiar in English as 'the Lord is my strength and my song'. Each of the two nouns, however, has been interpreted otherwise. The sense of זמר, it has been argued, is not 'sing' but 'protect' (cognate with Arabic *ḍamara*, and much used in theophoric names in ESA). Arabic words cognate with 'make music' have the first consonant /z/, not /ḍ/. Meanwhile עזי is interpreted as related to Arabic *ġāzī* 'warrior', *ġazā* 'go forth to war'. The total sense is then:

'Warrior and protector is Yah.'

Thus in a short phrase of three words (one of which occurs only thrice in the Bible elsewhere), two are given novel interpretations. On the other hand, the words are not such familiar ones as אדם and יקר, and the archaic style of the poem may lead the reader to expect unusual words.

[1] For example, Ullendorff in *VT* vi (1956) 191 f.

In favour of this interpretation the LXX may be quoted: βοηθὸς
καὶ σκεπαστής 'a helper and a shelterer'. Neither the Targum
(תוקפי ותושבחתי דחילא יוי) nor the Vulgate (*fortitudo mea
et laus mea Dominus*) support the LXX in this at Exod. 15. 2, while
it itself renders the same Hebrew at Isa. 12. 2 as ἡ δόξα μου καὶ ἡ
αἴνεσίς μου and at Ps. 118 (117). 14 as ἰσχύς μου καὶ ὕμνησίς μου,
following the sense 'make music, praise'.

Yet other philological treatments have been proposed. KB, also
alleging support in ESA, holds that זמרה means 'strength', cf.
the phrase זמרת הארץ of Gen. 43. 11, which might mean 'the
strength, i.e. the best products, of the earth'. If עזי were taken as
from עז 'strength', this would give a good parallelism. Rabin, on
the other hand, associates עזי with Arabic '*azā*' 'patience, con-
solation', and holds that a Hebrew cognate is found in the personal
names יעזיהו and יעזיאל.

(11) A grammatical example

The examples cited up to now have been mainly lexical in
character. It is by the new identification of a lexical item that
cognate languages have been used to clear up a difficulty in meaning. Problems of grammar, however, can be dealt with in the same
way, and sometimes the two are interlinked.

Semitic verbs may in some forms indicate gender. In normal
Hebrew, however, this is not so in the 3rd plural of the perfect
tense, where the form קָטְלוּ is used for both masculine and feminine.
In classical Ethiopic, however, there is a distinction here, with the
vowel /u/ used for the masculine and /a/ for the feminine. There is
reason to believe that this is the older Semitic state. Now consider
these three passages:

1. I Sam. 4. 15: וְעֵינָיו קָמָה

'his eyes had grown dim'
(*BH*[3] emends to קָמוּ, with the Oriental *Qere*).

2. Neh. 13. 10: מְנָיוֹת הַלְוִיִּם לֹא נִתָּנָה

'the gifts of the Levites had not been given'
(*BH*[3] emends analogously to נִתָּנוּ).

3. Gen. 49. 22: בָּנוֹת צָעֲדָה עֲלֵי־שׁוּר

perhaps 'daughters (i.e. branches) run up over the wall'

(*BH*[3] emends; Skinner, *Genesis*, p. 530, says the discord of number is harsh, in spite of GK § 145k, which tried to argue for a feminine singular verb with plural subject; Skinner himself thought the passage defied explanation altogether.)

Clearly, if it can be maintained that this is an isolated survival of the distinctive feminine termination in /a/ for the 3rd plural (which appears, incidentally, in certain readings in the Aramaic sections of the Old Testament), then the need for emendation is removed. This possibility is discussed in GK § 145k and § 44m but rejected; Brockelmann in his *Grundriss* stated that the distinctive feminine in this part of the verb had completely disappeared in Hebrew.[1] But in his recent work on syntax he takes the contrary view, citing two of our three passages explicitly, and saying that though the ending was no longer recognized by the Massoretes it was preserved by them because they understood it as a singular.[2]

It is evident that the choice between a textual and a philological treatment may be present in grammatical matters of this kind just as it may be present in matters of vocabulary.

(12) 'Enclitic *mem*'

This is another grammatical example. The Ugaritic poems contain a number of examples of /m/ added after a word; there is no certainty what the vocalization might be. This phenomenon has been called 'enclitic', which seems to mean little more than that it is written at the end of a word and as part of it, not having the word-divider between. There has been some discussion whether the enclitic means anything, i.e. whether its presence or absence makes any difference, and if so what kind of difference. Into this I shall not enter, except to say that philological treatments which have identified an enclitic *mem* in Hebrew appear for the most part to have treated it as if it had no distinct meaning. It may be added briefly that there are in a number of Semitic languages particles which appear at the end of words and include /m/; of these perhaps the most noticeable is the final *ma* of Accadian, which is fully discussed in the grammars of that language.

Now, if such a phenomenon was present in ancient Hebrew, and if it later ceased to be recognized or understood, it would not be

---

[1] *Grundriss*, § 262g, p. 575.
[2] *Hebräische Syntax* (1956), § 50a, p. 50.

surprising if it had left traces which to later scholars would constitute a difficulty, leading not improbably to emendation to remove
the unwanted *mem*s. Philological treatment, by exposing the *mem*s
for what they are, would remove the difficulty.

An example where this has been tried is Ps. 29. 6:

וַיַּרְקִידֵם כְּמוֹ־עֵגֶל לְבָנוֹן
וְשִׂרְיֹן כְּמוֹ בֶן־רְאֵמִים:

This text, by the traditional grammar, should mean:

'And he made them dance like the calf of Lebanon,
and (made) Sirion (dance) like the young wild ox.'

The difficulty is that one would expect Lebanon and Sirion to be
parallel, and the two animals to be parallel, so that the text would
be rather like this:

'And he made Lebanon to skip like a calf,
and Sirion (to skip) like the young wild ox.'

This happy result can be produced in more than one way. One
possibility is emendation; one can follow the suggestion of *BH*[3] and
emend the verb to וַיַּרְקֵד, thus simply removing the *mem* which
here, with its vowels, forms the suffix /em/ and gives the verb an
object 'them'; once this is removed, Lebanon becomes the object.

Alternatively, one can explain it as the enclitic *mem*. Since this
had slight or no effect on the meaning, it implies that the verb had
no object suffix and has the same syntactic function as if it were
וירקד without /m/. Thus the philological explanation has the same
effect as the emendation but involves no change of text.

The question also depends on the location of the caesura. The
division of the verse as it is cited above follows that printed in *BH*[3].
But the Massoretic division, marked with the *athnach*, fell before
the word 'Lebanon', so that the sense is:

'And he made them skip like the calf,
Lebanon and Sirion like the young wild ox.'

This is the division followed, for example, by AV. This division
makes sense of the *mem*, which is here the object suffix of the verb,
and this object 'them' balances with the other object 'Lebanon and
'Sirion' in the other half-verse. On the other hand it makes the first
half-verse much shorter than the second and thus appears to spoil
the parallelism in that way. In any case it is of interest to note how

the emergence of a difficulty in the eyes of scholars is related to a loss of confidence in the Massoretic accentuation.

The example which has just been described was one of the first where the existence of enclitic *mem* in the Bible was suggested, in fact by Ginsberg.

Another good example is a suggestion of Reider[1] at Nah. 1. 10, where the phrase: וּכְסָבְאָם סְבוּאִים has been a source of difficulty. If the first *mem* can be treated as enclitic, the text may be understood as 'and as the drunken are getting drunk'.

No grammatical philological treatment has been pressed harder than enclitic *mem*. Hummel's article in 1957, often taken as an exemplary discussion, listed thirty-one instances already discovered, and went on to suggest seventy-six others which seemed probable.[2] Though he admitted that some of these might be explained otherwise, Hummel was confident that this loss would be balanced with the discovery of many others still unnoticed. The large numbers cited appeared to put the phenomenon beyond reasonable doubt.

It therefore seemed a remarkable scepticism that Driver, himself an enthusiast for the philological approach if ever there was one, should doubt the existence of enclitic *mem* in Hebrew.[3] Moran wrote:[4]

After H. D. Hummel's completely convincing study on the subject, a scepticism which prefers to suspect the text rather than accept a linguistic feature attested in Amorite, Ugaritic and Amarna (Jerusalem!) should be virtually impossible.

We shall later consider some issues of principle raised by this kind of argument. Meanwhile one only will be stated: the issue is not only the presence of enclitic *mem*, but the scale or frequency of its occurrence, once this argument is granted. Very many Hebrew words end with ם; it is common as a plural ending and in pronoun suffixes. If in every such case it is likely to be suspected to be an enclitic of no meaning, a very large field of variability is laid open. Hummel's 107 instances are quite good *if we first assume* that enclitic *mem* was a frequent phenomenon; as a proof of its existence, if the latter is in doubt, the list is not very strong.

---

[1] *JJS* iii (1952) 79.
[2] *JBL* lxxvi (1957) 85–107.
[3] *CML*, pp. 129 n., 130 n.; *JSS* x (1965) 116.
[4] In Wright, *The Bible and the Ancient Near East*, p. 60.

(13) Some general statements

I have now given enough examples to indicate some characteristics of the philological treatment.

It remains to consider some general principles which have been stated in justification of the philological approach. Though the publication of strings of short notes has often left rather vague the general logic of the method, there are certain points of principle which frequently find utterance.

The first of these is the hostility to emendation as the way out of difficulties. Driver wrote in 1927:[1]

> The time has come to lay down the rule that *no word, and especially no verb, in the Hebrew Bible, if only it presents a truly Semitic form, may be emended.* Many, if not most, such words will find an explanation some day in the cognate languages, while there will generally be no reason to suppose that those which cannot be so explained have been incorrectly handed down although their meaning remains hidden to us.

Or let us hear Professor Winton Thomas:[2]

> It must be regarded as the first business of the Old Testament linguist to explain by comparative philology the forms he finds in Hebrew, and not, save in the last resort, to emend. Emendation is based upon the false assumption that all that can be known of Hebrew *is* known—it perpetuates the known as the norm by which language is gauged. Comparative philology, however, adventures into the unknown, and discovers new criteria by which language can be adjudged possible or impossible. . . . This revolt against emendation of the Hebrew text has restored the reputation of the MT.

That emendation was based on a false assumption of knowledge has also been suggested by Albright, who refers to:

> our ignorance of Hebrew poetic vocabulary, which has led in recent decades to innumerable erroneous emendations.[3]

Sometimes the hostility to emendation has become almost hysterical. Guillaume writes:

> Inasmuch as the text of Job has been subject to 'emendation', i.e. deliberate falsification of the evidence, to an appalling degree . . . I determined to read it as though it were an Arabic work.[4]

---

[1] *JTS* xxviii (1927) 287.
[2] In *Record and Revelation,* p. 401.
[3] Peake's *Commentary on the Bible,* 2nd edn., 1962, p. 62.
[4] In the Hooke Festschrift (1964), p. 108.

It is hard to see how such a phrase as 'deliberate falsification of the evidence' is justified. Emendations do not in any way falsify the evidence. The emendation is not inserted in the text, but only suggested in the appendix. Translations such as the RSV, when their renderings depend on an implied emendation, usually make this plain by a note in the bottom margin. The evidence remains intact for anyone who knows better. Nor can one see what is the basis for the term 'deliberate'; this could be responsibly said only if the authors of textual emendations actually knew perfectly well what the existing text meant, which clearly is not the case. Guillaume's statement shows no understanding or sympathy for the difficulties and uncertainties which led to the use of emendation. In any case our purpose at this point is only to note that hostility, sometimes intemperate, to textual emendation is common in the literature of philological treatments; yet, as we have shown and will show further, many of those who have used philological treatments have also used emendation quite lavishly.

The second important point of principle is that this devotion to the text, and hostility to any conjectural alteration of it, apply only to the consonants of the text, and not to the vowel signs or other aspects of the Massoretic punctuation. Sweeping and far-reaching rewritings of the punctuation are a frequent, though not quite a universal, feature of philological treatments. This can be found stated as a general principle. Thus Driver writes:

> The solutions of difficult words and phrases here put forward are based on the assumption that alteration of the consonantal text must wherever possible be avoided but that the vowel-points are only of secondary importance and may be emended with considerable freedom.[1]

Or again:

> On ne tient pas compte des voyelles, qui n'ont de valeur que celle d'un commentaire, presque médiéval.[2]

Such judgements seem indeed to be implied by the wide practice of philological treatments. The question then is whether it is ultimately consistent to look with such deep veneration on the Jewish transmission of the consonants of the Bible while holding such deep scepticism towards the Jewish transmission of the vowels.

Also we may ask whether an approach to Hebrew which considers

---

[1] *VT* i (1951) 250.   [2] *ETL* xxvi (1950) 348 n. 7.

the vocalization with such doubt does not thereby logically deprive us of a great deal of our existing knowledge of Hebrew. Does not the organization of Hebrew into a coherent body of knowledge depend on the vocalization system, which forms the logical basis for our analysis of the grammar? May not the philological treatment, starting out by claiming to extend our limited knowledge of the vocabulary and usage of Hebrew, logically end up by placing us in a thorough scepticism of even such knowledge as we have?

Thirdly, it is implied or stated that, where a difficulty is found in Hebrew, almost anything from anywhere in the Semitic languages can conceivably be invoked as a guide to the restoration of the right meaning. It is true that Semitic languages have not all been drawn upon equally; for the main body of philological treatments has depended on a central group of sources, represented especially by Aramaic, classical Syriac, Accadian, Ugaritic, and classical Arabic.

Nevertheless it does seem to be implied that any linguistic phenomenon in any one, or in any group, of these languages, if it appears to fit the needs for the healing of a difficulty found in the Old Testament, and if no obstacle or impediment is at once obvious, may be likely to have existed also in Hebrew. Existence in a cognate language is taken to constitute prima facie evidence for existence in Hebrew. We have just quoted Moran's argument[1] that if a phenomenon exists in Amorite, Accadian, and Ugaritic it is unwarranted scepticism to doubt its existence in Hebrew.

The implication is that there was a very close sharing of linguistic phenomena, and in particular of lexical items, between the Semitic languages. The picture is one of a group in which very great community of features existed. Driver wrote:

These languages stand far more closely together than, for instance, French, Spanish and Italian; but Ethiopic, like Rumanian, is in many respects farthest removed from the common type.[2]

And again:

The further back the enquiry is pushed the closer the resemblance between the various languages becomes. In fact, early inscriptions show Phoenician and Hebrew and Aramaic and even Arabic in a stage of development in which they stand in almost the same relation as

---

[1] See above, p. 33.

[2] In *The People and the Book* (1925), p. 75. But Driver goes directly on to argue that nevertheless great caution must be used in explaining an unknown word in one language from a cognate word in another.

Babylonian and Assyrian to each other and must indeed not so very far behind this stage have been a single language.[1]

We have now sufficiently illustrated the procedure of philological treatments and initiated some discussion of the principles involved. Before we study these more closely, something should be said about the history of the understanding of Hebrew. This will be done in the next chapter.

[1] *Analecta Orientalia* xii (1935) 70. Cf. the discussion below, pp. 184–7.

III

SOME HISTORICAL ASPECTS

THIS chapter will provide a brief survey of certain historical matters which are of importance for our subject. We are not concerned primarily with the history of the text or the history of the Hebrew language, or, again, with the history of exegesis and theological interpretation, though all of these are connected with our main theme. That main theme itself, however, is the history of basic linguistic understanding. How well did people at various times know what Hebrew sentences and words meant? If they were uncertain, where did they look for guidance?

(1) *The Disuse of Hebrew among the Jews*

Philological treatments generally imply that the meaning of a rare word came to be lost in the Jewish tradition, and for this reason has to be recovered by research in the cognate languages. We have therefore to consider the fact that Hebrew in the course of time ceased to be the normal daily speech of Jewish communities, and along with this the date and the manner of this disuse of Hebrew.

It is commonly held that before the time of Christ Hebrew had ceased to be a 'popular' language, and had been replaced among the Palestinian Jews by Aramaic. The language spoken by Jesus, which has been the centre of Christian discussion of the matter, is believed to have been Aramaic, though this view does not exclude the possibility that in discussion with Jewish scholars Jesus may have spoken Hebrew. It is commonly held also that the Hebrew of the Mishnah was an 'artificial' language of the schools, comparable with ecclesiastical Latin, and that it is in any case a strongly Aramaized form of Hebrew. Where such views are held, they may naturally encourage an emphasis on the early and cognate materials (such as Ugaritic), rather than on the literature of post-biblical Judaism, as the place to look for the true sense of biblical words.

The following considerations appear to be relevant:

(*a*) The view that the general language of Palestine in the first century A.D. was Aramaic, and accordingly that this was the language of Jesus, has come to be challenged in recent years; Birkeland has even tried to prove that Jesus spoke Hebrew.[1] Perhaps these newer theories will not in the end find acceptance, and the Aramaic theory will maintain its ground; even so it would seem that the older certainty about the dominance of Aramaic no longer holds good, and that fresh thinking about the matter is needed. This present book, however, is not concerned with the language of Jesus, and I mention it only as a striking example of the issue.

(*b*) It seems rather too obvious and simple to ascribe the disuse of Hebrew to the Babylonian Exile. It is true that some scriptural passages in Aramaic appear from the time of the Return, and the Jews of Elephantine used only Aramaic. It does not follow that this can be generalized completely and made to mean that Hebrew was universally in decline. If Aramaic had been generally accepted in Nehemiah's time, that statesman could not well have been shocked by the existence of children (obviously a minority of children) who could not speak Hebrew. Moreover, the wrath of Nehemiah may have had some success in reviving Hebrew, or may have been part of a wider reaction in favour of Hebrew than is indicated in the one saying of Neh. 13. 24 f. As for the passage Neh. 8. 2–8, where interpreters make plain the sense of the law, in spite of the ancient tradition which makes this the origin of the Targum and in spite of modern arguments to the same effect, the passage may be better construed otherwise: it is a reference to explanation, rather than to translation into a different language.

Late books of the Old Testament, including the great literary complex of the P Document, continue to use Hebrew, and certain linguistic changes (visible, for instance, in Chronicles or Esther) show relations with the later Mishnaic language. Sirach wrote in Hebrew, and in Daniel it is the parts more definitely connected with the time of Antiochus Epiphanes which use Hebrew. Of the Qumran documents, a larger body are in Hebrew than in Aramaic.

---

[1] Birkeland, *The Language of Jesus*; for further references and a summary of the issues see Emerton in *JTS* NS xii (1961) 189–202; extensive references in Fitzmyer, *The Genesis Apocryphon from Qumran*, p. 20 n.; recently Rabinowitz in *ZNW* liii (1962) 229–38, holding the New Testament word ἐφφαθα to be Hebrew.

Thus a widespread loss or disuse of Hebrew cannot be simply ascribed to the exilic period. It would appear rather that the disuse of Hebrew proceeded very gradually, or, indeed, that some initial decline of Hebrew in the exilic period was later compensated for by a certain revival, so that Hebrew actually increased in influence before it later began to decrease again. As late as the war of A.D. 132–4, when Simon son of Kosba wrote letters to his officers, he wrote them in Hebrew. It can indeed be argued that the preference for Hebrew was a product of the nationalistic upsurge of the time; and this might be true, just as the inscriptions on Jewish coins were in Hebrew. But even if this argument is right, it does not diminish the reality of the continued use of Hebrew; it rather furnishes one reason for that reality, and a reason not unsupported by Nehemiah's similar motives centuries earlier.

(c) It has indeed been argued that the Hebrew literature of Qumran (and equally of Sirach or of Daniel) uses an archaizing style. This could be so without implying the disuse of the Hebrew language. Hellenistic poets like Apollonius Rhodius were passionate archaizers, but this does not cast doubt upon the vitality and influence of Greek as a means of communication in their time. If Sirach or Daniel or the *Manual of Discipline* archaized in style, this means only that they chose to express stylistically their continuity with the earlier sacred literature. It does not mean, or even suggest, that the archaizing took place because Hebrew was no longer in use in any other form than that of a past literature. Moreover, as is commonly the case, attempts at archaizing were accompanied by clear evidences that the language was in fact in process of change.

(d) Mishnaic Hebrew is not an Aramaized Hebrew.[1] There are indeed words adopted from Aramaic, as was the case already in the Bible; but there are also many words, especially nouns, adopted from Greek. Especially striking is the fact that, in the stock of verbs, a significant group which was held in common by biblical Hebrew and by Aramaic is not used in Mishnaic Hebrew, while of the 300 verbs occurring in Mishnaic which do not appear in the Bible only a fairly small proportion are adoptions from Aramaic.[2] Typical Aramaic devices like the emphatic state were not generally adopted into Hebrew, and, of the lexical items which characteristically differentiate Aramaic from biblical Hebrew, most are

---

[1] See Segal, *A Grammar of Mishnaic Hebrew*, esp. pp. 1–20, 46–57, 98 f.
[2] Ibid., pp. 46 ff.

not found in the Hebrew of the Mishnah. Many features which appear similar, such as the particle שׁ, are nevertheless not derivations from Aramaic, though they might be conceived as Hebrew developments which have been encouraged or fostered by the presence of analogy in Aramaic. One has the impression that, though there was clearly much bilingualism, the separateness of the two idioms was in general well maintained; elements from the one were found in the other, but speakers knew whether it was Hebrew or Aramaic that was in use.

(e) The late Hebrew of Mishnah and Midrash is not an 'artificial' or an 'unnatural' language; it was formed by processes of growth and change such as are general in linguistic history. If it is true that its growth took place in particular geographic areas or in particular social or professional strata, this only means that these are the particular conditions for a linguistic development under normal processes. One suspects that the 'artificiality' often felt by the Western or Christian scholar lies less in the language system than in the content and style. The style fits the content, and expresses the conventions of a peculiarly stylized approach to the problems of Judaism at that time. This provides no ground for the idea that the language itself was artificial, as if it were a contrivance remote from the actual functioning of languages yet illegitimately pretending to the status of one.

(f) It is often said that Mishnaic Hebrew was not a 'popular' language or a 'vernacular', but only a specialized language of the schools. But the spread of its vocabulary is not such as to suggest use only in learned contexts. Its stock of words for such unlearned matters as shopping or cooking is much greater than that of biblical Hebrew. Similarly, in the Qumran period we find contracts for land transactions sometimes in Hebrew and sometimes in Aramaic. The terms 'vernacular' and 'colloquial' have lately come to be used once again for Mishnaic Hebrew ('vernacular' here not necessarily in the sense of *the* only vernacular or universal language of an area, but in that of a language having some general use apart from purely learned application).[1]

---

[1] See Rabin, *Qumran Studies*, p. 67 n., and in general his stimulating article in *ScrH* iv (1958) 144–61; also Greenfield in *HUCA* xxix (1958) 204, who refers to Mishnaic Hebrew as 'a vernacular raised to a literary language' and again 'a language with roots in the daily preoccupations of its speakers—agriculture, the handicrafts, animal husbandry'.

(g) The model of the 'vernacular', often openly illustrated by the example of ecclesiastical Latin among the medieval vernaculars, fails to recognize the distinctive sociology of the Jews. Jews were not like medieval Germans or Englishmen. On the one hand the Jewish scholar was socially closer than the medieval cleric to the occupations which in Christendom were 'lay'; on the other hand the relation of the 'lay' Jew to Hebrew texts as used in study, in prayer, and in the synagogue service, was infinitely closer than the relation of the medieval Christian to Latin texts. The respective places of study and of 'lay' vocation were very different.

Linguistically the model we have to consider is rather that of bilingualism, a situation quite different from the relation of Latin to the monolingual vernacular speakers of medieval Europe.[1]

(h) In any case, the question of the 'vernacular' status of Hebrew is not the decisive one for our purpose. It is relevant to our study to know how widespread the living use of Hebrew was, but in itself it is not decisive. Our question is not about numbers but about quality; it is about the mode and the precision of the transmission of Hebrew meanings. If Hebrew was not widely spoken, then the transmission of meanings was not accompanied by a continuing productive corpus of non-scholarly usage. This, if true, narrows down in an interesting way the field in which we conceive the mode of transmission to lie; but it in no way decides the question of the reliability or the perceptiveness of that transmission.

Therefore in arguing, as I have done, against an excessively early date for the general disuse of Hebrew, and against too categorical a denial of 'vernacular' status for late Hebrew, I by no means imply that those conceptions of the meaning of biblical words which were current in late times were therefore 'right'. Since Hebrew changed as all languages do, the survival of Hebrew in popular usage would not have universally favoured the correct transmission of the meaning of biblical words. Since the words which we shall discuss are *ex hypothesi* difficult or obscure ones in any case, it is possible that late colloquial Hebrew would furnish no guide to understanding, and may even have positively obscured it through the development of new forms and new senses. Thus the continuity of Hebrew from

---

[1] Such bilingualism is asserted by Kutscher, הלשון והרקע, p. 10; while Rabin in *ScrH* iv (1958) 152 speaks of a 'trilingual' situation in the Persian period, and Goshen-Gottstein, op. cit., p. 135, speaks of a 'quasi-trilingual' situation in the Qumran period. For modern studies of bilingualism see U. Weinreich, *Languages in Contact*; von Weiss, *Zweisprachigkeit*, and literature there cited.

the biblical down to the Mishnaic period does not in itself provide a clear basis for the preservation of the meanings of rare words in biblical texts. It does, however, make a significant difference to the perspective in which we approach the whole problem.

(j) If it is true that the Jewish transmission of meanings was of a scholarly rather than a 'popular' kind, this is not as unnatural or artificial as it has often seemed. On the contrary, the fact of historical linguistic change made natural and necessary a scholarly structure for the transmission and interpretation of meanings belonging to the older stages. The social preference for that which seems to belong to 'the people' and 'real life' should not be allowed to dominate our assessment of linguistic evidence. Even if it is true that the main burden of the transmission of Hebrew meanings was borne by a scholastic tradition, this does not prove anything about the accuracy of that transmission. That scholars should retain valuable knowledge of a language long out of popular use is not so very surprising a thing. Western Europe learned classical Greek from scholars whose life was lived in a milieu in which classical Greek, and even Hellenistic Greek, had not been popular usage for centuries. It is rather ironic that modern scholars, whose own experience of Hebrew is often formed exclusively through scholarly reading, should regard the transmission of meaning through scholars in ancient times as a ground for scepticism.

On the other hand, late Jewish scholarship was never of a purely linguistic type; its linguistic memories were maintained within the context of religious and legal interpretation, and this in turn may have reacted upon the senses ascribed to words in the biblical texts. We shall later examine some instances of this. Moreover, finally, there was a change not only in the linguistic medium of Palestinian daily life; there was also one in the medium of scholarly conversation, with the transition from the Tannaitic to the Amoraic period. It is possible that this scholarly move to Aramaic may have been, for the transmission of meanings, as important as the popular move to Aramaic which occurred earlier.

These, then, are some ways in which the situation of late Hebrew may be relevant for our study. These considerations do not in any way decide the importance or the place of late Hebrew; at least, however, they may clarify the perspective in which we regard it, and open some questions which have too often been taken to be closed.

(2) *Linguistic Elements in Jewish Interpretation*

Certain tendencies in Jewish biblical interpretation, though they did not depend upon ignorance of Hebrew or loss of command of Hebrew in the religious community, may perhaps have produced a climate in which it was factually easier for linguistic information to become confused, diffuse, or apparently immaterial.

Ancient Rabbinic interpretation differs from the modern philological approach. Firstly, there was a certain striving for the production of multiple meanings. The modern philological approach has on the whole looked for one 'correct' meaning, that which is justifiable on the basis of linguistic evidence. The production of multiple meanings seems to work in the opposite direction, and reduces the emphasis on linguistic evidence as the source of precise discrimination between interpretations. Discrimination is exercised rather through an evaluation of the *results* of interpretation (measured against the prevalent religious structure), and through comparison with *other* passages in the authoritative Scripture. The accuracy of the linguistic basis is not a supreme criterion.

Secondly, interpretation might not only fasten on to the literal form of the text but might attach meaning to segments of it which are, from our point of view, at a sub-meaningful level. Religious interpretation could be attached not only to words as a whole but to segments of words; it could be attached to letters of unusual shape or position; it could build on senses which the words have elsewhere, or on the senses of similar words or words associated in other passages; and it could build on senses excluded by the present context just as well as it could build on those favoured by the context. Thus, while the acceptance of multiple meanings diminished the centrality of a clear procedure from linguistic evidence, the finding of meaning in sub-meaningful elements enabled interpretation also to be closely literal. This 'linguistic-form allegory',[1] both literal and allegorical at the same time, favoured the multiplicity of meanings.

This style of interpretation, which in the later Jewish way we may characterize as the *derash*, by no means in itself directly occasioned a loss of command of Hebrew; nor was it logically dependent on such a loss of command on the part of the community. The

---

[1] For this phrase see my *Interpretation Old and New* (London, 1966), pp. 114 f., 117.

multiplicity of meanings meant that interpreters could produce extremely artificial senses while at the same time they knew perfectly well what we would now call the real meaning. The procedure did, however, make it less important and decisive that the meanings of words, as normal linguistic usage indicated them, should be kept in mind.

Several particularly relevant types of rabbinic interpretation should be specially mentioned.

Firstly, there is the finding of meaning by arbitrary analysis of strange words. B. *Ber.* 54b displays such an analysis of the words אבני אלגביש 'hailstones' to mean 'stones' (אבנים) which 'stood' or remained suspended 'on the back of' or 'for the sake of' a man (על גב איש) and came down for the sake of a man; the first 'man' was Moses, the second Joshua. The unusual word תלפיות similarly figures in B. *Ber.* 30a in an interpretation where the word is taken as the 'hill' (תל) to which all 'mouths' (פיות) turn—thus furnishing scriptural evidence for the practice of turning towards Jerusalem in prayer: for Cant. 4. 4 says that 'Thy neck is like the tower of David builded with תלפיות'.

Secondly, it is hard to separate this from the 'etymological' interpretation of words. Why, for instance, *Genesis Rabba* asks with reference to Gen. 1. 10, did God call the dry land ארץ? The answer is: because she 'conformed' (רצתה) to his 'will' (רצון). Etymologizing interpretation of this kind, though found particularly in connexion with personal names, is to be found in all sorts of other connexions also.

Pseudo-etymological connexions with similar words constitute one way in which multiplicity of meaning is achieved. In B. *Ber.* 29b the Mishnah speaks of a 'time of crisis' (פָּרָשַׁת עִבּוּר). What does this phrase mean? One speaker says that it applies to the time when God is filled with 'wrath' (עֶבְרָה) against enemies, like a 'pregnant woman' (אשה עוּבֶּרֶת). Another opinion refers it to the time when people 'transgress' (עוֹבְרִים) the words of the Torah. Thus the discussion gathers together the similar forms עבור, עברה, עוברת, and עוברים and provides from this connexion a multiple network of possible meaning.

One interesting variation, when exegesis of a biblical text is being attempted, is the *al-tiqre* (אל־תקרי) interpretation.[1] At B. *Ber.*

---

[1] See H. Torczyner in *Encyclopaedia Judaica*, ii. 74–87. Also Gordis, *Biblical*

64a, for example, a biblical passage (Isa. 54. 13), is quoted, which reads:

וְכָל־בָּנַיִךְ לְמוּדֵי יהוה :

R. Eleazar says:

'Do not read "thy children" but "thy builders" ' (בּוֹנַיִךְ).

This enables a connexion to be made with a series of other texts concerning building and houses. Again, at B. *Ber.* 57a, we read:

If one dreams he has intercourse with a betrothed maiden, he may expect to obtain knowledge of Torah, since it says: Moses commanded us a Torah, an inheritance (מוֹרָשָׁה) of the congregation of Jacob. Do not read 'inheritance' (מוֹרָשָׁה) but 'one betrothed' (מְאוֹרָשָׂה).

It should not be supposed that these adjunctions 'not to read' such and such imply that the text is still in a fluid state. On the contrary, they are if anything an evidence that the text was already largely fixed, even though the vocalization signs were not yet written. The text from which departure is made is the Massoretic text; it is it that is 'not' to be read.

Secondly, these interpretations are not confined to difficult vocabulary elements. Nor do they imply that the real meaning has been lost. The interpreter may know perfectly well the general usage and reference of a word at the same time as he is producing an artificial analysis of it in quite another sense. These are devices of the *derash*, and are by no means to be taken at quite their face value. Similarly, legends can be generated by linguistic peculiarities in the text. Num. 21. 14 has a phrase which in the AV margin is 'Vaheb in Suphah'. The Hebrew is אֶת־וָהֵב בְּסוּפָה. There is a certain linguistic anomaly in the word וְהֵב, for very few Hebrew words begin with /w/. A Tannaitic story, retold in B. *Ber.* 54a, resolves the terms into a sense 'Eth and Heb in the rear' and explains that Eth and Heb were two lepers who followed in the 'rear' (סוּפָה) of the camp of Israel and later saw the discomfiture of the Amorites.

These interpretative devices, then, do not by any means imply that meanings have become unknown; they are, very frequently,

Text, pp. 78 f. For a recent consideration of the relation with the New Testament, P. Borgen, *Bread from Heaven* (Leiden, 1965), esp. pp. 62–67. See also further below, pp. 212 and 214.

additions to the plain meaning rather than replacements of it. Nevertheless, in a general atmosphere in which such methods were not only possible but popular and attractive, it is understandable that certain useful and valid linguistic information, grounded in actual usage, would escape notice and come to be lost.

The etymologizing treatment of words has its roots far back in the history of Semitic literature. This popular etymology had no historical reference, and all the etymologizing of antiquity was alike in this.[1] It was a literary device used in the development of narrative or poetic effect, an interpretative device by which special meanings were extracted, and (as with Aquila) a translation technique by which features in the original text which must, because it is a sacred text, be pregnant with meaning, are reproduced, so far as is possible, in the translation.

The Bible itself has a number of examples of popular etymology, especially in personal names. The name Eve, Hebrew חַוָּה, was etymologized in Gen. 3. 20: Adam called her by this name because she was אֵם כָּל־חָי, 'the mother of all living'. Here the LXX rose remarkably well to the occasion, saying that her name was Zoe, life: Ζωή, ὅτι αὕτη μήτηρ πάντων τῶν ζώντων.

Such etymological plays are beloved of the early story-tellers, and form part of the dramatic colour, especially at the birth of a child, but also when a name is changed or some other significant turn in the course of events occurs. Etymologizing seemed very natural because most Hebrew names were phrases which had meaning as other phrases of the language had. Some were prayers, like יְחֶזְקֵאל ('may God strengthen'); some were declarations, like עֹבַדְיָהוּ ('servant of the Lord'); some were statements of events, like אֶלְנָתָן ('God gave'). The names etymologized in the old traditions, however, were for the most part not names of the normal Hebrew type. The explanations of names like Cain or Noah or Naphtali had an artificiality which did not attach to the understanding of actual Israelite names.

To us, indeed, it is clear that some of the etymologies do not fit. The name 'Noah', in spite of Gen. 5. 29, does not come from נחם 'comfort'; and in spite of I Sam. 1. 20 the name 'Samuel' is not

---

[1] For an article on another ancient literature comparable with the biblical see J. Gonda, 'The Etymologies in the Ancient Indian Brāhmaṇas', *Lingua* v (1955–6) 61–85.

connected with שאל 'ask, borrow'.[1] This latter discrepancy has sometimes been taken to show that the story is really about the birth of Saul, for the explanation would really fit that name. But this is being too logical; the etymologies did not depend on having the right 'root', as we should call it.

The phenomenon of popular etymology cannot be strictly separated from a whole series of other stylistic devices, such as assonance or paronomasia. To quote two familiar examples:

Ps. 137. 5: אִם־אֶשְׁכָּחֵךְ יְרוּשָׁלָ͏ִם תִּשְׁכַּח יְמִינִי׃

'If I forget you, o Jerusalem, let my right hand wither' (RSV).

This is, in respect of the meaning of the second verb, usually esteemed to be a better translation than the 'If I forget thee, o Jerusalem, let my right hand forget *her cunning*' of AV.

AV had to supply (from a supposed ellipse) an object for the second verb; but its rendering at least conveyed that there was an assonance, and thus caught something for which the writer was striving; for the point is that the verb in each case is שכח.

In Isa. 5. 7, on the other hand, though the consonants are not the same, a striking effect is produced by the partial similarity of the words:

וַיְקַו לְמִשְׁפָּט וְהִנֵּה מִשְׂפָּח לִצְדָקָה וְהִנֵּה צְעָקָה׃

'He looked for order, what he saw was murder;
he looked for right, what he heard was the cry of fright.'

(The writer's translation.)

Such literary devices attracted attention to the way in which words are made up and to the effect of their use in combination with other words containing the same elements.

The use by prophets of a keyword, as the divinatory guidance conveyed by the seeing of an object, probably also had an effect. Two famous cases are at Amos 8. 2, where the prophet sees a basket of summer fruit, קָיִץ, and on this basis God tells him that

---

[1] Sometimes a modern philological treatment can give a much more satisfying interpretation of these names. Cain is usually understood after Arabic *qain* 'smith', and this fits well with certain characteristics of the Kenites. For the name Noah we have the very attractive suggestion of Driver in *ETL* xxvi (1950) 350, after Eth. *noḥā* 'be long', that Noah's name meant something like 'long (in life)'. This would seem to fit with Oriental traditions of the relation between the Deluge and the quest for immortality, and accords with the Sumerian name ZI.UD.SUD.RA. These meanings, even if correct, had probably disappeared from consciousness by the time the biblical stories were written.

the end, קֵץ, has come upon Israel; and at Jer. 1. 11, where the prophet sees a rod of almond, שָׁקֵד, and indeed God is watching, שֹׁקֵד, over his word to perform it.

In Dan. 5. 26–28 the words 'Mene, Tekel, Peres' are already written; the situation is closer to that of interpreting an authoritative but mysterious written document. Its elements have a double or triple meaning, depending on words which have the same root or at least look similar. Thus, by a common interpretation, *mene* is the coin 'mina' but also the verb 'is counted'; *tekel* is the coin 'shekel', but also the verb 'is weighed'; and *peres* or *parsin* is the two small half-units, but also secondly the verb 'divided', and thirdly the name of the Persians, one of the two nations to whom Belshazzar's kingdom will be divided and given.

In late times, then, etymologizing interpretation is on the increase. A certain amount is found in the New Testament, related to personal names, like Melchizedek in Heb. 7. 2; and here there is also an etymologization of the place-name Salem as 'peace'. Hebrews, however, does not venture far into the etymological wilderness; both of these are simple cases, and the writer does not try us with a similar treatment of (say) Levi, or Aaron, or Phinehas. A more systematic etymologization of names, both of persons and of places, can be seen in Philo and in Christian commentators; it was, after all, a way of finding sense in lists of names, such as the bare lists of places where the Israelites stopped on their way from Egypt to Canaan. The symbolical use of place-names was on the increase, whether with or without etymologization; the symbolical interpretation of 'Lebanon', for instance, goes back as far as the history of post-biblical tradition can be traced at all.[1] In such cases, if an etymological slant was obvious, it was utilized; if not, no matter, the results could be reached without it. The explanations are usually based, more or less obviously, on Hebrew; they rest also in part upon the Stoic etymological tradition, but Palestinian Judaism fostered the process independently.

We may then sum up this point by saying that the growth of etymologizing interpretation was favoured by certain genuine elements in the nature of Hebrew language and literature; but that on the other hand the major cause of that growth was a loss of appreciation of the ancient literary styles for what they were, and

[1] Vermes, *Scripture and Tradition*, p. 36, and pp. 26–39 generally.

the passage to a more scholastic method of study. This newer method of study was connected with the status of the literature as a holy scripture and the corresponding expectations of the kinds of meaning to be derived from such a scripture, in whole and in its smallest parts. With the loss of sense for the original communicative literary forms, meaningful stress comes to be put upon elements which do indeed occur in the text but do not carry substantial independent meaning within it. The great etymologizers were also the great allegorizers. There grows up a self-conscious, undiscriminating emphasis on formal linguistic features, while the overall continuity of resultant interpretation is provided by legal and dogmatic systems.[1] It is not hard to see how some loss of awareness of exact linguistic meanings could have occurred in such circumstances. Moreover, as we shall see shortly, the characteristics which thus arose within Hebrew interpretation also affected the understanding of Hebrew words and texts on the part of translators who tried to put them into Greek and other languages.

(3) Early Intra-Linguistic Relations

The science of comparative philology as we know it is a modern creation. But the idea that Hebrew is related to other languages is very ancient.

There is a considerable period during which Hebrew and Aramaic lay together in the consciousness of many Jews. There is a lack of direct evidence in the form of actual statements about the relation between languages.[2] But some relations between the vocabulary of one language and that of the other must have been evident to those who knew something of both.

Four categories in lexical similarity or difference between the two languages seem obvious:

Firstly, there exists a long series of words in which a similarity between the two languages in form and meaning is fairly plain, for example:

king	Aram. מלכא	Hebr.	מלך
heaven	שמיא		שמים
hear	שמע		שמע
say	אמר		אמר

---

[1] On this generally see my *Old and New in Interpretation*, pp. 107 ff., etc.

[2] We can quote St. Jerome, however: *vicina est Chaldaeorum lingua sermoni Hebraico*: PL xxix. 25 f.

A perception of these similarities would probably be very natural.

Secondly, there are words in which one consonant differs but the similarity of the word as a whole and of its meaning may have made the correspondence fairly evident. The obvious instances are where Aramaic ד, ט, ע, and ת correspond to Hebrew ז, צ, צ, and שׁ. These are found in familiar words such as:

gold	Aram. דהבא	Hebr.	זהב
run	רהט		רוץ
land	ארעא		ארץ
sit, dwell	יתב		ישׁב

This series would not always be as evident as it is to the modern philologist. The relation between the Aramaic מטא and the Hebrew מצא might not be apparent, since the meanings differ, the Aramaic word meaning 'come' (Hebrew mostly בוא) and the Hebrew meaning 'find'; and while in Aramaic 'find' is אשׁכח, Hebrew שׁכח is normally 'forget'.

Thus a person who knew both Hebrew and Aramaic would be in a position to notice a long series of correspondences in form and meaning and also to be warned against generalizing such correspondences.

A third category is composed of words which exist in the one language but are very much more frequent in the other, though meaning more or less the same in both. The Hebrew אתה 'come' is poetical and infrequent, but the Aramaic אתא is frequent and standard. In biblical Hebrew the verb יהב 'give' is found only in the imperative, but in Aramaic it is the usual word for 'give', which in Hebrew of course is נתן.

A fourth category is the number of important and frequent words which are completely different between the two languages.[1] For example:

go up	Aram. סלק	Hebr.	עלה
go down	נחת		ירד
go in	על		בוא (נכנס)

---

[1] There are indeed very occasional cases in which the 'Aramaic' word is found in Hebrew, e.g. אָסַק in Ps. 139. 8 and a number of cases of נחת and שׁבח. I am not trying to argue that Hebrew and Aramaic are completely exclusive in this regard. The contrast is not between Hebrew and Aramaic, between which certain overlaps occurred, but between *normal* words which were closely similar in the two languages and normal words which were very different, even if sporadic overlaps bridged the gap.

serve	פלח	עבד
fear	דחל	ירא
witness	שהד	עוד
praise	שבח	הלל

Though the modern philologist may sometimes see contacts between the word in one language and some cognate in the other, in the ancient world the words would usually seem to be totally different.

Thus there was a basis upon which certain comparative insights could develop; but they would also be limited by other aspects of the material. The knowledge of Aramaic might confuse the tradition of the meaning of Hebrew; it might also assist the preservation of that tradition.

Though the similarities between Hebrew and Aramaic can hardly have escaped the Targumists, the differences were sufficiently frequent and obvious to save them from the temptation to read Hebrew as if it was Aramaic, even where a Hebrew word had the same consonants as those of an Aramaic word. The Targumists were in general too experienced to fall into the obvious mistake of writing the same root in Aramaic as they found present in Hebrew. For example, רחץ means 'wash' in Hebrew but 'trust' in Aramaic, and no sense could be got out of the frequent references to washing in the book of Leviticus if they were translated by רחץ in the Targum.[1]

In fact a survey of the Targums suggests that the cases where the Hebrew word is translated by an Aramaic cognate word, and where the meaning is also different, are not numerous. In other words, the Targumists did not generally pursue that etymological fancy in translating which might have led to a preference for a word like the Hebrew where such could be found.

There was an additional reason why such close adherence to the very forms of the original Hebrew was not pursued by the Targumists. Their translation is, more than most translations are, of the character of a paraphrase. Quite substantial interpretative additions are made. For those who are not accustomed to the characteristics of Targums, an example may be given from Isa. 40. 1–3. Here is the Targum text as translated by Stenning; and

---

[1] Cf., however, the Greek example below, p. 54.

in it we italicize all those elements which are substantial additions to the Hebrew:

O ye *prophets, prophesy* consolations concerning my people, saith your God. Speak ye comfortably to Jerusalem, and *prophesy* concerning her, that she is about to be filled with *the people of her exiles*, that her transgressions have been forgiven her, for that she has received the *cup* of *consolations* from before the Lord, as if she had been *smitten* twice for all her sins. The voice of one that crieth, Prepare ye a way in the wilderness before *the people of* the Lord, *tread down* paths in the desert before *the congregation of* our God.

Where there is no hesitation to insert either renderings which make precisions far beyond those required by the Hebrew or phrases which are pure quantitative additions to the Hebrew, it is unlikely that an attempt to represent the sheer outward form of the Hebrew text will be a normal procedure. It would have been quite possible for the Targum to exploit the Hebrew word צְבָאָהּ ('her period of service') and treat it as suggesting the Aramaic צבא 'goodwill'. This could have given a good sense: 'goodwill for her is fulfilled'. The Targum has rather followed the normal Hebrew sense, namely 'army, host', and expanded this with its comment 'the people of her exiles'. The tendency to expand and paraphrase has linguistic effects opposite to those produced by a painful concern for the formal and quantitative aspect of the Hebrew. Sometimes, however, the same source may use both approaches.

The LXX does not, like the Targum, generally introduce large amounts of matter quite unrepresented in the Hebrew; its tendency is often rather to abbreviate, as is evident especially in Jeremiah and Job. To take a simple example, χριστός 'anointed one' occurs in the Greek Psalms and Isaiah in exactly the same places (ten and one in number respectively) where the MT has מָשִׁיח; but the Targum has several cases of מְשִׁיחָא which are pure additions to the Hebrew. Similarly, it writes מְשִׁיחָא for the שבט 'sceptre (comet?)' of Num. 24. 17.

There are, however, cases where the other procedure seems to have been followed and the Targum uses the same root as the Hebrew.[1] At Amos 2. 13 there is a word מֵעִיק which the Targum renders by מיתי עקא '(I am) bringing distress'. In so doing it associates the rare Hebrew verb עוק, which in fact occurs only

---

[1] For some illustrations of the problems this may cause in the understanding of the Targum and the Syriac see below, pp. 263 ff.

here and has remained a point of uncertainty to the present day, with the Aramaic עקא. This is quite a common word, and is used quite frequently to translate Hebrew words like צרר 'to distress'.

The influence of Aramaic may be seen not only in the Targums, but also at times in other translations, and also in general Jewish comment and interpretation.

It has often been held that the LXX shows Aramaic influence in certain of its renderings. Aramaic usage seems to have affected the translators' understanding of Hebrew. This would not be surprising, since some Jews in Egypt had certainly spoken Aramaic, and one may surmise that most contacts with international Jewry were made in Aramaic. Two examples will be quoted:

At Isa. 53. 10 the Hebrew דַּכְּאוֹ means 'to crush him', but the Greek says καθαρίσαι αὐτόν 'to purify him'. This seems to be well explained if the LXX translator had in mind the common Aramaic word דכא 'purify'; this differs from the cognate Hebrew verb by the normal correspondences. We cannot, however, be quite sure of this explanation. The translator could simply have misread the דכאו of the text, or, looking at it cursorily, have been sufficiently impressed by the similarity to the Hebrew verb זכה, which would give the sense 'purify'. The explanation based on Aramaic, therefore, is not entirely necessary. It is, however, somewhat strengthened by the fact that the Targum takes the same line here, translating by

למצרף ולדכאה ית שארא דעמיה בדיל לנקאה מחובין
נפשהון:

'To refine and purify the remnant of his people, in order to cleanse their soul from sin'.

Another striking case, perhaps the most striking in the Greek Bible, occurs at Ps.60 (59). 10 and again at 108 (107). 10. MT reads:

מוֹאָב סִיר רַחְצִי

'Moab is my wash-bowl'.

LXX has:

Μωαβ λέβης τῆς ἐλπίδος μου

'Moab the bowl of my hope.'

This seems to depend upon the Aramaic רחץ, which has already been mentioned above. However, the Targum itself does not follow this interpretation, but reads at 60. 10:

בעטיית מואבאי

'I trod down the Moabites',

and at 108. 10:

דושישית מואבאי

'I trampled down the Moabites',

both of which, of course, are very rough paraphrases. The LXX renderings, though they seem to depend on a mental reference to Aramaic, are not the effect of the actual Targum, or not at any rate of the Targum which we now have.

Quite considerable lists of cases showing dependence by the LXX on the Aramaic rather than the Hebrew meaning of occasional words can be collected from the works of scholars.[1] Not all of the suggestions which have been made can be accepted, however, for sometimes other explanations are possible.

The Aramaic language continued to affect the understanding of the Bible long after it had itself fallen into practical disuse. Examples of renderings which depend upon Aramaic can be found in the AV. At Judges 7. 3 MT reads וְיִצְפֹּר מֵהַר הַגִּלְעָד.

Now the verb צפר is a *hapax legomenon* of very uncertain meaning. Aramaic had a familiar word of this root, צפרא, which means 'morning'. The later Jewish commentators, such as Rashi and Kimchi, took this into account in dealing with the passage; and AV, when it translates 'depart early from mount Gilead', is following this.[2] Interestingly enough, the Targum itself did not take this line; its translation is יתבחר, which has no apparent connexions with Aramaic words of the root צפר. Again, the translation of the obscure מַדְהֵבָה (Isa. 14. 4) as 'the golden city' in AV follows Kimchi and depends on the connexion with the Aramaic דהבא 'gold'.

---

[1] For a considerable list, some of them very dubious, see Wutz, pp. 150 ff. A few are quoted by Swete, p. 319 n., from Nestle; see also I. L. Seeligmann, pp. 49 f. Some scholars have gone so far as to suggest that Aramaic rather than Hebrew was the Semitic language truly known to the translators; see Vollers in *ZAW* iii (1883) 224 f.; also Flashar in *ZAW* xxxii (1912) 251, etc.

[2] See G. F. Moore, *Judges*, p. 203.

The Targum was productive in this way in the Middle Ages, in areas where Aramaic had not been spoken anyway, because it was studied by the commentators and its interpretations were often taken up by them. Many of these interpretations do not depend on the similarity between Hebrew and Aramaic words, but rather the opposite: the Hebrew being difficult or controversial, the Targum rendering may be free from these particular uncertainties and thus be taken up into the commentary. This continuing general esteem of the Targum, which had now become a sort of additional sacred text supplementing the Hebrew text, is a basis from which there could always spring interpretations depending upon particular linguistic phenomena of Aramaic.

In sum, then, the existence of the Targum, and the wide use of Aramaic in Jewry, formed a kind of practical introduction to problems of relating Hebrew to another cognate language, and thus occasionally introduced a kind of primitive linguistic comparison.

The influence of Aramaic and other languages on the understanding of Hebrew can not only be traced through indirect evidence from translations; Rabbinic sources sometimes give direct statements purporting to rest on the knowledge of other languages. An introductory phrase sometimes found is לא הוו ידעי רבנן מאי 'our teachers did not know the meaning of . . . until . . .', followed by the circumstances in which the sense came to be known.[1]

A famous instance is וטאטאתיה, of which the meaning was unknown until the maid of Rabbi was heard to say:

שקולי טאטיתא וטאטי ביתא

'take up the broom and sweep the house'.

Other examples cite languages heard when travelling in foreign parts. Rabbi d. Bar Hana tells that he had not known the sense of יהב in the verse Ps. 55. 23 הַשְׁלֵךְ עַל־יְהוָה יְהָבְךָ until one day when he was carrying a heavy burden and an Arab said to him

שקול יהבך ושדי אגמלאי

'lift up your *yehab* and throw it on my camel'.

Again, we hear that 'Rabbi says that in coastal cities (כרכי הים)

---

[1] See B. *Rosh ha-Shanah* 26a–b; also B. *Meg.* 18a. For a discussion of the relation to Arabic of these passages see S. Krauss in *ZDMG* lxx (1916) 321–53, esp. pp. 338–49.

selling was called 'כִּירָה; and this piece of philological information was supposed to be useful for the understanding of Gen. 50. 5: בְּקִבְרִי אֲשֶׁר כָּרִיתִי לִי.

Again, a tradition reports: 'R. Simeon b. Laqish said: When I was in the province קָן נְשֵׁרִיָּא, one called the bride נִינְפִי and the hen נִינְפִי שְׂכוִי.' נִינְפִי is applied to Ps. 48. 3: יְפֵה נוֹף מְשׂוֹשׂ כָּל־ הָאָרֶץ, and the word נוֹף is thus associated with the distantly similar Greek νύμφη. Similarly, the interpretation of שֶׂכְוִי is applied to Job 38. 36, a passage the obscurity of which often excited the interest of the older scholars.

Appeals of this kind to foreign languages are sometimes made at points where the Hebrew is intrinsically difficult or obscure; but sometimes also they provide an additional or midrashic explanation to a text where the normal sense must have been quite well known.

An instance of the former is found at Gen. 49. 5:

שִׁמְעוֹן וְלֵוִי אַחִים כְּלֵי חָמָס מְכֵרֹתֵיהֶם׃

In *Gen. R.* the last word is declared to be the Greek μάχαιρα 'sword', which of course gives a seemingly fitting sense. The word has long been considered difficult. BDB, p. 468b, registers it under כוּר, but seems doubtful; GB, p. 423a, is also at a loss, and KB, p. 523a, states only that the word is 'unexplained'. A very attractive philological treatment is to take it as cognate with the Ethiopic *mkr* 'advise' (in the theme II. 1, *'amkärä*, 'consilium dare, suadere', Dillmann, col. 199; cf. also III. 3); Ullendorff[1] mentions this connexion, already seen by Ludolf. The sense would then be: 'Weapons of violence are their counsels.' The appeal to a foreign word in the Midrash is related to an acknowledged obscurity in the Hebrew itself.

The position is quite different in the following example from *Pesikta de-R. Kahana*, xl.: the words spoken in leading up to the sacrifice of Isaac, שֶׂה לְעֹלָה 'a lamb for a burnt-offering' (Gen. 22. 7 f.), are interpreted with the statement that this is a Greek word, i.e. σέ 'thee'; thus the sense of שֶׂה לעלה is אתה הוא הקרבן 'thou art the sacrifice'.[2] There was, of course, no difficulty

---

[1] Index, no. 200; the discussion in Skinner's *Genesis*, pp. 516 f., shows the uncertainty of the older interpreters. None of the versions seems to have known the sense, cf. my remarks below, p. 270.

[2] See A. Brüll, *Fremdsprachliche Redensarten* (Leipzig, 1869), p. 26; this work gives many relevant examples.

in the word שֶׂה for the interpreter; but, by suggesting that it was a Greek word here, he was able to give apparently literal evidence for what was indeed, as every reader knew, the situation in the incident described. The introduction of a suggestion of a foreign word may thus be a means to a midrashic interpretation, and not connected with any intrinsic difficulty in the text.

These scraps of 'philological' information can of course by no means be solemnly taken at their face value. They do not necessarily represent the mode by which an interpretation was reached. Even when a tradition records that 'I did not know the meaning of word *x* until...' it is by no means certain that this is absolutely true even for the Rabbi concerned, and his interpretation might use the information from foreign sources only for one exegesis among others of a relevant text. Needless to say, there was no systematic approach to philological study and no attempt to distinguish between languages which are cognate with Hebrew (such as Arabic) and those which are not (such as Greek).

The examples are nevertheless significant, in that they may show us: (*a*) that some uncertainty about the sense of unfamiliar words was admitted, (*b*) that the legitimacy of appeal to other languages than Hebrew was already accepted, though in a very confused form, in the Talmudic period; and this held open the possibility of something which the medieval lexicographers used to much greater effect.

In general Greek lacked the obvious similarities to Hebrew which Aramaic had, and it did not provide, as Aramaic did, a potential entry into a rudimentary comparative philology. Nevertheless, the practice of Greek translators sometimes provides further illustrations of the tendencies we have been describing.

Occasionally they seem to have chosen Greek words which had some similarity to the Hebrew words being rendered. The rendering ἤχου for אֹחִים at Isa. 13. 21 is a probable example;[1] and at Isa. 51. 8, where the Hebrew has the two nouns עָשׁ and סָס, both meaning 'moth', σής is used for the rendering of the latter, though it usually renders the former; this may well be attributed to the verbal similarity. Stock examples from the later Greek translators are αὐλών for אֵלוֹן at Deut. 11. 30 and θεραπεία for תרפים at I Sam. 15. 23 (if this text is reliable).[2]

[1] On this passage cf. below, pp. 243, 250.
[2] See Swete, *Introduction*, p. 41, and Field's note 34 on I Sam. 15. 23.

Again, Greek translators sometimes put into practice in Greek the tendencies of arbitrary analysis and etymologization which we have already traced in Hebrew and Aramaic sources. The use of ἱκανός for the divine name שַׁדַּי depends on a resolution into שֶׁ 'which' and דִי 'sufficient'. For the enigmatic אֵשְׁדָּת of Deut. 33. 2, the Vulgate's *ignea lex* and later the AV's 'a fiery law' imply a resolution into אֵשׁ 'fire' and דָּת 'law, religion'. These methods continued throughout the Middle Ages, as in the resolution of שָׁמַיִם 'heaven' into phrases like שָׁם מַיִם 'water is there' or אֵשׁ+ מַיִם 'fire and water', mentioned by Rashi on Gen. 1. 1.

Such devices are an attempt to display or exploit in translation something of the formal characteristics of the original; it is easy for us to see how such an emphasis could damage the consciousness of linguistic meaning, though the intention was doubtless quite different. The literalizing emphasis on the formal and quantitative was pressed hardest of all by Aquila, and accompanied by extensive etymologizing.[1]

Up to the sixth century or so it seems fair to say that the main mental effort of Judaism took a form which favoured such methods. The elaboration of the halachic law implied a concentration on legal distinctions; while the Midrash, which followed the actual contours of the biblical material more closely, also included wide freedom for legendary expansion and, because of its fanciful and often more humorous style, allowed the plain sense of the text to be submerged under highly imaginative plays upon words and phrases. These conditions could have been detrimental to the maintenance of a good and sober awareness of meanings in biblical Hebrew.

An important change of direction is signalled by Qaraism. In spite of the compromises and uncertainties of the Qaraitic movement, it does seem to restore an emphasis on the commentary form and an appeal to the scripture. By this time (Qaraism takes its rise in the eighth century) there are several other changes of position to mention. The work upon the text of the Bible, which we associate with the name of the Massoretes, was under way. Codices were copied by the families of Massoretes and provided with vocalization and accent signs under a number of systems of increasing refinement. Systems of vocalization were being devised also for the Quran in Islam and for the texts of the Syriac-speaking Christians. It is not necessary for our purpose to fix the exact dates and

---

[1] For an introduction to Aquila's methods see Swete, *Introduction*, pp. 31–42.

priorities of these operations. In a later chapter we shall return to the Massoretes and the nature of their work.

In the Islamic period Jews were able to enjoy an expansion of their philosophical and scientific horizons. Grammatical studies began and expanded. The first considerable name in the history of Hebrew linguistic studies, Saadia Gaon (892–942), was also a considerable commentator on books of the Bible, and a philosopher of note.

Meanwhile Arabic quickly took over from Aramaic the place of prominence as the language with which Hebrew might usefully be compared. Many of the great Jewish thinkers normally used Arabic. Maimonides wrote his *Guide for the Perplexed* in Arabic, and it was Ibn Tibbon who translated it into Hebrew. The pious Jewish scholar still read his Targum in Aramaic and his Talmud which is mainly in Aramaic; but the linguistic medium for the most active Jewish thinking had come to be Arabic.

In contrast with the earlier Judaistic development, in which the tendency to *derash* had so been fostered, the period of the Massoretic development and of the rise of Jewish grammatical studies can be characterized as the time of the *peshaṭ*. It is reasonable to consider that a major stimulus towards this emphasis on the plain sense came from the confrontation with Qaraism within Judaism, and with Christianity and Islam without.[1] The religious values of the *derash* were by no means abandoned or forgotten; but for the questions which now became foremost in scholarship it seems no longer to have been supposed that answers would be found in a mere appeal to the tradition of *derash*. The new lexical and grammatical studies, rudimentary as they were, represented an attempt to find guidance in linguistic evidence rather than in traditional religious interpretations.

(4) *Aspects of the History of Jewish Grammatical Studies*

This section will provide some elementary introduction to a subject which has been widely neglected but is relevant to the historical understanding of our general theme. Scholars will perceive the extent to which I depend on the learned expositions of Bacher. Amid the complicated and varied work of the medieval Jewish

---

[1] For a simple presentation of this view see E. I. J. Rosenthal, 'Medieval Jewish Exegesis: Its Character and Significance', *JSS* ix (1964) 265–81.

grammarians I have picked out elements which concern us here. They help to illustrate, among other things, (*a*) the continuing presence of comparative methods, (*b*) the methods of analysis used on biblical words in medieval times, and (*c*) the nature of the Massorah, which will concern us again later.

'The Massorah is the real cradle of Hebrew grammar', writes Bacher.[1] It provided a careful registration of the written form of the Bible, and was a kind of school in which the mind was trained to recognize with painstaking care the detailed points which might discriminate between right and wrong reading. The Massoretes thus come to the verge of grammatical study. Their notes occasionally take cognizance of such distinctions as masculine and feminine, or the difference between final and penultimate stress.

Yet Massorah is not grammar, and the use of grammatical categories is not general or predominant in it. Its purpose is to assure the correct writing and reading of the text. Semantic problems are not generally discussed. This is not to be despised as a fault. The value of the Massoretic registration is its careful fixation of the formal characteristics of the text at a time when interpretative methods had long been too fluid to permit any simple perception of the relation between form and meaning. Only late in the course of the Massoretic activity, with Aaron ben Moshe ben Asher in the early tenth century (a time therefore to which certain important Hebrew manuscripts still extant go back), does a combination of grammatical discussion with Massoretic activity appear to be found. Even then it is not an independent linguistic description, but rather a setting forth of the rules implied in Massoretic work, under some influence from Arabic grammatical science.

It was either ben Asher or his greater contemporary Saadia who took the important step of first noticing and formulating the distinction between what would now be called root and afformatives.[2] The importance of this is to us so great (our Hebrew grammar having been developed upon the basis of this distinction) that it is surprising to realize how late in the history of Hebrew it was recognized. Saadia also concerned himself with the rare words of the Bible, mostly *hapax legomena*, and wrote a treatise on ninety of them. In his translations into Arabic, and in the commentary related to them, he made much use of Arabic material in the explaining of Hebrew

---

[1] *ZDMG* xlix (1895) 8.
[2] See the discussion by Bacher, *ZDMG*, p. 48.

words. He was deeply indebted to Arabic grammatical ideas, and followed an Arabic example in conceiving his task as the prescriptive one of teaching correctness to Jews who had not the slightest idea of what was correct Hebrew.

About the same time as Saadia, we find Yehuda ibn Koreish, shocked to hear that the Jews of Fez had discontinued the reading of the Targum, arguing for a kind of interdependence of the knowledge of the three great languages, Hebrew, Aramaic, and Arabic. Did not the Scripture itself make it clear that the Hebrew, Aramaean, and Arab peoples were genetically related through Terah, Abraham, Laban, and Ishmael? Aramaic words could be found in the Bible itself; indeed, the Bible contained words not only of Arabic, but of Romance and of Berber origin. There is, he argued, even a Greek word in the Old Testament, for the לְקֻלָּס of Ezek. 16. 31, which a millennium later was still troubling the editors of BH^3, is from the Greek word καλῶς. Thus Yehuda ibn Koreish represents a strong if rudimentary comparativist position. He wrote a long list of word-comparisons to illustrate these principles.

Menahem ben Sarūk (about 960), on the other hand, paid little attention to Arabic and departed from the Arab theoretical basis which earlier workers had adopted. He cited Aramaic and Mishnaic Hebrew more frequently. The emphasis of his work was lexical rather than grammatical; his dictionary is the first full dictionary of biblical language in Hebrew. Following a principle of explaining words from the context in which they are found, he was led to a heavy stress on the stylistic form of parallelism. 'One half of a verse teaches about the other.'

A particular emphasis is placed upon the strict separation of the various roots. Yet the carrying out of this was still under serious limitations, for the triliterality of roots was not yet an accepted principle. Menahem's dictionary had an entry on 'the root צ', which had seven sections. To these belonged (1) words meaning 'fly', like נֵצָא, צִיץ, (2) words meaning 'bloom', like נֵצָן, צִיץ, (3) words meaning 'quarrel', like מַצָּה, נִצָּה, (4) the word צִי 'ship', (5) the word 'drought', צִיָּה, (6) a kind of animal, צִיִּים, (7) the word צִיּוּן, taken to mean 'monument', 'mark'. Schooled by a long tradition to analyse by looking for a triliteral root, we find it hard to understand that in the tenth century this was still not an established procedure.

Menahem's work was bitterly criticized by Dūnash ibn Labrāt, who in particular was able to refine and improve the identification and discrimination of roots, and to emphasize the predominance of the triliteral against other explanations. He emphasized once again the value of explanations from Arabic and gave a list of about 170 words as examples of how explanation from the Arabic could be correct and necessary.

Yehuda ben David Ḥayyūg (early eleventh century) was afterwards remembered as the founder of a great advance in Hebrew grammar. His study laid particular emphasis upon the verbs with 'weak' radicals, i.e. consonants like *y* or *w* which appear only in some forms and disappear in others. Until this was clear, the triliteral principle could not be carried through consistently. By making it into a consistent one, he used this principle to sort out the verb into regularity and classify the behaviour of the various weak consonants. The performing of this work, needless to say, involved a careful study of the vocalization; for it is by the vocalization that discrimination can generally be reached between uncertain possibilities of weak consonants. Appeals to the vocalization had already been made by workers like Dunash in criticism of earlier suggestions; in the handling of the problem of weak consonants this appeal becomes more intensive and more exact.

Abulwalīd Merwān ibn Janāḥ produced, also in the eleventh century, a systematic approach to the grammar, including the parts of speech, the possible combinations of vowels, the principles of noun-formation, and (a particularly interesting departure) a discussion of the use of tropes, i.e. cases where a word is used (or, in the case of ellipse, omitted) for stylistic or rhetorical effect in places where another would have been more normal. The question how far a difficulty in the biblical text can be explained by appealing to an anomalous usage for the sake of effect is obviously one which runs through all of our present discussion. Later, for instance, the AV got itself out of all sorts of trouble by an implicit appeal to ellipse, which in the English it acknowledged by supplying the omitted elements in italic type.

Most of these latter advances took place in the Muslim lands, including Spain; and it was Abraham ibn Ezra (1092–1167) who brought these achievements most fully into the lands of Christendom. His works were written in Hebrew, and not in the Arabic which for northern Jewry had been an obstacle to the understanding of many grammatical researches. It was in southern France that

the Kimchi family lived—first Joseph, and then his sons Moses and
David. David Kimchi (1160–1235) wrote a grammar usually called
the *Michlol* ('completeness, compendium') and a dictionary known
as the 'Book of Roots'. In this latter he added further etymological
comparisons, taken from late Hebrew and Aramaic, to the many
which had come down from the earlier scholars.

The systematic study of Hebrew vocabulary, which is implied in
the production of dictionaries, poses the question of synonyms,
words which are different in form but identical or closely similar in
meaning, and also that of homonyms, words identical in form but
different in meaning. Whole books were devoted to the collection
and analysis of synonyms; we may mention in particular the *Ḥotem
Tokhnit* of Abraham Bedarshi (later thirteenth century). Homonyms
were handled by Isaac Ha-levi ben Eleazar in his work *Ha-Riqmah*.

Let us summarize a few salient aspects of this rise of grammatical
study.

Firstly, the development of grammatical science began, in spite
of its careful attention to many details, with what would seem to us
now a very poor analysis of Hebrew grammar, so that it was an
achievement to recognize and formulate the triliteral root and the
difference between radicals and afformatives. By the end of the
development, on the other hand, a position had been reached which
shows remarkable similarity to the grammar generally taught in
modern times.

Secondly, comparative elements, with a stress on Arabic and
Aramaic, were prominent; although scholars varied in the degree
of their reliance on comparative study, the possibility of it was
present throughout the discussion. Even those who did not speak
Arabic, which was the living language of the southern grammarians, had a strong basis for comparative linguistic consciousness
in the Targum. Comparative studies were hindered, however, b
the unsatisfactory degree of clarity then attainable about the phono·
logical correspondences. It is not that no correct correspondences
were known. Important correspondences such as that of Hebrew
שׂ to Arabic /š/, or of Hebrew שׁ to Arabic /t/ (e.g. שֶׁלֶג = talj
'snow'), were perfectly well known. But alongside these well-
founded correspondences there were many of more dubious character.[1]

---

[1] For many examples in a recent publication see Wechter, *Ibn Barūn*, pp.
54–60 and related notes.

Thirdly, the production and refinement of the grammatical analysis of Hebrew was related to the use of the Massorah. The grammarians found themselves required to refer to it with great care, for it afforded them means of discrimination within all the mass of originally undiscriminated material. The ability to distinguish, let us say, forms of the verb חיל from forms of the verb יחל, something that becomes particularly necessary once comparative information begins to press upon the possibilities of understanding one or the other, depends upon the careful collection and comparison of the vocalization in all relevant cases. For this reason it is important to realize that the basic fixation of the Massoretic pointing was already done before the rise of grammatical and lexical inquiries. Even the manuscript B 19a, from which the text of *BH*³ was taken, was written in 1008; the Cairo codex of the prophets was made in 895 by Moses ben Asher. The pointing was done from tradition, and did not depend on the results of the incipient scholarly inquiries. Conversely, the fact that a classification of the grammar was possible forms something of a witness to the value of the vocalization in general.

Fourthly, on the lexical side it appears that for many words, especially out-of-the-way words, the Jewish scholars of this period did not attempt to rely on tradition for information about meaning. Whether they worked from comparative sources such as Arabic, or used the guidance of parallelisms and other elements of the Hebrew text, they did not make a simple appeal to tradition or to current usage. This does not necessarily mean that they were indifferent to either; perhaps it was rather that tradition would give contradictory answers. The emphasis on the *peshaṭ* or plain sense made it impossible to accept the fanciful interpretations found in some currents of tradition.

(5) *More Recent Trends*

Only one or two remarks should be made about the general change of scene as we move into the modern period.

Firstly, one notices a certain shift on the part of Christian opinion away from dependence on the Jews for deciding the meaning of Hebrew items. St. Jerome, in his reliance on the *hebraica ueritas*, had had to turn to Jewish informants for his linguistic guidance. The same situation is generally true in the Middle Ages, wherever study of Hebrew among Christians went on. A particularly strong influence was that of Rashi (Rabbi Solomon ben Isaac, of Troyes, 1030–1105), who was, and among Jews has remained, by far the most popular of the Jewish biblical commentators.[1] By the mid-twelfth century Rashi's works were being used in the school of Hugo of St. Victor, and Hugo's notes include admonitions on the necessity of understanding the Hebrew—since, after all, 'the Greek texts are truer than the Latin, and the Hebrew texts are truer than the Greek'. It was, however, Nicholas of Lyra, who died in 1349, who most fully brought the effect of Rashi's exegesis into the currents of Christian thinking.

After the sixteenth century, however, when the great Christian Hebraists like Reuchlin made Hebrew an integral part of Christian culture and education, there seems to be a lessening in the sense of dependence on Jewish opinion. The central Jewish authority in the sixteenth century, in respect of influence upon the Christians, was Elias Levita (1469–1549).[2] But no equally central figure followed him in the respect of Christians, and the progressive current of discovery which had characterized Jewish biblical study through the Middle Ages seemed, once its fruits were passed on to the Christians, to have become somewhat torpid. The study of Hebrew was cultivated and passed on among the Christians, and the conditions gradually came about in which it was possible for the Christians to become unaware of their debt to Jewish grammatical study and to forget that the Jews might be the ones who would know what Hebrew words meant.

This, however, did not happen immediately. The Buxtorfs in their handling of the text showed very deep respect for the Rabbinic tradition; and in 1620 the elder Buxtorf published his *Tiberias sive commentarius masorethicus triplex*, showing a close and lively interest in the Massorah, here following in the steps of Levita. In more recent times, however, there has come about a tendency to give little attention to the Massorah, and the way in which it functioned for the clarification and classification of the language has been generally less well known.

Another relevant historical matter is the dispute over the inspiration of the vocalization signs. Against the tradition that the points were, like the consonants, given to Moses at Sinai, Ludwig Cap-

---

[1] See particularly Hailperin, *Rashi and the Christian Scholars*.
[2] See G. E. Weil, *Élie Lévita*.

pellus in 1624 published an argument showing that the points had been added after the fifth or sixth centuries A.D. The more traditional view, conversely, now extended the conception of biblical inspiration so as to include explicitly the divine inspiration of the vowel points. This debate led to renewed interest in textual criticism and to an increased awareness that existing texts could err. The remembrance of this debate has, on the other hand, left another and a less happy inheritance, in the form of a feeling that the vowel points are freely disposable at the pleasure of the critic. Actually, as we shall see, the vowel signs are historical evidence just as the consonants are, and while neither history nor dogma can affirm that they are certainly right, history does mean that they must be examined as evidence and not arbitrarily replaced.

The seventeenth century is also notable for improved knowledge of the Semitic languages, especially Arabic. Several polyglot lexica were published, the best known being that of E. Castell, the *Lexicon Heptaglotton* (1669), which gave comparative registration of Hebrew, Aramaic, Syriac, Samaritan, Ethiopic, and Arabic, along with separate listing for Persian.[1]

All this implies a departure from the older idea that Hebrew was in some way a divine or angelic speech, and leads towards a treatment of it as a human language; to this one had only to add that it was a derivative human language, and the movement of Hebrew study into a more historical realm was accomplished. Albert Schultens[2] made this notably plain, for he regarded Arabic as the purest and clearest of the Semitic languages and attached Hebrew to the Semitic group as one dialect among many.

His *Dissertatio theologica-philologica de utilitate linguae arabicae in interpretanda sacra lingua*[3] argued that Arabic was in principle just as old as any other Semitic language and could therefore be applied to the understanding of Hebrew passages. That צרה at I Sam. 1. 6 meant 'co-wife' (= Arab. *ḍarra*), and that וַיַּעַשׂ at I Sam. 14. 32 meant 'bent, turned',[4] are points which Schultens affirmed (not without the support of earlier scholars like Jerome or Kimchi) and which have enjoyed reiteration in the twentieth

---

[1] On this period see Kraus, pp. 70 ff.
[2] See in particular J. Fück, *Die arabischen Studien in Europa*, pp. 105 ff.
[3] Found in his *Opera Minora* (Leiden, 1769), pp. 487–510.
[4] For further comment on this example see below, pp. 69, 98, 246 f.

century. Many of his other suggestions are less happy, and the discerning modern Arabist Fück speaks of his work as a 'misuse of Arabic, driven to the farthest point'.[1] Johann David Michaelis (1717–91) may be mentioned as one who, following in Schultens's line, did even more to place the understanding of Hebrew within the framework of the philology of Arabic and other Semitic languages. But meanwhile a further change was under way, for Arabic studies were freeing themselves from the position of a servant to *sacra philologia*, i.e. the position of being consulted only when some obscurity in Hebrew required elucidation.[2]

In the nineteenth century the logic of textual emendation may be comparable with the logic of the source analysis which was equally dominant at the time. In source analysis scholars reacted against the artificial expedients by which the inconcinnities of narratives had been covered over. Such inconcinnities, they held, did not belong to the texts originally; rather, they had arisen by the careless compounding of different sources. The scholar could trust in his own sense of unity and sequence, and thus could analyse the material in a way which would remove the need for artificiality. Similarly, in the area of verbal difficulties, the scholar could rely on what he knew; if the text made no sense, one need no longer hide this fact, as the older exegesis had done, and one certainly need not try artificial explanations for the anomalies of the text. Rather let the text be emended to what it had been before careless scribes corrupted it, and the difficulties would be gone. In conjectural textual criticism the careless scribe plays a role somewhat analogous to the role of the clumsy redactor in source criticism. One does not need to press this parallel; but within limits it is true. Both at the level of the larger literary units (source criticism or 'literary' criticism) and at the level of the smaller verbal or graphic groupings (textual criticism) we have an outburst of activity by the scholar who does not recognize that the text, in the form in which it now stands, and in the continuity in which it has been transmitted, is final.

At any rate, in the highly productive scholarship of the later nineteenth century, it does seem that textual and literary criticism, rather than comparative philological operations, succeeded in occupying much of the time and energy of scholars. The great Wellhausen, who was later to achieve fame as an Arabist, in his textual

---

[1] Fück, p. 107.   [2] Fück, p. 122.

studies on the Old Testament seems to have concentrated almost
entirely on the textual approach, emphasizing the LXX in particular. At I Sam. 14. 32, for example, he does not even mention the
Arabic explanation suggested by Schultens, though more recent
scholars have reiterated it.[1] At Amos 7. 4, where the rendering
'creation' or 'creatures' for the obscure חֵלֶק is a fairly easy suggestion on the basis of familiar Arabic usage, Wellhausen as late as
1898 simply has nothing to suggest.[2] S. R. Driver's *Notes on the
Hebrew Text and the Topography of the Books of Samuel*, on which
whole generations of English-speaking students were trained, also
laid all its emphasis on textual and palaeographical, rather than on
comparative philological, insights; though occasionally it noted the
latter, as in the case of צרה 'co-wife' at I Sam. 1. 6.

The predominance of textual treatments can be best seen in the
standard critical text which emerged from this period, namely *BH*³.
This text gave space to hundreds of emendations, but quoted
rather few cases of philological treatment. In Hosea I find over 300
places where the editor has registered textual changes in the lower
apparatus; of philological treatments, however, I find only one.
This is at 7. 16, where the editor suggests the reading וְזָל לַעְגָּם
(itself assuming a conjectural rearrangement of the order of consonants, plus an assumed haplography); the suggested explanation
is that this זל would be the Arabic *zāla* 'ceased', or rather a
Hebrew cognate thereof, which in BDB is not recognized except
as the root of זוּלָת 'except'.

In Job, on the other hand, *BH*³ registers a much larger number
of philological treatments. The editor, Beer, registers in the lower
apparatus some fifteen cases where he explains the reading through
reference to other languages than biblical Hebrew.[3] In many of
these, however, the philological treatment does not go with a retention of the MT but with an emendation. These are, of course, only
a very small proportion of the philological treatments which have

---

[1] J. Wellhausen, *Der Text der Bücher Samuelis* (Göttingen, 1871), p. 93.
[2] J. Wellhausen, *Die Kleinen Propheten* (Berlin, 1898), pp. 7, 89. For a discussion of this possibility see below, pp. 260 f.
[3] See 3. 14, Arab. *haram* 'pyramid'; 15. 12, MH רמז 'nod'; 15. 30, MH נשר
'cut down'; 18. 3, MH טמם 'make blunt, stupid'; 19. 26, Accad. and Targ. חור
'look'; 20. 18, MH לעס 'chew'; 21. 24, MH עטם 'thigh'; 21. 27, Syr. המס
'think'; 25. 3, MH בור 'boorish'; 33. 25, Accad. *ṭapāšu* 'be sleek'; 36. 18, Aram.
חמה 'beware'; 36. 33, MH עלעולה 'storm'; 37. 21, Syr. בהר 'obscure';
41. 18, Syr. שדיה 'spear'.

been suggested for the book of Job; but it is interesting that they did find a place in this way in the apparatus of *BH*³. It is also interesting to see how many of these suggestions depend on late Hebrew, and how few are drawn from the Arabic and Accadian sources which have recently become considerably more prominent. In any case, in spite of the somewhat greater registration of philological treatments in Job and some other books, it remains true that *BH*³ in its notes remains overwhelmingly a monument to the textual approach.

Nevertheless the strength of the tendency towards textual treatment did not pass without challenge. Sometimes this challenge came from scholars of a conservative tendency, whether Jewish or Christian, who found it hard to accept the judgements now fashionable among scholars and felt that these solutions were arbitrary. Such scholars felt that it was better to explain the text than to rewrite it by emendation or to analyse it by source-critical methods; and if it had to be explained, the use of other languages was one way to explain it. Moreover, some of the scholars of such a conservative tendency were men of formidable philological ability. Franz Delitzsch (1813–90) is the most obvious example, and, in a somewhat different category, we may mention Dillmann also; from various points of view, indeed, scholars who disagreed with the reigning hypotheses, or who worked on aspects which were not then in the centre of interest, contributed to keeping the scene of scholarship varied.

The discovery of Accadian caused an important shift of emphasis in Old Testament study. We need not discuss the impact of the new knowledge about Accadian literature and religion. On the purely linguistic side the discovery greatly altered the perspective from which Hebrew could be seen, and in particular provided a very different angle of view from that which had been mainly informed by Arabic and Aramaic.

Friedrich Delitzsch in his *Prolegomena* (1886) is thus found using some arguments which were to be re-echoed again and again 70 or 80 years later. It is dangerous, he argued, to remove unusual locutions or *hapax legomena* by emendation, since ancient Hebrew literature is very fragmentary. Emendation can thus simply remove the genuine from the text. Accadian comes as a providential saviour to the MT, and much reserve must be used in emendation (p. 69). The whole study of vocabulary reflects upon the reliability of the

MT and thus upon all other text-critical questions (p. vii).
Delitzsch's work, not without its one-sided aspects, sets the tone for
much later philological work.

About the turn of the century we have two men who worked on
the text and whose notes provided numerous examples of both
textual and philological treatments, though with the emphasis
rather on the former than on the latter. Felix Perles in his *Analekten*
(1895, second series 1922) made many lexical suggestions; for
example he identified at Job 40. 17 a verb חפץ meaning 'make
straight, stretch out', different from the usual חפץ meaning 'be
pleased'. Arnold Ehrlich in his *Randglossen* provided a long series
of textual and philological suggestions. Both of these writers seem
to have been a stimulus to later workers on the philological side.

In spite of these varying influences, however, the use of textual
treatment remained generally dominant in the earlier twentieth
century, and we have registered already its place in the apparatus of
*BH*³. In the twenties and thirties, however, we should take note of
two points of view which stimulated discussion.

The first is the work of the voluminous if erratic scholar Wutz.
The main point of Wutz's work, the transcription theory, i.e. the
opinion that the LXX was translated from a Hebrew text which
had already been written in Greek script, may fortunately be passed
over here; it is fully reviewed in the standard works on textual
criticism. It does concern us, however, that in quite a large number
of cases Wutz, finding a Hebrew word to be translated in a surprising way by a Greek word, accounted for this, subject to the tortuous
complications of the transcription theory, by explaining that the
Hebrew word had a sense made evident to us today by a cognate
Arabic or Aramaic or other Semitic word.

For example, there are certain places where the familiar Hebrew
דֶּרֶךְ, usually meaning 'way', is translated by words for 'sin' like
ἁμάρτημα. Wutz believed[1] that the Hebrew word was actually an
(otherwise non-existent) דֶּרֶב, explained in his laconic notes as
identical with '*ar. darb vitium*'. That is to say, the original text had
this word דרב, which was quite rightly rendered by the LXX but
in the transmission of the Hebrew text was mistakenly corrupted
into the familiar דרך. Such explanations, often thrown out

---

[1] *Transkriptionen*, p. 462. The word ἁμάρτημα occurs in MS. B at Hos. 10. 13,
while ἁμαρτία is found at III Kingdoms 22. 53.

without any attempt at full justification, are quite frequent in Wutz's work.

Like the rest of Wutz's work this aspect has received some strong criticism. As for the 'Arabic *darb*' meaning 'vice', Nyberg[1] flatly denied the existence of this word, as well as the necessity for such an interpretation. At the best the suggestions of Wutz are often poorly argued or substantiated; at the worst, they seem often to be simple mistakes.

Nevertheless Wutz found an echo for his argument that LXX renderings might derive from real Hebrew meanings which are now recoverable only through appeal to the cognate languages. Driver in 1934 enunciated the 'important rule' that:

The origin of the Greek rendering must be sought in the vocabularies of the cognate, especially the Aramaic-Syriac and the Arabic, languages before assuming that it represents a divergence from the Hebrew text.[2]

In saying this he made reference to Wutz's arguments in *Transkriptionen* i. 150–2. So careful a scholar as Winton Thomas concedes that the writings of Wutz 'contain a great deal of material which will repay study by the Hebrew lexicographer'.[3] Thus the work of Wutz did something to stimulate the rise of philological treatments.

Another, and a more important, criticism of the common use of textual treatments came (1934–5) from the Swedish scholar Nyberg. Nyberg was highly critical of the proneness to emendation in contemporary scholarship. The proud *ich lese* and the dogmatic *legendum* seemed to him to be not a demonstration, but a denial, of good scholarship. It was assumed that the extant text was thoroughly corrupt; but, Nyberg argued, if the text was really corrupt, so that it became somewhat like the verse of Aristophanes supposed to represent Persian (*Acharnae* 100), then the honest thing was not to emend but to abandon altogether the attempt at interpretation. Nyberg set out what he held to be the tacit assumptions of the current fashion, and against these he formulated counterpositions of his own. The following points are those most relevant to our subject.

Firstly, the prevailing fashion, as Nyberg analysed it, assumed

---

[1] *Studien zum Hoseabuche*, p. 81 n. Wutz, one may surmise, based himself on the plural *'adrāb 'vitium, corruptio'* of Freytag, ii. 19a.

[2] *ZAW* lii (1934) 308. [3] *OTMS*, p. 255.

that 'the understanding of the Old Testament books in the Jewish community came very early to an end'. Since the text was only half understood, the transcription was a mechanical one. This led to all sorts of errors: words, meanings, and constructions which never existed in the living language. If this is the case, then

The punctuation is nothing but a quite late attempt to wring from this partially meaningless text a sense appropriate to a Rabbinic train of thought.

Against all this Nyberg thought that the transmission, being live and oral, though it certainly involved changes and the evolution of new understandings, had never been mechanical and had never consisted in mere guesses at the sense of a text mechanically preserved in writing.

Secondly, the fashion assumed that the Old Testament is written in a uniform language, with the exception of the Aramaic sections and the limited sections of 'late' Hebrew, such as Qoheleth and Esther. In thinking this, Nyberg held, scholars were deceived by the unitary punctuation system and the unitary grammar involved in it. There are, on the contrary, regionally and temporally distinct strata in the Old Testament.

Thirdly, the fashion supposed that the MT was a late and poor form of the text, and that better and earlier guidance was to be found in the versions, and especially the LXX. Nyberg refused to give wholesale judgements on this kind of thing. He emphasized the need for careful study of the origin of every variant, of the meaning of the versions and their translation techniques, and of the history of each version. In places he was ready to decide that the consonantal text behind the LXX was better than that of the MT.[1] But in general the emphasis of Nyberg's work was upon the reliability of the MT. The versions are derivative from MT; that is, they generally represent poor departures from MT or a text close to it, rather than good independent bases. He ended with a strong call to the scholar to get back to the MT as the text which he had to interpret.

Nyberg also held that the growth of the fashion for emendation had gone along with, and partly been a result of, an isolation of Old Testament scholarship from more general oriental philology.[2] The

[1] See the summary list, *Hoseabuch*, p. 114.
[2] Nyberg, *ZAW* lii (1934) 243; *Hoseabuch*, pp. 6 f.

Old Testament could not be isolated from what was known of the development of tradition in Islam, in Zoroastrianism, or in Mandaism. The use of these wider perspectives, he believed, would overcome the isolation in which the emending procedures had grown and flourished.

Nyberg in his general remarks did not discuss the place of comparative philology in solving difficulties through appeal to the cognate languages. In his detailed work on Hosea, however, he uses this method quite frequently. Thus at Hos. 8. 9 he finds it impossible to make sense of the word פֶּרֶא if it has the usual meaning 'wild ass'; it means a 'shoot', following the Accadian *pir'u*.[1] At 10. 10 he comments on the phrase בְּאָסְרָם. One would expect this to be 'in their binding', but this is meaningless. He argues therefore:

> The corresponding Arabic *bi-'asrihim* is a comprehensive expression of totality and means 'all without exception'. . . . If the Arabic expression has been able to undergo this development of meaning, why should the same be impossible for the Hebrew אסר which means exactly the same thing?[2]

Thus the sentence is to be translated: 'All the tribes without exception will assemble themselves against them.'

At Hos. 7. 16 he says that זַעַם obviously cannot have the normal sense, i.e. 'wrath'. But, he goes on, 'anyone who knows Arabic thinks naturally of *za'am*'. The LXX and Syriac, with their renderings of 'shamelessness, lack of discipline', were at this point more or less correct.[3]

Though some appeal was thus made by Nyberg to comparative philology, it would be wrong to exaggerate his dependence on this source. To a rather greater degree his arguments depend upon showing the existence of unusual or unrecognized usages within Hebrew. Himself the author of a Hebrew grammar, he strove to do justice to the variety of possible expression in the language. Thus the difficult phrase כִּמְרִיבֵי כֹהֵן at Hos. 4. 4 is dealt with primarily through a syntactic treatment, the main appeal being to other examples in the Hebrew Bible, and only a secondary appeal being to Arabic and other Semitic languages.[4]

---

[1] *Hoseabuch*, p. 64.   [2] Ibid., p. 79.
[3] Ibid., p. 60. Ar. *za'am* is approximately 'claim'.
[4] Ibid., p. 24.

In general, then, the importance of Nyberg's work for us lies (*a*) in its strong challenge to the fashion for emendation, and (*b*) in his insistence on raising important questions of principle, in particular about the relation between language and understanding.

In recent decades the original production of emendations has decreased, and the tendency to resort to philological rather than textual treatments has been growing. But the degree of movement towards the philological approach has been very varied. In England very distinguished philological work came from Professor G. R. Driver of Oxford and Professor Winton Thomas of Cambridge. In America some considerable emphasis on philological treatments, based especially upon Ugaritic, has been seen in the work of some of Albright's followers. Jewish scholars like Eitan and Tur-Sinai have also been extremely prominent.

German Old Testament scholarship, on the other hand, seems to have been less prolific in philological treatments. Some of the post-war commentaries continue to show a marked acceptance of the guidance of *BH*[3] at points of textual difficulty. A detailed work like Kraus's *Psalms* resists the zeal for emendation found in the older scholars like Duhm or Gunkel, but is not on the other hand very productive of new appeals to the cognate languages. While it discusses a number of those which have been made, the general tendency is a sober and moderate defence of the MT as Hebrew, rather than a fresh appeal to cognate material.

IV

ASPECTS OF COMPARATIVE
PHILOLOGICAL METHOD

As we have seen, there had long existed a certain somewhat rudimentary comparative approach to Hebrew, in which its words were
related to similar words in Aramaic and Arabic. It was only in the
nineteenth century, however, that comparative philology in its
modern form grew up. The modern movement can be distinguished
from the older in respect of (a) the degree to which it sought to state
consistent or systematic relations, as distinct from more isolated
examples; (b) the insistence on an historical approach. We shall discuss certain aspects of comparative philology as it is related (1) to
history, (2) to sound, (3) to meaning.

(1) *History*

Comparative philologists would normally claim that their approach to language is an historical one. The comparative perspectives
of medieval linguistic scholarship, even when accurate observations
of similarities and differences were made, and even when certain
historical data (like the difference between biblical and Mishnaic
Hebrew) were known, did not assume an historical form. The comparative philology which developed in the nineteenth century, by
contrast, was historical in method and outlook in the sense that the
comparative relations which it observed were set within an historical
framework of change and development.

The more obvious aspect of this historical approach was the
emphasis on the dating and the strict chronological control of the
available written sources. In biblical Hebrew this was connected
with the literary criticism which departed from the traditional
dating of books and evolved theories of their composition from
sources. New evidence, like inscriptions and the Amarna letters,
was likewise set in relation with previous knowledge through careful chronological ordering. It thus became possible to write a
history of a language, provided that evidence over a sufficiently

long period was available, as was very obviously so, for instance, with Greek or English.

More important for our purpose, however, the comparative relations between two languages like Hebrew and Aramaic were now worked out as the result of historical development from a common ancestor, and the reconstruction of this common ancestor language, though not necessarily undertaken in detail, was implied or assumed in comparative work. The characteristic of comparative philology was not only historical organization of extant evidence but also the use of extrapolation to produce a picture of previous stages, themselves not directly evidenced, which would serve as a basis for an historical and developmental account of the stages which are directly known from evidence.

It might indeed be supposed that there is a quite different task which is more properly 'comparative', that is, the study of the differences and similarities between languages which are not related in origin—Chinese and Hebrew, let us say, or Turkish and English. Comparisons of this kind, though not without their interest, are not what has usually been meant by the term 'comparative philology'. This term has meant the comparative study of language groups within which signs of a common historical origin can be detected; 'comparison' is not a general discussion of similarities and differences, but the construction of an historical common scheme within which the material of related languages can be placed. It is thus possible to say that 'comparative' was not quite the right word; Hoenigswald[1] refers suggestively to 'the process of triangulation known misleadingly as the *comparative* method'.

Obviously the historical emphasis fits in easily with this emphasis on the study of languages related in origin. If we are interested in the differences between Chinese and Hebrew, we do not necessarily advance the subject at all by tracing each back to an earlier historical stage, for at that earlier stage they will be still equally unrelated. If we are discussing Hebrew and Aramaic, however, the extension back into an earlier stage may bring us closer to their common origin. Thus to be comparative, as comparative philologists have construed the term, means to be historical.

Conversely, for certain early stages of development, it may seem that there is no way to be historical except by being comparative in one's approach. The point of origin of the Romance languages is to

---

[1] Hoenigswald, *Language Change*, p. 2.

a considerable extent directly evidenced in the form of Latin. But for the languages of the ancient world the previous historical stages are not directly known. We have no direct evidence for Hebrew before the earliest written texts in Hebrew. If we wish to know something of Hebrew as it was before these earliest texts, we can have recourse to the comparative study of Arabic or Aramaic. Moreover, we can no longer rightly confine our study to one such related language: in principle the prehistory has to be worked out from the evidence of the whole group of related languages. Prehistoric Hebrew was not related uniquely to Arabic or to Aramaic, but had its own history, for the reconstruction of which we may have to consider the evidence of Ethiopic or Mandaic or a modern South Arabian dialect. Comparative study therefore involves in principle the requirement that it should be the general comparative study of a language family.

The reconstruction afforded when the other Semitic languages are taken into account may enable us to state probable conjectures of the nature of Hebrew before the time of the existing records. We may then perhaps conclude that Hebrew at an earlier stage had case-endings in its nouns, as classical Arabic still has. Again, observing that Hebrew appears to have three sibilants, ס, שׂ, and שׁ, where Arabic has the two, /š/ and /s/, and that Hebrew /ś/ (שׂ) often corresponds to Arabic /š/ while Hebrew /š/ (שׁ) corresponds to Arabic /s/, and combining this with similar observations applying to other Semitic languages, we may perhaps conclude that the ancestor language had a series of three, which we may represent as /s/, /ś/, and /š/; and that these three have been reduced to two in Arabic in such a way that the Arabic resultant phonemes commonly appear to be opposite to the pair with which they are obviously comparable in Hebrew.

The total reconstruction of an ancestor language like proto-Semitic is, of course, understood to be extremely hypothetical. Indeed, for the purpose of the kind of philological treatment discussed in this book, no complete explicit reconstruction is required or assumed. Most treatments offer the particular evidence of a word with its meaning in two, three, or four of the known Semitic languages. Thus the very hazardous task of stating what the proto-Semitic form and meaning were is not necessarily required. Nevertheless the potentiality of such a reconstruction, within the limits set by our information, is a background assumption of the whole procedure. Most work, no doubt, has been done on the basis of what Murtonen calls 'the theory of the descent of all the Semitic languages from one single mother tongue structurally similar to them'.[1] Such a theory may be right or wrong, and certain points in our study may be relevant to a judgement on such a theory; but for our practical purposes here we do not require to determine what proto-Semitic was like, but only to observe that the existence of such an entity was and is one of the assumptions in method made by comparative philology.

The importance of the common ancestor of languages like Arabic, Aramaic, and Hebrew has not lain in our reconstruction of this language; rather, the reconstruction serves as a basis from which the extant languages can be described historically as the products of fairly consistent changes. How rigorous this consistency must be is one of the questions which will have to be discussed shortly.

Though comparative philology is thus historical in the sense that the relations it observes are set within a framework of historical change, there is another sense in which it is more ambiguously related to historical method. The construction of a common ancestor for extant languages is only a partially historical procedure, for no direct historical evidence of the common ancestor is available; the common ancestor is a hypothetical construction sufficient to account for later phenomena actually extant. Any addition to the evidence known (as, for example, the discovery of a language like Ugaritic) may mean that the picture of the common ancestor has to be revised. Conversely the discovery of a previously unknown language may provide confirmation of reconstructions which philologists had previously made.

This constructive character of the work of comparative philology is seen not only in the picture of ancestor languages like proto-Semitic but also in other relations. When it is said that such and such a form 'originally' had a certain sense, or that a Hebrew meaning had developed from such and such a pre-Hebrew meaning, these are constructions which rest upon evidence in the historically known languages but are not in themselves directly or empirically verifiable.

This constructive character of the work of comparative philology is important for several aspects of the argument which will follow

[1] *JSS* xi (1966) 150 n.

elsewhere in this book. Philologists have at times tended to speak rather apodeictically, as if their opinions rested on direct evidence. This is not always justified. To say this is not to question the validity of comparative philology; we are merely drawing attention to complications inherent in its methods. The construction of linguistic stages previous to those directly evidenced, though it is an important procedure of historical philology, is a complicated and precarious undertaking which may have to be subjected to constant revision. One reason for this is that, in the circumstances here obtaining, the law of economy of hypotheses does not apply: the simplest connexion between two phenomena need not be the best explanation, and much more complicated relations may be equally probable. This constructive character to which we have referred does not mean that comparative philology is unhistorical or without factual basis; but its operations are indirect rather than direct.

It is true that the comparative method is not the only one available for the reconstruction of previous historical stages of a language. Something can also be achieved by what has been called 'internal reconstruction'.[1] In Hebrew, for instance, the evidence of the 'segholate' nouns may suggest that the earlier form of מֶלֶךְ was *malk*, while the earlier form of סֵפֶר was *sifr*. This result is achieved primarily not through comparison with other cognate languages but through a consideration of phenomena within Hebrew, such as the suffixed forms מַלְכְּךָ and סִפְרְךָ. Much of our information about the prehistory of Hebrew is attained in this way.

Nevertheless a larger proportion of our historical reconstructions, and for our purpose a more important part, rests upon a comparative method using cognate sources. 'Much better opportunities for reconstruction exist where the older stage can be triangulated from two or more independent later stages into which the speech community has separated.'[2] The possibilities offered by internal reconstruction are restricted if it cannot be accompanied and strengthened by the presence of comparative method.

In summary, then, comparative philology has operated in the construction of a developmental scheme within which the material

---

[1] For a brief review, wrapped in impenetrable technical terminology, see Hoenigswald, *Linguistic Change*, pp. 68 ff.; more simply, Lehmann, *Historical Linguistics*, pp. 99–106.

[1] Hoenigswald, op. cit., p. 69. Cf. Thieme, in Hymes, pp. 585–97.

of related or 'cognate' languages may be set and seen historically. For persons who, like Old Testament scholars, work at a point near to the earliest available historical evidence of the language involved, i.e. Hebrew, comparative methods seem to be a principal resource for the obtaining of a view of the earlier history.

(2) *Sound*

In considering the modes in which the evidence of extant texts is used in comparative philology, we may first give attention to the study of sound and sound-laws. As is well known, this played an important part in the rise of comparative philology, and Grimm's law in the field of Germanic is particularly famous among the general public.

Actually much of comparative philology has avoided a real concern with sound in the strict sense, i.e. with phonetics and acoustics. Its work has, certainly in the Semitic field, been based for the most part on the written signs. Where work has been done on the modern languages and dialects, interest in phonetics has been more immediately necessary. For the older languages, however, where no direct phonetic information was available in any case, philology has often devoted its primary attention to correspondences of the written signs, and has shown considerable naïvety or vagueness when statements about sound going beyond this were attempted. When a philologist tells us that a correspondence exists between Hebrew /z/ and Aramaic /d/, and that these represent different developments from proto-Semitic /ḏ/, he to a large extent has in mind the letters ז and ד in the Hebrew or Aramaic script, along with the sounds generally associated with them in the various modern universities. He probably would not be able to give a description of the changes in voice production which are involved in his own statement, and the fact that his statement did not seem to be dependent on such a description is one main reason why a detailed philology, including assertions about 'sound-laws' and 'phonology', could grow up in the company of a very considerable ignoring of the description of sound.

Philologists have known, nevertheless, that it was in the sound rather than in the writing that the changes they trace had occurred, and a very important place is given to the correspondences between the different languages of a cognate group. Any comparative grammar will furnish a table of the sounds of the (constructed) parent language, with the sounds into which each has developed in the later languages. Thus we may hear that proto-Semitic had /t̲/ (*th*), Arabic /t̲/, Hebrew /š/, Aramaic /t/ and Ethiopic /s/. Hebrew /š/ then 'corresponds' to Aramaic /t/, as in שׁוֹר or תּוֹר 'ox'. If Hebrew שׂ has a corresponding שׂ in Aramaic also, as in קְדֵשׁ 'holy', this goes back to proto-Semitic /š/ or is explained in some other way. An exhaustive statement of such correspondences is part of the structure of a comparative grammar.

It has remained, however, a matter of some dispute how strictly the correspondences which are normal are to be taken also as certain and invariable. One school of nineteenth-century philologists maintained the position that 'sound laws admit no exception'. Others, however, have thought it possible to treat the normal phonological correspondences more lightly. Meir Fraenkel, for example, tries to argue that the familiar Hebrew חַזָּן 'synagogue cantor' is a 'Hebrew variant' of the Arabic *ḥaddām* 'servant'. This at once involves a conflict with the usual correspondences, since a Hebrew /z/ corresponds to a /z/ or a /d̲/ in Arabic, but not to a /d/ in that language. Fraenkel goes on, however:

> However, sound rules are not sound laws. Lagarde and Nöldeke point out exceptions in the Semitic sound rules. . . . The ears and the mouth of men are not machines, which follow iron physical laws and are without exception. We know how the sound laws of Grimm have been criticized. . . . The tables of sound correspondences, which we find in Bauer and Leander or in Brockelmann, are correct in general, but we cannot admit that they are right without exception for all linguistic phenomena. These are not laws, but only tendencies of sound change.[1]

Obviously the question is of vital importance for our subject. We may consider separately two questions: (1) how far the sound changes, by which the correspondences between cognate languages have evolved, are regular; (2) how this applies to the situation of difficult passages in the Old Testament.

As for the first of these questions the opinion of modern linguists seems to be distinctly in favour of the regularity of sound change. To argue this does not require, and indeed is not supported by, the use of the concept of 'iron physical laws', or indeed of 'laws' of any

[1] *HUCA* xxxi (1960) 69.

kind at all. Examination of the modes by which changes occur, including the statistical element and the fact that phonetic change is a social phenomenon, leads still to the assertion that 'phonetic change is regular' and that 'whenever the proper conditions obtain, phonemic change occurs without exception'.[1]

The consideration of dialect adds additional complexity to this picture without altering it in principle. On detailed examination the total entities called 'languages' may be found to break down into local diversities, which may have differences from the correspondences shown by the standard forms usually quoted. Thus, to take a well-known example, proto-Germanic /-k/ should become /-x/ (commonly spelt *ch*) over the whole High German area. Dialect geography, however, shows that the line between *ik* and *ich* is different from the line between *maken* and *machen*.[2] Thus 'the various isoglosses in any bundle seldom coincide exactly'.[3] The units examined in linguistics are not absolute and homogeneous entities which form separate 'languages'; remarkable local diversity exists.

This does not, however, in itself disprove the assertion that changes are regular under given conditions. It means that the statement of the conditions is more complicated than can be achieved through the simple specification of the language concerned as a whole. It is thus always possible that the detailed situation in some area was more complicated than is suggested by a normal correspondence such as that between Hebrew /z/ and Aramaic /d/.

The existence of dialect (which will be discussed further in the next chapter)[4] and other complications does not, then, constitute a valid objection to the conception that sound changes are regular.

This regularity is not only an important principle for comparative philological operations in general; it is one of particular importance for philological treatments in the Hebrew Bible. The passages under discussion are, *ex hypothesi*, obscure ones; the relations of meaning between them and known Hebrew words, and between them and suggested Semitic cognate words, are an open

---

[1] Quotations are from Gleason, pp. 394–7. Cf. already Saussure, who insists that phonetic changes are 'absolutely' and 'perfectly' regular, *Course*, pp. 143 ff., while this does not depend on the use of any simple concept of 'law', ibid., pp. 91–95. For another recent summary statement see Robins, pp. 311 f.

[2] For a simple statement, with diagram, see Lehmann, pp. 124 f.

[3] So Gleason, p. 401.

[4] See below, pp. 98–101.

question. Since this semantic relation is a very open one, it is desirable that the phonological relations should be very closely established; otherwise we have two loose probabilities or surmises, with no more coercive factor than the conviction that the result is a suitable meaning for the text. The looser the phonological correspondences, the more the weight of proof must fall on the semantic suitability of suggestions offered; but semantic suitability, under these circumstances, is perhaps not much more than mere guessing. It is wrong that such guessing should be justified by the argument that phonological correspondences are not rigorously mandatory, and that the sense achieved 'fits perfectly well'.

An otherwise unexpected variation from the standard correspondences can well be accepted as important evidence where there is no substantial doubt about the meaning of the terms in question (no one doubts that *ik* on one side of a German isogloss means the same as *ich* on the other side); but when the philological operation is being conducted in order to identify words previously unknown the matter is quite otherwise. The same is true of dialect; it is one thing to use evidence known to belong to a particular dialect, but quite another to call a form 'dialectal' when there is no evidence for its belonging to any particular dialect and no series of dialectal features into which to fit it; this latter procedure, in other words, is merely using the general idea of dialect irresponsibly in order to excuse an ignoring of the normal correspondences in a particular case.

Many examples in the history of philology show how the determination to take phonological correspondences rigorously has led to the discovery of new rules and thus to the extension of knowledge. It was precisely because rules such as those of Grimm were taken to be strict and universal that scholars were forced to worry over them and through this worrying produced new refinements, such as Verner's law relating stress to voicing. If the rules had not been taken as strict and universal in the first place, the phenomena would have been supposed to be haphazard and inexplicable, and no new results would have been forthcoming.

Thus attention to strict phonological correspondence is one of the ways in which suggestions, which seem at first to be semantically satisfying, can be further probed.

The average person would be very likely to affirm the philological identity of English *day* and Latin *dies*. Yet this identity does not conform to the normal correspondences, and it appears that in fact the words are not cognate. If phonological correspondences were treated as a light matter, these scholarly doubts would have been swept aside by the impatient sense that the semantic agreement made it unnecessary to consider the problem of the phonological difference. Only strictness in the application of sound correspondences prevents the student from quick and easy conclusions based on semantic identity or similarity.

In an article in 1956 Ullendorff, listing words held in common by Hebrew and ancient South Arabian, included the equivalence between Hebrew שׁפת 'place, set' and ESA *s̆ft* 'give'. This is semantically an easy equivalence, since a similar spread of meaning can be easily seen in the common verb נתן 'give'. Beeston, however, in a later note, observes that this equivalence involves an irregular correspondence of sibilants, for the ESA /š/ usually corresponds to Hebrew שׂ, as in שׂדה 'field', ESA *s̆dw*. This being so, Beeston is led to suggest a completely different etymology for the words in question.[1]

It is not necessary for us to argue between the suggestions advanced by these distinguished scholars. What is important is to observe that the desire to support the normal correspondence is the motive for further research into the matter. But for such a motive the semantic obviousness of the suggestion as formulated by Ullendorff would seem entirely satisfying. It is the desire to render justice to the normal correspondences that leads to a further examination of the question, and to the offering of solutions which are more out of the way. Conversely, one can say that where the rules of normal correspondence have been taken lightly, all sorts of vague guesses from cognate languages have been offered.[2]

The statement of the phonological correspondences, then, forms a kind of basic logic for the work of comparative philology.

[1] Index, no. 310.

[2] The results of an extremely cavalier treatment of the correspondences can be seen in the work of John Gray on Ugaritic. See examples quoted in the review of the 2nd edition of his *The Legacy of Canaan* by Pope in *JSS* xi (1966) 228–41. Correspondences work in only one direction: when we have established that Hebrew *x* corresponds to Arabic *y*, this does not constitute a proof that Hebrew *y* corresponds equally well to Arabic *x*. The correspondences are reversed if Ugaritic and Hebrew *rbṣ* are related to Arabic *rbq* and Ugaritic *'lm* to Hebrew *ṣlm*; see Pope, op. cit., p. 231. Pope writes: 'Gray appears to operate on the assumption that it is permissible to reverse any process of permutation or substitute freely on either side of a phonological equation.'

(3) *Meaning*

Thirdly, we observe that the structure of comparative philology includes an irreducible semantic element. Even where correspondences in form are emphasized, this should not disguise the fact that in the setting up of these same correspondences a semantic element is involved. If we argue that Greek β in certain positions corresponds to Latin *v*, and if we exemplify this by comparing Greek βαίνω and Latin *venio*, we do this because we think that the Greek word and the Latin are semantically close enough to be good evidence. If we use as an example the relation between Hebrew שָׂדֶה 'field' and Accadian *šadū* 'mountain, country', we imply also that we can see some kind of possible semantic relationship between the meanings of the two words, even though this is a relation of greater dissimilarity than that between βαίνω and *venio*. Putting it conversely, it is doubtful whether we would accept words as illustrations of a phonological correspondence unless we could perceive a semantic relation, or a possibility of such relation, between them.

It is true that a series of phonological correspondences can be set up without this dependence on semantic similarities. Elements such as inflexions, rather than words supposed to be of like meaning, may be taken as the basis for comparison. In early Indo-European philology it was the comparison of elements like verb endings that allowed scholars to avoid the traps involved in the use of words of like meaning.[1] The same can be done in the Semitic field. The comparison of the Accadian series *iprus*, *taprus*, *taprusi* and the Hebrew series תִּקְטְלִי, תִּקְטֹל, יִקְטֹל gives information about vowel and consonant correspondences, even though it is known that semantically the function of the Accadian tense is not the same as that of the Hebrew tense. It is thus to some degree possible for a series of phonological correspondences to be set up without major semantic decisions about the similarity or dissimilarity of the meaning of words.

Nevertheless only a sketchy comparative phonology could be built up on this basis alone. Comparative philological works usually contain long strings of actual word comparisons. Thus Brockelmann[2] gives a list of words all meaning 'beard': Arabic *ḏaqan*, Hebrew זָקָן, Syriac *daqnā*, Accadian *ziqnu*. No semantic

---

[1] On this see Jespersen, *Language*, p. 38, with reference to the work of Rask.
[2] *Grundriß*, i. 335.

difficulty is involved. But sometimes the semantic relations are more complicated. In Hebrew אָמַר means approximately 'say'; but the Arabic *'amara* is rather 'command', Accadian *amāru* is 'see', and Ethiopic *'a'märä, 'ammärä* is 'know' or 'show'. This may be in vague terms 'the same word'; but the relation between the meanings is much less simple and obvious than with the words for 'beard'.

A large number of the decisions involved in setting up a system of phonological correspondences contain, then, a semantic element. Where possible, philologists may try to use for their basic correspondences examples where the semantic element is minimal (such as inflexional affixes and the like) or where it would be accepted as highly obvious (such as a series of words all meaning 'beard', as quoted above). Nevertheless almost all comparative grammars will use semantic criteria in setting up their lists of correspondences and providing illustrations.

One reason for this is the statistical variation in the frequency of the different phonemes of a language. Where a phoneme occurs frequently and in a variety of contexts, it may be relatively easy to obtain evidence of series of cognate words in which it occurs. In other cases the evidence may be much more sparse, and therefore more ambiguous. In Indo-European, for instance, the incidence of the phoneme /bh/ was very much higher than that of /b/. It is correspondingly more difficult to produce a convincing multiple demonstration of the occurrence of realizations of /b/ in the various languages. This rarity means that scholars will probably scan with greater caution the semantics of words purporting to illustrate the correspondence. In Hebrew the incidence of שׂ is substantially lower than that of (say) עַ, and this is one of the reasons why the phonological correspondences involving the sibilants are a matter of greater uncertainty; and since there is some uncertainty about the normal correspondences, greater weight must lie on the semantic convincingness of examples quoted. Moreover, Semitic languages use in inflexional affixes and the like only a very limited number of their stock of consonant phonemes, and שׂ is not one of them. Thus all attempts to state correspondences for שׂ involve the semantics of individual words.

In the research operations of comparative philology the scholar uses a list of basic correspondences which have been built up wherever possible with plentiful examples and with the use of words (or grammatical elements), such as the words for 'beard' just cited, which do not present immediate semantic uncertainties. Only because this list is fairly stable can the more adventurous research into the highly doubtful words be undertaken with confidence.

This, however, introduces us only to the elementary aspects of semantic problems in comparative philology. The meanings of words were not only used in order to construct a basic series of correspondences; study had also to be given to the various meanings of cognate words in different languages, and to the historical change of meanings in temporal stages of the same language; and, as in our philological treatments of the Hebrew Bible, comparative methods had to be harnessed to the task of discovering meanings.

In the Semitic language field, one may assert without injustice, the classical discipline of comparative philology showed a much greater weakness in questions of semantics than in other aspects of its work. Its careful and meticulous erudition in the classification of forms and the tracing of their history was not matched by an equal sophistication in the semantic area. Here on the contrary a remarkable degree of naïvety and even some considerable guesswork is to be found, while purely quantitatively the work put into aspects like phonology and morphology was vastly greater than that put into semantics. In such respects one may say that semantics formed the Achilles' heel of comparative philology.

For this weakness on the semantic side it is not difficult to suggest some reasons. Firstly, the generally empirical emphasis of comparative philology encouraged an emphasis on forms rather than on meanings. Forms are empirically attested in a way that meanings are not. This is true in spite of the constructive character which, as we have seen, attaches to the work of comparative philology. Even schemes which are highly creative and constructive can cite actual forms which are attested, being reducible to visible signs on paper or other mediums of writing. Such forms are the hard core of evidence on which philological constructions rely and to which they can in the last resort be referred.

In contrast with forms, meanings are rather slippery to handle. What kind of empirical evidence is there for the meaning of a form at this time or that? The evidence for what was written at such-and-such a time, and, behind that, the evidence for what was audibly heard at such-and-such a time, appears to have a hard and tangible

character which does not apply to assertions about what was meant
at the same time.

The historical emphasis of comparative philology reinforced
this failure to develop semantic doctrine. In the history of forms
written evidence may enable us to know just when any particular
form was in use. Even within the history of forms, we may note, it
is a much more precarious matter to decide when a form came into
use or fell out of use; for the empirical evidence, in the nature of the
case, is normally only of use and not of non-use, so that for non-use
one is dependent on one of the less desirable forms of argument
from silence. It is a still more uncertain and complex operation when
we move from forms to meanings and try to state just when and
how and why one meaning changed and was replaced by another.
Such historical semantic judgements are indeed possible where the
development of a language and literature can be followed from a
series of contemporary documents, as is the case in medieval
French, or indeed, to some extent, in the Old Testament itself as we
move from the older documents to the later. But historical philology has never been satisfied to follow the course of development
documented by extant documents; it has also sought to reconstruct
the history of the time before such documents existed. But for this
period, naturally, no empirical evidence exists. This has damaged
the study of semantic changes much more than it has damaged the
study of form changes.

Phonological development, as traced by comparative philology,
seemed to show a remarkable unity. If the phoneme /t̪/ passed over
into /t/, it seemed to do this by a more or less universal drift, which
affected the language as a whole and was largely (though not necessarily entirely) independent of questions of meaning in particular
words. Such a change could be historically fixed in relation to
other changes, so that an historical account could be given in relative
sequence, even if no exact chronological data were available.

This kind of precision and logicality was not available for semantic change. Historical approaches did not succeed in making it
fall neatly into sequence. For instance, we may suppose that the
Hebrew מִנְחָה underwent a change of meaning from the more
general 'offering' to the more particular 'cereal offering' which is
its sense in Leviticus. This change of meaning, however, has
nothing to do with general characteristics of words with the consonants /m/ or /n/ or /ḥ/, and the understanding of it cannot be

reached by gathering evidence empirically discernible through the presence of certain consonants. The change is, indeed, something that can be well studied through considering other words in the same semantic field (such, for example, as the rise to prominence of קָרְבָּן); but the study of this involves us at once in a much more literary and less empirical type of analysis. The movement of word meanings is not easily statable in the general form which sound changes have, for it depends on forces operative within, and peculiar to, the particular semantic fields concerned.[1] Thus, though any semantic change may gradually have come to exert influence on the language more generally, semantic changes do not provide an easy means of setting up a relative linguistic chronology such as can be furnished on the basis of sound changes.

The comparative emphasis, like the historical, tended to make an appreciation of semantic realities rather more difficult. We all know the type of philologist who, when asked the meaning of a word, answers by telling us the meaning of its cognates in other languages. This over-etymological approach is the result of excessive reliance on comparative thinking. The meaning of a word is its meaning in its own language, not its meaning in some other. To say this is not to deny that it is of considerable interest to know the meaning of cognate words in cognate languages. But the characteristic procedure of many scholars has been to start with comparative data; and the attempt to state the meaning in the actual language under study (in our case, Hebrew) has often been biased by a striving to fit this meaning into a possible derivative process starting from the comparative material. Thus the comparative emphasis, which has done so much to clarify fields like phonology and morphology, has often tended to confuse the field of semantics.

One prominent semantic operation is the statement of analogies.

There is a familiar Hebrew word בטח which means 'trust, feel safe'. This is commonly related to the Arabic baṭaḥa; but this latter means rather 'prostrate, fall down, lie low'. Scholars have sometimes maintained that the latter sense exists in the Hebrew also. It has been identified at Jer. 12. 5:

ובארץ שלום אתה בוטח ואיך תעשה בגאון הירדן :

---

[1] Cf. below, pp. 170–3.

The more traditional type of rendering is:

> 'and though in a land of peace thou art secure,
> yet how wilt thou do in the pride of Jordan?' (RV)

Driver, however, offers:

> 'If thou fallest flat on thy belly in a land of peace,
> how then wilt thou fare in the rising surge of the stream?'
> (Cf. RSV 'fall down'.)[1]

Again, at Job 40. 23, Driver argues that the text

$$\text{יִבְטַח כִּי־יָגִיחַ יַרְדֵּן}$$

means that he (i.e. the crocodile) is lying flat on the mud.

Such a relation between a sense of 'trust' and one of 'fall' or 'lie down' has been cited not only for this word but for others also. The Hebrew שקט 'be quiet, be at rest' has been compared to Arabic *saqaṭa* 'fall, drop'. Within Hebrew הָשְׁלַכְתִּי literally means 'I was thrown' but in context seems to mean 'I was made to depend or rely'. Blau, more remotely, compares Arabic *nāma* 'sleep', along with *nāma 'ilā* 'rely upon'.[2]

Again, it may be argued that there is a relationship between יחל 'wait', חיל or חול 'writhe', and the root of חַיִל 'strength'. If this is argued, it may also be supported by adducing the example of קוה 'hope', which is said to be equivalent to Arabic *qawiya* 'be strong', while in Hebrew a cord is called קו because it is twisted.[3]

The use of chains of semantic analogy in this way is characteristic of comparative philology. The chains may cover different meanings in one language, or may adduce examples from several. At times we find Semitic philologists also offering examples from outside the Semitic area. Thus meanings in the area 'wind' and 'spirit, soul' can be found for related or identical words not only in Semitic languages but also in Latin and Greek. The relation between Hebrew אמר 'say' and Ethiopic *'ammärä* 'show' can be paralleled with that between Latin *dicere* and Greek δείκνυμι.[4]

---

[1] But contrast Köhler's example of a 'verfeinerte Semantik', in *OTS* viii (1950) 144 f., followed also in KB, p. 118b.

[2] In *VT* vi (1956) 244.

[3] Cf. also מתן (Index, no. 208), and המתין 'wait'. The problem with these chains of analogy is that they do not give direct historical information, and the process of development in one may be quite different from that in another which looks logically alike.

[4] This example already in my *Semantics*, p. 118.

(4) *General*

Thus far we have spoken of comparative philology as a study which sought to provide comparative historical statements organizing the data from the various languages of a group, in our case the Semitic family. But the period in which this work was at its height (the nineteenth and early twentieth centuries) was also the period in which large numbers of new texts from ancient times became known. It was a time of discovery; inscriptions were found and published, new texts and indeed whole new languages became centres of scholarly awareness. Accadian and Ugaritic are the most prominent Semitic examples; in Indo-European a similar situation was formed by the discovery of Hittite and Tocharian.

The importance of this is that philological scholarship had to deal not only with the organization of known linguistic evidence but also with the processing and interpretation of new material. In all this exploration comparative insights were of great importance.

Comparative methods, indeed, were not the only ones used. Egyptian hieroglyphic was deciphered, and the grammar and lexicon of this language worked out, without any substantial body of comparative material to serve as a guide; such help as was provided came from bilingual texts, and from later stages (Coptic) of the same language. Some languages, Sumerian for example, came to be known, even though no comparative affiliations have been certainly discovered.

Nevertheless comparative studies have often formed a very large part of the scholarly apparatus used in work on a new text or a new language. If a newly discovered Phoenician inscription contains a word not previously known, the scholar will at once start to look more widely around in the Semitic field. In the case of Ugaritic the meaning of the texts has been worked out through a network of comparative information which gradually became more refined. This network provided by comparative identification eventually fixes the contours of the poems sufficiently well for us to make good surmises of the sense of words for which no comparative explanation can at present be given.

The decipherment of entirely new texts thus gave a high practical importance to comparative philology; and the occupation of so many scholars with the study of new texts contributed to the great upsurge of philological, as against textual, treatments in recent decades. Nevertheless this practical application of comparative philology was not without its dangers to that subject itself. It meant that many scholars, when they used comparative perspectives on a language like Ugaritic, were not comparative philologists in the strict sense, and did not make themselves responsible for the total task of synthetic organization of data from the Semitic field. The primary interest of the scholar was to find an interpretation of a new text. In the zeal and pressure of discovery, he might use comparative methods in a way which, if it had been part of a truly systematic comparative philology, would have been seen to be inviable. The use of abnormal phonological correspondences is a prime example. If these occurred so freely and so generally as is implied by the philological suggestions of some scholars (if taken cumulatively), then their effect would be no less than to shake the whole fabric of comparison which philologists themselves have carefully worked out. Thus a wide use of and appeal to comparative philology does not necessarily mean that philological methods and insights have been properly used or observed.

Another aspect of comparative philology which calls for comment is that it has, on the whole, been lacking in introspection into its own methods and has often failed to provide a satisfactory justification for each decision as it was reached. To some extent this is a natural effect of the working out of the method, and can be seen in classic works such as Brockelmann's *Grundriß*. The logic by which comparative philological decisions are made includes the use of an extremely complicated series of examples, many of which present in themselves a series of different problems which demand different answers. The complication of providing a rigorous logical demonstration for every element in the structure of a comparative grammar would therefore be immense.

One of the ways in which this difficulty has been met has been for the philologist to present his results rather than his argument: a kind of great hypothesis, which asks the reader to accept it as true if he finds that it covers the data. Within such a corpus we often look in vain for an argued justification of any particular section. The method as a whole is taken to be common ground, and its practical success in accommodating the evidence is the reason for accepting it. This may help to explain the apodeictic and assertive air of many philological treatments: it springs from the general mode of operation of comparative philology.

In contrast with the historical and developmental emphasis of the older philology, modern linguistics has laid greater stress on the synchronic study of a language, as it operates at a particular time as the means of communication of a speech-community. This does not remove an interest also in the diachronic study of language. Indeed, it can be argued that language study can be truly historical only when it works with a picture of succeeding synchronic states of the language as a whole, and that in this respect the older philology with its emphasis on historical development, because it failed to see the languages as synchronically functioning systems, paradoxically failed to be historical. By isolating the elements from the system within which they worked, it sometimes actually tended to damage historical appreciation.[1]

To sum up, then: an appreciation of philological treatments of the Hebrew Bible has to include a sympathetic but also critical understanding of the discipline of comparative philology from which they arose. On the one hand, the earlier forms of this discipline contained certain weaknesses, the effects of which later appeared in individual suggestions applicable to Hebrew. Some of these weaknesses can be mended if account is taken of more modern developments in the study of language. But my argument by no means depends on a kind of linguistics entirely different in scope from the older philology. The questions which we shall have to uncover and develop were already very plainly present in the older procedures. And, on the other hand, where philological treatments of the Bible have been faulty, this has often been not because of weaknesses in the basic philological discipline, but because the canons of that philological discipline itself were poorly observed by those who built upon it.

[1] For an earlier criticism of 'atomistic' study see Goshen-Gottstein in *ScrH* iv (1958) 101 ff.

V

PRELIMINARY QUESTIONS IN PHILOLOGICAL TREATMENTS

(1) *General*

I F a word in the Hebrew Bible is to be identified, not as the Hebrew word which it has normally been taken to be, but as another word known from cognate sources elsewhere in Semitic, it is clear that an immense learning would be required for the proper handling of the matter. One would have to know not only that such-and-such a word exists in Arabic or Syriac or Ugaritic, but also where it is used, in what connexions, and with what frequency. One would have to consider yet other Semitic languages, since evidence in another such (possibly Accadian or South Arabian) might conceivably make it impossible to maintain the simple connexions conceivable if only Arabic or Syriac is taken into account.

Many philological treatments do indeed rest upon such an encyclopedic scholarship and upon a refined judgement in the wide fields of the Semitic literatures. It must nevertheless be confessed that this required degree of erudition has not always been present. It is possible, though it is not desirable, to short-circuit some of this learning. The instrument which permits such a short-circuiting is the dictionary. It is not a superhuman task to learn what the dictionaries of the various Semitic languages are, and to become familiar with their various scripts and their modes of ordering material. Once this is known, all that is required is to know the possible correspondences for any given Hebrew word and look them up one by one.

The number of such correspondences will depend on which consonants are involved, and which languages. For a Hebrew כתב the student would have to consider only one correspondence in the Arabic dictionary, namely *k-t-b*. For a Hebrew עזב, on the other hand, he would have to consider more. The ע could normally correspond with either a /ʿ/ or a /ġ/ in Arabic; and the ז could correspond with either a /d̲/ or a /z/. There would be theoretically at least four possibilities. In the event there might well be less, for not all of the groups theoretically possible might be in use in Arabic. But where 'weak' letters such as /w/ are involved, the number of possibilities may be large. Pope in a recent article on שָׁחַת in Job 9. 31 tells us that more than thirty combinations are theoretically possible in an attempt to state the root and thereby achieve a comparative philological contact;[1] only a few of these, however, are found to exist. Even in these more complicated instances, however, it is still easy to work out what the theoretical possibilities are.

The procedure, while a little laborious to describe, is thus quite a simple one, assuming some gift for languages and a fair amount of ingenuity. Some of the more facile examples of philological treatments probably rest on some such simple dictionary-searching procedure. From time to time, indeed, protests have been raised against philological treatments on just this ground, that they are based on searches in the dictionary, without any adequate knowledge of the literatures themselves.

One need not say more about this unfortunate situation. It is right, however, that it should be mentioned. Because philological treatments exude an air of immense linguistic scholarship, it is only right to point out that the procedure may be a quite simple one, even if applied with ingenuity. In any case, this leads us to some further discussion of the phonological correspondences, and, in due course, of the weaknesses in the available dictionaries.

(2) *Metathesis and Dialect*

Consonants cannot be treated entirely individually; a consonant may in a certain environment be altered in such a way as to produce a correspondence which in other environments is abnormal. This is normally described in the classical works as assimilation and dissimilation. Hebrew ט, for example, does not normally correspond with Arabic /t/. But there is little doubt that Hebrew קטל 'kill' corresponds to Arabic *qatala* with the same sense. The departure from the correspondence otherwise normal is related to the environment of the /q/ and the /l/.[2] Our certainty

---

[1] *JBL* lxxxiii (1964) 270; Index, no. 170.

[2] Brockelmann, *Grundriß*, i. 154, gives a note on the development from proto-Semitic /t/ following /q/ in Hebrew and Aramaic; some curious variations exist.

in accepting the unusual correspondence depends on the clear semantic closeness of the words in the two languages.

Further, a word may be represented in a cognate language by a word which has the same consonants but in a different order; in the standard works this is usually known as metathesis.[1] It may not only be found between one cognate language and another; one language may itself display alternative forms, with the same consonants in a different order. The standard Hebrew examples are שִׂמְלָה or שַׂלְמָה 'dress', and כֶּבֶשׂ or כֶּשֶׂב 'lamb'.

The probability of a metathesis will vary according to the language with which Hebrew is being related; Ethiopic, for example, seems to have a higher proportion of secure cases, in relation to Hebrew, than Arabic has.

Moreover, many explanations which have been based upon metathesis have not found general agreement, and must be considered uncertain. Brockelmann[2] relates Arabic /ḥanaš/ to Hebrew נחש, both meaning 'serpent'; but this is doubtful, and is rejected by BDB.[3] The attractive relating of Ethiopic mäḥärä 'have compassion' to the Hebrew stem רחם of the same meaning has been disputed,[4] though it is regarded as 'probably' right by Leslau in a recent discussion.[5] Often one has to consider carefully the possibility of a completely different explanation than metathesis, so that the words cited have no common origin at all. Scholars who have made liberal use of explanations depending on metathesis, such as J. Barth in his *Etymologische Studien*, have incurred a good deal of criticism as a result.[6]

In addition, the traditional comparative grammars have erred in lumping together two quite different phenomena. Firstly, it may be meant that a form existed historically and that thereafter a change in the order of its phonemes occurred. This, one presumes, is intended when it is said that שַׂלְמָה is a metathesis of שִׂמְלָה. Special reasons brought about a change of sequence in *this* word, but did not act so universally as to eliminate the older form from use. At any rate an historical change from one form to the other is supposed to have happened.

[1] For a survey see Brockelmann, *Grundriß*, i. 267–78.
[2] Ibid., p. 275. This involves also a doubtful correspondence with the שׂ; and other explanations of the Hebrew word have been given.
[3] BDB, p. 638a.   [4] Praetorius, quoted in BDB, p. 933a.
[5] Leslau, *Contributions*, p. 50.
[6] See for example Brockelmann, *Grundriß*, i. 268, and references there.

Secondly, what is meant may be not an historical change, but only the fact that the sequence is different from that which one would 'logically' expect if everything were without anomaly. We read that הִשְׁתַּמֵּר is a 'metathesis' from an assumed *הִתְשַׁמֵּר; but it is not necessarily true that *הִתְשַׁמֵּר actually existed at some previous historical point after which a shift was made. Perhaps, under the given conditions, the /t/ was always put after the first radical; there was no historical change, but only a difference from what happened with other consonants.[1] The incidence of metathesis should therefore not be exaggerated by the inclusion of false cases, and these latter should not make us overestimate the probability of historical changes of order of phonemes.

Moreover, 'metathesis' means a linguistic change of sequence observable in speech, and not a graphic disturbance, i.e. the mistaken copying of characters in the wrong order. Occasionally the word has been used in what appears to be the latter sense. For וַיַּעַשׂ at I Sam. 14. 32 Reider maintained that the verb 'must have been' שָׁעָה = Arabic sa'ā 'betake oneself', 'run'.[2] He continues: 'the error can be accounted for through metathesis, which is frequent in Hebrew as in other Semitic languages'. The mention of an 'error' appears to mean a graphic error. If so, this is different from 'metathesis' as it is usually meant in comparative grammars.

Explanations involving metathesis were already produced by the medieval philologists. Ibn Janāḥ, for example, at Ps. 45. 2 רָחַשׁ לִבִּי דָּבָר טוֹב, explains that the heart is 'sweating out' good words, a metaphor for 'producing'. This explanation depends on the use of the Arabic rašaḥa 'sweat'.[3]

In summary, then, we must judge that the existence of the phenomenon traditionally described as metathesis, in the relations between one Semitic language and another, is indubitable; but that the appeal to it, in cases where the identity of the Hebrew word is itself in considerable doubt, is statistically not very probable. Only occasionally can we expect it to lead us to a true solution.

To the matter of metathesis we may conveniently join also the matter of dialect. We have already discussed the place of dialect in

---

[1] The two types are still confused in Moscati, *Comparative Grammar*, p. 63.

[2] *HUCA* xxiv (1952–3) 85; cf. above, pp. 67, 69, and below, pp. 246 f.

[3] Cf. Eppenstein, p. 14. For a large number of additional examples, of which many luridly illustrate the dangers of reliance on metathesis, while some others are of substantial value and interest still, see Wechter, *Ibn Barūn*, p. 55, and especially n. 310, pp. 183 f.

general, and it remains only to show ways in which the appeal to dialect has worked in particular cases.

Discussing the use of Arabic in the elucidation of Hebrew words Guillaume writes:[1]

> Arabic is a language of far greater content than 'classical' Arabic which is based on the language of the poets of Najd. Arabic includes the dialects of all the tribes in all areas of the peninsula; consequently it is legitimate to cite dialectical forms that are known and forms that have arisen through metathesis or the interchange of consonants.

In the result, however, the acceptance of several variables, namely the use of (1) any or all dialects alike, (2) metathesis, (3) unusual consonantal correspondences, simply means a very vague relationship between the Hebrew words and the Arabic words to which they are being referred. The reader may judge for himself from a random selection such as:

Arab.	*laja'a* 'seek protection'	Hebr. גאל	'redeem'
	kamala 'be complete'	גמר	'finish'
	waraqa 'strip of leaves'	ילק	'locust'
	maqqa 'suck the breast'	נוק	'suckle'

Guillaume's articles[2] contain large numbers of examples no more convincing than the above, often involving multiple metathesis and/or abnormal phonological correspondences, plus great deviation on the semantic side between close agreement and remote distance. These examples may indeed have some interest when considered in relation to the theory of biliteral bases;[3] but as direct lexical equivalences they reduce to the absurd the very principles to which they appeal.[4]

This is no argument against the use of dialect forms in the search for guidance concerning difficult Hebrew words. There is every reason to expect that, if cognates of Hebrew words have been preserved in other languages, some of these have been

---

[1] Hooke Festschrift, p. 109.

[2] In *Abr-Nahrain* from 1959; republished as *Hebrew and Arabic Lexicography* (1965).

[3] See below, pp. 166–70.

[4] Cf. also the principle that 'if certain consonants are known to be interchangeable in Arabic . . . such changes can legitimately be used to provide a parallel from Arabic to a word in Hebrew', *Abr-Nahrain* i (1959–60) 4.

preserved in non-standard forms, such as the dialects of non-classical Arabic. Rabin, for example, has furnished some very probable explanations in this way. The Yemenite *kurkur* 'deep river gorge' provides an attractive annotation to the Hebrew phrase ככר הירדן.[1] This seems to make better sense than the usual explanation which relates the word to the sense 'circle' or 'round plain'.

Thus there is every reason to welcome studies which try to adduce non-standard Arabic dialect forms for the elucidation of Hebrew words. But there is also every reason to expect some consistency between various instances of relation between Hebrew and any one Arabic dialect, while the variety of dialects does not mean that any or every dialect form may be used as an obvious correlate to a Hebrew word which seems semantically to suit it.

Dialects not only exist in the cognate languages such as Arabic but may also have existed in Hebrew. The rather uniform grammar of MT may have smoothed out dialectal variations.[2] One may expect these especially in writers of particular known localities, such as Hosea. But, of all the obscure expressions in the Bible, not more than a small percentage are likely to receive convincing explanations on the ground of dialect, on the basis of the information at present existing. The attempt to press explanations based on dialect for a large number of examples is likely to be self-defeating.

These problems are particularly acute in special cases, such as Dahood's argument for a strong Canaanite background in Qoheleth. The argument includes some rather surprising elements. There is a familiar Hebrew word פעל, which means 'make, do'. There are several places in Qoheleth (and in other books) where forms with the sequence בעל have usually been taken to belong to the familiar Hebrew בעל 'master' or 'owner'; but where, Dahood argues, the word is in fact a dialectal variation with a /b/ replacing the /p/ of the standard form. Passages in question include Qoh. 8. 8b, where 'iniquity cannot save its doers (בעליו)', Isa. 54. 5, Job 31. 39 (where בעליה means 'her workers'), and Prov. 3. 27.

In support of this proposal Dahood adduces certain variations

---

[1] Rabin, *Ancient West-Arabian*, p. 28.

[2] Cf. the argument of Nyberg, cited above, p. 73. Some of the variations most commonly noticed, e.g. שׂלמה/שׂמלה and כשׂב/כבשׂ, can hardly be called dialectal in any case, since they alternate within the same sources.

which seem to occur in Canaanite dialects, including Ugaritic: Ugaritic *lbš* or *lpš*, *nbk* or *npk*, *t̲bt̲* or *t̲pt̲*; Ugaritic *ʿrpt*, but Hebr. *ʿrbt*; Ya'udi *nbš* or *npš*. So he decides 'that biblical Hebrew should possess a number of by-forms is, accordingly, no cause for surprise.'[1]

It is, indeed, no cause for surprise that this should be possible. It is quite another thing to suppose that it has thus been proved to be so, or even to be probable. Just to quote one counter-argument, one has to consider the possibility that the variations cited are produced only in certain environments and are, in the language of the traditional philology, assimilations and dissimilations; and, moreover, that these are related to the peculiar phonetic character of the sounds in Ugaritic and to the fact that this language had a total phoneme stock substantially different from that of Hebrew. Thus one of the variations occurs after /t̲/, a phoneme non-existent in Hebrew; two others occur before /š/. The word for 'soul' in Hebrew occurs not only elsewhere, but in Qoheleth itself, only in its normal Hebrew form with /p/; the same is true of שפט 'judge' (Qoh. 3. 17). It is thus an entirely precarious undertaking to argue that, when /b/ and /p/ may be free variants in certain Canaanite dialects in certain environments, this may then be simply extended and supposed to apply to quite any word in Hebrew.

In any case the series of proposals here under discussion, namely that words including the sequence בעל should be taken to mean 'do, make', naturally depends also on another circumstance, namely that the sense 'master, owner' does not give equally good or better sense; which, however, is far from clear.

It is important in general, therefore, in the circumstances of Old Testament research, that we should not allow the phenomenon of dialect to allow wild and arbitrary conclusions. As we have seen, a considerable degree of regularity in phonological correspondences has been fundamental to comparative philology. This is not altered by the fact that dialect exists; dialect only makes more complicated the statement of the relations.

(3) *Loan-words and Words of non-Semitic origin*

The lists of normal correspondences are made up for, and apply only to, the words which have descended straight into the various languages from their common ancestor. Many words, however,

---

[1] *Biblica* xliii (1962) 361 f.

were absorbed later from one Semitic language into another; Hebrew adopted many Accadian words, and Arabic adopted many from Aramaic. Such adoptions commonly diverge from the normal correspondences, and the philologist in setting up his lists of such correspondences must avoid using probable loan-words as evidence. The form which the word takes in the receiving language will depend on the way in which it was heard and phonemicized at the time and place of its reception and assimilation. If we have enough examples, it may be possible to state general rules. In the older Semitic languages, however, we sometimes have only the vaguest means of determining when and where a word was taken over, and we may not have enough examples to provide any consistent pattern.

Thus words of Arabic origin in the Ethiopic lexicon, or words of Aramaic origin in the Arabic lexicon, may not show the correspondences with Hebrew which are normal for Ethiopic and Arabic respectively; nor can they be used as evidence to establish the validity of unusual correspondences between these languages and Hebrew.

Sometimes, indeed, a philological treatment will depend on just this principle, and argue that a Hebrew passage can be understood because it includes loan-words from other Semitic languages which precisely for that reason do not follow the normal correspondences. The verb and noun כרה occur as *hapax legomena* at II Kings 6. 23, ויכרה להם כֵּרָה גדולה. This text may mean 'and he made for them a great feast'. The words are known in this sense in Accadian and are registered in BDB, though some faintheartedness made that lexicon rather doubt the text. Rabin argues that these are loan-words from Accadian, and that the real Semitic root is that found in Arabic *qarā* 'invite to a feast', cf. also Ethiopic *'aqräyä* 'invite or receive as a guest' (?), Ugaritic *qry dbḥ* 'offer a sacrifice as food'. If this root descended direct to Hebrew from proto-Semitic, its first consonant would be /q/ rather than /k/, unless a quite unusual exception were being made. Therefore it is more likely that the word has been absorbed from Accadian, where /q/ has passed into /k/ before /r/.[1] Thus there is no reason to doubt the text at II Kings 6. 23. Moreover, examples of this same Semitic *q-r-y* remain in Hebrew, spelled with a ק because they have not come in from Accadian. Rabin finds a pair at Exod. 3. 18,

---

[1] Rabin does not in his note give evidence for this shift in Accadian.

5. 3, where the somewhat puzzling phrase אלהי העברים נקרא עלינו is taken by him to mean 'God has asked us to hold a banquet for him'.

What has just been said about words absorbed from other Semitic languages applies much more forcibly to words which have been taken over from outside the Semitic languages altogether. Such words may not normally be used for the establishment of phonological correspondences between the Semitic languages; and they will be unlikely to provide solutions for difficult Old Testament passages except in special circumstances.

The situations which involve words of non-Semitic origin fall clearly into two types. The first is where a difficulty in a Hebrew passage may have been caused by the presence of an unrecognized non-Semitic word. The correct identification of this word, as a word already adopted into Hebrew and used by the biblical writer, would then remove the difficulty. The second situation is that which arises when information related to non-Semitic words comes to be unwittingly mixed up in the philological reasoning which seeks to discover the true sense of a Hebrew word.

The first type of problem does not require much discussion here. The main stock of words of non-Semitic origin in the Old Testament is well enough known.[1] Most of these are words about the meaning of which there is no real doubt, such as the familiar היכל, used of the temple or part of it (from Sumerian through Accadian), or פחה 'governor' (Accadian).

There are also words the meaning and derivation of which is in some doubt, but which bear unusual forms and thereby make probable a non-Semitic origin; the אַפִּרְיוֹן of Cant. 3. 9 is an example. Again, sometimes scholars have felt that a Hebrew word has no adequate etymological background in the Semitic languages and have therefore sought an explanation elsewhere. The prominent example is פסח 'passover'. Since the Semitic etymologies are not very satisfactory, some scholars have suggested explanations from Egyptian, and this can be supported by the tradition that the passover originated in Egypt. Some of these explanations have the peculiar feature that the פ of the Hebrew word is interpreted not as a root consonant but as the definite article of Egyptian (cf. Index, no. 262).[2]

---

[1] For a recent treatment see Ellenbogen, *Foreign Words*.
[2] Cf. the recent survey in J. B. Segal, *The Hebrew Passover*, pp. 96 ff.

Non-Semitic words are, it would seem, most likely to be identified if the words are nouns[1] and if the reference seems to be to
foreign officials, institutions of foreign origin, unusual artefacts
and foods likely to be transported from distant lands; and particularly, perhaps, if foreigners are depicted in the text as speaking
or being addressed. Many such identifications though interesting
do not pose a very critical problem for the understanding of the
text. Either the word is known generally, e.g. as a commodity in a
list of such,[2] so that the philological identification may serve to
clarify the exact identity of the referent; or the referent may be
taken to be known, as in the case of תֻּכִּיִּים 'peacocks', and the
philological task is rather to trace the source of this word. Sometimes philological study may do something of both. One of the
advantages which study of non-Semitic origins may confer on us
is freedom from bondage to false etymologies from within Semitic
or from within Hebrew itself; thus, if חָנִית is not a Semitic word,
we can be free from the dubious derivation of meaning from חנה
'bend' ('as *flexible*?', BDB, p. 333b),[3] and if שָׁלִישׁ should not be
Semitic, we may be free from a derivation from the 'third man in
the chariot'[4]

Where a non-Semitic origin for a word in the Old Testament is
considered, attention should be given to the date both of the
passage itself and of the events described in it. The probability of
Hittite words would be higher in the earlier period. Accadian
words may have come into Hebrew from very early times down to
the Babylonian exile. Persian words are conceivable from the
sixth century or so onwards, but acknowledged examples of these
(and also of Greek words) in the Hebrew parts of the Old Testament are few; the Aramaic sections contain many more.

Suggestions of Egyptian words have been most plausible when
they have been found in stories of the Israelite sojourn in Egypt,

[1] Of twenty-two likely Hittite words discussed by Rabin in *Orientalia* xxxii
(1963) 113–39, two are verbs in Hebrew (תרגם and קלס). The predominance
of nouns may be explained partly through the modes of cultural contact, and
partly because borrowed verbs are harder to trace on account of the forms which
they must assume; cf. below, p. 132. Ellenbogen's collection appears to include
only one verb (אסף).

[2] See for instance Rabin, 'Rice in the Bible', *JSS* xi (1966) 2–9.

[3] Cf. below, p. 291 n.

[4] A Hittite origin was suggested by Cowley, *JTS* xxi (1920) 326 f.; see discussion
by Rabin, *Orientalia* xxxii (1963) 133 f., who in the end returns to a Semitic
derivation, but not from the root which means 'three'.

or in materials like prophetic oracles against Egypt. A striking series of names among the Levitical lists—Moses, Phinehas, possibly Miriam, Putiel, Hophni—can be given plausible Egyptian explanations. It was in Egypt that the crowd shouted אַבְרֵךְ as Joseph went by (Gen. 41. 43), and it is reasonable to look for an Egyptian explanation, even if scholars have suggested too many such rather than too few.[1] The word יְאֹר 'river', mainly used of the Nile, has usually been taken to be the Egyptian 'itrw. The word 'passover' has already been mentioned. For the rare צֶאֱלִים, some plant under which Behemoth shelters in Job 40. 21–2, and taken by BDB to be a kind of lotus, Humbert[2] appealed to the Coptic čal 'branch', related to earlier Egyptian d̠'rt 'a fruit'.

Most examples of this kind, however, though significant for the appreciation of Hebrew meanings, are a little different from what has been meant in this book by a 'philological treatment'. They are mostly attempts to deepen our understanding of a strange word; but they are not generally a resort in situations where the understanding is in such uncertainty that only a new philological identification can save the text from emendation. We shall not go farther into this subject, because our main interest is in the use of the *cognate* languages for the illumination of the Bible. It is just because the languages are cognate that the appeal to them has seemed so powerful and so convincing. It will always be likely that some few difficult passages will find clarification through the identification of a non-Semitic word, but we must on our present knowledge expect such cases to be statistically infrequent in comparison with the examples for which solutions are found through the use of Semitic languages.

The second problem with non-Semitic words is, as we have said, the possibility that forms and meanings of non-Semitic words and information about them may involuntarily be taken up into discussions which are logically valid only if the material is Semitic in origin. To make mistakes in this regard is not as difficult as might be imagined. One source of it lies in dictionaries which do not differentiate words of foreign origin.

The lexical stock of Ethiopic, for instance, and still more that of the modern Ethiopian dialects, includes many words from

---

[1] See BDB s.v., pp. 7b–8a; *BH*[3] apparatus ad loc.
[2] Humbert *ZAW* lxii (1950) 206; cf. Driver in Levi Della Vida, i. 237.

Cushitic and other African sources. Perhaps the most striking example of all, however, because the most likely to be a cause of error, is Arabic. Classical Arabic in certain areas included many Persian words. In works of reference these are not always marked as Persian; and the risk of confusion is all the greater in that some of the shorter Persian words bear forms not unlike common Arabic formations.

Thus, to take a prominent example, Arabic has *dāna* (root *dyn*) 'borrow', of Semitic origin, and also *dāna* (root *dyn*), with a whole series of derivatives of standard Arabic form, meaning 'profess a religion', which is of Persian origin; and, moreover, it is possible that we should distinguish, in respect of origin, between *dīn* 'religion' (= Iranian *daena*) and *dīn* 'judgement' in the familiar phrase *yōm al-dīn* 'the day of judgement'. The latter probably involves borrowing from Aramaic or Hebrew, since the sense 'judge', basic to this phrase, seems to be characteristic of these languages rather than of Arabic itself.[1] A similar situation obtained within Persian itself, where we have pairs like *dār* 'gallows' (Iranian origin) and *dār* 'house' (Arabic), to say nothing of pairs which are very similar though not identical, such as *mehr* 'love, friendship, sun' (root as in the name Mithra) and *mahr* 'marriage portion' (Arabic, cf. Hebrew מֹהַר).[2] The ancient philologists knew of the existence of this problem, but certainly did not have the means to identify every case rightly.[3]

There is a Hebrew personal name יֶרֶד, and Noth in his *Personennamen* (p. 231) relates this to the Arabic *ward* 'rose'. This in itself is semantically a possible suggestion, since there are other Hebrew personal names which use names of plants, such as Habakkuk (a plant name known from Accadian) or Tamar (palm-tree). But, as Kopf points out,[4] the Arabic *ward* is of Persian origin. Noth's explanation will therefore not work. Kopf goes on to say that there is an Arabic word of real Semitic origin, *ward* 'bold, brave', which is actually used in Arab personal names and which fits the Hebrew name very well. Later Hebrew, of course, displays also the word

---

[1] For an analogous situation in Hebrew itself see below, p. 109.

[2] For these words see A. K. S. Lambton, *Persian Vocabulary*, pp. 65, 162.

[3] Use was made of a rudimentary study of the rules of consonantal compatibility, which will be discussed below, pp. 178–81; see references in Greenberg, *Word* vi (1950) 163.

[4] *VT* viii (1958) 179.

וֶרֶד 'rose'. This is an example where, as mentioned above, the Persian word is deceptively similar to a Semitic formation.

In fact quite large numbers of examples can be cited where scholars have cited words from Arabic without noticing that they are of Persian (or other non-Semitic) origin and therefore probably not relevant for texts like the Old Testament. The Arabic *kinnāra* 'piece of linen' is not of Semitic origin and therefore probably will not do to explain the Ugaritic *knrt*.[1] Wutz at Hos. 12. 2 discovered a word דִּשְׁמָן which he supposed to exist also at Ps. 68. 32 and which he explained as identical with 'ar. *dusfān nuntius leno*'—to quote the whole of Wutz's laconic note. As Nyberg points out, however, this word came into Arabic from Middle Persian and is not relevant.[2] Again, there is a somewhat obscure phrase אַגַּן הַסַּהַר at Cant. 7. 3. Most commonly, perhaps, it has been taken as 'a rounded bowl' (so RSV; English numbering, 7. 2) or the like. Reider, offering a different interpretation,[3] used the Arabic *jauna*, which he understood to mean 'disc' (of sun or moon). Kopf, criticizing this attempt, says that it rests on a misunderstanding of the Arabic dictionaries, which refer to the colour rather than the shape of the sun, and that in any case the word in question is a Persian word, the classical *gun* 'colour'. This word in turn, interestingly enough, did in the end find its way into Hebrew in the later גַּוֶון, cstr. גַּוֶון, 'colour, manner'; but this does not make it a valid comparison for Old Testament times.

This may be particularly troublesome if the sense obtained by reference to a word of Persian origin is not very far removed from the sense obtained by reference to a word of Semitic origin. For a moment of light relief, we may illustrate this from the case of 'checkmate' in English. One often hears that this means 'the king is dead', *shah* being the familiar Persian word and *mat* being taken as the familiar Arabic word 'is dead', cognate with Hebrew מֵת. I have often heard this example taught to beginners in Hebrew as a mnemonic to assist them in learning the word מֵת. But in chess the king is not dead; and if the word for 'king' were Persian one might expect the word for his death to be Persian also. Actually, both words are Persian, and mean 'the king is helpless', which

---

[1] Ullendorff, in *JSS* vii (1962) 342, against Gray, *Legacy*, p. 86.
[2] Wutz, *Transkriptionen*, p. 321; Nyberg, *Hoseabuch*, p. 94 n.
[3] Reider in *HUCA* ii (1925) 94; Kopf in *VT* vi (1956) 293 f. See Lane, p. 490c.

actually fits the situation of the game.[1] The *Oxford English Dictionary*, avoiding bigotry, gives one explanation under 'checkmate' and the other under 'mate'. The matter shows how easy it is to fail to notice the difference between Persian and Arabic words.

Sometimes a contamination of senses between words of different origin in the same language may have taken place. In Jer. 10. 18:

הִנְנִי קוֹלֵעַ אֶת־יוֹשְׁבֵי הָאָרֶץ

the verb is commonly rendered 'sling out'; the noun 'sling' is קֶלַע. Driver, however, has argued that the meaning is 'uproot' or 'remove', on the basis of the Arabic *q-l-ʿ* 'remove from its place'. He goes on to trace the semantic development, and his first series of words includes the following:

Hebr. קלע 'uproot'; Arab. *q-l-ʿ* 'extract'; *qalāʿa* 'a loosened clod' (as extracted from the ground), *maqlaʿ* 'stone quarry', *qalʿa* 'fortress' (as originally a rocky fastness), *q-l-ʿ* 'large stones' [=*qalaʿa* of Lane, p. 2992?]; Syr. *qulāʿā* 'clod, mud'.

The obvious weak point in the series quoted is *qalʿa* 'fortress', for the idea that this got its name from being a rocky place, while not impossible, is not immediately convincing.

In fact there has been some suggestion that this word for 'fortress', a quite common word, is not of Semitic origin.[2] Belardi in a recent article derives it from an Iranian *kalāta* 'hill fortress'.[3] If this is so, he goes on, any connexion made in the Arab consciousness with the verb *q-l-ʿ* 'sling' would be only through popular etymology trying to give an *a posteriori* justification to the sense by attaching it to a military function.

Whether Belardi is right in his suggestion I would not presume to judge; but it does indeed look attractive. It does not in any case have any immediate effect on Driver's suggestion in respect of Jer. 10. 18. But it does show us that words may be of non-Semitic origin even when they appear to fit in with some kind of Semitic

---

[1] It occurs to me that Arab users of the phrase may have *thought* it meant 'is dead', which would be a further interesting complication; but I do not know if this is so.

[2] Fraenkel, *Fremdwörter*, p. 237, already doubted that this word was originally Arabic. Siddiqi, p. 70, makes a suggestion similar to that of Belardi, but without the explanation of how the word came to be related to the stem *q-l-ʿ*.

[3] Belardi in the *Annali* of the Istituto Universitario Orientale, Naples, Sezione Linguistica, i (1959) 147–50, following H. W. Bailey, op. cit. 118–20.

etymology, and even when they may be felt so to fit by speakers of
a Semitic language. Though we can trace separately the origin
of Semitic and non-Semitic words in relation to a given language,
we cannot be sure of separating the two in their semantic interrelations once both have come to be used together. Thus non-
Semitic words may come to be fitted into existing linkages of
form and meaning in a Semitic language. This, if true, will greatly
complicate the task of tracing a semantic history and applying it to
biblical Hebrew in which the non-Semitic component will not be
relevant.

The same kind of problem may be illustrated for Hebrew with
the familiar word דִּין. Driver, I think rightly, holds that the example
at Esther 1. 13 is 'religion', from the Iranian *daena*; this is confirmed in the phrase as a whole, דָּת וָדִין, because the other word,
דָּת, is certainly Persian. The Hebrew dictionaries are therefore in
a sense wrong in listing under דִּין 'judgement'. But it is quite
probable that Hebrew speakers did the same thing themselves, so
that this word, in so far as it continued to be used, became con-
taminated with דִּין 'judgement, justice'. For 'religion' the Jews
later said rather דָּת.[1]

Where words from two different origins have come closely together in a Semitic language, it may be very much a matter of
chance whether we have knowledge to see their distinct origin.
There is a Syriac *mlaṭ* meaning 'to study, take care', and it would
seem theoretically a possible semantic development to relate it to
the sense 'rubbed', 'smooth', which can be related to Hebrew מלט
'escape' and in Syriac itself appears as *mlaṭ* 'smear' (with oil or
chalk). Analogies for such a development might be thought of—
for example 'polite', or 'erudite' (from *rudis* 'rough'). In fact,
however, the Syriac *mlaṭ* is derived from the Greek μελέτη and is
thus a homonym with the *mlaṭ* of Semitic origin.[2] Examples of
this kind may have been much more frequent than our information
enables us to know, and would be particularly difficult to detect if
the senses of the two words overlapped in some degree or if popular
etymology devised notions which bridged the gaps between.

Another example shows how one may be misled by non-Semitic
material and also by false trains of semantic analogy. The word for
'sailor' in Hebrew is מַלָּח. I have several times heard this taken as

---

[1] Cf. above, p. 106.

[2] Schulthess, *Homonyme Wurzeln im Syrischen* (Berlin, 1900), p. 37.

from מֶלַח 'salt'. Not only does it have exactly the same consonants, but the noun formation is the familiar one used for many occupations. A moment's thought, however, should suggest that the meaning by analogy would probably be 'salt-worker' rather than 'sailor'.

In fact, however, the word is of Sumerian origin, from *ma* 'ship' and *laḫ* 'propel'; so that there is no connexion with salt at all. (It is, when one considers the beginnings of navigation in the ancient Near East, not obvious why it would be connected with salt in any case.) Clearly, the impulse to interpret מַלָּח as something to do with 'salt' arises from the *English* usage 'an old salt' —itself a modern usage, first recorded for 1840 by the *OED*. This analogy is an entirely misleading one.

This leads us nevertheless to the interesting realization that the semantics of this Hebrew word, since it is the name of an occupation, have acted to draw it into the familiar *qaṭṭāl* pattern used for so many occupations. This may be the reason for the double /l/, which is not explained by the Sumerian original, or by the Accadian version of it. Thus, though the word was not of Semitic origin, and though it was not derived semantically in any sense connected with salt, nevertheless it took its place within the series of patterns available for words coming from the Semitic root *m-l-ḥ* and conformed in part to the semantic information conveyed by the choice of a member from that series. If we did not have clear information from Sumerian about the origin of the word, we would have been largely groping in the dark about the semantic development. Another striking example is the שֶׁלֶג of Job 9. 30, which is probably not 'snow' but 'soapwort'. This is not a semantic derivation from the sense 'snow', but a word from outside Semitic altogether. Yet the context, taken along with the natural connexions between water, snow, and washing, makes it very understandable that confusion should arise.

Thus non-Semitic words, even when we are in a position to identify them clearly, once admitted to a Semitic language can begin to have effects in word formation and semantics. There may be many hundreds of cases where this has happened but where we are unable to trace it, the only evidence left being a perplexing variety in the semantics of words which in form seem to be plainly Semitic.

To sum up this section, then, all philological treatments have to exercise caution lest words of non-Semitic origin are involved in the formal or semantic histories which they endeavour to trace. Some such words are fairly obvious from their form and are correspondingly less likely to cause confusion. Others may easily pass unnoticed. All philological treatments appeal to formal and semantic histories in cognate languages, but many of these histories may involve the influence of non-Semitic words, which influence is not necessarily, and not even probably, transferable to other Semitic languages.

(4) *Area Preferences Within Comparative Philology*

Are there, among the languages cognate with Hebrew, some which are likely to be more productive of philological suggestions than others? We shall later (ch. 7) discuss the extent to which the lexical stocks of the various Semitic languages overlap. Meanwhile it is right to mention some more general factors, which have influenced scholars in their preference for one group rather than another, within the Semitic languages, as the source for attempted elucidations of Hebrew.

One such factor, more social than genuinely linguistic, is the love of the scholar for his own specialization, e.g. Accadian, Egyptian, or Ugaritic. This is especially evident when a new area of study is being opened up, as with Accadian in the later nineteenth century and with Ugaritic in the twentieth. There is then a strong impulse to take the new knowledge and apply it to the solution of old problems. Driver thus speaks of the 'pan-Ugaritism' which has arrived and will pass as other fashions like the 'pan-Babylonian' have done.[1]

Sometimes these forces are supported by other kinds of interpretative special pleading. Yahuda, who produced a long if unreliable series of Egyptian terms in the Pentateuch, was animated among other things by a will to disprove the 'Wellhausen' type of historical criticism.

Scholars are also affected by the simple matter of what they generally get to know. To many Hebrew scholars Arabic has been the most familiar cognate language, because it is taught at most universities and made familiar through visits to the Near East. Post-biblical Hebrew itself, on the other hand, has often suffered

[1] In *JSS* x (1965) 117.

neglect in Christian scholarship, apart from special cases like the
Dead Sea Scrolls. The modern Ethiopic languages, and even
classical Geez, are also less widely known. Ugaritic, by contrast,
has had great prominence because of its closeness in time and style
to biblical texts, and the attention it has received has thus in
turn made it easy and natural to use it as a main source for philological explanations. Not without importance, conversely, is the
size of the vocabulary in the relevant languages. The immensity
of the recorded vocabulary of Arabic is a main reason for its
prominence in philological treatments of Hebrew. Given a consonant sequence in Hebrew, there is perhaps a better chance of
finding a possible formal correspondence in Arabic than in any
other cognate language. The extent of its vocabulary, and the
variety of senses attributed to its words, form the subject of not a
few jokes and proverbs. The size of the Arabic lexical stock,
however, carries with it certain dangers, which we shall discuss
shortly: especially there is the question whether all this vocabulary
is properly and accurately recorded.

   Though scholars have in fact often displayed a preference for
one cognate source as against another, it is doubtful if any decisive
reason in principle can be given for any such preference. In
principle all Semitic material is likely to be relevant. It is doubtful,
therefore, if it is a valid criticism to say (for example) that a
scholar depends on Arabic rather than Accadian or Ugaritic.
Such criticism in any case, apart from its logical precariousness,
has often been very unfair. Dahood, for instance, has sometimes
in his enthusiasm for Ugaritic let it appear that Albright, using
Ugaritic and Phoenician, forms a contrast with Driver who
appeals to Arabic.[1] Even if it were true that Ugaritic and Phoenician
had a higher value, it would be false to ignore the dependence on
Arabic (and Hebrew!) for the original decipherment of Ugaritic;
while it is mere folly to suggest that Driver's work has neglected
Ugaritic or limited itself to Arabic. There are, indeed, scholars
whose work has been vitiated by an over-exclusive attention to one
branch of the Semitic languages, but Driver can hardly be included
in this number; Dahood himself would be a more justified target
for criticism on this score.

   If any principle for preference between rival sources were to be
sought, three different scales might be considered: (1) Date:

---

[1] *Biblica* xxxviii (1957) 306; more recently, xlvii (1966) 403 f.

sources nearer to the Old Testament in time might be considered more likely to produce solutions. (2) Geographic proximity: sources closer to Palestine might be considered more reliable. Even if late in date, they might go back to similar earlier cultural conditions and might retain traces of common vocabulary. (3) Closer affinity within the classification of the Semitic family. This would favour North-west Semitic languages against East Semitic languages like Accadian or South Semitic languages like Ethiopic. Experience, however, suggests that lexical isoglosses do not coincide with the broader groupings of the languages and dialects; certainly many sound comparisons between Hebrew and Accadian have been made, and the same is true of Ethiopic.

In fact, while these scales deserve some consideration, it is clear that nothing can be decided by them for the individual case, though certain statistical trends may be noticed. Dialects of recent date, of remote locality, or of different group within the classification of Semitic, may yet provide good parallels. Ullendorff[1] cites the word *nfr* 'to fly', 'bird', as an instance of a word found only at the opposite local and temporal extremes of the Semitic spectrum, in Ugaritic and in Tigrinya, and doubtless other such instances could be found.

Sometimes preferences are made on the grounds of social, historical, and anthropological judgements. The most important example is Arabic; it has often been supposed that it is a very primitive tongue, barely differing from proto-Semitic. This linguistic view is associated with the social belief that the mode of life of the Arabian bedouin is identical with the cultural situation in which Semitic languages were first spoken.

Moscati, for example, in a recent work,[2] maintains that circumstances in Arabia, particularly poor communications, 'make for a greater degree of archaism, whether linguistic or ethnic', and concludes both that Arabic provides the best basis for the reconstruction of proto-Semitic and that the bedouin of Arabia come close to the ethnic type of the ancient Semites. Even in anthropology and social history, however, this view might be questioned;[3] while, on the side of linguistic history, a quite different view can be quoted from Bergsträsser:

---

[1] *Orientalia* xx (1951) 273 f.; *VT* vi (1956) 197.
[2] *The Semites in Ancient History*, p. 33.
[3] Cf. the works of Caskel cited in the bibliography.

In spite of these features of high antiquity [the reference is to the retention of the vocalic and consonantal stock of original Semitic], Arabic is on the whole the most complete representative of a *later* shaping of the Semitic linguistic character: old freedoms, individual anomalies and unevennesses are removed, in the morphology through the strict carrying out of unitary analogies, and in the syntax through firm regulation of the possibilities of usage and precise delimitation of the area of meaning of all syntactic means of expression.[1]

It would thus be wrong to suppose that the experts have given any clear or simple approval to the view that Arabic is peculiarly close to the ancestor of all Semitic languages.

Idiosyncratic elements in Arabic, that is points at which it has developed away from the original Semitic heritage and constructed patterns and elements peculiar to itself, will be less likely to provide evidence for the elucidation of Hebrew texts. For instance, Ps. 68. 9 and Jud. 5. 5, both ancient poems, have a phrase זֶה סִינַי, which has long puzzled commentators. Some have taken it as a rather stupid gloss, meaning 'this is (i.e. refers to) Sinai'; others have considered emendation to זָע סִינַי 'Sinai trembled'.

The modern fashion is to use a philological treatment, and to say that the sense is 'He of Sinai', 'the Possessor of Sinai'. God is mentioned immediately before and after, and this therefore gives a good parallelism. The treatment cites the well-known Arabic *ḏū* 'the possessor of'; and one may add the South Arabian names for deities, such as *ḏt ḥmym*.

This looks like a solution. Birkeland, nevertheless, has argued that it will not work.[2] For, he maintains, this development of *ḏū* 'possessor of' is peculiar to Arabic, and accordingly will not apply to this Hebrew text.

We do not have to decide the rights and wrongs of this here; but it illustrates the effect of lexical idiosyncrasy upon all arguments which seek to transfer phenomena and meanings from one Semitic language to the elucidation of texts in another.[3]

---

[1] G. Bergsträsser, *Einführung*, pp. 134 f.

[2] Birkeland in *Studia Theologica* ii (1948) 210 f., followed by Kraus, *Psalmen*, p. 467; but contrast very favourable acceptance by Albright and his followers, e.g. Moran in Wright, op. cit., p. 61. Some considerable semantic discussion would be required in order to decide whether the instances adduced by Moran from Ugarit and Mari are a real analogy.

[3] For other examples in which the question of idiosyncrasy is discussed see below, pp. 119, 172, 193 n., 224; also the discussion of Arabic vocabulary items,

(5) *Problems of the Lexicographical Tradition*

Mention has already been made of the danger in any excessive dependence on the dictionary. Such dependence, as shown by any simple procedure of searching the dictionaries for possible words, becomes even more dangerous if the dictionaries themselves are faulty.

Of modern dictionaries not so much need be said, since students will be aware of the main problems involved in the use of them. Nevertheless one or two points will be mentioned as particularly deserving caution. Many modern dictionaries have been affected by the etymological emphasis characteristic of much comparative philology.[1] This in itself can hardly be simply called a fault; but it is a source of greater difficulty for our present purpose than is at first evident. Because of it a dictionary may strive to state a 'basic meaning' or 'original meaning' in addition to the meaning actually found; or it may strive to give some other sort of comparative basis as the starting-point of the article. Once this is done, the structure of the article may be moulded in order to provide a justification for the claim that the extant meanings flow from this basis or origin.

If this method is followed, it becomes possible not only that doubtful etymological material will be inserted (because the article will seem incomplete without it), but also that the statement of meanings actually found will be distorted by the force of the attempt to provide an etymological rationale. Even where lexicographers only classify the meanings of words under various headings, this will very frequently imply theories of semantic history. Thus, paradoxically, for the investigator pursuing a philological treatment of an Old Testament text, the etymological interest which past lexicographers have had may be a very mixed blessing.

In some languages different dictionaries give different degrees of prominence to etymological information or etymological hypotheses. The *Chicago Assyrian Dictionary*, for example, does not generally give etymological comparisons except at the end of the article, and does not allow them to alter the information set out in the article on the basis of the actual Accadian literature. The corresponding dictionary of von Soden, on the other hand,

below, pp. 116, 162, 165 f., 169 n., and that of glottochronology in general, below, pp. 184–7.

[1] Cf. above, p. 90.

will normally classify a word at the beginning by reference to a Semitic comparative etymology.

Apart from etymology some modern dictionaries may include words and senses which are too specialized or too remote to form a good parallel to a Hebrew word.[1] When the sense 'deceitfulness, vain speech' for Arabic *ḫaraba* has to be found from Dozy (i. 356), and when even there it depends on the peculiar form *ḫurbayr*, this is strong evidence that the sense is a special development within Arabic, and unlikely to be applicable to Hebrew חרב (Index, no. 138). The normal sense in Arabic is 'destroy'.

Much more serious problems attend us when we consider the practice of the ancient and medieval lexicographers. Mention has already been made of the large size of the vocabulary recorded for Arabic, and anyone who has done even a little work with a large Arabic dictionary such as Lane's knows of the bewildering variety of meanings which can be registered in it. With some further experience the scholar often comes to have some scepticism of explanations which rest entirely upon the Arabic dictionaries, for experience has shown him how easily some kind of suitable sense for a difficult word can be gained from them. The best analysis known to me of the problems as they impinge upon the Old Testament is by L. Kopf; and, having no specialized competence in this field, I shall refer to his work and state the main points as I understand them to be.[2]

Firstly, the great Arabic dictionaries familiar to Western scholars, such as those of Freytag and Lane, do not rest directly upon the literature itself, and are not formed by excerpting and citation from actual texts, but are themselves compilations from older Arab dictionaries. Sometimes interpretations within these older dictionaries have suffered misreading or misunderstanding on the part of later workers, whether within the development of Arabic lexicography or in the process of translation into English or Latin.[3] So industrious a user of the Arabic lexicon as Driver can thus be

---

[1] Cf. also below, pp. 165 f., 265, etc.

[2] See Kopf in *VT* vi (1956) 286–302; *BO* xii (1955) 134–6 (a review of Al-Yasīn); also Fück in *ZDMG* cvii (1957) 340–7; Wild in *ZDMG* cxii (1962) 291–8; most recently Wild, *Das Kitāb al-'Ain*. Wild agrees in the main with Kopf (see pp. 41–57 of his book) while at one point qualifying the generality of Kopf's judgement (p. 57, n. 197). Haywood, *Arabic Lexicography*, does not contribute to our question.

[3] Instances in Kopf, *BO* xii (1955) 135, *VT* vi (1956), e.g. 290 ff.

found to deplore the lack of a really scientific lexicon of Arabic, which would have to be founded upon the actual literature.[1]

Secondly, the medieval Arabic lexicography did not act very critically or discriminatingly towards the material which it assembled. Quite secondary applications of words are found quoted alongside normal and frequent usages, and metaphorical applications may receive the same kind of treatment as normal ones. A striking case is quoted by Kopf from the *Qāmūs*. The familiar word *kursi* (cf. Hebrew כִּסֵּא) receives in this dictionary, alongside the normal sense 'chair', the very surprising one 'knowledge'. This goes back to the Quranic verse 2. 255 which says: 'His seat comprehends heaven and earth'. The tradition of exposition and theological discussion which has gathered around this verse has found its way into the lexicon as if it was one of the actual meanings of the word.[2]

Let us quote Kopf again:

The Arabic poets developed a great number of metaphorical designations for the limited group of things and ideas which formed the object of their descriptions. Hence the supposed richness of Arabic in synonyms, which are alleged to amount to hundreds of designations for the camel, the sword and so on. In fact in many cases these are adjectives which express only certain properties of the objects designated but because of frequent use developed into standard terms.[3]

Or again:

The Arabic dictionary, in the form in which we now have it, usually explains words empirically; that is, the explanations are mostly fitted to the use of the respective words in a particular context, and therefore are very often too specific. Herein lies one of the chief reasons for the very numerous senses, widely diverging from one another, which the Arabic dictionaries accord to various derivatives of the same root.[4]

[1] See *VTS* iv (1957) 6. Cf. also Fück's judgements in his *Die Arabischen Studien in Europa*; on Freytag—'only a somewhat enlarged and improved edition of Golius' (p. 166); on Lane—'in respect of method it does not go beyond Golius and Freytag, for it fails in principle to adduce the factual usage of the literary works extant' (p. 169); in general—'an Arabic lexicon resting on the texts themselves remains even today one of the most urgent tasks of Arabic studies in Europe' (p. 84).

[2] On this see also Kopf, 'Religious Influences on Medieval Arabic Philology', *Studia Islamica* v (1956) 33–59; also Wild, op. cit., p. 50, who cites other even more extravagant cases, such as the glossing of *ḍḥk* 'laugh' as 'menstruate' at Sura 11. 71.

[3] Kopf in *VT* vi (1956) 298.

[4] Ibid.

According to Kopf, the Arabic dictionaries explain expressions in a purely practical way, without indicating the basic meaning and the semantic development (p. 300). Or, as we might put it, there is no adequate discrimination between the information given by a word (which we might call its 'meaning') and general characteristics of that to which it refers (its 'reference').[1] To give a very simple illustration, we may call a woman a flower, but if we then make a dictionary and give 'woman' as a gloss under the entry 'flower' we shall be likely to cause some confusion.

Again, many of the meanings given are not real linguistic information but are a product of the lexicographical process itself. This can happen (*a*) through etymologizing, i.e. the effort to explain a word through a favoured derivation; (*b*) through the telescoping of past exegetical discussions;[2] (*c*) through the collection, and the representation as different existing senses, of the suggestions made by different scholars. On this last Kopf says:

A large part of the vocabulary, which the Arabic philologists listed and explained, was not known to them either from daily use or from extended reading. Their chief task thus lay not in the establishment of exact and fitting explanations for words which were current to every educated man, but in the discovery of the meanings of infrequent and unknown words, which they probably met for the first time in the course of their professional activity.[3]

Similarly Wild points out that the interest of lexicographers was not in ordinary daily speech but in literary usage. The examples cited are, where possible, taken from poetic passages, a fact which increases the possibility that very special applications of words may be cited misleadingly.[4] Genuine examples taken from the poetry could even be supplemented with instances constructed *ad hoc* by the lexicographer.[5] Meanwhile common and frequent words are by-passed without notice of any kind; Wild cites *kalb* 'dog', *kaṯīr* 'much', and *kull* 'all', left without any mention in the *Kitāb al-ʿAin*.[6]

Finally, the English of a dictionary like Lane's may be ambiguous, or may not be a certain rendering of its Arabic sources, matters well exemplified by Kopf.

---

[1] This distinction of information and reference is taken up again below, pp. 291 ff.   [2] Kopf, op. cit., pp. 299 f., if I understand him rightly.
[3] Kopf, op. cit., p. 296.   [4] Wild, op. cit., pp. 41 f.
[5] For an example see Wild, op. cit., pp. 44 f.
[6] Wild, op. cit., p. 41 and n. 2.

That the Arabic lexicographical tradition is not wholly reliable for our purpose (a purpose, needless to say, entirely foreign to Arab lexicography itself) is no new idea. Jouon in a memorable phrase wrote:

Si minces que soient les filets d'eau coulant de la source hébraïque, il est d'une bonne méthode de les exploiter à fond avant d'adresser ses pas aux eaux étrangères de l'infini et complaisant Qamous.[1]

Similarly Ullendorff, in discussing the *hapax legomenon* הבר of Isa. 47. 13 and proposing the sense 'worship, do homage' (which fits quite well), takes issue with the attempt made by Al-Yasin to connect the word with Arabic *habr* 'depressed land', and writes:

It seems to me impermissible to exploit the Arabic dictionary in this manner (thus treated it will yield almost any meaning desired of it) by detaching a highly idiosyncratic meaning-variant from a specific poetic context.

Similar problems are occasionally found with Syriac, where a meaning has been taken from the indigenous lexicography. They occur also in the use of Accadian lexical tablets. Sometimes the equivalences these offer have been construed as evidence for the existence of words and meanings not clearly found in continuous texts.

At Isa. 11. 15, והחרים יהוה את לשון ים־מצרים, the text has often been altered to והחריב 'dry up' (cf. LXX ἐρημώσει); the familiar verb החרים is not elsewhere used with cosmic elements like the sea as object. Driver wishes to retain the text, appealing to an Accadian *ḥarāmu* which he says means 'cut off'. This word appears to exist, however, only in a lexical list, glossing Sumerian *kud* 'cut'. One of the other words used to gloss *kud* is *batāqu*, and of this word the note *ša mē* 'with reference to water' is added.[2] It is quite precarious to extend this to *ḥarāmu*; von Soden rather attaches the latter to the Semitic root *ḥrm*, which would seem to imply the more general sense of 'separate'.[3]

Similarly, Driver, trying to show the existence of a שמר 'cast out, reject', quotes a syllabary which has the equation *šum-mu-ru* = *bu-us-su-ru* and argues that the latter is related to the Aramaic בסר 'despise'.[4] The former word is thereby identified with Syriac

---

[1] *Mélanges de la faculté orientale* (Beirut), iv (1910) 10.
[2] Von Soden, p. 114; actual use of this verb for interruption of water-courses can be quoted.
[3] Von Soden, p. 323.   [4] Von Soden, p. 142; cf. below, p. 141.

š-m-r 'send, dismiss, discharge; reject', and then in turn a Hebrew cognate is identified. Again, in the argument that there is a Hebrew יצא meaning 'shine', as of gold and silver, it is quoted that Accadian *aṣû* and *namāru* are used alike as synonyms explaining the same Sumerian verb.

A famous instance which involves these questions is the word שִׁילֹה in Gen. 49. 10; 'the sceptre shall not depart from Judah, nor the ruler's staff from between his feet' (thus far RSV) עַד כִּי־יָבֹא שִׁילֹה . . .

The meaning of this has long been a subject of dispute.[1]

It is not easy to know what function the place-name Shiloh would have, if it were meant here. Traditional Christianity took 'Shiloh' to be a Messianic name.[2] The too obvious emendation מֹשְׁלֹה 'his ruler' has been tried; and perhaps the commonest approach has been to construe as something like שֶׁלֹּה 'to whom it belongs' (so RSV, and cf. Ezek. 21. 32).

The philological treatment, made known independently by several scholars like Noetscher and Driver, and accepted by so distinguished a student of Messianic ideas as Mowinckel,[3] relates the Hebrew word to an Accadian *šelu* or *šilu* 'ruler'. This suggestion has had considerable influence. Yet, as Moran shows in a recent comprehensive survey,[4] there is considerable doubt whether this word with this sense exists in Accadian at all, though terms for kings, princes, and potentates are tolerably numerous therein.

It is from the lexical tablets that the word was first identified, and it provides a good illustration of the difficulties involved in the use of them.

The identification of *šilu* was based on the 12th tablet of the lexical series Id-A-nâqu, which gives thirty-five equivalents for the Sumerian sign U when pronounced *u*.[5] Among these thirty-five are *ši-lum* and also some words which mean 'ruler'. These latter (e.g. *šarrum* 'king' and *belum* 'lord') are separated from *ši-lum* by *i-lum* 'god', and the list contains such diverse items as 'totality', 'ear' (*uznu*), 'hand' and 'earth'. It was from this list that

---

[1] See for instance Rankin, *Jewish Religious Polemic*, index, s.v. Shiloh.
[2] Cf. now also the Qumran text 4Q Patriarchal Blessings.
[3] *He That Cometh*, p. 13 n.
[4] *Biblica* xxxix (1958) 405–25.
[5] The list is published in *Cuneiform Texts*, pt. XII (London, 1901).

Zimmern first identified the *šilu* or *šelu* which was then applied
to Gen. 49. 10. In this identification he seems to have been unduly
influenced by the context, and especially by the equivalences
which follow the word rather than those which precede it. In fact
the sense of *šilu* is now well known: it means 'hole', 'rent', or
'fissure'.

There is also a vocabulary list in which for the Sumerian *nam.
lugal* 'kingship' the Accadian equivalent is given as *ša-lu-tum*.
Landsberger, in editing these materials, himself declares this to
be an erroneous writing, and corrects the text to the familiar
šarrutum, which is of course the normal Accadian word for
'kingship'.[1]

Such, then, are some of the problems which may be met in any
attempt to use the older lexicographical writings as a means to
appropriate the material of the cognate languages.

(6) 'Aramaisms' and Similar Terms

We may end this chapter with an analysis of such terms as
'Aramaism' or 'Arabism', which we meet fairly often in the literature of philological treatments.[2] These terms are often lacking in
clarity. The following possibilities may be intended:

(1) The term may mean only a statistical displacement towards
what is more frequent in Aramaic but more infrequent in Hebrew.
It is common knowledge that אתא is the normal Aramaic word for
'come'. The same word occurs, however, in Hebrew, and there
are about twenty cases in the Old Testament. Most of these, if
not all, are in poetry. Suppose, then, that we find a text where אתה
becomes the more frequent word for 'come', or where it occurs
outside of the poetical context; then the situation in this regard is
more like that which exists in Aramaic, and someone may say that
this is an 'Aramaism'. But there is no question that the phenomenon
itself is real Hebrew; the only difference is in the distribution and
frequency. All discussions of 'Aramaisms' in late books of the
Old Testament like the Song of Songs should try to distinguish

---

[1] See *Materials for the Sumerian Lexicon* iv (Rome, 1956), p. 32, l. 55. For
some discussion of *šilu* see von Soden in *Orientalia* N.S. xvi (1947) 81–3, xviii
(1949) 402; Goetze in *JCS* i (1947) 256, n. 19. Goetze attaches the word to the
Arabic verb *sala'a* 'split, cleave'.

[2] For a helpful survey see Driver, 'Hebrew Poetic Diction', *VTS* i (1953)
26–39; earlier, Kautzsch, *Aramaismen*. A recent full survey is by M. Wagner.

between phenomena which are not normal Hebrew at all and phenomena which are only statistically unusual.

(2) Secondly, usage may be identified by means of an appeal to Aramaic, where this usage has not previously been recognized as existing in Hebrew though it is well known in Aramaic. The identification is intended as an identification of a normal, if uncommon, usage in Hebrew. Many cases which probably fall into this category can be found in the literature. Thus at Isa. 57. 13,

$$\text{בְּזַעֲקֵךְ יַצִּילֵךְ קִבּוּצַיִךְ}$$

Driver says that the word קִבּוּץ is here an 'Aramaism', used in the same sense as the Syriac *qbāʿā* 'fixing' and then 'statue' (cf. *qbaʿ* 'fix, found'; *qbiʿtā* 'fixation, form, sign'). The sense would then be:

'Will your statues save you when you call?'

Driver surely means that the usage is a native Hebrew one, inherited from earlier Semitic; and when he calls it an Aramaism, this means that the sense was discovered from Aramaic. If the word had been actually taken over from Aramaic, or used as a deliberate imitation of Aramaic usage, it would surely have retained the ע of the Aramaic form.

Sometimes it is not so clear what was meant. At II Kings 3. 27, where the text reads:

$$\text{וַיְהִי קֶצֶף־גָּדוֹל עַל־יִשְׂרָאֵל}$$

Driver feels it hard to explain this as the wrath of a Moabite god. The noun קֶצֶף therefore may be supposed to have a 'weakened Aramaizing' sense, comparable to the Syriac *qṣap* which means 'be angry' but also 'be sad'; cf. also *qṣipā* 'sad', and Mishnaic קְצוּפָה 'sorrow'. A Greek variant, he notes, reads λύπη here.

'Aramaizing' here could mean that the biblical writer, aware of the shades available in the Aramaic word, applies the same to the Hebrew word. More probably, however, it means not an imitation of Aramaic usage by the Hebrew writer, but the use of normal Aramaic usage as evidence to uncover occasional Hebrew usage.

(3) Thirdly, a term like 'Aramaism' may mean that an expression of Aramaic type was deliberately used, or that, if not deliberately, at least in fact, the existence of an Aramaic phenomenon is actually affecting the choice and the character of Old Testament

usage. It is sometimes plausible that contact with Aramaic speakers may explain unusual locutions by northern Israelite speakers like Hosea. Contact with Accadian is also a possibility; it is somewhat less likely than Aramaic influence, because Accadian must have been to the average Israelite a much more strange and difficult language than Aramaic.

A possible case for such an Aramaism would be the מֶלֶךְ יָרֵב of Hos. 5. 13. The 'King Jareb' of AV has long been discredited, since no such name appears to exist. A generation of students has been taught that this text should be read as מַלְכִּי רָב, meaning 'the great king'. The termination /-i/ is interpreted as 'an old nominal termination'.[1]

The case for an accidental wrong word-division is not strengthened by the fact that exactly the same phrase appears again at Hos. 10. 6. This leads to the search for another explanation. Driver argues that the text is quite right, and that the word is an adjective identical with the Syriac *yireb* 'be great', cf. *yaributā* 'size'. That the MT is right is shown by LXX Ιαρειβ and Pesh. *mlk' dyrb*. Thus, in Driver's opinion, the word is an 'Aramaizing form' from the root רבה or רבב, 'and is nothing but *šarru rabū* [the Accadian for "the great king"] in Aramaic guise.'[2]

(4) A term like 'Aramaism' may be used when scholars hold that a text was originally written in one language and then translated into another, and that characteristics of the diction of the former state have been carried over into the latter. This has been argued particularly for the book of Job. Tur-Sinai in a lengthy commentary has maintained that Job was written in Aramaic and later translated (rather badly, it would seem) into Hebrew.[3]

Similar problems arise with those theories of other books, such as Qoheleth, which attribute their linguistic peculiarities to translation from another language.

These problems will receive no further attention in this book. They depend on special theses which have to be specially proved for the books concerned and which, whether valid or not for those

---

[1] So, somewhat obscurely, BDB, p. 937a, who further add confusion by citing the word under the root ריב 'contend', although they do not themselves believe this to be the right meaning.

[2] Nyberg, *Hoseabuch*, p. 38 f., also wants to retain the text; he thinks of an Assyrian deity, referred to in the text as 'the Melek Yareb'.

[3] Cf. also the quotation from Guillaume, above, p. 34.

books, cannot be extended therefrom over other books which are not the product of the same translation process. Some particular examples which will be cited in this book do, nevertheless, come from works which contain these special theses.

To sum up, then, the above four categories classify the ways in which terms like 'Aramaism' seem to be used.

VI

THE DISTRIBUTION OF HOMONYMS

(1) General

PHILOLOGICAL treatments tend to increase the number of homonyms known to exist in Hebrew. The method frequently implies that a familiar word had alongside it another word of identical or almost identical form. The rarer homonym then became concealed or forgotten through mistaken identification with the more familiar, or may otherwise have fallen into disuse. Philological research is able, from its resources in the cognate languages, to identify a homonym thus lost; and since treatments do not generally identify words which previously were *formally* completely unrecognized (to do so would usually mean departure from the consonantal text) a substantial proportion of new identifications are homonymic with a word already known. Nevertheless the cumulative implications of this multiplication of homonyms have seldom been noticed.

A good example is עִיר, familiar in the sense 'city'. A homonymic עִיר 'excitement' (root עוּר 'arouse') has been identified for one or two places, principally Jer. 15. 8 עִיר וּבֶהָלוֹת 'excitement and terror', by BDB and others.[1] Driver, however, here finds another word, עִיר meaning 'invasion', cognate with Arabic *ġāra*. At Deut. 34. 3 (customarily 'city of palm-trees') and some other places he identifies an עִיר which is not 'city' but 'small depression'. At Job 3. 8 he finds yet another word, the root of which is עִיר, meaning 'revile', in the phrase הָעֲתִידִים עֹרֵר לִוְיָתָן 'those who are ready to revile Leviathan'. This involves taking the parallel phrase as אֹרְרֵי יָם (MT אֹרְרֵי יוֹם), meaning 'those who curse the Sea (i.e. sea-monster)'. This verb is cognate with Ethiopic *tä'ayyärä* 'revile', Arabic *ġāra* II 'revile'. This sense 'reviling' was also applied by Guillaume to the phrase at Hos. 11. 9: וְלֹא אָבוֹא בְּעִיר, which was put by BDB under the word for 'excitement' (though with some doubts about the text).

---

[1] BDB, p. 735b. The word עִיר 'city' is registered on p. 746.

Nyberg meanwhile had seen at this same place an ancient word עִיר for 'fire' or 'heat'. Gray discovers another עִיר 'inmost recess (of temple)' at II Kings 10. 25, and Dahood has an עָרִים 'gods' which at least in the plural is homonymous. To all this we may add a verb עִיר (?) meaning 'bore', found only at Isa. 50. 4, and cognate with the Arabic *ǧāra* 'sink in the earth', *ǧār* 'pit', which gives to the phrase אָזֶן לִי יָעִיר the sense 'he boreth me an ear'.

The reader, unless he is experienced in the literature of philological treatments, will probably have found this account somewhat bewildering. Yet the situation I have described is far from an uncommon one. There are several homonyms if all, or even if most, of the scholars concerned have been right in their identifications. Something can, indeed, be done to sort out this list of real homonyms, near-homonyms, and apparent homonyms, and we shall shortly offer some distinctions which will help in classification. But one could continue indefinitely with the mere listing of new homonyms in Hebrew identified in the course of philological treatments.

What I have not found is any perception that the production by scholars of such large and increasing numbers of homonyms constituted any kind of problem or difficulty. The identification of roots and the organizing of the vocabulary with adequate distinction of meanings has long involved the discrimination of homonymic roots, and this has been a creative and salutary part of the progress of lexical studies. One does not therefore see at once how a process which has solved problems for so long may now begin to create fresh problems.

Several aspects of homonymy will now be discussed in general, in order to establish some preparatory approaches to the matter.

The following distinctions provide a preliminary analysis of various kinds of homonyms relevant to our subject:[1]

(1) <u>Some homonyms are products of phoneme mergers</u> traceable through reference to other Semitic languages, and when this is so it may be possible to separate them clearly.

---

[1] Homonymy was known to Arab and Jewish medieval scholarship; the usual Arabic term was *muštarik* and the Hebrew שֵׁם מְשׁוּתָּף. Distinctions of types of homonymy were drawn up, but are more logical than linguistic in character and do not correspond with our present series. Homonyms for our purpose mainly fall within the class which Maimonides called 'absolute homonyms', see Efros, *Maimonides' Treatise on Logic*, p. 59. For the Arabic term see Ibn Khaldūn, *Muqaddimah* (ed. Rosenthal, 1958) iii. 26.

(2) Some homonyms are complete, in that all items in the paradigm of a word are identical with those of its homonym; others are partial, the coincidence extending over only certain forms within the paradigm.

(3) Accordingly, roots may be identical without the production of homonyms in actual forms, and the difference between identity of roots and homonymy of actual forms must always be kept in mind.

(4) Accordingly, problems with homonymy are likely to be particularly noticeable in the case of verbs.

We now turn to consideration of these points in greater detail.

(1) It is useful to make a distinction between two classes of homonyms, according to the relation they have to phonological changes perceptible between one Semitic language and another. If proto-Semitic has two phonemes, *x* and *y*, and if these merge to form *x* in Hebrew, then words of the patterns *xab* and *yab* will probably become homonymous. If there is another language in which this merger does not take place, then the homonyms in Hebrew may be distinguishable through comparison with that language. The two phonemes which in Arabic are /ʻ/ and /ġ/, and which correspond to a phonemic distinction in proto-Semitic also,[1] find their representation in Hebrew in the one phoneme /ʻ/, i.e. ע. The verbs עֲנה 'sing' and עָנה 'answer' form such a pair of homonyms. Among the Hebrew consonants, the phonemes which can normally be so analysed, stated as set against Arabic, are six in number: ז (/ḏ/ and /z/); ח (/ḥ/ and /ḫ/); initial י (/w/ and /y/); ע (/ʻ/ and /ġ/); צ (/ṣ/, /ḍ/ and /ṭ/); and שׁ (/t/ and /s/).

Where a word has more than one of its consonants belonging to groups which have converged in this way, multiple possibilities of homonymy may theoretically emerge. Thus Hebrew, as BDB sets it out, has חָצֵר 'enclosure, court' (cf. Arab. ḥaṣara 'encompass, surround'), חָצֵר 'village, settlement' (cf. ḥaḍara 'be present, settle, dwell'), and חָצִיר 'herbage' (cf. ḥaḍira 'be green'). Seldom, however, are there actual occurrences of homonymy in the same number as the merger of phonemes from proto-Semitic would theoretically allow.

In cases of this kind, other things being equal, it will commonly

---

[1] The view that /ġ/ was proto-Semitic has been questioned by Růžička, but his view has not been generally accepted. In any case it makes no difference to my argument; I could equally well use the illustration of /ḥ/ and /ḫ/.

be possible to distinguish homonyms quite clearly by pointing to cognates possessing phonological differences which are no longer operative in Hebrew. Such an identification makes quite clear that an actual homonymy has occurred and precludes the possibility that the multiplicity of meaning should be explained in some other way, e.g. by derivation of the sense of one word from the sense of the other. For instance, I have heard עָנָה 'sing' derived from the phrase עָנָה בְשִׁיר as an instance of sense-derivation by ellipsis (from the sense 'answer in song'); but the Arabic cognates eliminate this possibility. Thus homonyms which can be identified by reference to different words in another language, such as Arabic, in which the phoneme mergers found in Hebrew have not taken place, form peculiarly certain examples of homonymy in comparison with other types.

Not all homonyms which have been detected, however, can be dealt with in this way. In fact, only a minority of the Hebrew consonantal phonemes permit an analysis by comparison with multiple phonemes in a cognate language. In languages like Arabic, in which we know of relatively few mergers of phonemes from proto-Semitic,[1] correspondingly few of the homonyms existing can be classified or accounted for in this way.

The historical question of the date when the various mergers took place may be mentioned briefly. It is conceivable that some Hebrew texts originated at a time when the relevant merger was not yet complete, so that (for instance) /ʿ/ and /ġ/ were still distinct at the time of the original production, in spite of the identity of letters in the text now extant. At the difficult place Jer. 12. 9,

הַעַיִט צָבוּעַ נַחֲלָתִי לִי הַעַיִט סָבִיב עָלֶיהָ MT

Driver identified the first word עַיִט as a word meaning 'lair, den', cognate with Arabic ġāṭa, and thus different from the more familiar עַיִט 'bird of prey', which follows. If this is right, the sense is roughly:

'Is my heritage a hyena's den, with birds of prey around it overhead?'[2]

---

[1] The obvious case in Arabic is /s/. One may contrast s-k-r 'be drunk' (= Hebr. שׁ) and s-k-r 'close' (= Hebr. ס in סגר); likewise in the verbs samara, samura, one would distinguish the sense 'converse by night, stay awake' (= Hebr. שׁ in שׁמר, if BDB, p. 1036a, is right; otherwise GB, p. 847b, KB, p. 993a) and the sense 'nail' (= Hebr. ס as in סמר).

[2] This solution involves also the identification of צבוע as 'hyena'; cf. below p. 235. For ġāṭa (y) intravit et latuit cf. Freytag, iii. 306b.

—rather than the more familiar (but not very clear)

'Is mine heritage unto me as a speckled bird of prey? Are the birds of prey around it?' (RSV).

If this identification at Jer. 12. 9 were right, and if /ʿ/ and /ġ/ had merged into one phoneme in Hebrew before Jeremiah's time, then the two words were homonyms, and it is possible that play on the two homonyms may have been part of the writer's intention.[1] If, on the other hand, the merger had not yet become complete, there would be no homonymy and the words would be distinct in sound as well as in meaning; the writer might then still be supposed to have played on assonance, but not on homonymy. It was long thought that in the biblical period /ʿ/ and /ġ/ were still distinct and that Greek transcriptions like Γαζα and Γομορρα proved this even for quite late times; but, since the incidence of these Greek spellings appears not to coincide with the difference between the consonants in the probable etymologies of the Hebrew words, this opinion is no longer generally held.[2] In my judgement, the mergers listed above (p. 127) were probably already complete in the later biblical period, if not earlier. We may only mention also that, if שׁ were pronounced generally like ס (cf. Judges 12. 6), this would produce certain homonymies, while if שׂ were pronounced like שׁ it would produce certain others. In general, however, it does not appear that study of the date of the mergers will make a very great difference to our estimate of homonymy in general, though it may pose intriguing problems in particular cases.

To summarize, then: it is useful to distinguish, among the total group of homonyms, between those which can be related to phonological mergers and those which, within the limits of our present knowledge, cannot be so related.

(2) Secondly, it will be useful to consider a distinction between complete and partial homonymy. Where homonymy is complete, all items in the paradigm of a word will coincide with the corresponding parts of its homonym. Where homonymy is partial, it will be found only in part of the range of the paradigm. There is a rare construct plural שְׁבֻעֹת which is found from both שָׁבוּעַ 'week' and שְׁבוּעָה 'oath' and is thus in a way a homonym; but

---

[1] Cf. below, pp. 151–4.
[2] See recently Moscati, *Comparative Grammar*, p. 40; earlier, Růžička in *ZA* xxi (1908) 293–340 and elsewhere.

there is no homonymy in other parts of the words, and the statistical degree of overlap is extremely low. Similarly, the words בֹּקֶר 'morning' and בָּקָר 'cattle' would have partial homonymy in all probability in the plural; but it is doubtful if overlapping cases are textually sound; and since both words occur with an overwhelming predominance in the singular, the degree of overlap, if any at all, is extremely low.

Partial homonymy, though it is a source of trouble to language learners,[1] is not a very serious obstacle to the use of a language in communication. For the native speaker in the vast majority of examples the combination of grammatical and semantic contextual indications selects the right sense infallibly. The situation is not particularly different from that where two different items in the paradigm of the same word coincide, though in other words of the same class they generally differ. Thus in Hebrew יַעֲלֶה may be 'he goes up' (qal) or 'he puts up' (hiphil), though these are normally marked as distinct. Paradigms do not always provide equal marking for every distinction which has a place within the paradigm.

We may argue then that, while partial or occasional homonymy or overlap of forms is something with which the language system may be expected to deal in its stride, complete homonymy, where two words will overlap in all their forms, may be a more serious matter.

(3) Thus, thirdly, it is important to see that the problems relating to homonymy depend primarily not on the overlap of roots but on the overlap of forms.

Under the sequence עלם BDB classifies three different roots. But, though the radical sequence is common to all three, there are extremely few cases in which any homonymic forms occur. One of the three roots, for instance, appears only in the noun עוֹלָם; but this form does not appear in the other two roots. In fact, of all the forms registered for the three roots, allowing some leeway for textual uncertainties and so on, I think there is only one homonymous form, the qal passive participle which occurs once from the root meaning 'conceal' at Ps. 90. 8 and coincides exactly

---

[1] There are old books of homonyms for learners of Latin, which are designed to enable them to see synoptically the various possibilities of forms like *facies* (either 2 sing. fut. of *facio* or nom. sing. of the noun *facies*); many hundreds of such instances can easily be found.

with the noun meaning 'youth' which occurs several times. Thus, out of quite a large number of forms registered under the three roots, only very few fully overlapping homonymic forms, and possibly in fact none at all, actually occur. It is possible, of course, to register עוֹלָם 'eternity' under the root עוּל, but this does not materially alter the situation.

The problem of understanding how homonyms functioned as discriminatory communicative signals depends on sound rather than on writing, and depends on the whole sound of the word concerned and not upon the abstraction we call the 'root'.[1] There may be two roots סלל, but since the forms from one of them (סַל and סַלְסִלָּה, both meaning 'basket') do not occur with the other (a verb meaning 'lift up, cast up'), there is no factual homonymy in the extant texts. This is particularly evident when a root is not used as a verb and is recorded in the dictionaries only in order to state a root for particular noun formations.

(4) It should now be obvious that the phenomenon of homonymy will, under the conditions of Semitic languages, be especially noticeable in verbs. The noun דְּבִיר is not homonymous with the noun דָּבָר or the noun דֶּבֶר, whether they come from the same root or not. עֹרֵב 'raven' is never homonymous with עֶרֶב 'evening', though the root sequences are identical. Nouns have particular patterns of formation which, not in all cases but in many, will distinguish them from other nouns of a different pattern, whether the root sequence is the same or not.

In verbs, however, this is not so to anything like the same extent. Semitic does not have the verb-classes or 'conjugations' which are so prominent in Indo-European languages. In Latin, for example, we can cite two verbs with stem *vēn-*; but *vēnor* 'hunt' will not be confusable with *vēneo* 'be for sale'. The stem *fer-* can be found in two verbs which will nevertheless usually be distinct: *ferio* 'strike' and *fero* 'carry'. In Avestan we can list two verb stems *kar-*. One means 'make' and is cognate with Skt. *kṛṇoti* 'build'; its present is *čar-* (class I). The other means 'enter' and is cognate with Skt.

---

[1] Similarly in Greek there is no homonymy between pairs like ἄρα and ἆρα, καλῶς and κάλως, since the pitch accent is distinctive; the difference had, however, no written marking until late times. Strictly, a more correct term for our study would be *homophone*; two words alike in writing but not in sound would be *homographs*. I have ventured, however, to retain the more traditional term *homonym*.

carati, Greek πέλομαι, Latin *colo*; its present is *čara-* (class IV).[1] Distinctions of this kind are not normally available in Semitic; identity of radical sequence in verbs will produce homonymy.

In Hebrew it is necessary for the functioning of a verb that it should fall within a number of formation patterns; if it does not, it just cannot mean anything. A form like */qītīl/ could not function as a verb. In this respect nouns are different. A noun may be taken over from another language and offer (as in אַפִּרְיוֹן or שַׁעַטְנֵז and many post-biblical words of Greek origin) a pattern quite unexampled in Hebrew, but this does not prevent its functioning. A verb, on the other hand, functions only through its having one of the patterns such as /qåtal/ which are used for verbs. If therefore two verbs are homonymous in their sequence of root consonants, they will necessarily, through the nature of the verb system, be homonymous in their entirety, with only the following qualification.

There are in Semitic the themes or *binyanim*, that is, the types like qal and piel. Sometimes a distinction in use of theme prevents verbs of identical root from being homonymous. In Hebrew there are the two 'homonymic' verbs חלה 'be weak, sick' and חלה 'appease'. But the latter is found only in the piel, while in the former the piel is infrequent and other themes are frequent. Though the radicals are the same, only limited overlaps in usage occur, and homonymy is only partial. The analysis of ערב in BDB sets out six roots with this sequence; but of these only three have verbs extant in biblical Hebrew, and of these three only one is found in the hithpael and one in the hiphil. All three, however, are registered for the qal. Again, זמר 'make music' occurs only as piel, while זמר 'trim' occurs only as qal and niphal. Similarly, לוה 'join, accompany' occurs in qal and niphal, לוה 'borrow, lend' in qal and hiphil. Here are some other examples: ברא—I 'create', qal, niphal only; II 'be fat', hiphil only; III 'cut down (trees)', piel only; חלל—I 'bore', qal, piel, pual, poel, poal; II 'play the pipe' (denom.), qal, piel, polel; III 'pollute, profane', niphal, piel, pual, hiphil; IV 'begin', hiphil, hophal only; ענה—I 'answer', qal, niphal, (hiphil once, but doubtful); II 'be occupied', qal only; III 'be afflicted', qal, niphal, piel, pual, hiphil, hithpael; IV 'sing', qal, piel, only.

These statements have to be made with caution when verbs are rare in any case, so that we cannot say with certainty that particular

---

[1] Quoted from Reichelt, *Awestisches Elementarbuch*, pp. 434 f.

themes were not used. Nevertheless there is sufficient ground to be confident that a certain number of verbs, the roots of which were alike, were in practice partially discriminated because only limited themes were used and these differed between one verb and another. In general, however, it remains true that the conflict of homonyms may have been rather more prominent in the verb.

Certain wider ramifications are implied by points (3) and (4). Philological treatments have generally emphasized the search for a cognate root rather than the word formations in which the forms are found. Many treatments give the impression that, so long as a root sequence suitable for the Hebrew consonants can be established, and so long as this sequence can provide an adequate meaning, the existence of the corresponding formation in Hebrew can be merely assumed. We shall later discuss the suggestion that Hebrew had a לְאֹם 'ruler', cognate with Accadian *līmu*, *limmu* 'magistrate, eponym'. Hebrew לְאֹם, however, seems to belong to the formations *qutul* or *qutl*, while the Accadian belongs to *qitil* or *qitl*. This fact has to be given due recognition in any argument which seeks to derive the sense of one word from the sense of the other.

This requirement is avoided, of course, if it is roundly declared that the vocalization in Hebrew is wrong and should be emended, e.g. to a form like *לְאָמִים. This drastic step, however, carries with it other consequences which we shall have to consider. For the present we observe simply that the low valuation placed upon the vocalization in many philological treatments agrees with the comparative neglect of the word formations.

The semantic importance of word formation applies to all uses of comparative philological information, and not only to cases where the Hebrew text is itself in difficulty. Hebrew עוֹלָם and Arabic *'ālam* not only have corresponding roots, but the formation also is closely similar or identical. If, on the other hand, we compare the famous word עַלְמָה 'young woman' with the Aramaic עולימא or עולימתא, though the root is the same, the formation is a different one; the Aramaic had the pattern *qutail* (with or without feminine ending). Any drawing of semantic conclusions from one word to the other has to take account of the different formation.[1]

---

[1] This is one reason why the meaning of Hebrew עַלְמָה cannot be quite simply and directly established through citation of forms like the Palmyrene עולימתא 'hetaira'; cf. the use of this argument (among others) by Driver in *TLS*, 19 May 1961, p. 309, with reference to the translation of Isa. 7. 14.

These then are some distinctions which may help us in studying the possible interactions of homonyms in Hebrew.

(2) *Homonyms and Communication*

I have already mentioned the atomistic nature of philological treatments. The scholar is seeking a solution to one detailed verse or phrase. The solution may involve the identification of a new homonym in Hebrew. In producing this solution the scholar may not notice that the cumulative effect of his work, especially if the work of other scholars working on similar lines is added, produces a new question. It has long been common knowledge that homonyms exist in Hebrew. If we have two words formally identical, why not four or six? Under the circumstances, the question whether homonyms can be infinitely increased in number is not usually asked. In this the scholar is looking at things from a somewhat self-centred point of view. He is thinking of how he, the modern scholar, can identify this word in relation to other languages. He is not thinking about the other question, namely, how did the Israelites under these circumstances know what they were talking about? The production of new homonyms raises a question about the communicative efficiency of Hebrew.

So far as I have found, the producers of philological treatments have taken notice of this question only in very isolated cases. Tur-Sinai notices it, for instance, when he proposes the suggestion that the word רב should in certain places be understood not as 'great, numerous' but as another word meaning 'weak, powerless, afraid'.[1]

Job 4. 3   הִנֵּה יִסַּרְתָּ רַבִּים וְיָדַיִם רָפוֹת תְּחַזֵּק:

can then read:

> 'If thou hast supported the powerless
> and strengthened the weak hands'

—which, of course, gives a good parallelism. Other instances suggested by Tur-Sinai are Job 4. 14, 26. 3, 35. 9. He goes on to remark that:

The pronunciation of this word was apparently different from that of רב in the ordinary sense; otherwise, it would not have been possible effectively to contrast רב 'numerous, great' with אֵין כֹּחַ 'powerless' (II Chron. 14. 10).

[1] Tur-Sinai, *Job*, p. 76 f.

The text at II Chron. 14. 10 reads:

אֵין־עִמְּךָ לַעְזֹור בֵּין רַב לְאֵין כֹּחַ׃

Whatever we may think of Tur-Sinai's solution, it is of real interest that he has noticed the problem of reduction of communicative efficiency caused by homonymy, and has adjusted his solution to it by the virtual addition of a qualification making clear that in the original situation there cannot, in his judgement, have been a homonymy.

In very general terms, this question of the communicative efficiency of Hebrew is the question which we now have to discuss. In putting it in this way, we do not suggest that homonymy in itself constitutes any insuperable obstacle to communication. That homonyms exist in many languages is very well known.

We do have to consider, however, such questions as these: can we say something more definite about the conditions in which homonymy exists in Hebrew? Are these conditions such that the addition of still more homonyms through philological investigation is favoured or disfavoured? Can we see in homonymy a factor which worked for linguistic change in Hebrew? What effect does the recognition of homonymy have upon our judgements about Hebrew style? When a high incidence of homonymy is established in Hebrew through comparative studies in the cognate languages, how far does this situation in Hebrew agree with the situation in each or all of the cognate languages considered for themselves? What effect does this in turn have upon the making of comparisons between Semitic languages?

One or two more distinctions may help us to discriminate between ways in which homonymy affects communication.

Firstly, we may distinguish between the homonyms of like grammatical function and those of unlike grammatical function. This can be easily illustrated from English, in which there is a high number of homonyms but the number is greatly reduced if we remove those which are of unlike function.[1] Thus if we take *see* and *sea*, one is a verb and the other a noun. *Week* is a noun, but *weak* is an adjective. In these circumstances the context, or in

[1] This is already noticed by Menner, *Language* xii (1936) 231. Arguing that homonyms are not likely to interfere unless they are the same part of speech, he cites Old English *earm* 'poor' and *earm* 'arm'. Similarly, while *cleave* 'sunder' is usually transitive, *cleave* 'adhere' is intransitive and always has a preposition; these verbs, now homonymous, were not so in Old English.

other terms the slot occupied by the unit, does a very great deal to select for us between the possible homonyms and exclude as irrelevant what would be significant if the word occupied a different slot. In French, something similar can be said for *ou*, *où* and *août*. There are, of course, many cases where this simple distinction does not apply: *pair* and *pear* are both nouns; so are *piece* and *peace*. Nevertheless the distinction serves to overcome a great deal of the ambiguity which one would expect to arise from homonymy. In Hebrew, of course, patterning and inflexion are such that a verb will relatively seldom be homonymous with a noun. The relevance of the point is that the high incidence of homonyms in English is much reduced in its effect upon communication through this difference of grammatical function, and therefore cannot be used in a simple fashion as an argument for the viability of large numbers of homonyms where the circumstances are different.

Here, however, we can add another discriminating factor, namely the more general context, which may establish a semantic field within which a word will fit. We know that in the sentence *They're a happy* . . . the next word is likely to be *pair* rather than *pear*. General context will similarly form a good guidance in most cases for the choice between *piece* and *peace*.

Now it would be of general interest to know how far the incidence of homonyms (or alleged homonyms) in Hebrew is correlated with the existence of general contexts which, by defining a semantic field, serve to select the correct word from among several homonyms in the lexical stock. We may illustrate this first from the group of three homonymic verbs צלל, which occur in precisely identical forms.

In the first instance, at Exod. 15. 10:

כִּסָּמוֹ יָם צָלֲלוּ כַּעוֹפֶרֶת בְּמַיִם אַדִּירִים׃

the first phrase 'the sea covered them' has already done much to define the semantic field; and, after the verb צללו has come, the unambiguous words 'like lead in the great waters' form very substantial guidance to select the meaning 'sink' rather than that of the homonyms meaning 'tingle' and 'be dark'.

For the second verb צלל, in every one of the four cases known the semantic field is defined by the presence of a subject which is an organ of speech or hearing (ears or lips). These subjects follow the verb, but in each context the semantic field of hearing has already been established, before the utterance of the verb, by other phrases or words.[1]

The third צלל occurs at Neh. 13. 19, in a phrase apparently meaning 'and it happened, as the gates of Jerusalem became shadowy at the beginning of Sabbath'. I do not see that the semantic field has been so clearly defined by the context as in the other two. The reference to the coming of the Sabbath might furnish some indication. At Ezek. 31. 3, where the subject is an enormous tree, the definition is better. In any case, even if the third צלל was used without much clear definition of the semantic field, the presence of clearer definition for the other two may have been sufficient to avoid much ambiguity.

Sometimes the presence of homonymy, along with usage of both homonyms in closely related semantic fields, may lead to the coalescence of the two senses. Orlinsky suggests that there were two homonyms שכב. The former has the familiar sense 'lie';[2] the other means 'pour out', like Arabic *sakaba*. The Hebrew phrase שִׁכְבַת־זֶרַע then means 'outpouring of seed'. The original sense was forgotten, because (a) the sense 'lie' was normal for the verb, while (b) the semantic field was close to that of שכב as 'lie with'. Indeed both words occur together in Num. 5. 13:

וְשָׁכַב אִישׁ אֹתָהּ שִׁכְבַת־זֶרַע

This being established, Orlinsky goes on to expound Job 38. 37:

וְנִבְלֵי שָׁמַיִם מִי יַשְׁכִּיב

as:

'Who can pour out the bottles of heaven?'

Such a treatment, whether in the end it is right or not, shows an intelligent judgement of the possible effects of homonymy, gives a relation to a well-established Arabic sense, and perhaps makes more sense of Hebrew שכבה than a derivation from שכב 'lie'.

It is a quite different matter if homonyms not only lie within the same semantic field but mean something quite different, or even directly opposite, within it.

---

[1] The cases are: I Sam. 3. 11; II Kings 21. 12; Jer. 19. 3; Hab. 3. 16.

[2] Cf. already GB, pp. 824 f. The phrase שִׁכְבַת הַטַּל at Exod. 16. 13, however, seems to mean a 'layer' more naturally than an 'outpouring' of dew; this somewhat weakens Orlinsky's suggestion. The LXX has καταπαυομένης τῆς δρόσου, i.e. כ plus שבת.

A classic case is English *let*. Alongside the common *let* meaning 'permit' there is a *let* meaning 'prevent'. This is a homonym produced by convergence through sound changes; in Old English the words are respectively *lætan* and *lęttan*. Hamlet says: 'I'll make a ghost of him that lets me', and AV renders at Rom. 1. 13: 'I purposed to come unto you, (but was let hitherto)'. In the seventeenth century this use was already becoming archaic. But the corresponding noun *let* is still found in special contexts, like the legal *let and hindrance*. (Note that there is no noun form *let* meaning 'permission'; though there is a *let* referring to house rental.)[1]

The existence of two homonyms with directly opposite senses within roughly the same semantic field may have led to the disuse of one of the homonyms. 'After it had become homonymous with *let* "permit", this word must have been singularly ineffective', says Bloomfield.[2] Thus, he goes on, 'it is likely that homonymy plays more than an occasional part in the obsolescence of forms'.

If we apply this to the Old Testament, two possibilities emerge. If the existence of a homonymy was such as grossly to damage the communicative efficiency of language, possibly we should regard a proposed new homonym as on that ground unproved. If, on the other hand, homonymy can be a factor in the obsolescence and disappearance of words, this may explain why a rare homonym became unknown, and thereby confirm the identification of one.

A good illustration is the disappearance of words developed from Latin *gallus* 'cock' in south-western France, because the word would have become homonymous with the word for 'cat' (/gat/). This explanation was put forward by Gilliéron.[3]

---

[1] Even in the AV the grammatical context usually selects the sense: *let* ('prevent') is absolute, with no following infinitive, and *let* in *let me go* could not mean 'prevent'.

[2] *Language*, pp. 398 f.

[3] An exposition is conveniently available, with map, in Bloomfield, *Language*, pp. 396 ff. Other sources I have found helpful are Elise Richter, 'Über Homonymie', in the Kretschmer Festschrift (Vienna, 1926), pp. 167–201; Menner, op. cit. Another instance is that of *queen* and *quean*, which are different words, though connected by *Ablaut*, OE *cwēn* 'princess, queen' and *cwene* 'woman, servant, harlot'. Menner, p. 232, says that: 'a survey of the distribution of *quean* in English dialects clearly corroborates the view that confusion with *queen* is the cause of its disappearance'. He also suggests that semantic interference may not develop to the point of excluding one homonym from the language but may result only in a limitation of meaning or a new division of meanings. This may have happened also in Hebrew.

The view of Gilliéron is still a matter of controversy; but the discussion remains suggestive for Hebrew. Here are some examples.

The familiar word עָזַר means 'help'. At Job 30. 13, however, Driver detected a homonymic עָזַר meaning 'hinder' in the phrase לֹא עָזַר לָמוֹ. Dillmann, followed by BH³, had emended to עָצַר, meaning 'restrain, hold back'. This is the conjecture probably followed by RSV:

> 'They break up my path,
> they promote my calamity;
> no one restrains them.'

Driver, however, argued that the conjecture was unnecessary, for the Arabic '-z-r 'reprove, hinder' shows that the phrase means 'not hindering them' in any case, without emendation of the text. He added that the Accadian *ezēru* 'scold' attests the early diffusion of this root.

The difficulty is the conflict between two homonyms, identical in all forms, of which one means 'help' and the other means 'hinder', so that they lie within approximately the same semantic field. We cannot argue that the word meaning 'hinder' is normal in Job and remove the difficulty in this way. Job 26. 2 מה עזרת ללא־כח is a clear case of 'help', while 29. 12, only one chapter before our example, has the phrase

ויתום ולא־עֹזֵר לוֹ

'an orphan with no one to help him'.

This phrase, with its very close similarity to that at 30. 13, makes it difficult to suppose that the same writer would make such a change in so short a space.

These considerations in themselves are far from final; but they do indicate the kind of problems involved in homonymy. These cannot easily be simplified, for yet another homonym, עָזַר 'be valiant', has been identified by Driver for three passages in Chronicles and one in Psalms; it is cognate with *Ugar. ǵzr* 'hero, heroic might'.[1] At I Chron. 12. 1 the sense of

וְהֵמָּה בַּגִּבּוֹרִים עֹזְרֵי הַמִּלְחָמָה

---

[1] *CML*, p. 142; Ullendorff in *JSS* vii (1962) 347 adds the comparison with Eth. *'zr*, *tä'äzrä* 'impetum facere' (Dillmann, col. 1003) and other comparative information. Dillmann himself, however, by no means accepts this sense. The application to Ps. 89. 20 is found also in Albright, *The Archaeology of Palestine* (1949), p. 233, but with the sense 'youth'. Cf. further Index, no. 236.

'and these are among the mighty men, heroic in war'.

Meanwhile for Zech. 1. 15 Eitan appealed to yet another Arabic word, *ġazura* 'be copious, abundant'. Arguing that the usual word 'help' cannot really be extended to mean 'help forward, increase, further' (cf. RSV here), he argued that the contrast was between God who was angry a little and the nations who were copious or abundant in the affliction.

Again, the verb עָזַב is familiar in the sense 'leave, abandon'. At certain places, however, Driver has identified a sense 'help', which is known for the Ethiopic *'äzzäbä* (Dillmann, cols. 1003–4). At Jer. 49. 25 the MT is difficult:

$$\text{אֵיךְ לֹא־עֻזְּבָה עִיר תְּהִלָּה:}$$

Taken literally, this would seem to mean:

'Oh how the city of praise has not been abandoned!'

Rudolph in *BH*[3] and in his commentary (p. 252) preferred to omit the word 'not' (which, indeed, is not represented by the Vulgate). He argued that the particle is an angry gloss by a reader who thought that the title 'city of praise' could not apply to Damascus, of which the oracle is speaking.

The omission of the negative by the Vulgate is not so very powerful an argument when all the other versions have it. If we follow the Ethiopic word 'help', Driver argues, we have the good sense:

'How helpless is the city of praise'.

He then goes on to find another case in Jer. 49. 10–11, and an even more striking one in Exod. 23. 5. If one finds one's enemy's ass in trouble, the text says:

$$\text{וְחָדַלְתָּ מֵעֲזֹב לוֹ עָזֹב תַּעֲזֹב עִמּוֹ:}$$

'and (if) you are reluctant to help him,
(nevertheless) you must certainly help him.'[1]

RSV had already seen the advantage of a sense like 'help' and actually translated in this way; but since they note only that the Hebrew was 'obscure', they probably did not have a clear idea how their rendering could be justified.

---

[1] The more traditional approach is to say the sense is 'let loose, set free' and make this a component in the usual sense 'leave, forsake'.

At Job 9. 27, אֶעֶזְבָה פָנַי וְאַבְלִיגָה, Driver found yet another homonym, meaning 'be cheerful, be agreeable', with its cognate in the Arabic '-*ḏ*-*b*. The sense therefore is 'I will look cheerful'.

Once again, then, we have in addition to the familiar word 'leave, abandon' a homonym which means 'be cheerful' and one which means 'help'. Of these two, the former presents less of a problem; it may be that the context of facial expression would suffice to select the right homonym. The latter, however, is a homonym which almost exactly contradicts another homonym within the same semantic field.

In addition to these the standard dictionaries themselves recognize a homonym עזב at Neh. 3. 8:

וַיַּעַזְבוּ ירושלם עד החומה הרחבה:

and this is usually taken as 'restored' or 'paved'; it is the only occurrence. Once again, then, we have a total of perhaps four verbs עזב, all homonymic.

In the case of the עזב 'help' suggested by Driver, we have, indeed, a philological difficulty of a more orthodox kind, in that there is some uncertainty about the existence of the Ethiopic usage cited as comparison. Dillmann cites only one case, with the careful qualifications '*ut videtur*' and '*incerta est haec significatio*'. Leslau in his *Contributions* offers nothing on this root.

A similar example can be seen in Driver's treatments of שמר. Even for the verb 'keep' he identifies a sense 'tend, cultivate' (Accadian *šummuru*), which, applied to Hos. 4. 10–11, with re-pointing, gives

כִּי־אֶת־יהוה עָזְבוּ לִשְׁמֹר זְנוּת:

'For they have forsaken Yahweh to cultivate whoredom'.

A second verb is שמר 'rage' (Accadian *šamāru*). A third verb שמר means 'cast out, reject'. Hitherto recognized only in Syriac, it is now identified at Ps. 37. 28b:

לְעוֹלָם נִשְׁמָרוּ וְזֶרַע רְשָׁעִים נִכְרָת: MT

Here many scholars, noting that from the acrostic form the half-verse should begin with ע, have exploited the ἄνομοι of the Greek to write a subject עַוָּלִים; and, since this makes the wicked into the subject of the first verb, either one must emend to נִשְׁמָדוּ

or follow Driver and say that the נִשְׁמָרוּ of MT means 'are cast out'.[1]

In any case, our example shows how the familiar שָׁמַר 'keep' is taken to have a homonym which is so sharply opposed in sense as to make confusion likely. A context in which persons are 'preserved' by God is a context in which we might also hear that they are 'cast out, rejected'. A similar treatment by Tur-Sinai at Job 14. 16 gives the sense:

MT   לֹא־תִשְׁמוֹר עַל־חַטָּאתִי

'thou dost not overlook my sin'

(reading as piel, and with the Syriac-Mandean sense of not 'watch' but 'release, absolve'; parallelism with 'thou numberest my steps').[2] If this is right, conflict of homonyms is again likely.[3]

Having given these illustrations, we now have to consider another matter of general interest. It is rather difficult, and perhaps not absolutely necessary, to draw a clear line between homonyms, i.e. words which are alike in form but mean different things, and the phenomenon of polysemy, or the existence in the same word of a number of different senses.

At least some linguists have held that there is no absolute distinction between the two assessments of a phenomenon. Bloomfield, for example, writes: 'In many cases we hesitate whether to view the form as a single form with several meanings or as a set of homonyms.'[4]

In some of the illustrations I have given, as the discriminating reader will have noticed, it is possible to argue that the number of homonyms is less than I have represented, because two of the homonyms quoted are alternate senses of the same word. Thus, for instance, I cited טוֹב meaning 'good' and טוֹב meaning 'perfume' as two homonyms. The philologist whose mind is accustomed to

---

[1] I myself think the MT to be right in its normal sense: 'they [i.e. the saints, just mentioned] are preserved for ever, but the seed of the evil is cut off'. The acrostic sequence ignored the particle לְ; cf. 37. 39, where the ת verse begins with ו. The Greek ἄνομοι is from a variant or doublet.

[2] Eitan treats the same passage in the opposite way, keeping שָׁמַר as 'keep, watch' and holding that חטאת is 'step' (Arab. ḫaṭā, ḫaṭwa).

[3] The verbs here discussed are of course additional to the II and III שמר registered as the putative roots of שְׁמָרִים 'dregs' and שָׁמִיר 'adamant'.

[4] Language, p. 150; cf. also p. 145. It may be that the decision between homonymy and polysemy can be reached through componential analysis, as outlined, for instance, by Nida, Science of Translating, pp. 90 ff.

working on comparative, etymological, and historical lines may reply that these are actually 'the same word', and that the sense 'good' is derived from the sense 'sweet-smelling' of the same word, a relation made visible through the South Arabian *ṭyb*, a word for a kind of incense. One sense, accordingly, may be said to 'derive' from the other. Similarly, with עֲזֹב, where we noted a homonymy between the word with sense 'leave, abandon' and the word with sense 'help', Driver himself, whose interpretation we have been considering, thought that a continuous semantic development could be seen from a sense 'left' through the passive sense of 'left; let alone; was indulgent to' to the active sense of 'helped'.

It seems to be wrong, however, to suppose that the difficulties and problems caused by the recognition of homonyms are in any way disposed of if we are able to see that an historical development has taken place from one example to another. This is a clarification only for the historically oriented philologist, not for the normal user of the language. Menner seems to be right in arguing:

> From the point of view of the speaker ignorant of origins, the embarrassment and confusion caused by multiplicity of meanings is likely to be as great when a form represents two or more etymologically distinct words as when it represents one. Most students of homonyms and most semanticists pay little attention to this fact, but Jespersen pertinently remarks that 'the psychological effect of those cases of polysemy, where "one and the same word" has many meanings, is exactly the same as that of cases where two or three words of different origins have accidentally become homonyms.'[1]

In other words, טוֹב meaning 'perfume' may, for the etymologically oriented philologist, be 'the same word as' טוֹב 'good'; but from the point of view of the communicative problems related to homonymy, it makes little difference. The Hebrew speaker did not know the history of the language; and, since there is a difference between 'perfumed wine' and 'good wine', nothing is achieved

---

[1] Menner in *Language* xii (1936) 243 f. Cf. the procedure of the *Chicago Assyrian Dictionary*, which provides a separate entry (marked by A and B, etc.) where meanings are sufficiently different, thus providing for clarity and distinctiveness even at the price of increasing the number of apparent homonyms. There is no striving to secure a clear distinction between polysemy and homonymy. See the statement in the preface of the first volume to be published, vol. vi (Ḥ), p. v. In not striving for any absolute distinction between homonymy and polysemy, we appear to be in accord with the medieval Hebrew and Arabic approach. The medieval tendency was to treat the matter as one of varying senses of the same word. See Maimonides, in Efros, pp. 59 f.

to overcome the difficulty by saying that יֵין הַטּוֹב historically may
have meant both.

Finally, an instance which shows how conflict of homonyms
may, through the perplexity it caused, have produced a graphic
confusion in the text. I Sam. 14. 25–26 uses the word יַעַר 'honey-
comb'. The MT is difficult, and a clever restoration by Wellhausen[1]
suggests that the normal word דְּבַשׁ 'honey' was added as a gloss to
יַעַר; the gloss in turn rendered יַעַר itself unnecessary, so that it
came to be understood in its other and commoner sense, i.e. 'wood'.
Meanwhile the gloss דְּבַשׁ through its similarity caused a confusion
and loss of a form of דְּבֹרִים 'bees'. Even if hardly quite certain,
this reconstruction illustrates the interdependence of linguistic and
textual transmission. Apart from the LXX, the versions follow the
sense 'wood'.[2]

In order to indicate succinctly the kind of problems involved in
the suggestions which have been made, I attach now, without
detailed discussion of each case, a list of some typical examples in
which homonyms have been detected in recent philological
treatments. The second column gives the homonym (or the sense)
which is generally familiar; the third that which has been recently
suggested.

1. אהבה	a. 'love'	b. 'leather'	
2. ברית	a. 'covenant'	b. 'splendour'	
3. מְבַשֵּׂר	a. 'messenger of good'	b. 'refuter, opponent'	
4. גוי	a. 'people'	b. 'field, land'	
5. דלק	a. 'burn'	b. 'pursue'	
6. דעך	a. 'be extinguished'	b. 'attack'	
7. דשן	a. 'be fat'	b. 'be hidden, shrouded'	
8. חזון	a. 'vision'	b. 'magistrate'	
9. חטאת	a. 'sin'	b. 'step, walk' c. 'penury'	
10. עברה	a. 'excess'	b. 'wrath'	
11. עמס	a. 'hoist, support'	b. 'set in cement, lay bricks'	
12. עש	a. 'moth'	b. 'pus, rottenness' c. 'bird's nest'	

---

[1] Set out in detail by S. R. Driver, *Notes on Samuel*, pp. 113 f.

[2] Most do not, however, fail to recognize the feminine יערת (which has no
homonym) at 14. 27, or יער itself at Cant. 5. 1 (but LXX there ἄρτον).

13.	רוּץ	*a.* 'run'	*b.* 'break in' (a horse)
14.	רשׁע	*a.* 'evil'	*b.* 'ample, rich'
15.	שׁב (participle)	*a.* 'returning'	*b.* 'running about, straying'
16.	שׁיר	*a.* 'sing'	*b.* 'travel'
17.	אתנן	*a.* 'gift, price (of harlot)'	*b.* 'effigy'

(3) *The Count of Known Homonyms*

In estimating the likelihood of any suggestion which involves the addition of a new homonym to the Hebrew lexical stock, it is obviously relevant to know how many homonyms we have already. Conceivably scholars may suppose that, since Hebrew has a large number of homonyms in any case, there is no valid reason for objecting to the addition of a few more.

We may try, therefore, to estimate the number of 'agreed' homonyms, that is, of homonyms the existence of which is generally recognized and which provide a base for measuring any increase of homonyms. I have not, however, found previous studies which have produced counts of homonyms on a basis of modern knowledge and in a form adapted to the questions I am seeking to answer. The obvious source is the registration in the standard dictionaries. The organization of these dictionaries is, however, far from well adapted to our question. One cannot simply go through them and count the number of places where words are distinguished as I עבר, II עבר, and so on. These include many cases where the root is identical but no actual overlaps in form occur. They use the same distinction for homonyms in the normal sense and for words of special kinds such as personal names and place-names. Moreover, the dictionaries vary between themselves in the way in which they organize the differentiation of various words. Nevertheless some approximate counts may be made on the basis of the existing dictionaries.

Using as a criterion the formal one of enumeration under Roman figures such as I and II,[1] BDB is found to list just over 500 homonymic nouns. A very large proportion of these, however, are proper names, which we may ignore for the purposes of this study. The proper name 'Smith' is homonymic with the noun 'smith', but communication allows for this fact and it should not commonly

---

[1] The figures are, very occasionally, inadvertently omitted by BDB.

stand as an example of interference with communication through homonymy.

Once personal and place-names are removed, there are about 200 cases of homonymy involving nouns, counted from BDB's entries. Among these, however, some are limited in their degree of overlap or of potential conflict.

A few are instances of homonymy between a noun and a word of some other class. Thus the homonymy between אוּלָם 'porch' and אוּלָם 'but' is not a likely source of confusion.

Sometimes the semantic fields are so completely distinct that overlapping is not significant. There is little serious overlap between בַת 'daughter' and בַת meaning the measure 'bath'. Moreover, these words are formally distinct in the plural, and may have been so in the suffixed forms also.

Sometimes one noun belongs to a fairly general semantic field, while another is much more technical, being the name of an animal, an instrument, a measure, or the like. This applies to pairs like אֲנָקָה 'crying' and אֲנָקָה 'ferret, shrew-mouse'; דְּרוֹר 'release' and דְּרוֹר 'swallow'; and the two words בַת, just quoted.

Again, sometimes there may have been no homonymy within the same text, or the same period. It has often been argued in favour of philological treatments that Hebrew is not a uniform mass but has variations according to place, time, and style. This same argument, however, may reduce the number of agreed homonyms and thereby may reduce the probability that should be accorded to suggestions of new ones. In other words, the homonymy is a product of the lexicographical process, in which all Hebrew words are gathered together; but in the original situation, the homonymous words did not all exist together in the same register, place, or time, so that homonymic conflict did not take place.

A real homonymy in the same texts is that of אִיִּים (1) 'foreign coastlands, islands', (2) 'wilderness animals' (traditionally jackals).[1] Though this is a full homonym within the same register of speech, the words are easily distinguishable because 'foreign coastline' is excluded in the contexts which imply an uncanny howling being, for all cases of the latter are in a list of several wilderness animals. Similarly, the Song of Songs has not only the common מִדְבָּר

---

[1] Torrey, *Second Isaiah*, pp. 289 ff., and KB take these senses as related in origin; even if true this does not much affect my argument.

'wilderness' but also the *hapax legomenon* מִדְבָּר, usually taken to mean 'speech' or 'mouth'. Occurring as it does (4. 3) within a list of the physical characteristics of the woman, the use runs little risk of confusion. But at least these examples are found together within the same texts.

It is different with the אִי 'not' of Job 22. 30 אִי־נָקִי. Assuming that this is not a textual error (as KB takes it to be), it is possible that it belonged to the vocabulary of Job but not to that of the classical prophets. Conversely, Job does not use אִי for remote lands, islands, jackals, or goblins, although these are all themes which might well come within the purview of his poem. Thus it is possible that this homonymy, though it appears in the catalogue structure of the lexicon, did not in fact operate; and the same argument could be made for the אִי which appears twice in Qoheleth. Thus although a dictionary is forced to register perhaps four words of the form אִי, it is also possible that in the usage of a particular place, time or style only two possibilities, or even only one, existed.

Once all these various considerations and qualifications have been taken into account, the gross number of some 500 homonymies involving nouns may be reduced to a number of practical homonymies, involving nouns in such a way as to create any real ambiguity or conflict, of a few dozen in all.

We should consider not only how many forms there are which have homonyms but also, where a form has homonymy at all, how many homonyms it is likely to have. The received dictionaries may from time to time list as many as four, five, or six homonymous words, but such cases form a small proportion of the total number of homonymies.

Thus under אַיִל, according to BDB, there are four homonyms, meaning 'ram', 'chief', 'pillar', and 'tree'. One may wish to modify this: the first and second might be classed as a polysemy; the second and the fourth do not actually appear in the absolute singular form which we have quoted. But there are still probably three or four homonyms, and we can even add more if we take the construct form אֵל (the writing as אֵיל makes no difference for our purpose); for then there is the familiar divine name אֵל, and also, whether it is 'a different word' or not, the אַל (sometimes taken to mean 'power') of the phrase יֶשׁ־לְאֵל יָדִי. Thus for the form אֵל (אַיִל) we could possibly speak of six homonyms.

Perhaps a better example is that of כֹּפֶר. BDB, GB, and KB register four homonyms, with meanings of 'ransom', 'pitch', the name of a plant, and 'village'. But the third is a plant name and the fourth is conceivably a dialect form.

In any case this situation with four homonyms or more is relatively rare. There are four also with חָרוּץ and with צִיר, and more precariously with צַר. But of the total number of forms where homonyms occur, the vast majority among the nouns offer only two possibilities, once proper names are excluded. Only quite rarely have large clusters of identical homonyms, with like grammatical function and excluding proper names, achieved general recognition.

With verbs, as with nouns, the dictionaries often list what appear to be homonyms, but on examination these turn out to be from texts of widely separate provenance, so that no synchronic homonymy occurred. Of the four homonymic verbs עָנָה, the second ('be occupied') occurs only in Qoheleth, which book, however, does not use the third ('be afflicted')—though affliction, one might say, is a prime theme of this author—or the fourth. Possibly עָנָה 'sing' was losing ground before the more frequent שִׁיר (which alone had a noun 'song' to go with it), and by the time of Qoheleth was obsolete, thus enabling the newer עָנָה 'be occupied' to find a place.

The word גָּאַל 'defile' occurs in Deutero-Isaiah, in which גָּאַל 'redeem' is also prominent. One might expect therefore to find some considerable conflict. It is interesting therefore that practically no overlap of actual forms occurs, the only case being the form נְגֹאָלָה at Zeph. 3. 1. The forms usually registered as niphal and hiphil are both unusual forms, which do not occur for גָּאַל 'redeem'—נִגְאָלוּ and אֶגְאָלְתִּי. Thus actual homonymy of forms is very slight, and possibly the avoidance of homonymy has fostered the production or retention of the peculiar verbal forms. Caution must, however, be exercised, because forms which are not attested may nevertheless have occurred.

Another relevant test is a comparison of the incidence of homonyms in Hebrew and in the other Semitic languages. It would be paradoxical if philological treatments produced in Hebrew an incidence of homonyms greater than that which is found in the other Semitic languages themselves.

The incidence of homonyms might be expected to vary in

relation to the phonological changes in the prehistory of each language. Where phoneme mergers have been frequent, the incidence of homonymy should be expected to be higher. Other things being equal, there should be more homonyms resulting from such merger in Hebrew than in Arabic and Ethiopic, but fewer than in Accadian or Mandean. It is in fact not unlikely that Hebrew roughly occupies such an intermediate position. This, however, is far from an exact account of the matter, because phoneme merger is not the only cause of homonymy. The influence of loan-words, for instance, has also to be considered, and is quite high in Accadian, with its many Sumerian words.

Preliminary surveys I have done in two languages fairly close to the circumstances of Hebrew, namely Ugaritic and Syriac, do not encourage us to suppose that Hebrew had an incidence of homonymy substantially higher than has already been recognized; on the contrary, they suggest that the normal degree of homonymy was somewhat lower. The Ugaritic glossary, when studied cursorily, appears to display numerous homonymies; but most of these would disappear when the texts were vocalized. One can, for instance, expect that *ḥmr* 'ass' would be as distinct in Ugaritic from *ḥmr* 'clay, mud' as is the case in Hebrew. The same would apply to *rḥ* 'spirit' and *rḥ* 'smell'. In Ugaritic verbs a number of homonymies can be found, but not very many. With *ḥwy*, for example, there is no overlap of themes; the verb 'bow down' occurs only in a theme unknown for *ḥwy* 'live'. In some cases, homonymy appears by the reconstruction of one scholar but not by that of another. There are two homonyms *šlḥ* according to Gordon (i. 'send', ii. 'cast' or 'beat out' a metal), and Driver construes the situation in the same way; but Aistleitner tries to include both under the same word (his no. 2610). The form *tdʿ* from the verb 'sweat' is registered under *ydʿ* by Driver and thus becomes homonymic with *ydʿ* 'know'; but Gordon has it under *dʿ* and Aistleitner under *(w)dʿ*, in which cases it would probably not be homonymic when vocalized. The number of clear cases of homonymy in the Ugaritic stock of verbs, once the necessary qualifications are made, is quite low.[1]

---

[1] Driver's glossary appears to yield 16 cases, if we exclude cases like *nd* (i.e. *nwd*) and *nd* (i.e. *ndd*); they are: *'any, b'l, ḥwy, ḥrr, ḥss, tʿn, ydʿ, kss, ʿms, ʿny, qry, šbʿ, šlḥ, tr, tʿr, tʿr*. But a considerable number of these would be considered doubtful and are otherwise construed by other scholars. Some others are not true homonyms by the criteria we have already established above.

Syriac is another language which like Hebrew can present, when surveyed in the dictionary form, remarkable groups of 'homonymic' roots. A good instance is that of '*rb*, for which Brockelmann registers ten separate entries as against the six in Hebrew according to BDB; but very few of these have really overlapping homonymic *forms*. In Syriac we have the advantage of a discussion of homonymy on fairly modern philological principles, by Schulthess (1900). His discussion, however, is of homonymic roots, and does not explore the somewhat different problem of homonymic forms. The total number of roots discussed by him is forty-eight.[1]

I have also tested Syriac by taking the number of homonyms beginning with a particular letter. Brockelmann marks only four real homonyms with first radical /d/:

dgl	(1) 'aim'	(2) 'lie, deceive'	
dwl	(1) 'move'	(2) no real homonymy	(3) 'serve, be humble'
dwq	(1) 'pound'	(2) 'inspect'	
dšš	(1) 'neglect'	(2) 'cover, close'.	

Dll and *drr*, though marked, are perhaps not real cases.

In Syriac, if the general incidence of homonymy were the same as in Hebrew, one would expect the proportion including /d/ to be higher than in Hebrew, because Syriac /d/ results from merger of /d/ with /ḏ/, while pre-Hebrew /ḏ/ became /z/ in Hebrew. In so far as such merger is a cause of homonymy, one would expect a higher incidence in Syriac. In fact the incidence is lower than that already recognized for Hebrew. BDB, even if we eliminate some improbable entries (like two words דגל), offers fairly good examples such as

מדבר	(1) 'wilderness'	(2) 'speech' or 'mouth'
מדוה	(1) 'sickness'	(2) 'garment' (p. 551b)
דל	(1) 'door'	(2) 'poor'

---

[1] Though Schulthess discusses the way in which homonyms come into existence, he has, typically of the older philology, no thoughts about the problem of communicative efficiency, and he does not really offer anything relevant for our present discussion of homonymy in general. Nor are the problems which concern us seen by Nöldeke in his review, *ZDMG* liv (1900) 152–64. For our purpose the study of Schulthess is of interest mainly for its count of homonymic roots, and for some careful establishments of distinctions between homonyms. The forty-eight homonymic roots treated by him are: *bdl, bl', b't, glb, gpp, dgl, dšš, zhr, zw', zll, ḥbl, ḥgg, ḥm', ḥsd, ṭw', kwš, kss, mkr, mlṭ, ngl, sbr, shr, 'll, 'md, 'rb, prg, pr', ṣw', ṣll, ṣpp, qbb, qṭm, qpl, qṣr, rhb, rhṭ, r'', rpt, šgm, šgr, šḥm, šḥr, šwḥ (šyḥ), šll, šlp, šqp, šrb, tkk.*

דלה	(1) 'hair, thrum'	(2) 'the poor'
דמה	(1) 'be like'	(2) 'cease'
דמם	(1) 'be silent'	(2) 'wail'
דרור	(1) 'freedom'	(2) 'swallow'.

Modern philological suggestions would certainly, if accepted, add to this number; see Index, nos. 81–4, 87–101. One would expect Syriac to be a suitable comparison for Hebrew—not far removed in period, in cultural situation, or in type of literature. Yet, if the sample can be generalized, the incidence of homonymy in Syriac is actually lower than that already recognized in Hebrew, to say nothing of the substantial additions to Hebrew consequent on philological suggestions. It would then seem possible that philological treatments, though assuming a close overlap in lexical resources between the Semitic languages, nevertheless bring about a large disparity between them in respect of homonymy.

It is conceivable, on the other hand, that there have been periods of unusually high homonymy in the development of a language, and that in Hebrew the biblical period was such an epoch; by the end of the biblical era many such homonyms had been eliminated and a certain levelling of the vocabulary brought about. Syriac would then be more comparable with the post-biblical era in Hebrew. This possibility, though difficult to prove, deserves further research.

(4) *Homonymy and Style*

Another aspect of homonymy in Hebrew is its relation to style. It is by no means intrinsically impossible that Hebrew contained larger numbers of really interchangeable homonyms than (let us say) Syriac or modern literary Arabic. If this were so, however, it would almost certainly have an effect upon style. Certain kinds of Chinese poetry are said to build much of their stylistic effect upon the homonymic and ambiguous nature of the elements used. This is not an argument that Hebrew is like Chinese in this regard, unless we go on to say that Hebrew style, like the corresponding Chinese style, is actually built upon the subtle appreciation of ambiguities in language. Such an assertion about Hebrew style I have never seen. But in any case, if homonymy was a major feature of classical Hebrew, we might expect it to have an effect on style, whether by the development of devices through which clarity in ambiguous contexts might be found, or alternatively by the development of a style through which the effects produced by recurrent homonymy are prized and cultivated. A style of this latter kind is found in some medieval Hebrew poetry.

Now there are quite a large number of places at which scholars have claimed to identify the use of a pair of homonyms in juxta-position as a literary device. Not all of these command agreement by all scholars, but some can be considered very likely. A widely accepted case is Ps. 137. 5, already quoted.[1]

Play upon homonymies and double meanings was a feature of the ancient riddle style. A clear instance comes from the master of this style, Samson:

Judges 15. 16:

בִּלְחִי הַחֲמוֹר חֲמוֹר חֲמֹרָתָיִם
בִּלְחִי הַחֲמוֹר הִכֵּיתִי אֶלֶף אִישׁ׃

'With the jawbone of an ass, mass upon mass,
with the jawbone of an ass I slew a thousand men.'

There is exploitation of the homonymy between חמור 'ass' and חמור 'heap'. Even if the phrase חמור חמרתים is taken in an-other sense (e.g. 'shave, scrape, flay', supposedly after an Arabic *ḥamara*—accepted by GB, p. 242b),[2] the play on homonymy remains.

A play on homonyms is probable also in the answer to the riddle about the honey, Judges 14. 18:

מַה־מָּתוֹק מִדְּבַשׁ וּמֶה עַז מֵאֲרִי׃

There is an Arabic '*ary* 'honey', and the riddle played upon a Hebrew cognate, more or less homonymous with אֲרִי 'lion'.[3]

Play upon homonyms merges into the more general juxtaposition of words which merely have some similarity; this can produce all sorts of effects, from the emphatic to the comic. Isa. 5. 7 has been

---

[1] See above, p. 48.

[2] Cf. *BH*[3]. The Greek ἐξαλείφων ἐξήλειψα does not support the interpretation followed by GB. More probably it was influenced by the other verb חמר, used of the wiping on of pitch in Exod. 2. 3 (wiping on and wiping off can probably be covered by the same verb, cf. the history of כפר). It was also influenced by the range of ἐξαλείφω in Greek, which could be used for the 'wiping out' of people, e.g. Aes. *Ch.* 503, μὴ 'ξαλείψῃς σπέρμα Πελοπιδῶν, and thus fits nicely with the total sense found in the Greek.

[3] See J. R. Porter in *JTS* N.S. xiii (1962) 106–9.

quoted already.[1] A striking case is Isa. 42. 1–4, with the assonance of רצץ and רוץ, and the use twice of כהה (perhaps two homonyms meaning 'be dim' and 'rebuke'). The exact image of this song, however, remains obscure.

At some other places, at which the stylistic exploitation of homonymy has been argued, stylistic considerations seem to tell against the suggestion. At Isa. 55. 1, for instance, it has been suggested that כֶּסֶף is used firstly to mean 'food' (cf. the Accadian *kispu, kasāpu, kusīpātu*, etc.; von Soden, pp. 487, 453, 514) and then with the usual sense of 'silver, money'. The text would then mean something like:

Ho, everyone who thirsts, come to the water; and he who has no food (כסף), go, buy and eat; and go, buy without money (כסף) and without price wine and milk.

The effect of the collocation, if this suggestion were right, would surely be to produce a poor and stupid comic jingle.[2] That the text repeats twice the familiar sense of 'money' seems infinitely more probable.

Elsewhere, again, a collocation of homonyms may have taken place more or less accidentally, without any deliberate striving after effect. At Qoh. 7. 6:

כִּי כְקוֹל הַסִּירִים תַּחַת הַסִּיר

סִיר means firstly 'thorn' and secondly 'cauldron', but it is possible that the homonyms are juxtaposed without either the intention of an effect or the result of one. Or does this passage from one meaning to another of a rather unimportant word symbolize futility and foolishness?[3]

Other places where the collocation of homonyms has been suggested include:

Isa.	32. 6	עשׂה	(1) 'do'	(2) 'conceal'[4]
Jer.	12. 9	עיט	(1) 'den'	(2) 'bird of prey'[5]
Mic.	1. 7	אתנן	(1) 'effigy'	(2) 'harlot's hire'
Ps.	5. 4	בקר	(1) 'morning'	(2) 'offering for oracle'
Ct.	3. 8	חרב	(1) 'war'	(2) 'sword'

---

[1] Above, p. 48; for others, see Driver in *VT* iv (1954) 242.

[2] A good deal worse in this respect is Dahood's discovery of עָרִים 'gods' at Jer. 2. 28, and 19. 15, giving for the former a sense 'For your gods, O Judah, were the number of your cities/gods'.

[3] Gordis, p. 259, takes this to be an example of the writer's literary skill.

[4] Eitan, p. 58.   [5] Cf. above, pp. 128 f.

Several places suggest play on the similarity of יָרֵא 'fear' and רָאה 'see', e.g. Ps. 40. 4, 119. 74, Job 6. 21.

Sometimes, where a pair of homonyms is held to exist but where the text in question uses only one of them, it is possible that paronomasia or punning is intended; that is, that one form is used with the intention of suggesting two quite different meanings. For example, a word אַהֲבָה 'leather', in addition to the familiar אַהֲבָה 'love', has been found at Hos. 11. 4

$$\text{בְּחַבְלֵי אָדָם אֶמְשְׁכֵם בַּעֲבֹתוֹת אַהֲבָה}$$

where the senses in question are 'bands of leather' and 'bands of love' (parallel 'cords of hide'?), and Cant. 3. 10, where Solomon's palanquin is

$$\text{מֶרְכָּבוֹ אַרְגָּמָן תּוֹכוֹ רָצוּף אַהֲבָה}$$

In this latter example, since the parallels are substances like 'silver', 'gold', and 'purple', there seems to be strong reason for accepting the rendering 'leather'.

On the other hand one can hardly ignore the fact that love (אהבה) is precisely the main theme of the Song of Songs, and, in a somewhat different sense, of Hosea also. It is therefore a little hard to contemplate that a word אהבה would be used prosaically for 'leather' in these two works, without the striking similarity to the word 'love' being noticed.

To sum up, on the one hand it is a reasonable possibility that, when a rare homonym occurred in the Old Testament, its own homonymy was a factor in its own desuetude and thereby in the loss of understanding of its meaning. Where philological treatments claim to uncover homonyms previously not detected, this circumstance is in their favour. In relatively few cases, however, so far as my research goes, have such treatments tried to document with evidence this obsolescence of words because of homonymy. Treatments which use this argument should in principle attempt to show in what way semantic confusion may have arisen, in the circumstances of the relevant contexts, and in relation to the historical distribution both of homonyms which coincided with the word in form and of synonyms which, by coinciding roughly with it in meaning, may have taken over its semantic function when it came to be lost.

On the other hand we have not found evidence that homonymy

was a very widespread feature of biblical Hebrew. Its total incidence of homonymy, though probably higher than that of Greek or Latin or Arabic, was much lower than that of English or French. Philological treatments, if too many of them are accepted uncritically, would seem arbitrarily to raise the incidence of homonyms above the level justified by general evidence, and thereby to make Hebrew a language more troubled by homonymy than the very Semitic languages (apart from Accadian) which are being used as sources; and this procedure, in turn, must carry peculiar implications about style and communication in Hebrew, which implications have not generally been realized. These arguments favour reserve in accepting large additions to the count of homonyms in Hebrew.[1]

[1] Cf. recently D. F. Payne, 'Characteristic Word-play in "Second Isaiah": a Reappraisal' in *JSS* xii (1967) 207–29.

VII

THE DISTRIBUTION OF LEXICAL
RESOURCES IN THE
SEMITIC LANGUAGES

(1) *General*

PHILOLOGICAL treatments often appear to depend logically on the assumption of a high degree of community or overlap between the various Semitic languages in their use of lexical resources. It is implied that, a cognate word having been found, this will form a probable lead to (a) the existence of a related Hebrew word and (b) the meaning of that Hebrew word. The existence of a word in a cognate language is taken as a sort of prima-facie case for the existence of a corresponding word in Hebrew, and this prima-facie case is then clinched by the fact of a Hebrew text which seems to fit this word and give good sense.

The question of principle can be put in a quite simple form. How great is the degree of coincidence (leaving aside words of non-Semitic origin) between the various Semitic languages in their use of vocabulary? If this degree is high, then there will be a high degree of probability (other things being equal) in a claim that, if a word exists with a known meaning in language A (let us say, Arabic) it can therefore confidently be expected to occur in a recognizably related form and with a recognizably related meaning in language B (in our case, Hebrew). If the general degree of coincidence is low, then there will be a correspondingly low degree of probability in this claim. When we find it argued or implied that the existence of a word or form in a cognate language is prima-facie evidence for its existence also in Hebrew, such an argument or implication clearly rests on the assumption that the degree of coincidence is very high.

It should be noted that the question of related form cannot in this context be treated usefully apart from the question of related meaning. Where the same form, or a form corresponding under known conditions, is found in more than one language, is the meaning also substantially the same?

If we have 'the same word', but if it is found with a different meaning in language B from that known in language A, this does not make it difficult to claim that the word exists also in B, but it means that it will be hard to know what it means in B, and that therefore we shall have less chance of reaching any solution of the problem at all. For, we must remember, the whole situation under discussion is one in which the existence of the word in language B has not hitherto been recognized; and this means that there is a lack of evidence for its meaning in language B, apart from the evidence of the cognate language.

Moreover, since we are using as further evidence the context of a particular passage, the relevance of that context is itself dependent upon the degree of assurance we have about the meaning of the word we now claim to recognize for the first time. To put it simply, it will not help us much if we identify the root x-y-z, well known in Arabic, if we still do not know what this would mean in Hebrew. For these reasons it is of real importance to consider, from our general knowledge of the Semitic languages apart from the exigencies of particular difficult passages, what is the degree of community in the use of formally corresponding lexical items, and what is the degree of community in the meanings with which they function in the various languages of the group.

Now there is no difficulty, to begin with, in assembling a substantial list of words which in form (allowing for the normal correspondences) and in meaning (allowing for slight and easily explicable differences) run fairly uniformly across the whole series of the ancient Semitic languages or a large number of them. Such a list is offered by Bergsträsser in the appendix to his comparative study of the Semitic languages.[1] It contains about 170 items, of which Bergsträsser claims that they comprise the 'relatively certain correspondences of the five chief branches of the Semitic languages' (excluding loanwords from one branch to another). This, he says, is far from exhausting the lexical stock of proto-Semitic; for all words which are lacking in one or more of the branches, or which have been altered beyond recognition, are omitted.

This list contains some very fundamental words: basic words for human beings and relations, animal names, parts of the human

[1] G. Bergsträsser, *Einführung*, pp. 181–92.

body, some cosmic elements like day and night, and a number of common verbs, along with the numerals and a few prepositions. We may quote a few of the words in their Hebrew form: אָב 'father', יָלַד 'bear' (a child), עַקְרָב 'scorpion', זֶרַע 'seed', עַיִן 'eye', דָּם 'blood', יוֹם 'day', מַיִם 'water', בַּיִת 'house', נָשָׂא 'lift', קָרֵב 'approach', בָּכָה 'weep', שָׁבַר 'break'.

For all these words, about 170 in number, close correspondences in form and sense can be found running across the whole field of the basic branches of the Semitic languages.

The closeness of the agreement running through this list should not, however, impress us too much. This list is itself a very limited segment of the vocabulary of any one of the languages. Against it we have to set the vocabulary which is used in one language, or in two, but is not represented in the others. It is easy to produce impressive lists of words which are common in two or three of the relevant Semitic languages, but which are entirely absent from others or else occur in them only with meanings substantially different.

Dillmann[1] gave a list of about twenty-five important words which are shared by Hebrew and Ethiopic but do not appear in Arabic at all or appear in it only with very different meanings. They include, for instance: אֵשׁ 'fire'; עֵץ 'tree'; אֶבֶן 'stone'; אֶשֶׁךְ 'testicle'; יָכֹל 'be able'; יָצָא 'go out'.

Following this, Ullendorff[2] offers a list of 'an impressive number of words shared by Hebrew and South Arabian for which either no equivalent roots are attested in the other Semitic languages or else with such sharply differing meanings as to make the semantic and structural identity doubtful'.

Ullendorff's list comprises twenty-two examples and includes such prominent words as אִישׁ 'man'; הָרַג 'slay'; יָרָה 'shoot'; יֵשַׁע 'salvation'; קָהֵל 'assembly'.

Delitzsch used similar lists in his arguments against the priority of Arabic for the elucidation of Hebrew vocabulary. One such list endeavours to show how Arabic presents, in comparison to Hebrew, Aramaic, and Accadian, narrowed or clearly derivative meanings.[3] This he applies, for example, to:

---

[1] *Ethiopic Grammar*, pp. 6–7. Some of these words are shared also by Accadian and Ugaritic. [2] *VT* vi (1956) 195 ff.

[3] *Prolegomena*, pp. 27 f.; list showing Hebrew–Aramaic community, pp. 32–35, and Hebrew–Accadian community, pp. 45 ff. Cf. above, p. 70.

אמר 'say'—Arabic *'amara* 'command'

בוא 'come'—Arabic *bā'a* 'return home'

בעל 'possess' and also 'marry'—Arabic *ba'ala* specifically 'marry'

עזב 'leave, forsake'—Arabic *'-z-b* particularly 'be unmarried'

These indications, then, encourage us to pursue further the question of the degree of overlap in lexical stock between the various Semitic languages.

While Bergsträsser's list took a particular meaning and showed the correspondence of words with that meaning throughout the Semitic group, there seem to be other meanings (such as the words for going in a direction) which tend to have different words in the cognate languages:

	Hebrew	Arabic	Aramaic	Accadian	Ethiopic
'go down'	ירד	*n-z-l*	*n-ḥ-t*	*arādu*	*wärädä*
'fear'	ירא	*ḥāfa*	*d-ḥ-l*	*adāru*	*färhä*
	פחד			*palāḫu*	
'know'	ידע	*'-r-f*	*y-d-'*	*edū*	*'a'märä*
		'-l-m			

In some of these one language has a form closely similar to that of another in the same line, but with a meaning substantially different. Arabic *w-r-d* means not 'go down' but mainly 'arrive'; Hebrew נזל means not 'go down' but 'flow'; Arabic *f-r-h* is 'be lively'; very few Semitic languages show a cognate with Hebrew ירא 'fear';[1] though Arabic *'-r-f* is a very common word 'know', the relevant Hebrew ערף exists only as a noun 'neck' and as a denominative verb 'break the neck'; Hebrew עלם means 'hide'.

These differences, which refer to the *normal* words in use, are not removed by the *occasional* appearance in Hebrew of a form normally Aramaic, such as נחת 'go down', סלק 'go up'.

Conversely, one may take a given form and, allowing for the normal correspondences, consider what meanings attach to it in the other languages. For example: (*a*) Hebrew אמר 'say': the senses of cognates are—Accadian 'see', Arabic and Aramaic mainly 'command', Ethiopic 'show, know'. (*b*) Hebrew לקח 'take': in Arabic this is 'conceive' or 'impregnate'; Ethiopic *läqḥä* means 'lend', not 'take';[2] in Syriac the root does not exist except for *laqḥā*

---

[1] It occurs in Ugaritic, but not frequently; Leslau, *Contributions*, p. 42, gives a rather remote parallel from Tigre for פחד.

[2] Leslau, *Contributions*, p. 29, against KB.

'*planities circa urbem*',[1] which is semantically remote. For 'take' the Aramaic word is נסב, which is not found in Hebrew; the Aramaic 'ithpeel of לקח is rare and means 'be taken as a wife'; Ethiopic '*aḥäzä* is cognate with a Hebrew word, but also often appears with the sense 'begin'. Cognates of the Hebrew are found in Ugaritic and Accadian (*lqḥ, leqū*).

Our purpose, we should remember, is not to discover an etymology or identify the same root in another language. The traditional etymological consciousness, because it is directed towards questions somewhat different from ours, can indeed cause us some confusion. In particular, (1) it may be content to find in the cognate languages a word which has the same root, though that word is actually in a quite different formation; (2) it may overemphasize the fact that a cognate has the same root and underemphasize the fact that the meaning is substantially different, or it may emphasize the historical connectedness of the two meanings in such a way as to ignore their difference in function; (3) it may fail to balance the recognition of cognates with a recognition of the number of languages in which a cognate is *not* found. For example:

(1) There is a familiar Hebrew word חוֹמָה 'wall'. The etymologist will probably connect this with verbs meaning 'protect' in cognate languages. This, however, does not in itself mean that such a verb, which would be חמה, is in use in Hebrew with this meaning. The etymology of any particular word does not establish the existence of other formations from the same root.

It is useful to distinguish between roots which are productive and those which are not. Hebrew has a root לאך, which appears in the familiar words (*a*) מַלְאָךְ 'messenger', (*b*) מְלָאכָה 'work'. An obvious cognate is the common Ethiopic *lä'akä* 'send'. Unlike the situation in Ethiopic, however, it is improbable that the verb לאך existed in Hebrew as a free form. Though the root לאך exists, it cannot therefore be used to predict occurrence in other formations; nor, for the purpose of calculating the extent of lexical overlap, can it be counted in the same way as free and productive roots. Moreover, while we could rightly divine the Hebrew meaning of מלאך from that of the Ethiopic verb, it is doubtful if we could do this for מלאכה if the meaning of the latter were in fact unknown.

---

[1] Brockelmann, *Lexicon Syriacum*, p. 370.

Other examples can easily be added, e.g. the roots of תָּמִיד
'always'; נָבִיא 'prophet'; כֹהֵן 'priest'; קוֹל 'voice'.

(2) There is a familiar Arabic *jalasa* 'sit'. Hebrew גלשׁ provides
an exact correspondence and is probably cognate; it seems, however, to mean 'glide down', and is used of a herd of goats coming
down a hill (Cant. 4. 1, 6. 5). Perhaps etymologists can surmise a
mode of semantic connection between the two. But, if the meaning
in Hebrew were in fact unknown, it is very unlikely that we should
be able to reconstruct it correctly from the Arabic.

The following are some other words, the meanings of which in
Hebrew could probably not be divined from cognate languages, if
the meanings had not been known in the first place: דבר 'speak';
פחד 'dread'; ברא 'create'; גבול 'boundary'; ברית 'covenant';
and עלם 'hide'.

Sometimes, even if the root is known, the derivation of particular
meanings does not follow the same analogy in different languages.
We know that דֶּרֶךְ means 'road'. The verb דרך means 'tread'.
But the words in other Semitic languages which mean 'road' are
not cognates of דרך; and, moreover, they are often not related
to the word which means 'tread' in the relevant language. Aramaic
אוֹרחָא appears to associate itself with the verb 'travel', Arabic
ṭarīq with a verb 'knock', *šāri'* with a verb 'enter, begin', and
Ethiopic *fənot* with a verb 'send'. It is by no means certain that,
even if a 'root-meaning' is known, analogy will be available in such
a way as to ensure a right conclusion to the meaning of a given form.

(3) It is important to register not only the presence but also the
absence of cognate words. The latter is frequently neglected. Non-
existence of cognates is not usually made explicit by the dictionaries, and it is dangerous to treat their silence as evidence that
forms are not found. Moreover, because they are trying to explain
or illustrate a Hebrew word, they will often cite a form in another
Semitic language with a meaning which comes close to the Hebrew
meaning, without making it clear that in the language quoted this
is not by any means the usual meaning. In these three respects,
then, our purpose is something different from the traditional
interest in etymology.[1]

Another test is to go through the known vocabulary of a given
language and consider how many of the items have a Hebrew word

---

[1] Cf. again below, p. 299.

which shows adequate correspondence with them in form and in meaning.

In Arabic, as has already been implied, a very little thought is enough to disclose a large number of familiar words which either have no formal correspondence in Hebrew or else have a formal correspondence only where no close semantic similarity exists. Let the reader consider, for example, such familiar Arabic words as the following:

šayḫ	'old man, sheikh'	*ʿaql*	'intelligence'	*ġayr*	'other than'
ʿilm	'knowledge'	*faḍl*	'favour'	*ḥasan*	'beautiful'
jamaʿa	'collect'	*fiqh*	'legal science'	*jarā*	'run'
jihād	'holy war'	*ʿajūz*	'old woman'	*jānib*	'side'
jahila	'be ignorant'			*ʾarsala*	'send'

Some of these Arabic words have, indeed, been 'found' in Hebrew by scholars: עֶלֶם at Qoh. 3. 11 has been interpreted as like Arabic *ʿilm* 'knowledge',[1] the root of *jihād* has been found at II Kings 4. 34 (MT וַיִּגְהַר),[2] and Tur-Sinai identifies in the וְיַקְהִיל of Job 11. 10 a verb קהל 'forget' cognate with *jahila* (Index, no. 277). Such suggestions must, at this stage of the argument, be held in suspension; we cannot allow our comparison to be dominated at the start by large numbers of suggested words, some of which have hardly come to be widely known, much less accepted.

Again, <u>samples taken from various kinds of Arabic literature</u> (e.g. early poems, modern legal documents) <u>suggest that the percentage of words used which have a cognate of similar sense in ancient Hebrew will seldom exceed 30–40 per cent.</u>

In order to follow out this procedure more systematically, one may set out an area of the vocabulary of a Semitic language, e.g. all words beginning with a certain consonant, and set against them the cognates in Hebrew which have, or do not have, reasonably close similarity. I have done this, for example, with the Syriac verbs beginning with /b/, as listed in Brockelmann.[3]

I have listed the Syriac verbs, and set against them in several columns a mark indicating the degree of their agreement with cognate Hebrew verbs. If the cognate Hebrew word is close in sense to the Syriac, the mark is in column A; if it is remote, the mark is in column B; if a word from the same root appears in

---

[1] So Hitzig, according to Gordis, *Koheleth*, p. 221.
[2] Montgomery, *Kings* (ICC), p. 372.
[3] See Appendix, pp. 305 ff.

Hebrew, but not as a verb, the mark is in column C; and if there is no cognate in Hebrew, the mark is in column D. The total number of roots under which an entry was made is sixty-nine; the total number of entries is seventy-eight. The difference is because I have followed Brockelmann in entering two homonymous verbs in Syriac, or else have given separate entries to separate meanings of a Syriac verb, where these differ in their relation to meanings found in Hebrew. I have also noted some occurrences in Mishnaic Hebrew, which may also be relevant in several ways. The entries by columns come out as follows:

A	B	C	D
(sense close to Hebrew)	(sense remote from Hebrew)	(Hebrew, but not as a verb)	(not found in Hebrew)
26	13	9	30

These figures cannot be applied very strictly, for a number of uncertain factors exist: one may be uncertain what to do with denominative verbs, one may doubt the real existence of some of the meanings registered in dictionaries, one may be uncertain where to place a word which deviates from the normal phonological correspondences. For deciding whether a meaning in Syriac is close to or remote from one in Hebrew, my rough criterion has been the judgement whether one meaning is close enough to the other for us to be able to divine the meaning rightly from the cognate in the situation of normal philological treatments.

In spite of these qualifications the sample seems to be a reasonably fair one. Syriac and Hebrew are languages which one would expect to be fairly comparable, since they belong to roughly the same culture area and their literature is to a fair extent devoted to similar subjects.

If the sample is a fair one, it suggests that even in quite comparable languages like Syriac and Hebrew the number of verbs in the one which have closely corresponding cognates in the other with closely similar meanings may be only about 40 per cent., while the number of verbs which have no cognate verb at all in the other language is actually higher than this. Another survey I have done, of Syriac and Hebrew verbs beginning with /ʿ/, suggested that the number of verbs showing close correspondence in form and meaning was about 25–30 per cent. of the total number of Hebrew verbs and about 33 per cent. of the total number of Syriac verbs. Samples with other Semitic languages confirm the general direction of this argument. In Ethiopic verbs beginning with /'/ I find the number having reasonably close agreement with Hebrew cognate verbs to be about one in six, along with a number of places where we find less direct agreements (e.g. Ethiopic has '*of* 'birds' but not a verb corresponding to Hebrew עוּף).

Thus the evidence on the whole, while confirming some considerable community in the use of lexical resources in the Semitic languages, appears not to favour a degree of overlap or coincidence so high that the presence of a phenomenon in one language will easily form a prima-facie case for its presence in another. The overlap is somewhat higher if it refers only to roots, or to purely formal correspondences; but the philological treatments of which we are speaking go further than this. They involve a relation between the form-sense relationship in one language and the form-sense relationship in another; and this is just what is not, on the evidence from known examples, predictable in a very high degree.

At this point we may profitably recall experience with Indo-European, where similar phenomena occur. Words may show formal correspondence of some closeness, but not mean the same thing. German *sterben* is from the same root as English 'starve', but the sense is not 'starve' but 'die'. At first sight one might suppose this to be an analogy to the relation between Arabic *jā'a* 'be hungry' and Hebrew גָּוַע 'expire, perish', a familiar term of the P document. It would be unwise, however, to accept this impression; for *sterben* and *starve* appear to go back to a sense 'be numb, stiff' rather than 'be empty, hungry'.[1]

If we take a particular term or concept and collect the words in that field in the various Indo-European languages (the approach taken by Bergsträsser in his list already quoted for Semitic), we usually find not one root in use but a large number.[2] For 'die', for instance, Buck lists about seven different roots. If we take subdivisions of Indo-European, such as the Germanic languages alone, we find a greater community of use; but this does not apply to the Indo-European language group as a whole. It is of course possible to suppose that Semitic never became so diversified in this

---

[1] This example illustrates how the logical study of features of the referent, producing the argument that 'if you starve you die', misrepresents the linguistic facts entirely; on this see below, pp. 290 ff.

[2] For a compendious display of this procedure see Buck, *Dictionary of Selected Synonyms*.

regard as Indo-European did; but at least it is salutary to consider the position of the latter.

It may be briefly mentioned that the view that Hebrew is a 'mixed language' has sometimes been used as part of a plea for the existence in Hebrew of a large incidence of agreements with several cognate languages. There is some difficulty, however, in knowing just what is meant by 'mixed', and I think that it is a confusing term. I shall not, therefore, pursue the matter farther.[1]

It is also possible that one could find certain semantic fields in which a higher degree of lexical community is found between Semitic languages than in other fields. For instance, Löw in his researches on Aramaic fish-names observed that very few fish-names of common Semitic origin were to be found.[2] One might with further research be able to list fields in which considerable community existed, and set against this other fields in which the degree of community was low; if this were done, then the probability of success for philological treatments would be high in the former and low in the latter.

Finally, the scholar must bear in mind that a sense quotable for a cognate language like Arabic may be a rare or specialized development of that language and therefore not represent an older Semitic stage likely to be shared also by Hebrew.[3] Even if the sense 'stay in a place' is a legitimate one for ǧaniya, is not this a doubtful basis for an identification of Hebrew עֶנֶה (Index, no. 251), when the major Arabic sense is 'be rich' (Lane, pp. 2301 f.)? Can the sense 'advise' be ascribed to הֵשִׁיר (no. 306), when the main sense of the Arabic is 'sign; make a sign'? Arabic bīn (no. 54) is handled by Lane (p. 288) and Freytag (i. 179–80a) in a way that suggests clear dependence on the sense 'between', and it is unlikely that an independent sense 'region, field' existed in such a way that it could plausibly be attributed to Hebrew also. Does jarama mean 'complete' (no. 79) and so justify a word for a 'landing' on a stair, when the statistically dominant sense is 'commit a crime' and the likely

[1] The 'mixed' character of Hebrew was argued particularly by Bauer. For developments of this kind see Driver in *The People and the Book*, p. 109; *JTS* xxxi (1930) 275; Winton Thomas in *Record and Revelation*, p. 401. For a critical note see Harris, *Development of the Canaanite Dialects*, p. 11 n.; for a judgement that the term 'mixed' is confusing, Goshen-Gottstein, *ScrH* iv (1958) 135.

[2] 'Aramäische Fischnamen', p. 550. This circumstance tells against Löw's own identification of a Hebrew עֲמָלֵץ, see below, pp. 236 f.

[3] Cf. already above, p. 116.

primitive sense is 'cut off' (wool, fruit) (Lane, pp. 412 f.)? The identification of דהה 'be astounded' (no. 86) depends on an Arabic cognate 'be stupefied', but *dahiyy* and related words surely mean 'be smart, be cunning' (Lane, pp. 927 f.). When *dāna* means mainly 'be vile, weak' (adj. *dūn*), is it likely to yield a Hebrew sense of יָדִין 'provide abundance' (no. 87) on the limited grounds of V '*perfecta opulentia fruitus est vir*' (Freytag, ii. 73–74)? Though *bāha* is glossed as '*cognovit, dignovit*' by Freytag (i. 181b), does not the general Arabic usage suggest a basically sexual reference, 'lie with (a woman)' and the like (cf. Lane, p. 278b), which makes unlikely a Hebrew cognate 'remember' (no. 53)? When *kadama* really means 'bite', and when the sense '*firmiter vinctus fuit (captivus, ut effugere non posset)*' (Freytag, iv. 18a) is probably derivative from the sense 'bite', is it likely to provide a sense 'hold fast (in fetters)' for a newly identified Hebrew כדם (no. 172)? Is there enough evidence in the solitary V *inbaqaʿa* 'he went away quickly' (Lane, p. 235a) to justify 'go away' for בקע (no. 62)?

Thus, even when dictionary entries are quite accurate for their respective languages, one has to consider whether senses registered are likely to be central enough and old enough to allow of a sharing with biblical Hebrew.

Sometimes, however, research in other Semitic languages will confirm the probability of an early date. One might have doubted the early date of the sense 'mortgage, pledge' for Arabic *rahana* (no. 110), but its antiquity is made certain by its frequent use in Nabataean inscriptions. A Hebrew חטאת 'penury' has been identified on the basis of Ethiopic *ḫāṭiʾat*. Dillmann himself (col. 621) characterizes this Ethiopic sense as 'extremely rare'; but the verb and other noun forms in Ethiopic tend to suggest that this is indeed an ancient element of meaning, such as might be found in other Semitic sources much earlier (no. 126).

(2) *Biliteral Theories*

The normal elementary picture of the structure of the Semitic word is that of a triliteral pattern formed by three consonants which, with certain known exceptions, are fairly stable in all changes of the word. Biliteral theories, on the other hand, maintain that the triliteral structure is itself the product of extension or supplementation of a base of two consonants, through the addition of a third. The important class of 'hollow' verbs, like קוּם 'stand', is then <u>the residuum of an earlier state</u>. A number of roots have in common two consonants, but not three, and it is possible that they represent the supplementation of a basic biliteral form with different third consonants. Again, there is often a similarity between verbs with two main consonants (the 'hollow' and 'geminated' types) and those which have this base supplemented by a 'weak' consonant (most commonly /y/ or /w/ or /n/) either before or after.

The various theories here involved deserve much discussion in themselves. Their relevance to our theme in this book, however, is as follows. The classical picture of development from a parent language ('proto-Semitic') implies the theoretical construction of this parent language, and the use of correspondences which reflect the phonological changes in words the consonantal sequences of which were already formed in the proto-Semitic period. If, however, the supplementation of biliteral bases by the addition of a third radical had not already occurred in any standard way in the proto-Semitic period—if, in other words, the development of some words did not take place by normal sound changes from pre-existing full forms, but occurred *einzelsprachlich* with individual development from earlier bases—then some questions fall upon the entire system of comparison which has been understood up to now in this book.[1]

A comparative philology which operates by close control of the phonological correspondences found in cognate languages appears to assume that the root sequences were already firm in the ancestor. The root being x-y-z in proto-Semitic, it will have in the various Semitic languages in normal circumstances the normal correspondents of x-y-z. Suppose, however (and this is what biliteral theories appear to suggest), that in the proto-Semitic stage the only firm root for this case was x-y, for which a rather vague meaning can be given. The forms which will appear from this root will then (in most cases) not be correspondents of x-y. They will take a variety of patterns; in one language we shall find x-y-z, in another x-y-y, in another x-z-y, in another z-x-y, in another x-y-p, in another q-x-y.

In the circumstances envisaged by such hypotheses, only a rather vague statement can be made either about the formal

---

[1] A survey of the literature concerning biliteralism up to 1952 is given by G. J. Botterweck, pp. 11–30; more recently, Moscati, *Comparative Grammar*, pp. 72–5.

characteristics of the root or about its meaning. The biliteral bases cannot be fitted into strict phonological correspondences in the way that is pictured in Bergsträsser's list (which applies to known complete words). For instance, Driver, offering long strings of examples, talks of a base *gz-ks-kš-qs/ṣ* 'sever', for which he cites fourteen words in Hebrew alone.[1] Another base is *ẓr-sr-ṣr-śr-šr* and *dr-ṭr-tr* 'surround' or 'turn round'. This can be evidenced from a number of cognate languages in tables like this:

Hebr.	צור	'besiege'	צרר	'tie up'
	אצר	'store up'	חצר	'enclosure'
	עצר	'restrain'	עצרת	'band (of people)'
Arab.	'aṣara	'confine'	ḥaṣara	'surround'
Accad.	qaṣāru	'bind'		

Such tables, repeated for other forms of the manifold and variable character which such bases are supposed to assume, total up to between forty and fifty words from assorted Semitic languages, all of which have some form of the base contained in them and all of which can in some degree be explained semantically (or so it is argued) from the meaning of the base.

Out of these very numerous words, however, only very small groups, usually of two or three here and there, present the kind of precise phonological correspondences of which we have previously spoken, while very considerable diversities in meaning also occur. Consider, for instance, the semantic relation between Hebrew חדר 'room', glossed by Driver as 'enclosed chamber', and Syriac *ḥdar* 'go round'. Even if one accepts that this relation is rightly stated, one can hardly claim that, if the meaning of one of the words was unknown, the meaning of the other would supply an adequate guide to its discovery.

The normal correspondences function in a kind of prediction. Given, let us say, a normal Arabic form such as *šimāl* 'left (hand)', we can predict with fair accuracy what the normal Hebrew form or Aramaic form would be. But, given the base *ẓr-sr-ṣr-śr-šr*, and even given an Arabic word which is an instance of its use, we cannot predict whether a Hebrew word using the same base will have a third root consonant or what that consonant will be,[2] or whether it will use the same one (or the corresponding one) of the five forms

---

[1] Driver, *Problems of the Hebrew Verbal System*, pp. 4 f.

[2] '*All* consonants may be used as "determinants" ', writes Moscati, p. 74; italics mine.

of the base; nor can we tell what it would mean, except that it will be something to do with (or something which in its past semantic history may have had something to do with) surrounding, turning round, going round, or being round.

If there is some truth in biliteral theories, they may help to explain certain points which have already been discussed. For instance, where words in two Semitic languages do not show normal correspondences but are very similar in meaning, it may perhaps be possible to say that they are different expansions of the same base. This would account for their closeness without requiring the argument that sound correspondences in general should be treated loosely. Similarly, some of the words which have been cited as instances of 'metathesis' might rather be regarded as different expansions of a biliteral base, with the third consonant put in a different place.[1]

It is doubtful, however, whether this argument can be used helpfully in the context of philological treatments, where the meaning of the word in Hebrew is itself not certainly known. For reasons which have already been stated,[2] such treatments are not likely to carry cogency and conviction if phonological correspondences are fluid and uncertain. Where the relatedness of cognates depends on the appeal to a hypothetical common base, the chances of a convincing philological treatment are not good.

Conceivably there were two sectors in Semitic vocabulary. The first was already in a fairly fixed form in the proto-Semitic period. The words of this sector will then appear in the historical languages in forms showing the normal correspondences. In the second sector, however, the root sequences were still not firm in the proto-Semitic period, and various branches developed their words independently later, through expansion of a vague common base.[3] If this were so, philological treatments would work mainly in the first sector of the vocabulary, while in the second they would have a very much lower degree of probability.

---

[1] Cf. above, pp. 96 ff.

[2] Cf. above, pp. 83 ff.

[3] An example might be the words meaning 'naked'; the common base for this seems to be the sequence represented in Hebrew as ערה; but Hebrew and Arabic develop types like ערום, and Syriac develops ʿrṭl and Ethiopic ʿrq. One cannot help wondering whether Arabic, which may be held to have become separate at an early stage in Semitic language separation, did not develop many of its characteristic lexical items thereafter on its own; if this is so, its idiosyncratic productions are not helpful for philological treatments in Hebrew.

Thus, in general, while the hypothesis of original biliteral bases is relevant to the general assessment of philological treatments in the Old Testament, it is nevertheless unlikely that specific appeals to biliteral bases will, in the present state of our knowledge about the prehistoric stages of Semitic languages, provide an important or independent basis for the plausibility or probability of particular suggestions. On the contrary, emphasis on biliteral bases, carrying with it some implication that these bases were expanded independently in the separate languages, tends on the whole to undermine rather than to support the use of philological treatments.

(3) Semantic Fields

In each language words function in relation to other words in the same or contiguous semantic field.[1] The meaning of מנחה, for instance, can be described only in relation to the other words existing in the Hebrew of a certain time in the field of sacrifice, gift, and tribute. Its meaning is then a choice within the series of possibilities available within Hebrew. Again, the sense of a familiar word like חטא 'sin' depends on its relation to other words in similar fields, such as רשע and פשע, and to other words in opposing fields. Sometimes quite systematic structures can be stated, such as the terminology of the sacrificial system in Leviticus, or the two pairs:

קדש	'holy'	טהור	'clean'
חול	'not holy'	טמא	'unclean'

What is טהור is not thereby קדש; and what is חול, traditionally 'profane', though not 'holy', קדש, is not thereby in any way wrong or evil. It is wrong, however, if the distinctions between members of pairs are obscured, or if that which is טמא is mixed with that which is קדש.

Not all semantic fields are systematically diagrammed in this way; rather than a system, there is a bundle of meanings. Even then, however, the meanings are dependent on the meanings of other words in the same language at the same time. Even though languages are cognate and have a large number of individual cognate words, the make-up of these bundles may be, and indeed is likely to be, very substantially different.

This may explain why, when in language A form x-y-z is found with a certain meaning, no corresponding x-y-z may be found in

[1] Cf. above, pp. 89 f., 136 ff.

language B. In language A it has a significant function through its contrast with forms *a-b-c* and *p-q-r*. In language B, however, *a-b-c* does not exist, while *p-q-r* has developed a different meaning and therefore moved into a different semantic field, and the ground occupied by *x-y-z* is occupied by *d-e-f* and *l-m-n*. The method of identifying cognates works only for individual words; but the semantic functioning of words is within word-groupings which are quite asymmetrical in one language as compared with another, even when the languages are closely cognate.

We can illustrate this from the identification of the verb טבב interpreted as meaning 'announce' (hiphil) at Prov. 15. 2. MT reads: לְשׁוֹן חֲכָמִים תֵּיטִיב דָּעַת. Driver, reading the verb as תַּטֵּב or תֵּטֵב from the root טבב, gives the sense as 'the tongue of the wise announces knowledge'. A sense like 'understand' or 'heal' might similarly, we may add, be proposed for Prov. 17. 22. This root טבב is indeed found in several Semitic languages. In Syriac it seems to have the sense 'know, discover'; but it occurs chiefly in nouns like *ṭebbā* 'knowledge; story' and adjectives like *ṭbībā* 'famous, experienced', and in derived verbal themes with meanings like 'make known' and 'announce'. In Arabic also it is registered as 'know', but the most familiar form is *ṭabīb*, mainly specialized as 'doctor'; and the modern sense of the verb is mainly 'treat medically'. In Ethiopic it means 'be wise', while verb forms exist meaning 'educate, inform'.

This information, however, should be related to our knowledge of other words in the semantic field. Ethiopic, for instance, does not have the common root *ḥ-k-m* in this field; and while it has the root *y-d-ʿ*, from which Hebrew has יְדַע 'know', this is not used in Ethiopic in the sense 'know', but only in the causative 'announce, inform'. Again, while Ethiopic has the root *b-y-n*, which supplies a sense 'know, be intelligent' in certain contexts in Hebrew, the sense in Ethiopic is rather different, being rather 'distinguish, notice, make clear'. Again, the normal word for 'know' in Ethiopic is *ʾ-m-r* in the theme II. 1, as has already been observed in another connection.

Thus, though all of these elements in Ethiopic can be given parallels and connections in other Semitic languages so long as they are taken individually, the make-up of the total bundle is quite different from what we find in other Semitic languages. The fact that *ṭ-b-b* is present and important in Ethiopic, therefore, has to be related to the other relevant elements, and may be partially explained by them. The fact that *ṭ-b-b* exists somewhere in the Semitic languages by no means implies that it will necessarily exist in a language which also has *ḥ-k-m*, *y-d-ʿ*, and *b-y-n* in the senses in which they are found in Hebrew.

Similar changes of balance in the lexical stock can be traced in the languages which have *ḫ-s-s* in this semantic field, such as Accadian and Ugaritic.

Another example is the organization of words for social systems, such as government. *Šarru* in Assyria was the king's title, as מלך was in Israel. Hebrew had a word שׂר, cognate with the Accadian *šarru*, but it not only did not mean the same thing, it does not appear to have designated one clearly institutionalized political office at all. Most other Semitic languages appear not to have a cognate with *šarru* at all. Another term representing an institution in Accadian was *līmu*, *limmu*. Against the idea that words cognate with this should be identified in Hebrew[1] one has to set the possibility that the Accadian semantic development was peculiar to the institutional framework of Mesopotamian society. In general, though cognates can usually be found for any of the terms for government office in any Semitic language, the make-up of the group of terms in any one is likely to be markedly different from that of any other.

This point deserves very much more extended research. For our present purpose it must, however, be left here, and its importance can be summarized as follows. Firstly, traditional comparative method has tended to deal with individual words and has failed to give equal place to their function in relation to other words. This in itself may be a weakness in the method. Secondly, the consideration of the groups of words within a semantic field in a Semitic language may help us to understand how particular words, of which cognates are known in other languages, may yet not be present in the vocabulary of the one principally being studied. Thirdly, the same consideration may show how the semantic development of words may not follow directly from an original 'basic meaning' and may thus be quite other than is foreseeable even from accurate information about cognates. Given a form in one Semitic language, we can predict what form there may be in another, if normal correspondences are followed; but the meaning

[1] Cf. pp. 133, 254 f.

cannot so easily be predicted from the sense of the former, because in both cases it is dependent on interrelations with still other words, which interrelations are not predictable at all.

(4) *Words with Opposite Meanings* (*'Aḍdād*)

This section will consider briefly the position of those words which either (*a*) in the same language have two opposite meanings or (*b*) in one language have a meaning opposite to that which is found in another cognate language.

For this phenomenon Arabic grammar has used the technical term *'aḍdād* (singular *ḍidd*). In Arabic studies this is normally used for the former of the two cases specified, i.e. where a word exists with two opposite meanings in Arabic itself. Some recent studies, however, such as those of Guillaume, have extended the term and applied it where the opposite meanings are found in two different but cognate languages such as Arabic and Hebrew.

The subject of *'aḍdād* was considerably cultivated in the work of Arabic philologists, and there grew up a genre of literature with the title *Kitāb al-'Aḍdād*. Sometimes opinions have become prevalent according to which Arabic is particularly rich in words of this type; and one hears half-joking references to a language in which every word can mean a certain thing and also the opposite of that thing. Modern studies, however, have indicated that this picture of the Arabic vocabulary is extremely exaggerated. Weil writes:[1]

The opinion which has long been maintained, that Arabic, contrary to all the other Semitic languages, contains a very large number of such *'aḍdād* is no longer tenable. If all that is false and all that does not belong here are cut out of the list, there remains also in Arabic only a small residue.

We may then abandon the conception that words having two completely opposite meanings are extremely common in Arabic or any other Semitic language, and that our semantic decisions can be taken on the basis of such a view.[2]

---

[1] G. Weil, *Encyclopaedia of Islam*, 2nd edition, vol. i, p. 184. The first ed., p. 131, interestingly enough had itself included the false but deceptive example of Hebrew עֹשֶׁר 'riches', Arabic *'usr* 'poverty'; the words are not in fact cognate (cf. Aramaic עֲתַר).

[2] For a careful study of the Arabic words see Nöldeke's article '*Wörter mit Gegensinn*'; an earlier survey of the problem in Hebrew is Landau, *Gegensinnige Wörter* (Berlin, 1896).

It is rather more common to find that words have a meaning in one language opposite to that which they have in another cognate language. Arabic *waṯaba* commonly means 'spring up', while the corresponding Hebrew יָשַׁב means 'sit' or 'sit down'. There are Arabic dialects (Himyarite) which are said to have the same meaning as the Hebrew. Hebrew itself has the interesting וַיַּשֵּׁב at Gen. 15. 11, where the meaning seems to be that Abraham 'started up' or 'set in flight', i.e. 'scared away', the birds. LXX has συνεκάθισεν, following the ordinary sense of יָשַׁב. Aquila, though usually an etymologizer, renders with ἀπεσόβησεν, which is the right sense; the Vulgate similarly has *abigebat* and the Syriac *makkeš*. The Targum has אֲתִיב 'turned away', a word which probably seemed close in form to the Hebrew; but some MSS. have אַפְרַח, 'made to fly (away)', giving the sense but not the word-similarity. Rashi understood the word as from the verb נָשַׁב 'blow'.

The existence of words, where apparently obvious cognates yet had opposite senses, was already known to the medieval lexicographers. A familiar instance was אָבָה 'be willing', which means the opposite of the cognate Arabic *'abā* (*y*) 'refuse'.[1]

The development of opposite meanings may often have occurred through semantic change. A word having a certain range of meaning, the middle of the range drops out of use (perhaps through being taken over by another word altogether), leaving two extremes, which we may or may not have clues to connect. This is another of the main causes of homonymy, in addition to phoneme merger and the adoption of loan-words, discussed already above.

The following examples have arisen in the context of modern philological treatments:

The verb יָרַד usually means 'go down', but it is sometimes said that it also occasionally means 'go up'.[2] Driver says that it sometimes means 'go south', while עָלָה in the same circumstances means 'go north'; in any case there are places where some special explanation seems to be needed, e.g. Judges 11. 37, where Jephthah's daughter says וְיָרַדְתִּי עַל־הֶהָרִים. Cf. also David's 'going

---

[1] See, for instance, Wechter, *Ibn Barūn*, pp. 56, 61. Similarly contrasting meanings have been pointed out for familiar words like לָאָה and יָכֹל; see Driver, *CML*, p. 158; Botterweck, *Triliterismus*, p. 39.

[2] See KB, s.v., and literature there cited; Driver, *ZAW* lxix (1957) 74–7; Leslau, *ZAW* lxxiv (1962) 322, who gives the support of Ethiopian parallels.

up' from Maon to Engedi, I Sam. 24. 1. Driver, discussing this instance, cites some other paradoxical phenomena, such as Arab. *fara'a*, said to mean either 'go up' or 'go down' a mountain.

Again, Kopf, discussing the meaning of בטא in Hebrew, says that if this means 'thoughtlessness, over-hastiness', and if we compare Arab. *baṭu'a* 'be slow, hesitate' (بطؤ), then this is an example of opposed senses in the two languages.[1]

Discussing שׁרב 'heat', Driver[2] takes note of an Accadian *šarbu* 'shower', *šurubbū* '(cold) fever', *šuribu* 'cold', and says that the connection between the senses of cold and heat is illustrated by Lat. *urere*.

Going back to the Middle Ages we may remark that Saadia, discussing the difficult גילו ברעדה of Ps. 2. 11,[3] argued that the peculiarity could be explained by use of the analogy of the Arabic *ṭ-r-b*, which serves as an expression of both fear and joy.[4]

Perhaps the most striking example, however, of the way in which philological treatments have produced an alleged double opposition of meaning within Hebrew itself, is the familiar word בּ, normally supposed to mean 'in'. Ugaritic evidence in particular is interpreted with the sense 'from'. This sense, says Gordon, is common, and is 'in accordance with a Hamitic-Semitic feature whereby prepositions meaning "in" or "to" tend to connote also "from" '.[5] There are indeed places in Hebrew where the sense 'from' would at first sight appear to make good or better sense, e.g. Ps. 68. 19, לָקַחְתָּ מַתָּנוֹת בָּאָדָם, which would then mean 'thou hast received gifts *from* men' (so easy a solution that it may be *too* facile). There has been no shortage of voices assuring us that Ugaritic evidence makes it clear that 'from' is the actual meaning, all difficulty being thereby removed. There are, however, certain objections against this course of argument.

The first is the question of the communicative efficiency of a language in which the word for 'to' and the word for 'from' are apparently identical. This is, as we have seen, one of the obvious problems of homonymy. Possibly Ugaritic *b*, when meaning 'from', might have had a different vocalization from *b* with the sense 'in',

---

[1] *VT* viii (1958) 165.
[2] *JTS* xxiii (1922) 410.
[3] Cf. above, p. 5, and below, p. 284.
[4] See Eppenstein, op. cit., p. 9. The sense given by Wehr for *ṭariba* in modern literary Arabic is 'be moved (with joy or grief)'.
[5] *UH*, p. 217. Cf. also Gordon's detailed discussion, *UH*, pp. 83 f.

so that no homonymy existed. Again, it is possible that 'from' is not the sense of *b* in itself but only the sense of *b* when in collocation with certain other words, which supply the guidance to select the sense 'from'. If this were so, it might follow (*a*) that the sense 'from' could not be defined as such apart from such contexts, and (*b*) that the relation of *b* to such contexts might be confined to Ugaritic and certainly could not automatically be transferred to Hebrew. For instance, one of the most convincing cases for the sense 'from' appears in *tbʿ bbth* 'they departed from his house'. But perhaps the sense of *b* here is defined by collocation with *tbʿ*; and since *tbʿ* does not have a cognate in Hebrew we cannot be sure whether this is relevant for comparison with Hebrew at all. In *ṭrd bʿl bmrym ṣpn* or *td ʾišt bbhtn*, which Gordon cites with translations as 'drive Baal from the heights of Ṣapan' and 'the fire went away from the houses', a great deal depends on the exact usage and sense of the verbs, which may be beyond our power to determine.

Secondly, the whole setting of *b* in Ugaritic is not comparable with the setting of בּ in Hebrew, for the simple reason that Hebrew has מִן 'from', while Ugaritic does not. The meanings of words are functions of choices within the given vocabulary at one time; and in Hebrew the choice between בּ and מִן furnished an opposition entirely lacking in Ugaritic in the literary texts. In any one language the meaning of the prepositions is a highly subtle, difficult, and idiosyncratic structure of possibilities and choices, which cannot be broken into by clumsy assertions that a cognate language has another meaning for a given item. Some Semitic languages have *bn* for 'from', but not *mn*;[1] some Ethiopian languages have *k* with the meaning of 'from' but not with the familiar Semitic sense of 'as, like'. In each case the differences between prepositions depend on the total stock in each individual language, and these meanings cannot be arbitrarily shifted around from language to language merely on the grounds that the languages in question are cognate.

Thirdly, some question may be raised about the kind of 'meaning' which attaches to the sense 'from' for *b* in Ugaritic itself. Not

---

[1] South Arabian *bn* has been regarded as a product from the common *mn* by phonetic change; so Brockelmann, *Grundriß*, § 252b η (p. 497), § 84e α (p. 226). But the existence also of *ln* and *hn* may suggest rather that 'the whole ESA series *bn*, *ln*, *hn* are morphologically only enlarged forms of *b-*, *l-*, *h-*, to which the differentiated meaning "from" has been attached'. (So Beeston, *Descriptive Grammar*, p. 57.)

all cases which have been quoted are incapable of interpretation in another way. Thus:

štym bkrpnm yn bks ḥrṣ dm 'ṣm

is translated by Gordon as:

'drink wine from jars, the blood of vines from cups of gold'.

But it is not wholly impossible to consider the sense 'in'; one may drink 'in' or 'with' a cup, as well as 'from' one. This can apply also to *bph rgm lyṣ'a bšpth ḥwth*. While it seems to us natural to speak of a word going forth 'from' the mouth or lips, it is not impossible to see the sense as 'in her mouth (or, by her mouth) the word goes forth' etc. The insistence of scholars on the sense 'from' may sometimes rest on no more secure foundation than the fact that an English translation will use the word 'from'. But a translation can give a correct *general* rendering of a passage, without providing in its equivalences a correct understanding of particular lexical items.

These paragraphs are not written in order to deny that the meaning of Ugaritic *b* may be stated as 'from'. They do, however, indicate some of the problems implied if it is really thought that in Ugaritic the same word could freely and equally mean either 'to' or 'from'; and they suggest that, whatever is true for Ugaritic, the position is likely to be different in Hebrew because the presence of מן in the latter language makes the whole network of prepositional meanings quite different. These points have commonly been neglected when prepositional meanings discovered in Ugaritic have then been indiscriminately discovered in the Hebrew Bible; the same applies to the case of *l*.

Such, then, are some difficulties which may arise when homonymy takes the acute form of completely opposite meanings for the same form, or when forms which correspond in cognate languages nevertheless display quite contrary senses. In general, if it is supposed that cognate words are yet likely to have quite contrary senses, this consideration reduces the probability of success with philological treatments on any large scale. Such treatments imply that, where a cognate form is discovered, its (known) meaning will suggest that of the (hitherto unknown) Hebrew word. If it is to suggest this meaning only by a reversal of its own meaning, the process is likely to degenerate into guesswork.

(5) *Patterning of Roots and Compatibility of Consonants*

In the familiar triconsonantal root pattern Semitic languages do not tolerate any three phonemes in any order, but only certain combinations. The rules under which consonants are compatible differ, however, to some extent between the various languages.

(1) Certain combinations do not occur, or are very rare. While it is common for the same consonant to occur in positions 2 and 3, it is not generally tolerated for it to occur in positions 1 and 2. In positions 2 and 3, according to Moscati,[1] the same consonant may be found twice, but not two different consonants with a similar point of articulation (e.g. Hebrew ב and פ). Exceptions to these restrictions are more frequent in nouns, e.g. שֶׁרֶשׁ, שֶׁמֶשׁ, לַיְלָה; a number of noun patterns find their way into verbs through the formation of denominatives, e.g. Hebrew שֵׁרֵשׁ 'uproot; take root'.

(2) The restrictions on compatibility may have somewhat broken down in the course of time. Greenberg, whose article is the starting-point for recent research,[2] tries to detect distinctions between the restrictions attributable to the ancestor language and those observed in historical times; he adds a control comparison with Egyptian. Similarly, words of Aramaic origin may eventually have disturbed the patterns observed in native Hebrew.[3]

(3) Rules of compatibility are not identical in all Semitic languages. According to Moscati,[4] 'in Accadian /g/ and /z/ are never found in third position, nor can all three radicals be voiced'. If this is true, Accadian will not contain a word corresponding to Hebrew בָּגַד under the normal correspondences for individual consonants.

Similarly, Moscati says that in Hebrew the sequences /t-q/ and /q-ṭ/ are compatible, but not /q-t/; while in Arabic /q-t/ is found, but not /t-q/.[4] This does not quite agree with Greenberg's tables, which show one case of /t-q/ in Arabic in positions 1-2, and four in 2–3. It may be remarked in passing, in any case, that the study of compatibility rules may give a much better account of the phenomena which were traditionally handled under assimilation, dissimilation, and metathesis; thus the difference between Hebrew

---

[1] Moscati, *Comparative Grammar*, pp. 74 f.

[2] *Word* vi (1950) 162–81.

[3] The calculations of Koskinen, *ZDMG* cxiv (1964) 16–58, eliminate certain words from consideration on the grounds that they are 'clearly' of Aramaic origin.

[4] Moscati, pp. 74 f.

קטל and Arabic *qatala* is to be ascribed to differing compatibilities rather than to an 'assimilation'. We should then have an approach to general pattern systems, instead of lists of individual assimilations, dissimilations, and metatheses; and these lists could not be used as an argument in favour of exceptions to general linguistic statements.[1]

Again, Hebrew has no verb with ה in position 2 and a sibilant in position 3.[2] But in Arabic there are several (in Greenberg's tables 4 before /š/, 1 before /s/, 2 before /z/, none before /ṣ/: a total of 7 out of 127 verbs with /h/ in position 2). Similarly, according to Koskinen /ʿ/ and /h/ can occur in Arabic and Syriac in the same verb (e.g. /ʿ-h-d/), but not in Hebrew (nor Ugaritic and Palestinian types of Aramaic).[3]

Again, in positions 2 and 3 Hebrew greatly prefers the sequence /l-p/ over the sequence /l-b/. No true verb has the latter: חלב and כלב are noun roots only, שלב is probably a denominative verb, and גלב is commonly taken to be a loan-word. With /l-p/ real verbs seem to include about seven or eight; this depends on how far roots are distinguished: אלף, דלף (two roots?), חלף (two roots?), שלף, עלף, סלף. The ratio in Hebrew is thus six, seven, or eight to zero.[4] In Arabic verbs, however, Greenberg's corresponding figures for /f/ and /b/ are sixteen and fifteen. If these figures are even approximately right ,we should not expect to find in Hebrew words cognate with familiar Arabic words like *ṭalaba* 'slander', *jalaba* 'get, gain', *ṭalaba* 'seek'—not, at any rate, with the regular sound correspondences.

Thus in general there appear to be some differences in statistical preference, either for one consonant as against another, or for one position of the same consonant as against another, between cognate Semitic languages.[5]

An interesting illustration can be provided from Ugaritic. Ugaritic, like Arabic, has a phoneme which we mark as /ṯ/, and its normal correspondent in Hebrew is שׁ. But the statistical

---

[1] Cf. the discussion above, pp. 96 ff.
[2] Koskinen, p. 57.   [3] Koskinen, p. 29.
[4] Koskinen, p. 55; his reckoning, including some non-verbal roots, is not identical with mine, and is less suitable for direct comparison with Greenberg.
[5] Some remarkable differences emerge from a direct comparison of Koskinen's figures with Greenberg's; e.g. /ṯ/ is in Hebrew least common in position 3, but in Arabic it is most frequent in that position. But little can be done with this until exactly comparable figures are worked out.

frequency of /ṭ/ in Ugaritic seems to be different from what it is in Arabic. By Greenberg's figures, in Arabic /ṭ/ occurs in first position with exactly the same frequency as does /t/, namely fifty times. In Ugaritic verbs the frequency is different. Driver's glossary registers eighteen Ugaritic verbs with /ṭ/ in first position, and this excludes special denominative types such as derivatives from numerals, e.g. *ṯnn* 'do a second time'. For verbs with /t/ in first position, the corresponding figure is only eight.[1]

This might be accidental, but a real difference in root patterning between Ugaritic and Arabic is more probable. A notable instance is the verb *ṭt'* 'fear', which is cognate with the Phoenician שׁתע and has served to identify שׁתע in Hebrew also. The sequence /t-t/ in positions 1 and 2 is not a compatibility allowed in Arabic; Greenberg registers no instance at all. In Hebrew, on the other hand, where there is no phoneme /ṭ/, a word like שׁתע falls within the very frequent type of words with שׁ in position 1, followed by a stop in second position (cf. especially שׁתל, שׁתם, שׁתק). Clearly roots may come to be used in one branch of the Semitic languages when in another they do not fall within the accepted patterns.

One reason for this may be the very different phonetic realization in each language of the phonemes to which we apply the same conventional signs (such as /ṭ/) and through which we establish our comparative correspondences. Though Arabic /f/ and /j/ 'correspond' to Hebrew פ and ג, their phonetic realization is very different, and analogous differences in ancient times may have affected the degrees of compatibility.

To sum up, it is not likely that these considerations will frequently provide a *direct* criterion for the evaluation of philological treatments. No excessive reliance should be placed upon the statistics until Hebrew lexicography has been tested afresh in this respect. Nevertheless the rules of patterning and compatibility are a matter of real importance, and they probably affected the make-up of the different Semitic vocabularies. In addition to the semantic considerations which have already been touched on,[2] they suggest some reason why non-coincidences in lexical stock exist on the formal level also. They show how each of the languages has a

---

[1] Even if we identify the words in a way different from Driver's, the results are in this regard not very different; e.g. Gordon's positive identifications of verbs in *UH* seem to be about 2 with /t/ in position 1 and 10 with /ṭ/.

[2] See above, pp. 170 ff.

certain individuality, which cannot be broken down on the ground that other languages are cognate and that many individual words have close correspondences of form and meaning. Conversely, they permit no excessive optimism that a known form and meaning in one language will guide us directly to the meaning of a mysterious form in another.

(6) *Words Known Through Personal Names*

A number of words which are well known in other Semitic languages appear in biblical Hebrew only in personal names.[1] These words seem to constitute a prima-facie argument for the idea, which we shall see to be probable on other grounds, that the vocabulary of ancient Hebrew was substantially larger than that which is found in the Bible. Sometimes we might hardly know the meaning of these elements in Hebrew names but for the evidence of cognates, so that they seem to represent a primary success for a philological approach.

This list is chosen to illustrate some words of fairly general interest; it does not include words of narrowly specific types such as names of animals or plants. The words are listed in the order of the root as it would normally be quoted in Hebrew, assuming the interpretation cited to be correct.

אוש   'give', found in the name Jehoash (יהואש), also in the Elephantine form יאוש; Noth, p. 171. Some derive the name Josiah also from this; for an alternative see the item two below.

אשר   'rejoice', found in the name Asarel (אשראל), interpreted by Noth, p. 183, on the basis of Ar. *'aŝira*, as 'God has filled with joy'.

אשה   'heal', which may perhaps be found in the name Josiah (יאשיהו); Noth, p. 212, prefers this to the explanation through אוש 'give'; it gives a name parallel to ירפאל.

ברע   The name Beriah (בריעה) is taken by Noth as related to Ar. *barā'a* 'excellence'; p. 224 n. Contrast popular etymology from רע, I Chron. 7. 23.

דרק   'hard'—the name Darkon (דרקון); so taken by Noth, p. 225, on the basis of Ar. *darq* 'hard' (?—so Freytag, ii. 24 b).

---

[1] Some names which occur in the Bible are names not of Israelites but of Midianites and others (cf. אלדעה, above, p. 23); linguistic elements contained in such names, even though genuinely Semitic, are not necessarily evidence for actual Hebrew.

הדה 'lead', in the name Jahdai (יהדי); see Noth, p. 196. הדה at Isa. 11. 8 may be the same word; but if so, then the sense ('to put' the hand) is rather different from that suggested by the name (divine guidance, cf. Ar. *mahdī* 'guided one').

זבד 'give', Noth, p. 46 f.; common in names, e.g. Elzabad, Zebadiah, but very rare before the exile (one under David and two during the monarchy). The verb, and also the noun זֶבֶד, occur elsewhere only in the explanation of the name Zebulon, which of course is not from this verb, though the words have a similarity (Gen. 30. 20).

זמר 'protect', Noth, p. 176. The familiar biblical name is Zimri (זמרי), but the Samaritan Ostraca provide names with the fuller form such as בעלזמר and זמריהו. The cognate verb is common in South Arabian names.

חמה 'protect', found in names like Jahmai (יחמי); Noth, p. 196 f. Cf. the noun חומה 'wall', but no verb; see above, p. 160.

נמה 'bring tidings', suggested by Guillaume to fit the Qumran reading at Isa. 41. 27 (see below, p. 193). The name involved is Nemuel (נמואל). Against the idea that this name contains a verb נמה there are two arguments: (1) this gives no sense paralleled in Israelite names (2) the forms ימואל and למואל, which look related, count against a derivation from נמה.

עוש 'help', in the name Jeush (יעוש), Ar. *ǵāṯa*; Noth, pp. 176, 196. This verb actually occurs in the MT at Joel 4. 11, but the text has been doubted (e.g. BDB, p. 736a), perhaps unnecessarily. The sense 'help' seems to have been unknown to the ancient versions (συναθροίζεσθε, יתכנשון, *erumpite*).

עמר 'live', in the name Omri (עמרי); Noth, p. 63, who mentions that this name might be of Arab origin. The cognate is the frequent Ar. *'amara* 'live'.

ערש 'plant', suggested by Noth, p. 203, for the name Jaareshiah (יערשיה), on the basis of Ar. *ǵarasa* and Accad. *erēšu*, the latter of which is extremely frequent in personal names.

עתל 'tall' (so Noth; or perhaps 'carry', Ar. *'atala*?); found in the name Athlai (עתלי), and cognate with Accad. *etellu* 'high', ('prince'?); Noth, p. 191.

קות 'nourish', found in the name Jekuthiel (יקותיאל); Noth, p. 203. Cognate with Ar. *qāta*. Cf. the place name יקתאל, BDB, p. 430.

תרה 'protect'. Noth's interpretation of the name Ithream (יתרעם), p. 197, on the basis of Accad. *tarū* (Bezold). Noth admits the possibility of a relation rather with the known Hebrew root יתר 'be more, be left over', and this is on the whole more likely.

If these identifications are right, they seem to be indubitable evidence of Hebrew words beyond the normally recognized vocabulary. Some of these names were used quite frequently. There were three Omris besides the great king of that name, and a whole host of Zebediahs, Zabdiels, and others with names from the root זבד. Nowhere would philological solutions be so compelling as when Hebrew personal names themselves provide evidence for the words suggested. Yet, of the list given above, few examples have figured in philological treatments known to me; and some of those which do so figure, such as נמה, seem to be rather precarious ones. The recognition of new words from the cognate languages in Israelite personal names themselves does not, as one would expect, lead to clear identifications of related words in the running text. Can some other explanation be found?

The fact of poetical parallelism should also be taken into account. Of the words listed above a number relate to concepts quite common in Hebrew literature—'give', 'nourish', 'heal', 'protect', 'help', and 'live'. We should expect that unusual words might appear as second elements ('B-words') in parallelisms, even if they were not used independently of such contexts. This is particularly so where there is no adequate normal parallel for a word. Thus 'give' is very common in poetry, yet there is no adequate common parallel for נתן. It is surprising that זבד was not used with some frequency to provide such a parallel. The same can be said of עמר 'live', which would give an excellent parallel for the heavily-worked חיה.

Thus the evidence of personal names hardly encourages us to suppose that, simply because a word may have had currency in Israelite onomastics, it may therefore confidently be expected to be found in the running text of the Bible. The non-usage, or very limited usage, of plausible terms like עמר and זבד tends to lead us to the opposite conclusion, surprising as it is: that, even when a good explanation from cognates is available and even when usage in personal names is quotable, the lexical stock used in the biblical text was rather closer to the traditional picture than to that which would be constructed by the addition of numerous new words deduced from cognate parallels.

We may suggest a reason for this. It is possible that certain words existed in Hebrew but were used only in the formation of proper names; or, alternatively, that they were used, but only in other registers of the language than those which found their way into the biblical text. This is, of course, no more than a suggestion, which may not be capable of proof. I would mention, however, one analogy which, though not complete, is at least partially valid. The 'Amorite' names are names which notably diverge from the standard Accadian of the running texts in which they are found; so that in these materials the names are 'Amorite' though the general language is not. It may be that Israelite personal names used lexical elements which were not general in Hebrew; and possibly social and linguistic history might provide some such explanation.[1]

(7) *Lexicostatistics or Glottochronology*

Finally, some mention should be made of the recent approach known as lexicostatistics or glottochronology.[2] The basic conception is this: since the rate of change of vocabulary is fairly constant, the study of changes between cognate languages in a basic central word list will indicate the chronology of the separation of the different cognate branches from their ancestor. The procedure involves several assumptions, which have been partly tested in certain linguistic areas, and in particular:

- (*a*) the assumption that some parts of the vocabulary are less subject to change than others; this enables the investigator to set up a basic core vocabulary, the rate of change of which is used in the calculation;
- (*b*) the assumption that the rate of retention in the core vocabulary is constant through time; thus a certain percentage of words will be lost every thousand years;
- (*c*) the assumption that the rate of retention and loss of basic

---

[1] Noth lays a heavy emphasis on an Aramaic stratum; e.g. *Personennamen*, pp. 43–7, 171 n., 176 n. One might speculate that such a common Aramean background in Israel's prehistory has left behind in personal nomenclature some words which ceased to be general in other usage. We may compare names like *Jacob* (יעקב), which surely meant '(God) protect' but which is not accompanied by any free use of the verb in this sense in the biblical text.

[2] See Sarah C. Gudschinsky, 'The ABC's of Lexicostatistics (Glottochronology)', *Word* xii (1956) 175–210, reprinted in shorter form in Hymes, *Language in Culture and Society*, pp. 612–22; and cf. the bibliography of the subject there also, pp. 622 f.

vocabulary is approximately the same in all languages. According to Gudschinsky, this has been tested in thirteen languages, and the results range from 86·4 to 74·4 per cent. of words retained per thousand years. All but two of these thirteen, however, were Indo-European languages.

The procedure is then to set up a basic core list of words and compute from the incidence of cognates in a pair of languages the date of division of the primitive speech community to which both belonged. Needless to say, the technique is of particular interest for groups of languages which are known to be cognate but of which no historical records over a long period of time exist.

A good deal of uncertainty appears still to surround the approach of glottochronology, and I do not suggest that it is a certainly valid one. In any case its object is in principle a different one from that of the present study. We are not trying to establish the date at which the proto-Semitic ancestor speech community broke up, but rather to establish the degree to which cognate elements can be expected to appear in the various Semitic vocabularies. Thus it is by no means my purpose to argue for the rightness of the approach of glottochronology.

Nevertheless this approach may well be suggestive for us. Even the question of the date of separation of the proto-Semitic language community is not without some interest for us. Where scholars speak as if a very high degree of community in the use of lexical resources existed between Semitic languages, one sometimes has the impression that they suppose the proto-Semitic stage to be chronologically not very greatly removed from the appearance of the first linguistic documents—rather, indeed, as if the story of the Tower of Babel had rightly portrayed the remoteness of the origin of linguistic diversity! If the diversity of the Semitic group goes back not four or five thousand but ten or twenty thousand years— and it is at least conceivable that the approach of glottochronology might demonstrate this statistically—our expectancy for the finding of cognates in Hebrew because a form exists in another Semitic language must be somewhat reduced.[1]

It may be that the discussion of glottochronology may prove

---

[1] Cf. Driver's statements on the closeness of the Semitic languages to one another, quoted above, pp. 36 f. The Romance languages, with which comparison is there made, can be traced from a known ancestor over a very limited period. Driver's argument appears to disagree with the approach of glottochronology.

stimulating in the following regards. Firstly, the idea that there is a core vocabulary, in which the rate of change is lower than for other words, might fit with the observation we have already made in this chapter, namely that while one sector of the vocabulary can be found to have a high degree of agreement in many Semitic languages, outside of this sector other sectors can be found which have much greater non-agreement (e.g. words for going in a direction—up, down, out, and so on).

Secondly, however, it might be that the contents of such a core vocabulary would have to be set up differently for Semitic from the group which has been used for other languages.

Thirdly, it is conceivable that, for reasons which we cannot at present decide, the rate of vocabulary change in Semitic languages has not been the same as that found in the study of other language groups.[1]

Thus the approach of glottochronology remains potentially constructive and actually suggestive for our problem. Our study has tended to suggest that, while philological treatments of the Old Testament text have assumed a high degree of community in the use of lexical items, the degree actually observable in the Semitic languages may be somewhat lower. Where languages are cognate, only a limited percentage of their vocabulary can be expected to occur in cognate and corresponding forms. This has been indicated from other observations already in this chapter; the difference made by glottochronology is to relate this to a statistical scheme of probability over a chronological scale. If, as Gleason indicates,[2] the rate of loss of items is about 19 per cent. per thousand years for the core vocabulary, then two cognate languages after a thousand years will probably have about 66 per cent. of the stock in common, and 44 per cent. after twice that period. Since the rate of loss outside the basic core vocabulary is even higher, the probability that unusual and obscure items in one language can have their sense predicted on the basis of another is not statistically very high.

It remains to summarize the results of the discussion in this

---

[1] Some limited application of the approach through glottochronology to Arabic dialects will be found in Hymes, 'Rate of morpheme decay in Arabic', *IJAL* xxv (1959) 267–9.

[2] Gleason, *Introduction*, p. 450. The calculation assumes the most probable event, i.e. that the two languages will not lose the same items; language A will retain 81 per cent. of those retained by language B, and also 81 per cent. of the 19 per cent. lost by language B.

chapter. The discussion has not been conclusive, and has not produced any clear and definite estimate of the probability that lexical elements found in one Semitic language will be shared by another. It has shown, however, that caution has to be exercised in this matter, and that it is premature and injudicious to assume that the presence of material in one Semitic language forms a prima-facie case for its existence in another. Comparative study, when directed squarely upon the problem, itself shows that this is not so. Thus, in arguing against too quick an assumption of lexical overlap between the Semitic languages, we are not arguing against the comparative method, but applying it properly, and applying it to the lexical stocks as wholes, rather than to individual items within them. To put it negatively, a hyper-comparative approach, which has been overconfident in a high assessment of the degree of lexical overlap between languages, has been damaging to a truly comparative understanding of the situation.

VIII

THE MASSORETES, VOCALIZATION
AND EMENDATION

(1) *General*

MANY philological treatments hold firmly to the consonantal text, resisting suggestions that it should be emended; they are extremely free, however, towards the vocalization, often implying that it is a late and ill-informed interpretation which may be modified by scholars at will.[1]

Exceptions, indeed, can be found. For the enigmatic וְאַל־תִּרְהוּ at Isa. 44. 8 Driver's suggestion of an explanation on the basis of Arabic *dahā* implied an emendation to וְאַל־תִּדְהוּ affecting the consonants only, or even to וְאַל־תִּדָּהוּ affecting also the vowels and making the verb a niphal.[2] In this approach the philologist uses his imagination to detect forms close to, but not identical with, the consonantal text, which promise a successful philological treatment.

Conversely, a philological treatment will sometimes start from, and use as evidence, a feature of the existing pointing; and, after using a cognate language to explain the meaning, it will return to the existing pointing, which it has thus explained and justified.

At Neh. 5. 7 Kopf notes the unusual niphal in the phrase וַיִּמָּלֵךְ לִבִּי עָלַי and, comparing the Arabic sense, 'take possession', construes as 'I was beside myself'. Though the clue to the sense is found in Arabic, the suggestion starts from and returns to the Massoretic pointing.

A similar example is found at Hos. 8. 4. Here the verb מלך is taken by Driver to mean 'advise', after the sense in Aramaic. The verse reads:

הֵם הִמְלִיכוּ וְלֹא מִמֶּנִּי הֵשִׂירוּ וְלֹא יָדָעְתִּי׃

---

[1] Cf. Driver, cited above, p. 35; Dahood in *Biblica* xliv (1963) 291, with reference to Albright in Peake, pp. 62 f.

[2] Cf. above, pp. 6 f., 166, and below, p. 231.

and the meaning found by Driver is:

> 'they have taken counsel, but not of me;
> they have got advice, and I know not of it.'

The first verb means 'caused advice to be taken', thus justifying the hiphil; and the second is related to Arabic *'asāra* and is in Hebrew a denominative hiphil meaning 'obtained advice'. Thus, though the senses suggested are novel, the interpretation supports and justifies the hiphil pointing of the MT.

These illustrations show, then, that philological treatments can and do at times either (*a*) involve emendation of the consonantal text or, conversely, (*b*) confirm the punctuation as well as the consonantal text. It nevertheless remains generally true of philological treatments that many of them involve a departure from the Massoretic punctuation. The exceptions can hardly hope to become the rule.

Moreover, many philological treatments, though they do not abandon or emend the major consonants (generally speaking, the radicals, apart from 'weak' letters), nevertheless involve other changes (commonly supposed to be 'minor'), such as displacements of word divisions and confusion between *w* and *y*. If these 'minor' changes are used with high frequency in a small space their effect is not greatly different from that of outright emendation. When this is so, it is legalistic to claim that the consonantal text is being left intact. Even if basic root consonants are not altered into others, the text may be in effect rewritten. The following examples will show different degrees of this process. Moderate changes are involved in the quite attractive treatment of Ezek. 27. 19 by Millard. The MT offers the rather impenetrable:

$$\text{וְדָן וְיָוָן מְאוּזָּל}$$

Of this AV made

> 'Dan also and Javan going to and fro.'

BH[3] emends, so also RSV. Millard takes the text as:

$$\text{וְדַגֵּי יַיִן מֵאִיזָל}$$

meaning:

> 'and casks of wine from Izalla'.[1]

---

[1] *JSS* vii (1962) 201 ff. Cf. the identification of Izalla already in GB, p. 15 b.

The word דֵּן 'cask' is identified on the basis of Accadian *dannu*
(cf. also Ugar. *dn*). The textual alterations are fairly minor.

Other suggestions are more complex and involve very far-reaching changes in word division and vocalization. Hab. 3. 6–7 has the
very difficult passage:

$$\text{הֲלִיכוֹת עוֹלָם לוֹ} : \text{תַּחַת אָוֶן רָאִיתִי} \quad \text{MT}$$

These are the words rendered by the 'his ways were as of old' and
'I saw . . . in affliction' of RSV. Albright, reconstructing this,
produces a text which reads (apart from the last word):

$$\text{הלכות עולם לתחתאון} :$$

and means:

> 'eternal orbits were shattered'.

This suggestion, while not changing any consonant, is an extremely radical reshuffling of the consonants into a completely
different series of words and clauses. Such a reconstruction is
really no less an emendation than a conjectural alteration of one or
two consonants would have been; the effect is entirely as drastic.

We may add Tur-Sinai's reconstruction of Job 37. 17:

MT: $\quad\quad$ אֲשֶׁר־בְּגָדֶיךָ חַמִּים בְּהַשְׁקִט אֶרֶץ מִדָּרוֹם

Tur-Sinai: אֲשֶׁר בִּגְבֹר כֹּחַ הַמַּיִם בְּהַשְׁקִיט אֶרֶץ מִדָּרָם

The meaning of the reconstructed text is said to be:

> 'So that, when the waters become forceful
> and cause their wet clay to fall down.'

The new philological identification is that of a מֶדֶר, cognate with
Ethiopic *mədr* 'earth', Arabic *madar*. Though some of the textual
changes are individually easy ones (e.g. interchange of ר and ד),
the reconstruction is in fact extremely far-reaching, with a liberal
assortment of dittographies and haplographies in the space of some
nine consonants. Though Tur-Sinai says that 'the punctuators
failed to understand the text', it is hard to see how they failed to
understand the supposedly original בגבר כח המים, which is not
difficult in comparison with most of the text they had to point in
Job.

These instances show that changes of vocalization, or shifts in
consonant order or word division, implied in philological treatments may sometimes be so drastic in effect as to make it legalistic

to claim that the consonantal text is unchanged. We may now go on
to consider the questions more systematically.

(2) *Fallibility in the Consonantal Text*

Philological scholars, then, though critical of emendation, have
often been inconsistent and have used emendation, or else, as
argued above, have produced virtual emendations through reshuffling of the consonants. It may be answered, indeed, that
inconsistency is not a serious charge, since the transmission of the
text was itself subject to inconsistency, so that a responsible scholar
will have to use different methods at different times. In particular
it may be suggested that emendation is legitimate, but only after all
attempts at a philological treatment have resulted in failure.

This, however, hardly goes far enough. To admit the legitimacy
of emendation at all is to admit that the consonantal text is fallible;
and to admit this is to admit that the basis for philological treatments in the consonantal text is not wholly secure. Wholesale statements that emendation is illegitimate, if meant literally, imply that
the consonantal text was infallibly preserved. Given the conditions
of transmission of the Hebrew Bible, if the consonantal text is not
necessarily right, then emendation may at times be necessary.

Once this is admitted, it follows that from the beginning the
alteration of the text has to be considered on equal terms in principle with the possibility of a philological explanation. It is not
enough to agree that emendation may be considered only after all
forms of philological explanation, however remote, have been
exhausted. The difference between the two approaches lies from
the beginning in a balance of probabilities. This follows from the
admission that the text may be faulty, and is not invalidated by the
argument that many textual emendations in the past have proved
to be wild and arbitrary; the same is true, after all, of many philological explanations.

There is substantial, and indeed decisive, evidence that consonantal texts could be written and transmitted incorrectly. Such evidence can be found in the Old Testament itself in passages which
appear twice; it can be found in the Qumran documents; and it
can be found in the literature of cognate languages such as Ugaritic.

A comparison of passages which appear twice, such as Ps. 18,
which is also II Sam. 22, suggests that errors in the copying of the

consonantal text are probable. One cannot, indeed, assume that all such differences between parallel texts are a result of textual corruption; some may go back to free variants in oral tradition. The variation between כַּף (II Sam. 22. 1) and יַד (Ps. 18. 1) may perhaps be explained in this way; on the other hand, it could easily be a scribal change.

It is also possible that some of the differences between parallel passages are genuine linguistic, rather than textual, differences; that is to say, the parallel texts have words genuinely different though approximately parallel, rather than forms which have arisen by scribal error.

Ps. 58. 11 has a phrase which seems closely parallel to one in Ps. 68. 24. The former is:

$$\text{פְּעָמָיו יִרְחַץ בְּדַם הָרָשָׁע}$$

'he washes his feet in the blood of the wicked'.

This presents no difficulty. But at 68. 24 the words in MT are:

$$\text{לְמַעַן תִּמְחַץ רַגְלְךָ בְּדָם}$$

Now since מחץ in Hebrew usually means 'strike', it has been common practice to emend the verb at 68. 24 to תרחץ, thus producing agreement with 58. 11; so for example *BH*[3], with the alleged support of the versions.[1] Delitzsch,[2] however, argues that there was an Accadian *maḥāṣu* meaning 'pour over' (synonymous with *balālu*), and gives actual examples in literature. If this is right, the phenomenon has to be treated as a linguistic rather than a textual one. Finally, the sense is possibly only the normal Hebrew one 'strike': 'that you may strike your foot in the blood . . .'.

Nevertheless, it is not likely that all differences in parallel passages could be removed or explained in this way, and many of them should probably be ascribed to scribal errors, as textual critics have generally done. Ps. 18. 11 has an uncommon verb in the phrase:

$$\text{וַיֵּדֶא עַל־כַּנְפֵי־רוּחַ}$$

which means perhaps:

'and he swooped upon the wings of the wind'.

[1] Recently Kraus, p. 467. It is doubtful whether the versions really support this emendation. LXX for example has (67. 24) ὅπως ἂν βαφῇ ὁ πούς σου ἐν αἵματι. This is not very good evidence that the Hebrew translated was רחץ, which is never rendered with βάπτω in the LXX. Contrast 57. 11 (verb νίψεται). The Greek just gave a rendering such as the context seemed to demand.

[2] *Proleg.*, pp. 69 ff. More recently cf. von Soden, p. 581a, '(5) *besprengen mit*'.

The parallel II Sam. 22. 11 (along with some manuscripts in the Psalm) has the reading וַיֵּרָא, which would mean:

> 'and he appeared upon the wings of the wind'.

Probably this latter is simply a wrong text, and shows clearly the mistaking of ד for ר by copyists and its influence even in the text of the Psalm.

Thus the parallel passages afford strong evidence for occasional scribal corruption of the consonantal text. That such corruption exists is, of course, no new idea, and has in fact been the normal accepted belief among scholars. There should indeed be no need to repeat the evidence for it, were it not that arguments in favour of philological treatments have sometimes come close to regarding the consonantal text as sacrosanct; and for this reason it is right to reiterate some evidences of its fallibility.

The Qumran material also shows quite clearly that the consonantal text has been liable to corruption. This is so of course whether the Qumran texts are right or wrong when they differ from MT.

There are indeed places where it has been suggested that the Qumran text will yield to a philological treatment while the MT will not. An interesting example is the difficult Isa. 41. 27:

ראשון לציון הִנֵּה הִנָּם ולירושלם מבשר אתן׃

This, the MT, seems to mean literally:

> 'A first for Zion, behold, behold them;
> and to Jerusalem I will give a messenger of good.'

The obscurity of this text has led to numerous emendations, for which see *BH*³. The Qumran text 1QIsA has הנומה where MT has הנם. Guillaume argues that נומה is clearly a participle, in parallelism with the מבשר of the second part. It is to be explained, he says, from the Arabic *namā* 'bring tidings', for which he quotes cases in old Arab poems.[1]

---

[1] On this word see above, p. 182. Driver, *The Judaean Scrolls*, pp. 435, 444, gives the same interpretation as Guillaume. He appears also to find this word in 1QIsA 35. 7, where the MT has וגמא 'and papyrus'; but from the photographs the word seems clearly to be וגומא, exactly as in the MT except for the added *waw*. The Arabic *namā*, while certainly a real verb the use of which can easily be checked in early poetry, is probably an idiosyncrasy of Arabic, and seems to have no cognates in other Semitic languages. Thus the evidence for its existence in Hebrew is weak; nor, in Isa. 35. 7, is it clear what sense it would make.

In any case the Qumran text, whether better or not, adds to the evidence that texts varied. If readings in the Qumran texts are superior, it means that in the absence of the Qumran evidence (which might, after all, never have been discovered) the conjectural emendations might have been right and would certainly have been justifiable. There are in fact cases, as is well known, where the Qumran scrolls have been found to contain readings which had previously been conjectured by scholars.

A third place where we can see evidence of faulty transmission of consonantal texts is the Ugaritic literature. In places this is highly repetitive, quite long sections being reiterated in almost exactly the same words. In such passages some fairly obvious spelling errors have been detected;[1] and this is a literature the line of transmission of which to us ceased in the fourteenth century B.C.!

There is every reason to expect, therefore, that the transmission of texts has included errors in the consonantal as well as in the vocalized writing; and, in spite of the exaggerated reliance on textual emendation which has sometimes been shown, it will always remain an important possibility that difficulties have arisen by graphic error rather than by loss of linguistic understanding. Textual criticism must retain its traditional place and not be completely displaced by a too purely philological approach.

In order to make further progress, we have now to give closer consideration to the transmission of the vocalization.

(3) *The Importance of the Vocalization*

The picture implied in philological treatments is one of (*a*) a long period during which the consonantal text was carefully cherished and transmitted, and (*b*) a late and arbitrary process by which a vocalization was more or less imposed on this text by men who indeed tried their best to understand it but were handicapped by the limitations of their knowledge of Hebrew (now to them a long-dead language) and by the narrowness of their understanding of these particular texts. Is this a credible picture? Does it not raise in another form the question which Nyberg raised against the older textual criticism, namely that it assumed that the Jews very

---

[1] For some examples see Gordon, *UH* 4. 16 (pp. 17 f.). For instance we have the word *bt'rth* 'in its scabbard', once written *bt'rtp* (3 Aqhat i 29). This can be assuredly explained as the writing of the two strokes of Ugaritic *p* in place of the three of *h*.

early lost the understanding of what their own Scriptures meant, while they transmitted it by a mechanical copying procedure?— And, it would appear (in this we go beyond what Nyberg argued), having transmitted this consonantal skeleton of a Scripture by a mechanical copying procedure, did they then centuries later attempt to clothe it in the flesh of a newly created vocalization?

Firstly, the vocalization of the Hebrew Bible was not invented when the written marks of vocalization were invented. A distinction has to be made between the actual existence of vocalization and its written marking.

Biblical manuscripts long ago had no marking of vocalization in the form now dominant, i.e. the Tiberian point system. This system grew up from about the sixth century A.D. But long before this some degree of discrimination of vowels had been provided in the form of the vowel letters or *matres lectionis*. While it is possible to write Hebrew with no vowel letters at all, this was not the practice in any extant biblical texts. Even the Siloam inscription, from Hezekiah's time, has some vowel letters, though not exactly the distribution to which we have become accustomed from the MT. The Qumran scroll 1QIsA, as is well known, has a more copious use of vowel letters than the MT, and (somewhat like modern Hebrew) uses them in indicating 'short' vowels which were not so indicated in MT. Thus, even in the period before the pointing system was introduced, a written indication of vocalization did exist; and indeed in certain texts the written indication was greater than is to be found in the MT if the pointing of the latter is removed.

Thus even when it was without vowel points the text was not without indications of vocalization. Certainly this vocalization was not 'complete'; it did not try to indicate or discriminate all the phonemes of the text. But this is no absolute peculiarity of Hebrew; it is true of most writing systems that they do not systematically mark all the phonemes. For instance, stress and pitch are phonemic in English, but there is no way of representing this in the normal writing system.[1] In classical Greek vowel length was phonemic, but it has graphic representation only for certain of the vowels and not for others; and the pitch accent was phonemic, but was not marked until long after the classical period.[2] Consonant length is

---

[1] On this see Gleason, pp. 40–50.
[2] See Gleason, p. 419.

phonemic, and is extremely important, in Ethiopian languages, but has no written marking (though some modern grammarians have introduced it). In failing to provide a clear one-to-one marking for all vowel phonemes, the Hebrew *matres lectionis* departed from the consistent early Phoenician writing system, which had systematically omitted the entire sub-system of vowels; instead, they formed a series of optional markings for certain groups within the vowel sub-system.[1] The fact that at this stage there was not a well-proportioned correspondence between the phonemic and the graphemic systems is nothing extraordinary. Thus the texts of biblical Hebrew, even when they were still 'unvocalized', were not devoid of sensitivity to the indication of vowel distinctions in writing. When the complete vocalization, which included not only the vowel points but also other diacritic signs like the *daghesh* and also the accent system, came to be applied, it was related to a more rudimentary series of vowel indications which was already present.

More important, however, for our purpose is the tradition of vocalization which was passed on in addition to the written indications. Week by week and year by year, Moses and the prophets were read. It is a mistake to think of a written consonantal text which was handed on through generations without vocalization and then afterwards was 'vocalized'. This is true of the stages of the written text when taken in a somewhat artificial isolation; but it is not true of the history of the tradition. The Massoretes began with a text lacking vowel points and proceeded to point it and accent it; but this does not mean that they invented the vocalization. What they invented was a series of increasingly subtle systems for the marking of the vocalization which was already in use.

Thus the term 'vocalization' is somewhat ambiguous. The system of points was applied late (after the completion of the Talmud), and previously texts were unvocalized in the sense that these signs were absent; even then the vowel letters provided a partial marking of vowels. But the biblical text was transmitted also in a spoken form; the text was publicly read and the mode of reading was passed on. There is no evidence of a stage at which this *linguistic* transmission of the text had come to be interrupted, so that Jews had to start again with no material but a written text, from which the further linguistic elements such as vowels, which were unmarked in writing, had to be deduced or invented.

[1] See Gleason, op. cit., p. 419.

It is not probable that Jews learned to read the biblical text by looking at the written signs and guessing at the vowels which may have accompanied them. Rather, they learned by reading with a teacher, or listening to a synagogue reader; and this teacher or reader knew from his own learning how the text was to be read.[1] In this respect there was a difference from the reading of a casual communication like a letter, which would certainly have to be read without any tradition of vocalization, but in which the intrinsic difficulty of the text would be likely to be less, while a wrong reading would not carry religious consequences.[2]

It is commonly held to be a characteristic of the Semitic languages that the consonants are a basis or backbone and provide all the cardinal ideas, while the vowels indicate only modifications of these ideas. Only to a limited extent is this true.[3] Often one cannot tell a 'basic idea' from the consonants alone. The mere consonants אב do not make clear whether the idea is 'father' or 'ghost' or 'bud'. The vowels are critical as the consonants are. In the reading of an extended passage discrimination is made through the context. This can be done even when the vowels are not marked. It is not that the ideas come through to the mind independently of vowels; rather, the context guides the reader to select the vocalization which makes sense of the passage (or—and particularly if a passage is read silently—to select senses which imply a particular vocalization, and thereby to select, from the number of vowel patterns possible within the consonant sequence, the ones which make sense). The consonant sequences do not in themselves furnish the basic sense; taken just as they are written, they do not make clear which consonants are 'root consonants' and which are not. While *we* have learned to look for triradical consonantal roots and work outwards from these, we should be aware that (*a*) this procedure was developed by a grammar which itself presupposed the vocalization as its means of analysis, and (*b*) this procedure is not necessarily the way in which ancient and medieval Jews read the text (or any other document). This is relevant especially because the ancient reader normally read aloud and not silently.

[1] Cf. the Talmudic passage quoted below, pp. 213 f.

[2] Cf. my article 'Vocalization and the Analysis of Hebrew', p. 4, and below, pp. 208 f., where I suggest that the procedure of translators like the LXX differed from that of normal reading in Hebrew.

[3] Cf. Ullendorff, *Orientalia* xxvii (1958) 69 ff.; Moscati, *Comparative Grammar*, p. 72.

The mainly consonantal nature of Semitic writing systems, however, might be thought to show the contrary and demonstrate that the consonants were after all regarded as the main centres of meaning. But is it true that Semitic writing systems are so over-whelmingly consonantal? It is not true of Accadian writing; nor is it true of Ethiopic, in which the consonants cannot be written without an attached vowel. Ugaritic script indicated vowels for one of the consonants, namely *aleph*. Arabic script, when not pointed, does not mark *all* vowels; but it is equally characteristic of it that it always marks *some* vowels: normally, in fact, all long vowels are marked,[1] and only short vowels are unmarked. The commoner Semitic characteristic is not the marking of consonants exclusively, but the marking of only *some* vowels. The use of a script which is strictly without marking of vowels is indeed rather exceptional. The undoubted fact that writing systems which can work without any vowel marking are among those which have emerged in the Semitic world is not sufficient cause for us to conclude that there is a mysterious identity between the consonants and the basic meaning. Thus the relation between vowel and consonant in the writing of Semitic languages does not in itself give us reason to treat lightly the tradition of vocalization or to suppose that the vocalization was marked without very considerable guidance from previous tradition.

It is possible, indeed, to suggest explanations of the primarily consonantal nature of many Semitic writing systems without making any reference to a bearing of the basic meaning by the con-sonants, and indeed without making reference to meaning at all; such explanations would depend rather on the actual formal struc-ture of Semitic languages.

It is possible that the marking of a phoneme in writing was con-nected with the occurrence of that phoneme in initial position. In the Semitic languages which are relevant for the early development of the alphabet, all word patterns of importance had a consonant in initial position, while none had a vowel in initial position. Con-versely the alphabet provided a grapheme for each phoneme which might occur in initial position. The arrangement thus automatically segmented words into syllables with a consonant in first place. If this is plausible, the character of the system had nothing to do with the idea that consonants bore the core of

---

[1] Morag, *Vocalization Systems*, p. 13.

meaning; it derived from the formal structure of languages which had no relevant patterns except with consonants in initial position. In Greek adaptations of the script, however, vowels were early marked, and the necessity to do this may similarly be associated with the fact that many important Greek patterns have vowels in initial position.

We can state this in another way. The common and traditional view is that the basic meaning lay in the root, i.e. the consonants of the root, and that the vowels indicated modifications of this idea. But, even within the terms of this view, we observe that 'modifications' may equally include consonants, in which case they are marked in the script, or not include consonants, in which case they are not (we assume at this stage an absence of *matres lectionis*). Thus if קָטֵל is to be taken as a 'modification' of the basic קָטַל, surely exactly the same status belongs to הִקְטִל; but the latter has a consonantal addition which is marked in the script. If the consonantal nature of the script had had anything to do with the idea that the consonants should be marked because they formed the basic meaning, then it would have been natural for a script to develop in which the ה of the hiphil was not marked any more than the vowels of the piel. It is more consistent to maintain that what was to be marked was decided by structure. The traditional view comes nearer to the truth in this respect, that the pattern of many Semitic words, and especially verbs (where we can best use the term 'discontinuous morphemes'),[1] favoured the practicability of some such writing system. Even so, as we have seen, most systems quite rapidly introduced the graphic marking of *some* vowels.

This suggestion is made here only to show that alternative ideas about the primarily consonantal nature of the scripts can be entertained; but the remainder of my argument does not depend on the rightness of this suggestion.

It is well known that the pronunciation of Hebrew has changed historically. Certain spellings in the Qumran texts, for instance, have suggested to scholars that the 3rd masculine pronoun was pronounced as /hu'a/ in the Qumran period, while in the Massoretic period it was pronounced as /hu/. None of the pronunciations

---

[1] The term will be found in Gleason, p. 72 f. Gleason correctly states that Hebrew is unusual for the high number of such discontinuous morphemes which it contains; it is inexact when we go farther and make this the basic principle of Hebrew, as the popular view often does.

extant in modern times, probably, preserves a series of distinctions identical with those intended by the Massoretes. That Hebrew pronunciation should have changed historically is only what we should expect from our knowledge of languages generally.

Equally we know that the pronunciation of Hebrew has differed regionally and dialectically. This was already so in ancient times, and in more modern times there are the whole series of differences between Ashkenazi and Sephardi Hebrew.[1] These differences may be considerable. The vowel sign *qameṣ* is an [a] vowel in Sephardi, but an [o] vowel in Ashkenazi. A ת in post-vocalic position is an [s] in Ashkenazi, a [ṯ] in older Sephardi, and a [t] in modern Israeli. There have also been different written systems of marking the texts: the Babylonian punctuation, for example, not only uses signs of different shape from the Tiberian, but is a different system, having a different total number of vowels.

All of these, then, are ways in which the pronunciation of Hebrew has varied along co-ordinates of time and place. The question now is whether this variety is any reason why the tradition of vocalization should be considered intrinsically unreliable and therein separable in principle from the tradition of the written text. It would seem that many scholars, knowing of the existence of this variation in pronunciation, have concluded that the tradition of vocalization is an unchartable chaos, the produce of arbitrary decisions on the part of men who were out of touch with the realities of the texts under treatment.

This, however, does not necessarily follow. The fact of historical change and regional variation in the pronunciation of Hebrew, including the known existence of different written systems of vocalization, does not in itself prove that the vocalizations existing in tradition are unreliable or arbitrary in relation to the questions which are being studied in this book.

Firstly, we are not concerned with achieving a phonetically accurate reproduction of the words of, let us say, the prophet Isaiah. Since the pronunciation of Hebrew has become phonetically different, this would be a very difficult task. Such questions, however, are quite marginal to our subject. The existence of phonetic change in time is irrelevant except in so far as it can be shown to have led in actual evidenced cases to the obscuring of

---

[1] For a statement describing nine different Jewish regional pronunciations see Bauer and Leander, *Historische Grammatik*, pp. 170 ff.

information given by linguistic elements, for example, through producing a situation where one word comes to be confused with another.

One might have expected that philological treatments where they involve a change in the traditional vocalization might include an argument that known historical examples of phonetic change apply to the words under treatment. Not all elements of Hebrew have been equally affected by phonetic change. If such change were a main cause of the unreliability of the vocalization, we should expect the incidence of philological treatments to be heaviest at points where phonetic change is known to have occurred and lightest at points where no substantial change has occurred. No such correlation, however, is observable in a survey of philological treatments, nor have I seen reason to believe that scholars who produced treatments have considered the possible importance of such a correlation.

Moreover, sound changes do not operate at a constant rate on all sounds. While certain sounds in a given language may alter very greatly in a very short time, others may persist with little change over thousands of years. It is therefore wrong to expect that the undoubted fact of sound change in Hebrew will necessarily mean that the late pronunciation traditions are *in a level and general manner* unrepresentative of ancient practice. Moreover, a language may preserve important distinctions even though very great changes in phonetic character have taken place. A striking example is that of the stress accent in modern Greek, the position of which is to a large extent the same as that of the pitch accent in ancient Greek, even though the general pronunciation of Greek and the whole character of the accent itself have changed very greatly.[1]

Where philological treatments have involved a departure from the traditional vocalization, not only have they not generally given evidence of relevant phonetic change, but they are themselves mostly inconsistent with the possibility of explanation by appeal to phonetic change. One of the important aspects of phonetic change is its high relative constancy, such as is found in the differences between Ashkenazi and Sephardi pronunciations. Where philological treatments have required a change in vocalization, however, they have seldom or never implied phenomena of high constancy. Generally they have demanded the revocalization of *this one* particular word, irrespective of the effects this would have on other

[1] Cf. Thumb, *Handbook*, p. 28.

words employing the same patterns. For instance, it is not uncommon for scholars who find a verb pointed as (say) hiphil in the
Massoretic text to rule that it should in fact be a piel. Quite possibly
this kind of decision may be right. But it cannot be justified on the
ground of phonetic changes general in the transmission of Hebrew
pronunciation. All known forms of Hebrew pronunciation provide
distinctions adequate to discriminate between piel and hiphil in
normal circumstances. This is so even if the various pronunciations
are very different from each other. A confusion in transmission
between piel and hiphil could normally be attributed to historical
phonetic shifts only on the hypothesis that these obscured the distinctions between the two sets of forms. Since, in the texts under
examination, this does not appear to be so, and since adequate
marking of the distinctions continues to be accepted apart from
the isolated cases where the vocalization is emended, the phenomenon can hardly be attributed to general phonetic shifts. It is not
easy to see how such shifts could mean that the vowels of a word
somehow got picked up and redistributed, as seems to be implied
when we regard the vocalization as something which the scholar
can redistribute at will.

For instance, at Prov. 26. 28, MT לְשׁוֹן־שֶׁקֶר יִשְׂנָא דַכָּיו
apparently means 'a lying tongue hates its victims'. It has been
suggested (Index, no. 91) that the last word be read דְּכוּי 'ac-
quittal' (as Aram. דְכָא = standard Hebr. זכה). If this suggestion
means that an original writing דכוי came to be written as דכיו
and was followed by a change of vocalization, then it is basically a
graphic corruption and belongs to the textual rather than the
philological type of treatment.[1] But even then it leaves unclear
how communities, in which /dikkuy/ had been read, suddenly
changed over to the reading /dakkaw/.

If, on the other hand, a noun pronounced /dikkuy/ came to be
pronounced /dakkaw/, this is no 'mere' change of vocalization, but
a complete shift from one word to another, which cannot be explained by phonetic drift or other change of pronunciation. Any
such change would have affected also other words of the type
גְּלוּי, such as צְפוּי or שְׁקוּי.

In fact philological treatments have generally implied a more
semantically based process of vocalization; they have suggested

---

[1] Cf. again below, p. 218.

that the Massoretes were governed, not by the antecedent tradition of pronunciation, but by opinions about the meaning of the text. Seeing a consonant group in the unvocalized text, they are thought to have analysed it for grammar and meaning and marked it with the points implied by the results of this analysis. If the vocalization is 'wrong', this is because the Massoretes identified the word wrongly and, failing to discern the meaning, attached an erroneous vocalization.

There are, however, some serious difficulties in the way of this conception of the work of the Massoretes. One such difficulty is the traditionalism which appears to have inspired their work. There have, indeed, in recent years been some opinions according to which the Massoretes were rather linguistic innovators. This will be discussed shortly. But it seems better for the present to follow Bergsträsser's view:

> What we know of their activity shows an obstinate clinging to the smallest details of what was transmitted to them.[1]

Similarly Bacher had earlier written:

> These signs [i.e. the vowel points] are the embodiment of the vocalic pronunciation, which the Massoretes had received in oral tradition over many generations along with the written text of the biblical books. The knowledge of the linguistic forms, handed down in the reading of the text, reaches back into times not too far distant from that in which Hebrew was still a living language.[2]

It is true that various schools and stages of punctuation existed. But the process is an increasingly detailed attempt to mark what was already there, rather than the making of decisions entailing a departure from it.

The discussion traceable to the Massoretes is of a primarily non-semantic nature. The Massoretic treatises known to us, such as the *Ochlah we-Ochlah* or the *Treatise on the Shewa*, are concerned with classification of phonemic and graphic differences. These are not, indeed, wholly unrelated to semantic differences. But the mode of discussion hardly leaves room for the conception that the Massoretes first made up their minds what the text meant and then pointed it accordingly.

---

[1] *OLZ* xxvii (1924) 582–6. See Kahle, *Cairo Geniza* (2nd ed.), p. 188.
[2] *ZDMG* xlix (1895) 13.

The same can be said about the marginal notes, commonly called the Massorah, appended to the Hebrew Bible. These are not to any great extent of lexicographical or of semantic nature. Most commonly they are listings of *writings*. In these listings the obvious semantic questions—for instance homonymy—are commonly ignored. For the sense of a biblical passage the right identification of a homonym can be of obvious importance, but the Massorah gives little such guidance.

There are two homonymic nouns מַקֶּבֶת; one means 'hammer' and the other means 'hole, excavation'. The latter occurs only at Isa. 51. 1, but the Massorah of the Aleppo Codex neither marks it as an unusual form nor gives any indication that it should be understood otherwise than its homonym. In the same sentence, however, the Massorah marks the phrase אֶל־צוּר 'unto the rock' with an annotation that this group with this writing occurs thrice, though no semantic problem is touched by this. Again, at Isa. 13. 8 the form לְהָבִים 'flames' is marked with a note that it occurs thrice in all. The other two cases are לְהָבִים at Gen. 10. 13, I Chron. 1. 11, where the meaning is 'Lybians'. The Massoretic note, being concerned with writings and not with meanings, makes no attempt to separate the two types.[1]

It is true that certain notes of semantic type may be found, but these are so occasional as to show that the exception cannot be made the rule. For instance, at Prov. 25. 14, where the word נְשִׂיאִים occurs in a sense other than the common 'prince', the *Massora Parva* of Codex B 19a gives the note ד׳ מילין לשון ענן 'four (occurrences of) words in the sense of "cloud"'.[2] There are other places where the Massorah, using the technical term לשון 'has the sense of', provides some semantic guidance, very often in relation to unseemly expressions. Such notes, however, form so infinitesimal a proportion, in relation to the total number of Massoretic notes or in relation to the total number of places where semantic uncertainty is found, that we may suppose that they were usually prompted by some special reason; and thus these exceptions do not alter the fact that the main body of Massoretic annotations was non-semantic in nature.

Hapax legomena indeed are often marked with the sign ל (for

---

[1] See Weil in *VTS* ix (1963) 276 n.; cf. *Textus* iii (1963) 119.
[2] The other three cases are at Jer. 10. 13, 51. 16; Ps. 135. 7.

לִית 'there is none', i.e. no other instance).[1] But the identification
of rare words in our lexical sense is by no means the *purpose* of
these notes. The mark לֹ is used on *graphic* forms which are unique,
and this has nothing intrinsically to do with the uniqueness of the
word in a lexical sense. A form will be so marked even if the word
is a very common one, provided that the writing is an unusual one
(e.g. in respect of מלא or חסר in mode of writing) or one otherwise liable to confusion.

Generally, then, the Massoretic lists concern the exact writing
and reading. Often the procedure is semantically indifferent,
though it is important to the scribe, whose concern is with exact
copying of text. Even where the lists have semantic implications,
these often remain implications rather than express conclusions,
and the statement expressly made by the lists is one about the
pronunciation. There is a list which, under the consonantal form
יחל, records the number which have the vowel *patah* and the
number which have *qames*.[2] To us this involves the two different
roots חלל and יחל, and thus different meanings; but the form
which the Massoretic annotation takes is a declaration about the
variation between one vowel and another. All this makes it difficult
to sustain a view of the Massoretes as men who pointed the text as
they 'understood' it; if this had been so, one would have expected
a primarily semantic sifting and cataloguing of the material.

The picture of the Massoretes as interpreters who worked out,
or guessed, from the consonantal text what its meaning might be
and then vocalized it accordingly, has other difficulties which appear after very little thought. One of these is the fact that it is
extremely difficult, in cases where a text is intrinsically obscure,
to know how the Massoretes 'understood' it at all. If they had in
fact worked out an understanding of it, and then pointed the text
on this basis, one would expect it to be rather more transparent
what they intended than is actually the case. The difficulty of the
existing text tends at many points to suggest that the Massoretes
transmitted a received text with its own difficulties, rather than
iron these out into something which by their then knowledge was
smooth and satisfactory.

[1] Cf. Rabin, 'Millim Bodᵉdot', in *Encyclopaedia Miqra'it*.
[2] Weil, *VTS* ix (1963) 280 n. Weil rightly points out that this failure to make
a distinction between forms from different roots cuts entirely across our lexical
approach and forms a substantial difficulty for the modern student of the
Massorah.

This is a somewhat different matter from the standardization of grammar. It is often held that the dialectal and temporal variations in ancient Hebrew have been overlaid by the fairly unitary system now represented in the pointing. Such a standardization does in fact seem to have taken place, though I think it was not the work of the Massoretes, i.e. of those who introduced the pointing, but rather was introduced in the liturgical reading tradition much earlier (which seems much more natural). It is reasonable to suppose that this tradition introduced a more uniform and standard morphology. It would, in fact, be necessary to do so unless the readers of the Bible were endowed with phonetic, historical, and literary discriminations of a quite exceptional order. The synagogue reader could no more be expected to imitate the different Hebrew pronunciations of the Song of Deborah, the prophet Amos, and the wisdom teacher Qoheleth than the modern English reader tries to reproduce the phonetics of Shakespeare, Pope, and Scott when he reads these authors. Intelligibility would require that a levelled system should be employed. It is quite a different thing to suggest that within such a levelled system the discriminations between morphemes were arbitrarily altered by the Massoretes in order to achieve a meaning which seemed to them to be satisfactory. Thus the fact of the standardization of the grammatical system, if it is a fact, does not in itself justify the conception of an arbitrary moulding of the text by the Massoretes on the morphemic-semantic level.

One must also ask how the Massoretes, if their work involved innovations on the level of meaning, succeeded in getting these innovations accepted by the community, in view of the inertia of religious traditions and practices. Substantial changes on a semantic level would lead immediately to exegetical and theological decisions. How could such innovations be carried through, amid the sensitivity to such questions in the contemporary controversy between Qaraites and Rabbanites? How could the opposite party fail to point out that the reading of the text had been wilfully altered by the new traditions in the vocalization?

It should be added that the term 'the Massoretes' seems sometimes to be used in two senses, a narrower and a wider. I have used it in the narrower sense, to denote the scholarly families which worked upon the copying of the text and the provision of vocalization and accents in the period of roughly A.D. 600–1000. But the term may also be used of the more general transmission of the text, without special and exact reference to the punctuators. When we read in the context of modern philological treatments that 'the Massoretes failed to understand the text' this may be meant to apply not to the actual punctuators like the Ben Asher or Ben Naphtali families, but rather to the general tradition which already lay behind them and was assumed by them. If this is so, then some of the arguments I have just made do not apply in the same way. The conception that the text was misunderstood, if no longer applying to the Massoretes in the stricter sense, is not liable to the criticisms I have just advanced. The meaning may be that the misunderstanding, and the 'correction' of the text in order to fit a new understanding, had already taken place before the Massoretes recorded the tradition.

If this is what is meant, then my arguments do not have the same effect; but neither is the problem solved thereby. For if 'the Massoretes' is a term used to designate the general tradition of reading and understanding over some centuries, then the work of the actual punctuators can hardly be stigmatized with terms like 'artificial'; for their decisions were not produced in the process of providing a punctuation but must, right or wrong, have been inherent in the tradition long before the process of punctuation began. The decisions now are no longer 'late', but may have taken place at any time between the formation of the original text and the fixation of the Massoretic punctuation. Only detailed research can tell us whether they had already been made by the time of the Qumran texts, or even by the time of Ezra.

The difficulty of attributing to the Massoretes great initiative in semantic interpretation leads on the whole to the judgement that the source of confusion often lay early, rather than late, in the history of transmission.

(4) *Evidence for Pre-Massoretic Vocalization*

The last section discussed the general relation between the Hebrew vowels and the language as a whole, along with some relevant aspects of the work of the Massoretes. We now go on to discuss some areas in which evidence may be found for the vocalization of Hebrew before the Massoretes registered it with points. The evidence is complicated, and will receive only a partial survey here. Moreover, it is not new evidence; but it has generally been used in the study of different problems from our present one. Our concern is not with purely phonetic or even purely grammatical differences, but with differences which have a substantial effect on meaning. My purpose is to show that certain often-quoted sources and theories do not, on examination, disprove the continuance of a tradition of vocalization long before the time of the Massoretes. Finally, the many anomalies of the Massoretic pointing itself are an argument against the idea that the vocalization was the product of an artificial process.

One of the early sources of evidence is the Septuagint. The standard works mention with some emphasis that the text, from which this translation was made, was unvocalized. Thus Swete writes:

Lastly, almost every page of the LXX yields evidence that the Hebrew text was as yet unpointed. Vocalization was in fact only traditional until the days of the Massorah, and the tradition which is enshrined in the Massoretic points differs, often very widely, from that which was inherited or originated by the Alexandrian translators.[1]

What is true of the Alexandrian translation, however, does not necessarily apply to the way in which the Hebrew text was preserved within those communities which read in Hebrew and/or Aramaic.

Firstly, all the evidence indicates that knowledge of Hebrew in the Egyptian Jewish community was poor.[2] Philo, their most learned man, is usually supposed not to have known any. The Egyptian synagogue did not (according to the usual view, at any rate) read the Bible in Hebrew at all, in this respect differing from the other practice in which the Hebrew text was read along with a Targum into another language. For this reason LXX renderings which would seem to imply erratic vocalizations in Hebrew do not necessarily reflect the transmission of the text where the Hebrew was read in the synagogue.

Secondly, it is a possible hypothesis that the use of the then written text alone, i.e. the unpointed text, was a special feature of the work of some translators, which in this respect differed from the processes used in the transmission of the Hebrew text. These translators worked from the written text, deciphering it and providing a sense in Greek which seemed to correspond. It is not necessarily correct to say that they 'vocalized' it. Rather, given the

---

[1] *Introduction*, p. 322.
[2] For further comment on this see below, pp. 267 ff.

sequence of written signs, they may have selected, out of the various possibilities of meaning which were provided by that sequence, one which seemed to them, from a number of varying and sometimes competing criteria, to be good, and this they represented in Greek. They did not submit the text to a grammatical analysis, and for this reason we do wrong when we say, as we sometimes do, that they took such and such a form to be a participle, or that they supposed it to be a piel when it is really a hiphil, and the like.[1] These considerations were quite foreign to their situation. Given a sequence of characters *x-y-z*, they may have neither vocalized this nor analysed it grammatically, but may have had in their minds a series of Greek words which might be the meanings of *x-y-z*, and from these they chose one.

Thus the LXX were actually doing, if this suggestion is right, what common scholarly theory has depicted the Massoretes as doing: given an unpointed text, they deduced a sense and fixed that sense by their translation, just as the Massoretes are pictured as having deduced a sense and fixed it thereafter by their pointing. The difference is, however, that the Massoretes were in fact doing something quite different: they were not fixing a sense, but recording a tradition of reading.

The suggestion here advanced is consistent with the fact that the word divisions are often placed by the LXX at points which not only are different from those of the MT but also are intrinsically extremely improbable. In construing the sequence of written signs, they permitted themselves greater latitude than that which the language system, as we know it, in fact allowed, both to take elements out of sequence and to vary the boundaries between one element and another. Until the Middle Ages there was no grammatical analysis which made clear the conditions under which Hebrew consonants might seem to disappear, to intrude, or to occur in peculiar positions; and, until this analysis was done, phenomena which to us seem quite regular may have seemed to justify other kinds of disregard of sequence which to us are entirely irregular. The task of perceiving and fixing a sense, forced upon the translator by the nature of his task, was greatly eased by this latitude in the sequence in which elements might be taken.[2] In this notional

---

[1] Cf. also below, pp. 265 f. Contrast the picture of St. Jerome, below, pp. 211 ff.: he, following the work of the later Greek translators (and the Hexapla), knew that the vocalization could not be neglected.   [2] Cf. examples cited below, p. 267.

altering of the sequence, the translators were not, like the modern textual critics who have done something similar, trying to establish the original text. They did not 'read' something different; they worked in such a way that, if sense could be found by what for us implies a change of sequence, then that sense would do well enough.

To resume the main point, then: in some ancient translation techniques it was possible to work from a text which did not register in writing all the phonemes of the language, without this implying that no tradition of these phonemes existed.

The later translations into Greek and Latin may also furnish evidence for the vocalization (a) through their renderings, which may, when due account is taken of the techniques of the same translator elsewhere, constitute evidence for a mode of reading and therefore implicitly for a vocalization (b) through their transcriptions of Hebrew words into Greek or Latin scripts.

The former is illustrated at Ps. 68. 32 (Gk. 67. 32):

MT   כּוּשׁ תָּרִיץ ידיו לאלהים

Aq.   Αἰθίοψ δρομώσει χεῖρα αὐτοῦ τῷ θεῷ

For 'run' (רוּץ qal) Aquila uses τρέχειν (δραμεῖν), e.g. Ps. 19 (18). 6, Prov. 6. 18, Qoh. 12. 6 (though in this last the sense is different). The formation δρομοῦν is his characteristic coinage to represent the hiphil type. Aquila certainly did not know the form תָּרֵץ suggested in *BH³*—one of its excursions into the philological approach—but either (a) he knew the vocalization to be /tåriṣ/ as in MT (or something semantically equivalent), or (b) at least he deduced the same consequence from the graphic form.

Aquila's renderings, however, do not necessarily agree with the implication of the MT vocalization: e.g. his μετὰ σοῦ ἑκουσιασμοί for MT עַמְּךָ נְדָבֹת at Ps. 110 (109). 3, or his οἴσουσιν for יְאָתָיוּ at Ps. 68 (67). 32. While this could be ascribed to poor discrimination of vowels later clearly separated in MT, another explanation is possible: the renderings may be attributed to Aquila's etymologizing technique. This technique, by concentrating on the consonantal shape of words, tended to depreciate the discriminatory importance of the vocalization. With these qualifications, however, and with adequate understanding of the translation techniques, the renderings of Aquila and others often support the vocalization of MT against any alternative grossly different in its semantic effects.

Secondly, evidence may be found in the transcriptions of Hebrew in Greek or Latin scripts. Aquila can cite quite out-of-the-way words in forms close to MT, e.g. Isa. 60. 13 θαδααρ καὶ θαασουρ (תִּדְהָר וּתְאַשּׁוּר). The second column of the Hexapla wrote Ps. 46 (45). 1-3 as follows:[1]

λαμανασση λαβνηκορ αλ αλμωθ σιρ ελωειμ λανου μασε ουοζ εζρ βσαρωθ νεμσα μωδ αλ χεν λω νιρα βααμιρ ααρς ουβαμωτ αριμ βλεβ ιαμιμ.

A high proportion of vowels are very close to MT.

Similarly, Jerome has many words which suggest a firm tradition of vocalization.[2] The following are taken from the early chapters of Genesis: bresith (בראשׁית), eden (עדן), meccedem (מקדם), hissa (אשׁה), arom (ערום), thardema (תרדמה), hatath (חטאת). Here is a complete sentence (Gen. 4. 15):

MT ויאמר לו יהוה לכן כל־הרג קין שׁבעתים יקם

Jerome: *uaiomer lo adonai lochen chol oreg cain sobathaim ioccamo*

There is, indeed, reason to inquire about the phonetic basis of some of these words (e.g. *sobathaim, ioccamo*); but they do not support any claim that vagaries of vocalization were such as to produce any widespread *semantic* confusion.

Jerome has a comment on the word דבר at Jer. 9. 21, which has often been quoted as evidence for the absence of vocalization.[3] He writes:

uerbum Hebraicum, quod tribus litteris scribitur 'daleth, beth, res'— uocales enim in medio non habet—pro consequentia et legentis arbitrio si legetur 'dabar' 'sermonem' significat, si 'deber' 'mortem', si 'dabber' 'loquere'.

From what has already been said, we are in a position to see this remark in a wider context. Jerome's remarks cannot be universalized into the conception that in vocalizing the consonantal text every man did that which was right in his own eyes. It is by no

[1] Quoted after Swete, *Introduction*, p. 62.
[2] On Jerome's use and analysis of Hebrew see my articles in *BJRL* xlix (1966–7) 281–302 and *JSS* xii (1967) 1–36.
[3] e.g. B. J. Roberts, *Text and Versions*, p. 49.

means normal for him to offer us a choice between every possible vocalization of a consonant sequence; his normal procedure is to give a vocalized transcription without any sign of hesitation. At Jer. 9. 21 Jerome is facing a particular problem, i.e. that the earlier translators had been divided. The original LXX had missed out the word altogether, in accordance with its common tendency to abbreviate the text in Jeremiah. The Hexapla added θανάτῳ, which came from Theodotion. Aquila and Symmachus had λάλησον (= MT). Thus translations already existing had provided for two of the three possibilities which Jerome enumerates.[1] For this reason (and perhaps some other reason which we do not know) he mentions the possibility that the written characters can be construed in these different ways. The observation therefore does not represent either Jerome's normal practice or that normal in his own time. We may add that Jerome may very probably have known, and been influenced in his remarks here by, the practice of the *al-tiqre* interpretation,[2] which was certainly current in the Jewry of his time, but which, as we have seen, by no means implies any uncertainty in the tradition of vocalization.

That the temptation to use for literary or homiletic effect other vocalizations which are theoretically possible and which provide attractive extra meanings or levels of meaning (which, as we have seen, is the essence of the *al-tiqre* interpretation) was known to Jerome, can be seen from examples like his handling of רֹעִים at Jer. 6. 3.[3] If the word is read as *reim* it will mean 'lovers'; read as *roim*, it will mean 'shepherds'—*satis eleganter*, Jerome remarks, revealing the literary appreciation which he has of the double meaning. For in the previous verse (6. 2) Zion has been compared to a beautiful woman who attracts lovers, while now (v. 3) we hear of the gathering of shepherds for the attack on the city. Thus the alternative vocalization is a fancy which suggests an additional way in which two sides of a metaphor are linked. Jerome knew perfectly well that רֹעִים meant 'shepherds' and was vocalized as *roim*; this is fixed by the following עֶדְרֵיהֶם, and the versions, including Jerome's own, took it so.

The striking difference made by gross variations in implied

---

[1] Cf. also Hab. 3. 5, where a similar discussion by Jerome notes the LXX λόγος for דָּבָר, but Aq. λοιμός.

[2] See above, pp. 45 f., and below, p. 214.

[3] Text in *CC* Series Latina, lxxiv, pp. 63 f.

vocalization can be seen well in the Psalms, where Jerome's own translations represent, firstly, a version remote from MT, and, secondly, one close to it. This is Ps. 102 (101). 24 f:

(i) LXX ἀπεκρίθη αὐτῷ ἐν ὁδῷ ἰσχύος αὐτοῦ
τὴν ὀλιγότητα τῶν ἡμερῶν μου ἀνάγγειλόν μοι.

Psalt. Gall.

respondit ei in uia uirtutis suae
paucitatem dierum meorum nuntia mihi.

(ii) Symmachus

ἐκάκωσεν ἐν ὁδῷ τὴν ἰσχύν μου
ἐκολόβωσε τὰς ἡμέρας μου. ἐρῶ, ὁ θεός μου . . .

Psalt. iuxta Hebr.

adflixit in uia fortitudinem meam,
adbreuiauit dies meos. dicam: deus meus. . .

The Hebrew implied is:

(i) עָנָה בְדֶרֶךְ כֹּחוֹ קִצַּר יָמַי אֶמֹר אֵלַי׃

(ii) עָנָה בַדֶרֶךְ כֹּחוֹ (ק׳ כֹּחִי) קִצַּר יָמָי : אֹמַר אֵלַי

The vocalization implied by Symmachus and the *iuxta Hebraeos* is semantically equivalent with the MT and departs wholly from the approach of LXX, though the latter can be attached to exactly the same consonantal text.[1]

Similar remarks may be made about the Talmudic evidence. Here is *Baba Bathra* 21a–b, which deserves to be quoted in full, and is one of the passages commonly cited to show that vocalization signs were not yet in use:[2]

It is written: *for Joab and all Israel remained there until he had cut off every male in Edom* (I Kings 11. 16). When Joab came before David, the latter said to him: Why have you acted thus [i.e. killed only the males]? He replied: Because it is written: *Thou shalt blot out the males* (זָכָר) *of Amalek* (Deut. 25. 19). Said David: But WE read, *the remembrance of* (זֵכֶר) *Amalek*. He replied: I was taught to say זָכָר. He [Joab]

---

[1] See Gordis, *Biblical Text*, p. 59, who cites it as a passage where the Gallican Psalter 'substantiates beyond the shadow of a doubt a full verse and more of our Massoretic Text and yet has not one word in common with it!' The reconstructed pointing for LXX is that of Gordis.

[2] Quoted here after the Soncino version. The passage is mentioned by Roberts, *Text and Versions*, p. 49.

then went to his teacher and asked: How didst thou teach me to read? He replied: זָכָר. Thereupon Joab drew his sword and threatened to kill him. Why do you do this? asked the teacher. He replied: because it is written: *Cursed be he that doeth the work of the law negligently.* He said to him: Be satisfied that I am cursed. To which Joab rejoined: [It also says] *Cursed be he that keepeth back his sword from blood.* According to one report, he killed him; according to another, he did not kill him.

This passage not only shows that at the time no system of vowel points existed. It also shows that a reader of the biblical text was understood to receive the vocalization from a 'teacher', who himself in turn received it from the tradition of teachers before him. This is, after all, not entirely unlike the situation in modern English, another language in which the orthography represents the linguistic realities with at least as little precision as the representation of Hebrew in unpointed script. Children therefore learn at school the spelling and pronunciation, i.e. the socially accepted linkage between the language system and the writing system. In the situation of the Talmudic legend the reader stood within a tradition, even if more than one such tradition existed, and did not invent the vocalization for himself. This need for teaching and learning was perpetuated in Jewish usage even after the vocalization was written, because the synagogue practice is still to read from an unpointed text.

Moreover, the passage shows that a pronunciation tradition agreeing with the later Massoretic marking was already in existence. The play in the legend on זֵכֶר and זָכָר is a midrashic device very similar in type to the *al-tiqre* interpretations; and these, as we have seen, are not evidence that the received text was not in existence or was in any way in doubt. David's reading, characteristically, was the same as the Massoretic.[1]

Some discussion should now be given to Kahle's well-known theory according to which the Massoretes made substantial innovations or restorations in the grammar of Hebrew.

The three points of Kahle's argument are the following. Firstly, for centuries before their time the laryngals or gutturals were not

---

[1] It is slightly misleading when Roberts, p. 49, says that 'it is significant that the argument was settled, not by resorting to textual study, but by an authoritative statement of exegesis'. More correctly, there never was any argument at all, but only a legendary story built up on the similarities and differences of two texts, with the familiar device of a change of vowels worked into a narrative form.

pronounced; the evidence for this is found in transcriptions, statements by Jerome and so on. The Massoretes made every guttural carry a consonantal value, followed by its own vowel. Secondly, and on the basis of similar sources, plus non-Tiberian punctuation and certain considerations of comparative philology, he held that the 2nd person pronoun suffix was /-ak/, and the Massoretes altered this to /-ᵉka/. Thirdly, in the MT the six letters *bgdkpt* have a double pronunciation, but according to Kahle there is no earlier evidence of this. The double pronunciation fixed by the Massoretes 'was earlier completely unknown to the most authoritative Jewish circles'.[1]

Now if Kahle was factually right in claiming that these changes were made by the Massoretes, it is conceivable that certain of them might produce or contribute to confusions and losses of important distinctions, and thus bring about the mistakes concerning the sense of a word which only a philological treatment can disentangle.

These possibilities are for the present, however, no more than simple theory. In my long list of philological treatments I have not found examples which attributed the loss of understanding of the text to the specific changes upon which Kahle has laid so much weight. Conversely, we may say, philological treatment has not so far confirmed the hypothesis of Kahle by producing solutions the explanation of which would be assisted by his hypothesis.

The double pronunciation of *bgdkpt* is not important for our present problem. The difference is non-phonemic and the two possibilities are allophonic;[2] the phoneme is realized in one form or the other, determined by position. Taken alone it is not of great semantic importance. This may, indeed, be one reason why some early transcriptions ignored the matter; another reason is the defectiveness of transcriptions in the writing systems of Greek and Latin, in which the sets of possible phonemes and allophones are very different from those of Hebrew.[3]

Thus, though Kahle's view that the Massoretes were linguistic innovators has had great influence, the innovations alleged by him, even if true, are not such as to prove that the vocalization is *generally* arbitrary, and especially so in its effect on meaning. Rather, they are a group of limited alterations which in themselves could not be

---

[1] *Cairo Geniza*, p. 182.
[2] Morag, *Vocalization Systems*, p. 24 and note.
[3] See my article in *JSS* xii (1967) 1–36, especially pp. 9–13.

responsible for large-scale changes of vocalization, intended to produce a particular sense. Thus the position I have argued is not in itself affected if Kahle's views are correct.

In any case these views may be mistaken; they were disputed when they were first announced, and important arguments have recently been directed against them.[1] Views of the Massoretic activity based on them must now be reconsidered.

Moreover, philological considerations themselves raise certain difficulties against the conception of the Massoretes as men who, often ignorant of the older state of the Hebrew language, vocalized it to fit their own conceptions of the meaning of the text. One such consideration is offered by those philological treatments in which the word studied is pointed anomalously in relation to the normal Massoretic procedure. In such cases the existing pointing fits with and supports the philological treatments, and can hardly be regarded as a screen of normalization cast over an ignorance of the meaning. A good example is דְּעָה at Prov. 24. 14, which has been interpreted as meaning 'call' or 'seek'.[2] If this was the familiar verb יד‎ע 'know', then the vocalization is anomalous; GK (§ 48 l) is at pains to discuss it, and has no good analogy to offer. If the verb is a דעה 'call' or the like, the anomaly of the form is much less. But if we accept this solution, we must also accept one of two alternatives: either that the Massoretes actually knew the right sense here, or that, though they took the word to be a form from ידע 'know' (or simply did not analyse it semantically at all), they did *not* normalize its punctuation into what would be expected under their own usual procedure.

A similar case is the word תָּרְמָה 'treachery'.[3] The anomaly which made this a difficulty in the first place lay in the vocalization, which did not conform to usual MT patterns. The Accadian parallel advanced by Dossin, if right, confirms the Massoretic vocalization. If the philological explanation is right, then the Massoretes refrained from interfering with the vocalization of a word which was abnormal.

In addition to the existence of anomalies among the forms of

---

[1] See in particular the (in my opinion devastating) criticisms of Kutscher, *JSS* x (1965) 21–51; also, *inter alia*, Goshen-Gottstein in *ScrH* iv (1958) 117 f., and 'The Tiberian Bible Text', esp. pp. 90 ff.

[2] Cf. above, pp. 23 ff.

[3] Index, no. 299. On the anomaly see Moore, *Judges* (ICC), p. 259; 'an unexampled and really inconceivable type of noun'.

MT the apparent linguistic antiquity of many such forms has to be taken into account. Wherever comparative philology succeeds in fitting data from the MT into a comparative framework which also accommodates material from other Semitic languages, this success is a testimony to the general plausibility of the tradition of MT.[1] Phenomena like the *waw* consecutive were doubtless often marked wrongly in detail; but the general nature of the phenomenon would hardly be known to us if the Massoretes had not registered it adequately in many places, though it was something they could not possibly have known about from the contemporary linguistic environment. A vast amount of the detail in our comparative grammars presumes and permits an affirmation of the linguistic credibility of the work of the Massoretes.

(5) *Conclusions*

The traditional philology gave little place to the antiquity of a liturgical style of reading a sacred literature such as the Bible. Much philological study has preferred to find certainty in comparative evidence, rather than in the analysis of received streams of tradition, and has been sceptical towards the tradition of reading. But modern linguistic methods have reopened the question, and striking results have been achieved by the work of Morag on the reading traditions of the Yemenite Jews.[2] It is by no means true, as scholarly prejudice has often supposed, that such traditions are 'artificial'—which would mean, presumably, the product of factors unconnected with, and irrelevant to, the original situation of the literature being read. The agreement between certain Yemenite phonetic features and elements in the Babylonian system of pointing, the fact that the Yemenites have different pronunciations for their reading of the Bible and their reading of the Mishnah, and the existence in their reading of biblical Hebrew of phones non-existent in their own Arabic vernacular, all suggest the presence of valuable historical evidence.

[1] This argument is logically the same as that which Bergsträsser is said to have made when Kahle first announced his theory of an innovating activity by the Massoretes. The innovators, Bergsträsser argued, must in that case at least have read Brockelmann's smaller comparative grammar; how else could the innovations have been reconcilable with use in a comparative reconstruction? See Hempel in *ZAW* lxi (1945–8) 251; Kutscher in *JSS* x (1965) 43.

[2] S. Morag, העברית שבפי יהודי תימן (Jerusalem, 1963). See review article by E. Y. Kutscher in *JSS* xi (1966) 217–25.

Morag has discussed the question whether such traditions were stabilized at a time when the original language was still a living one. Such may be the case, he has suggested,[1] when three conditions are fulfilled:

(a) that the system used is stable and consistent in itself;

(b) that it does not conform to features known in the vernacular of the time;

(c) that its structural relation to other forms of the same language group is capable of formulation in terms of historical linguistics.

The growth and preservation of a liturgical reading tradition is no doubt a special case within linguistic history; but its special character by no means makes it unrelatable to the general processes of linguistic change: only the conditions for such change are peculiar. If, then, the Massoretes registered in their pointing the state of such a tradition in their own time, there is no reason to doubt that this tradition was connected with earlier stages of the Hebrew language by lines of development analogous to other known processes of linguistic change.

In preference to the sharp distinction between a reliable consonantal text and an unreliable vocalization, one might rather hold that the two aspects were interdependent. For example, graphic error in the written text has sometimes been the occasion for confusions in the vocalization. I would take this to be so in the parallel texts quoted above, where Ps. 18. 11 וַיֵּדֶא is likely to be the right text.[2] The easy graphic error וַיֵּרָא (II Sam. 22. 11) then generates the vocalization וַיֵּרָא which is natural to this writing.[3] This leads towards a textual rather than a philological solution; indeed, what we are saying is only what was logically implied in the traditional textual criticism. Moreover, this argument suggests that it is quite wrong to believe in a reliable consonantal text later wrongly vocalized through misunderstanding. The two are interdependent, and an erroneous writing may sometimes generate a vocalization which is suitable for that writing.[4]

---

[1] In a paper given to the International Conference on Semitic Studies, Jerusalem, 1965.   [2] See above, pp. 192 f.

[3] Cf. similar remarks about the case of דְּכִיר, above, p. 202.

[4] If we suppose a stage at which the /d/ and /r/ were marked by the same grapheme, then the case would be one of error in interpretation of a grapheme which had two phonemic values.

Sometimes we can see how analogy with another biblical passage could have caused a new but wrong vocalization. One of the most convincing philological treatments is Ginsberg's suggestion that at Prov. 26. 23, where MT has

$$\text{כֶּסֶף סִיגִים מְצֻפֶּה עַל־חָרֶשׂ}$$

we should read rather כספסגים 'like glaze', as in Ugaritic *spsg*, itself from Hittite or paralleled in Hittite. This gives a sense of: 'like glaze set over an earthen vessel . . .'. The close association of כֶּסֶף 'silver' with סִיגִים in several other passages (Isa. 1. 22, Ezek. 22. 18, and above all Prov. 25. 4, just a little before our passage) may easily have suggested the reading of MT, once the original ספסג was forgotten. Even here a graphic disturbance (shift of word division) was probably included in the corruption.

Where wrong readings of the text have grown up, the indications are that we should generally attribute them not to the ignorance of late Massoretes but to a much earlier stage in the tradition. The following points should be considered:

(*a*) The earlier period (let us say, before the second century A.D.) was the time in which wide variations in the written text still existed. These are not mere scribal errors, i.e. failures to copy correctly a text already fixed in its letter. The state was a much more fluid one, with different orthographies and different ways of reading. It is comparatively easy to picture how false readings may have arisen, where, for instance, a text written in one orthography is construed as if it had been written in another; or, again, where a text previously known orally came to be written down in the conditions of varying orthographies. All this was before the selection of one text-type limited the variety which gave licence to error. We may contrast the great vagaries in the Hebrew text of Sirach, a book which presumably did not enjoy the stability accorded by this kind of official status for the text.

(*b*) Wrong vocalizations might well arise if a work had circulation as a written document in certain narrow circles for some time before it came to be read in the wider community, i.e. as a holy text in the synagogue. Even if an esoteric group, such as a circle of prophetic disciples, had known the right reading of a text, this knowledge of theirs might fail to be passed on to the wider public; and in a more extreme case, a book might be taken up as a written document, without any mediation of a tradition of reading (must not this have happened to Josiah's Book of the Law?). Once a document had come to be generally accepted reading in the synagogue, a careful transmission of readings would begin. The absence of an efflorescence of substantial variants in the centuries from the second to the eighth or ninth confirms this. The early stage provides a far more plausible setting for confusions of vocalization than the time of the Massoretes, or even Talmudic times, where there already was a very firm tradition of reading.

(c) Something would depend on the degree to which the status of 'Scripture' at the times concerned was deemed to imply close and exact respect for the letter of the text. Such close and exact respect, when applied at points where the text had in fact already suffered graphic error, might be the origin of forced vocalizations.

(d) The testimony of the versions very often agrees with this. It is often, and rightly, observed in philological treatments that the versions like LXX, even if they understand the text wrongly, testify to the same text as MT; and, where this text is taken to be in error, it implies that the origin of the error was early, possibly going back to several centuries B.C. To take the example of Prov. 26. 23 studied just above, the vocalization and division כֶּסֶף סִיגִים can hardly be ascribed to 'the Massoretes'; the various versions, though otherwise differing, are clear that the word is 'silver'. The text was already like MT in this respect, at a time the best part of a thousand years before the Massoretes.

(e) This suggestion may also help to deal with a question which may have arisen from our discussion of the vocalization. Since the pronunciation of Hebrew changed, is it not likely that the Massoretic vocalization is increasingly unreliable the older the text we are considering? Will there not be varying degrees of reliability in the vocalization, and perhaps in the text generally, between the Song of Deborah, the sayings of Jeremiah, and the Hebrew parts of Daniel?

The most drastic changes probably took place quite early within the Old Testament period itself. Phonetic and grammatical change may have caused obscurity in the Song of Deborah, but such changes had probably already done their work by the time of Jeremiah. A simple progression along a time scale therefore does not at all measure correctly the degree of change. The changes in question have the character rather of quanta, discrete steps of change. To take an obvious example, it is possible that the Song of

Deborah had vocalic inflexional endings; any disorganization caused by the loss of these took place early, and probably took place in one major step. On the other hand, since some of the confusion of vocalization has arisen from the graphic form of the text, a late text like the Hebrew Daniel is not thereby necessarily particularly lacking in confusion.

It is now time to sum up the issues involved in the evaluation of the Massoretic vocalization stated or implied by so many philological treatments. The following general estimates seem at present to be possible.

Firstly, no one doubts that the traditional vocalization is subject to error and may deserve emendation by scholars under the safeguard of proper consideration of the factors involved. There is no evidence, however, that entitles us to carry this so far that we begin to regard the vocalization as entirely arbitrary or chaotic and therefore subject to alteration on no greater basis than the liking of the modern scholar. The vocalization is historical evidence just as other aspects of the text are; it has to be explained and not merely altered. In very few cases examined by me have philological treatments given any full and adequate explanation of the vocalization.

Secondly, not only is the vocalization historical evidence formed in the transmission of the text, like the consonantal or written text; but it also is a part of the text which goes back to origins long before the graphic marking of the vocalization by the Massoretes began. This does not mean that the vocalization is 'right'. It does mean that it has to be investigated in relation to the modes of interpretation existing in Israel from early post-biblical times on; and only through reference to the history of these modes can we determine whether the vocalization is a natural linguistic growth from earlier stages.

Thirdly, philologists in their constant appeal to the cognate languages, when it is linked with a low evaluation of the vocalization of Hebrew, often fail to realize how much their own system of knowledge depends upon and draws upon the Massoretic vocalization of Hebrew, both directly in that they repeatedly continue to quote it as if it were reliable, and indirectly in that the modern organizations of Hebrew grammar are themselves lineal descendants from the earlier Hebrew grammar; and this earlier grammar succeeded in making order out of the chaos of extant Hebrew forms only because it carefully followed the Massoretic vocalization as a guide. The tendency to ignore the Massoretic vocalization is a tendency to bring Hebrew into the category of languages such as Ugaritic where no intermediate tradition of pronunciation exists. But the possibility of organizing a scientific study of these languages depends, perhaps more than has been realized, upon the existence of the languages where an intermediate tradition of pronunciation does exist.

All in all, of the various aspects in which one has to evaluate modern philological treatments of the Old Testament text, the position of the vocalization appears to be the most unsatisfactory. Many of the necessary preliminary studies have not been done; adequate proofs are seldom given; and the wide learning of comparative philology has often failed to give precision and care to the establishment with evidence of the position it accords to the Massoretes. In future, philological treatments will have to account for what the Massoretes did, and not simply push it aside as the product of ignorance.

IX

LATE HEBREW AND THE LOSS OF VOCABULARY

PHILOLOGICAL treatments imply that our difficulties have arisen because words or their meanings came to be forgotten; correspondingly, the vocabulary of Hebrew in biblical times must have been larger than has normally been recognized. In order to consider these implications, and to study the method of philological treatments properly, we have to examine the vocabulary of post-biblical Hebrew.

In such an examination there are a number of different aspects, and, since these are commonly interlinked in the discussion of any single example, I shall first mention five, and thereafter go on to give illustrations which will involve some or all of them. The aspects are the following:

(1) Most obviously, the disuse of a word in late times may be the reason why its meaning ceased to be understood. If this is so, the sense has to be recovered from cognate languages precisely because within Hebrew itself it was lost from consciousness at a relatively early date. This argument is particularly persuasive, of course, in the case of those words which (*a*) are very rare within the Old Testament itself, or (*b*) occur only in very early sources within it, or (*c*) occur only in certain very specialized contexts within it.

The situation is the same if a word, instead of ceasing to be used in later Hebrew, came to be used with a different sense. This also might explain why the older meaning came to be forgotten.

In neither of its forms, however, can this argument be used without some examination of the evidence of post-biblical Hebrew. One cannot *assume* that disuse in late Hebrew provides an argument for the loss of understanding of a word unless one has first examined the resources of the post-biblical vocabulary, in order to see how far they included words similar to or related to the biblical word in question.

Our present reference works do not make this task easy for us. The dictionaries of biblical Hebrew generally make no effort to tell us about the history and currency of items after biblical times, with some exception made only for Sirach and the Qumran texts. The dictionaries of post-biblical Hebrew, on the other hand, suffer from some defects in their planning, their comprehensiveness, and their degree of scientific discrimination. The use of these reference works is in any case made more uncertain for many biblical students by their poor training and experience in post-biblical texts. These difficulties, however, do not remove, but actually increase, the importance of a proper consultation of post-biblical Hebrew for any study of the transmission of linguistic understanding.

(2) Secondly, a number of philological treatments do in fact make their identification of obscure biblical words through appeal to post-biblical Hebrew, or else include post-biblical Hebrew evidence in addition to evidence from cognate languages. It may be held that a treatment which can quote post-biblical Hebrew evidence has more to be said for it than one which can quote evidence only from other languages. At least it has succeeded in showing that the word or the root in question did at some time exist in Hebrew. It is thus free, other things being equal, from the suspicion that the word and meaning appealed to are entirely an idiosyncrasy of the vocabulary of another language; and it does not require to use the doubtful principle that anything which occurs in any Semitic language may be supposed to have occurred in Hebrew. In this respect the use of post-biblical Hebrew evidence appears to be a source of strength.

Against this, however, we have to weigh another consideration. If late Hebrew evidence for our word is readily available, and affords a sense which clarifies the biblical passage, it is no longer quite so easy to see how a failure in understanding took place and led to a loss of knowledge of the sense of the biblical word; thus some additional explanation may be required. Relatedness to a post-biblical Hebrew phenomenon is a kind of evidence which may work negatively as well as positively.

(3) Thirdly, as we have seen, philological treatments commonly tend to enlarge the vocabulary of Hebrew, and it has been argued that the vocabulary must, for all the purposes of everyday life, have been very much larger than that which is preserved in the Bible. I

think that this is certainly true, but that its bearing on our present discussion has not commonly been rightly seen.

The argument is that there are many objects which the Israelites had, and actions which they did, in biblical times which are not mentioned in the Bible and for which we therefore do not know the name in biblical Hebrew. Thus Driver, for example, has repeatedly emphasized that Hebrew vocabulary was larger than has previously been recognized.[1] It is, he urges, mistaken 'to consider that which is preserved in the MT sufficient even for the limited needs of daily life in ancient Palestine'.[2] Albright has stated that 'the known biblical Hebrew vocabulary cannot represent over a fifth of the total stock of North-west Semitic words used between 1400 and 400 B.C.'[3]

In a sense, probably no one would doubt this. The Bible is a very limited segment of all that was said in ancient Hebrew. Words have been found in our quite small inscriptional material which were certainly normal Hebrew but which do not appear in the Bible. The אשוח or אשיח which appears in Moabite in the Mesha‘ inscription, and in later Hebrew at Sir. 50. 3, meaning 'reservoir', was surely normal Hebrew. The form פים at I Sam. 13. 21 was not recognized, and the text was regarded as corrupt, until quite recent times, when the evidence of artefacts showed that this was the name of a weight, 'pim' or the like. Nevertheless modern discoveries of extra-biblical documents earlier than the Mishnaic period should make us cautious about claiming that a very large additional vocabulary is likely quite easily to be found. Though Palestinian inscriptions, the Hebrew Sirach, and the Qumran documents have produced some new words, their number should not be exaggerated; it is in fact quite limited.

Good examples from Sirach are שרק 'shine' (43. 9; 50. 7; cf. Arab. 'ašraqa), רצד 'observe' (14. 22; cf. Arab. raṣada) and לקות 'punishment' (9. 4; cf. the place-name Eltekeh, which indeed implies rather a sense of 'meet'). The Dead Sea Scrolls also show only a limited number of words of Semitic origin not found in the Bible; a good example is the phrase אוחזי אבות 'intercessors', known in Syriac and going back to Accadian.[4] Driver himself

---

[1] e.g. *JTS* xxxi (1930) 275.
[2] *JBL* lxviii (1949) 57 f.
[3] In Peake's *Commentary on the Bible*, 2nd ed. (1962), p. 62.
[4] For discussion see Wernberg-Møller, p. 53.

Q

asserts only that 'a very few' words require explanation from other languages; he identifies among others a דְּנַת 'vehemence' (with Accadian cognate), a שָׁאוֹן 'purpose' (cf. Arab. *šā'a*), and an עֵין 'company, group'.[1] Of other new words found in the Qumran documents, a number are not of Semitic origin, e.g. נֶחְשִׁיר, usually understood as 'hunting, pursuit'.[2] In some cases the interpretation is itself highly controversial. Anyway, it cannot be said that the discovery of fresh documentary evidence has produced a *large* number of words not already known in biblical vocabulary.

It nevertheless remains true that we should expect some considerable number of words for things and actions not mentioned in the Bible, and the lack of such in Sirach and at Qumran could conceivably be accounted for on the ground that these documents are devoted to the same general kind of subject matter which is found in the Bible. Now post-biblical Hebrew contains a large number of just such words, i.e. names for things which are not named in biblical Hebrew. It is generally probable that the words designating such objects in the Mishnah or the Talmud are also the words which were used in biblical times, unless there is some particular reason to the contrary. Doubtless some of these words are new formations, replacing an older word of which we have no knowledge; but it remains probable that many of them are old. I have in mind such words as כָּבֵשׁ 'preserves', נַחַר 'jetty', זוֹל 'cheapness', חֲטֶרֶת 'hump', צְלֶקֶת 'scar', שָׁעָה 'hour',[3] גָּפֶה 'stone fence', and גְּבָבָה 'rakings'.

Thus, in so far as the argument for philological treatments involves the appeal to objects and actions which are not named in the Bible, we should expect it fairly frequently to point to the language of Mishnah and Talmud as a source of evidence—always providing, of course, the necessary safeguards against mistaken use of words for processes which were technologically new in the Hellenistic period, or other innovations of post-biblical times, such as new religious or political developments.

Here, however, we come to another important distinction.

---

[1] See Driver, *The Judaean Scrolls*, p. 435. The suggestion of עֵין (or עוֹן) by Yalon is discussed by Wernberg-Møller, p. 59. Even among the suggestions listed by Driver, not many have found general agreement among scholars.

[2] Cf. de Menasce, *VT* vi (1956) 213 f. Rabin, *Orientalia* xxxii (1963) 132 f., interprets it rather as 'terror, panic'.

[3] On this word see my *Biblical Words for Time*, pp. 102 ff.

Though the point we have just made justifies us in expecting that research will make more extensive the Hebrew vocabulary known to us, this does not apply to quite any area of that vocabulary. It applies well, as we have seen, to objects for which we do not have a name in the Bible. It does not, however, apply so well to objects or actions for which we already have a name, or even two or three roughly synonymous names, in the Bible. In point of fact, in the philological treatments which I have collected, not a large proportion refer to objects or actions for which we hitherto have not known the name. On the contrary, the larger proportion have reference to objects or actions for which names are already well known.

Thus the argument that the vocabulary of ancient Hebrew must have been much larger than is known from the biblical text, while undeniable in itself and in theory, does not serve to justify a particularly large number of the new identifications of words which philological treatments have produced. The validity of the argument depends on the semantic field of the words concerned. For the semantic fields which were primarily involved in biblical literature (particularly religion and the human states and institutions connected with it) it is quite possible on the contrary that biblical usage exploited almost all of the lexical resources which were available.

(4) Fourthly, we have the problem of detecting what I shall call 'restorations' in the post-biblical literature. When a word used in biblical Hebrew appears also in post-biblical material, this may mean that a continuity of general usage existed throughout both periods. It may, however, also mean that a word found in the biblical text has been taken up and renewed in later literature, on the basis not of continuity in general usage but of reference solely to the limited biblical texts where the word occurs. The word is thus one quoted, and from this quotation it enters into a new lease of life. The sense which it now has, however, is not necessarily identical with that meant by the author in the original biblical milieu. On the contrary, it may be a sense attached solely to an occurrence in the biblical text as it was later read and understood; and this text may have been affected by graphic accidents and errors of transmission which have nothing to do with the continuity of linguistic meaning.

It may not be easy to decide in a post-biblical text whether restoration of this kind has taken place. Two criteria may be helpful: firstly, literary type, and secondly, frequency of occurrence.

Restorations, in the sense here intended, are most common in a highly allusive style, in which deliberate arcane reference is made to known biblical locutions. Such locutions may become technical in an esoteric current of exegesis, or may be cultivated in a learned poetic style. The Qumran hymns and books of discipline, and the type of liturgical poem called *piyyuṭ*, are examples. If the stylistic setting is more conversational and straightforward, the likelihood of such restorations is somewhat lower.

Frequency of occurrence is a criterion which more or less follows from the above. If a usage occurs with some frequency in the large late Jewish literature, it is on the whole less likely that an arcane reference to a particular biblical text is being made. This is not a *certain* criterion, for a usage might arise by restoration and then spread so as to become popular; but at least it is a consideration worth some weight.

(5) A fifth consideration is the influence of Aramaic. Those Jews who, in post-biblical times, were in a position to discuss the meaning of biblical words and to relate them to current usage would generally know Aramaic as well as Hebrew. Thus, for the purpose of studying the transmission of understanding and the loss of understanding, similarities between biblical words and Jewish Aramaic words have to be taken into account in the same way as similarities between biblical and post-biblical Hebrew. A distinction should also be made between types of Aramaic which were probably current among Jews and types which were not; lexical idiosyncrasies of the latter should not usually be brought into this comparison.

These then are the five general considerations which should be borne in mind. I shall now proceed to discuss some examples in which one or more can be seen in practice. I shall first of all exemplify some restorations, since of the various considerations this is the one which is most easily isolated from the others.

A good example is the word חלכה or חלכאים which occurs thrice in the difficult Ps. 10.[1] BDB doubted the text, but also tried an explanation of the word as related to an Arabic *ḥalaka* 'be

---

[1] The division of the word into two parts, חֵיל כָּאִים, by the Qere at Ps. 10. 10 is an example of what might begin as a graphic change but achieve an effect on later linguistic restorations, as suggested above, p. 218.

black', and passing from there into the sense 'unfortunate'. This is itself not a difficult semantic shift, being paralleled by קדר for example. KB has even greater doubts, and declared the word to be 'unexplained'. Komlos suggested that the ל was a formative element, and derived the word from חַכָּה 'hook'.[1] There continues to be some doubt about the sense and etymology.

Now the Qumran hymns show four examples of this word (1QH 3. 25, 26; 4. 25, 35). For the most part scholars seem to take the sense to be something near the 'unfortunate' of BDB, but make it perhaps a little stronger. Mansoor, on the other hand, pointing out that the parallelism at 3. 25 and 4. 35 is with 'the wicked', thinks that the sense is 'wicked, tyrants'.[2]

Even if we can certainly work out what the word means in the scrolls, we do not thereby necessarily show that this was the sense in the Bible. At several places in the scrolls it seems likely that a particularly obscure word or phrase in the Bible is picked up and given a heavily loaded sense; and one of the reasons for this may be precisely that the word was so enigmatic in the first place. This is likely to be done by any exegetical technique which holds the very details of the Bible to contain mysterious, yet quite specific, references to incidents and persons of a later time.

Meanings may have changed during the long history of use of the texts. Firstly, if it is true that certain stock parallelisms were held in common with pre-Israelite poetry, it is possible that items which are formally identical with Canaanite or Ugaritic materials may nevertheless have come to be understood and used with another sense in Hebrew. Secondly, within Hebrew itself, in texts like the Psalms which were used over a long period, it is possible that another sense has sometimes taken the place of that originally meant, and that homonyms which we can distinguish philologically may have come to contaminate the sense of one another.[3] Where literature was in continual use, like the Psalms, therefore, it is an oversimplification to suppose that there is *one* Hebrew meaning which has to be found. Changes of meaning may have taken place not only as biblical texts came to be interpreted in post-biblical times, but

---

[1] In *JSS* ii (1957) 243–6.   [2] Mansoor in *VTS* ix (1963) 316.

[3] Thus the words ירה 'throw' and ירה 'instruct', though probably philologically distinguishable (so GB, pp. 317 f.; KB, pp. 402 f., but not BDB, p. 434b; the older tradition is to derive the latter sense from the former in the meaning of throwing or casting lots), may have come to contaminate each other in the course of time, especially through certain forms such as תורה.

also within biblical times themselves, if these texts were used and re-used over a prolonged period.

Another instance is the חֹזֶה or חָזוּת which occurs only in Isa. 28. 15, 18. A sense of 'agreement, contract, covenant' is suggested by the parallelism with ברית and also by the evidence of most versions (LXX συνθήκας; Vulg. *pactum*; Targum שלם 'peace'; but Syriac *ḥezwā*, perhaps meant as 'vision', and in any case a calque on the Hebrew word). A completely different understanding is found only in the Hexaplar entry ἄλλος· καταφυγήν.[1]

Driver has provided comparative evidence which confirms this sense (ESA *ḥdyt* 'agreement', especially in the phrase *bḥdyt* 'in conformity with'). This seems greatly to surpass the attempts to explain the word, on the basis of the verb חזה 'see', as some kind of prophetic advice (so BDB, p. 302b; GB, p. 221a; KB, p. 285, accepts emendation into חסד for both cases). We may hold it very probable that the versions quoted were right. The word is then cognate with Arabic *ḥ-ḏ-'* 'be opposite' etc., and thus also with the familiar חָזֶה 'breast (of a sacrificial animal)'.

This example is interesting because the meaning has survived into medieval and modern Hebrew. Curiously, however, I do not find a case quotable from the Talmudic period. Perhaps the later Hebrew use is a restoration, prompted by the parallelism with ברית; but if so it is a right restoration. I am on the whole inclined, however, to consider it more likely that the tradition of meaning survived; but, if this is so, I am uncertain how to account for the lack of use in the Talmudic period.

A similar case is the obscure word תָּכּוּ. This *hapax legomenon* occurs only at Deut. 33. 3. BDB, GB, and KB have no explanation of the meaning; *BH*[3] offers the choice of two colossal emendations. The sentence is:

וְהֵם תֻּכּוּ לְרַגְלֶךָ MT

Vulg. *et qui appropinquant pedibus eius*

Now Stummer has pointed out[2] that in a *piyyuṭ* of Yannai (sixth century A.D.?) the verse occurs:

יען תוכה לרגלך ובצדק קרא
על כן לרגלו צדק הוקרא

---

[1] Is this the result of taking the Hebrew word as one related to מחסה, which is translated καταφυγή by LXX at Ps. 45 (46). 2, 103 (104). 18?

[2] Nötscher Festschrift, pp. 265 ff.

meaning perhaps:

> 'because he approached your foot and called in righteousness;
> therefore righteousness is made to meet his foot.'

This may possibly be evidence that the verb was used in a continuity of meaning from biblical times down, and may thus serve
towards a recognition of its actual sense in the biblical text; it may,
on the other hand, be deemed to have been a restoration.[1] In that
case, Yannai belongs to the same tradition which is represented by
Jerome; but this would not mean that this tradition is 'right'.[2]

Again, medieval Hebrew has a verb להק 'gather together', and
the noun לָהָק. The prayer by Qalir for Rosh-ha-Shanah has the
phrase שׁוֹאֲגִים בלהק 'shouting aloud in unison'; similarly,
Saadia writes וְהַמֶּלֶךְ יִקְרָאֶנָּה לעם בַּלְהָקִים. It would seem
likely that this is a restoration (and new formation) on the basis of
the assumed sense of להקת at I Sam. 19. 20.[3]

Two *hapax legomena* which are mentioned elsewhere in this book
are the אַל־תִּרְהוּ of Isa. 44. 8 and the וַיִּנָּהוּ of I Sam. 7. 2.[4]
Both of these occur in later poetry. A *piyyuṭ* published by Dr.
Wallenstein includes the lines:[5]

וְדַבֵּר יְדַבְּרוּ וּבַל יִרְהוּ

מְמַסִּיכֵי רַעַל שִׂדְמוֹתָם

> 'And they will surely speak and not be afraid
> of those who pour confusion (on) their fields.'

A poem ascribed to Saadia[6] includes both of our two words together, and the senses are 'fear' for רהה (here hiphil, 'frighten')
and 'follow obediently' or the like for נהה:

רְאִיתָה צָרֵי לִמְחִתָּה לְכָל־נוֹהֵיהֶם

שֵׁבֶט רוֹדֵיהֶם מְיָרְאֵיהֶם וּמַרְהֵיהֶם

---

[1] For a recent discussion of the evidential value of late (medieval) poetry in
textual criticism see A. Mirsky in *Textus* iii. 159–62.

[2] Another treatment is to read as one word והמתכו and construe as from
מכך 'be low', giving the sense 'they prostrate themselves': so, for instance,
Cross and Freedman, *JBL* lxvii (1948) 200 f.

[3] See above, pp. 25 f.

[4] See above, pp. 6f., 166, 188, and below, 264 f.

[5] Wallenstein, *Piyyuṭim*, p. 26.

[6] Siddur R. Saadia Gaon, p. 417, l. 21.

We may translate:

> 'You have fated the destruction of adversaries along
> with all their followers—(the destruction of) the
> scourge of those who dominate, frighten and terrify them.'

Both of these words, then, have to be considered as possible restorations.

In order to give a full estimate of the nature and course of probable restoration, one would have to trace the development of styles in the use of vocabulary right up to the Middle Ages. Rabin writes:[1]

> When the written use of biblical Hebrew was revived, after a long pause, in the middle ages, all stages of biblical Hebrew served equally as model, with special emphasis upon poetic and rare expressions.

Rabin traces the beginning of this revival of biblical Hebrew to the ninth century.

A possible test for restorations may be the following: if a word is found in both post-exilic and post-biblical sources, the chances for linguistic continuity in use are greater; if the word is found in the Bible only in very early sources, and then not again until late post-biblical times, the likelihood of a restoration is the greater. For example, להקה falls within the latter type.

Having exemplified the problem of restorations, we may now go on to look at other possibilities.

As we have said, the disuse of a word in late times may be a reason why its meaning ceased to be understood. There are a number of ways in which this may have happened.

A difficult example is the history of understanding of ישפיקו at Isa. 2. 6:

$$\text{כִּי מָלְאוּ מִקֶּדֶם . . . וּבְיַלְדֵי נָכְרִים יַשְׂפִּיקוּ:}$$

The root שפק or ספק 'be enough' actually occurs in the Bible (the verb in I Kings 20. 10, a noun form שֶׂפֶק at Job 20. 22), and several cases are found in Sirach, there spelt ספק. The sense 'have enough' is very familiar in later Hebrew, and in Isa. 2. 6 it provides a good parallelism with the other verb מָלְאוּ. Yet most interpreters have rather turned to the somewhat artificial

---

[1] *ScrH* iv (1958) 149.

interpretation as 'strike hands' (i.e. in a bargain), which has some support in Arabic idiom and, with limitations, in the rendering of Symmachus, quoted by Jerome as *et cum filiis alienis applause-runt*. Buchanan Gray,[1] rejecting the sense 'be enough', says that 'the use by Isaiah of a verb with such a history is not very probable'. But it is probable that the LXX *understood* the word as 'be enough' or 'be plentiful', in rendering:

καὶ τέκνα πολλὰ ἀλλόφυλα ἐγενήθη αὐτοῖς.

The Vulgate has *et pueris alienis adhaeserunt*, and this also illustrates the influence of late Hebrew. Jerome writes:

> pro quo scriptum est in Hebraeo, *iesphicu*, quod Hebraei interpretantur, ἐσφηνώθησαν, et nos uertimus, *adhaeserunt*.[2]

The ἐσφηνώθησαν of the 'Hebrew' interpretation seems to depend on the post-biblical verb פְּקְפֵּק 'drive in a wedge' (Jastrow, p. 1211a).[3] It is not clear to me how Jerome got from this to his *adhaeserunt*.

The sense 'strike the hands', already known in antiquity, came from the biblical verb סֶפֶק or שָׂפֵק.

It is interesting that the more obvious late Hebrew sense, that of 'be enough' or 'have enough', which is also the more probable sense philologically,[4] nevertheless did not succeed in maintaining itself in ancient times against other interpretations, one of which also rested on post-biblical Hebrew but on a much less satisfactory basis in it. It may be something in the exegetical tradition of the passage that has caused this. In any case, it is clear that the influence of post-biblical Hebrew did not always work in the way that would seem to us most obvious.

At Hos. 8. 13, MT זִבְחֵי הַבְהָבַי יִזְבָּחוּ, one suggested interpretation follows a post-biblical word הַבְהֵב 'singe, roast light-ly';[5] the meaning would be something like 'burnt-offerings'. At

---

[1] ICC, *Isaiah*, p. 58.

[2] Jerome's *iesphicu* here is another vocalization, which, whatever we say about the *e*, is clearly in agreement grammatically with the hiphil form of MT.

[3] A שׁ, where it is first radical in verbs, is sometimes taken as if it were a pre-formative as in shaphel forms. Cf. Isa. 41. 10 אַל־תִּשְׁתָּע, LXX μὴ πλανῶ—surely a construction as from the common תעה 'go astray'.

[4] This sense is supported for Isa. 2. 6 by Winton Thomas in *ZAW* lxxv (1963) 88 f., and also in KB, p. 928.

[5] Index, no. 103; cf. earlier BDB, p. 396b; GB, p. 172b.

Prov. 30. 15 a similar word could then mean 'burn (with erotic passion)'. Yet it is doubtful if the versions show evidence of influence from the post-biblical word. Renderings with ἀγαπᾶν suggest simply an analysis as from אהב, while those with φέρε φέρε are an analysis as from the exhortation הב, הבה. The Targum's דבחין דמגבן מן אונים 'sacrifices which they collect from extortion', and the Syriac dbḥ' dgbyt',[1] also suggest that the existence of הָבְהַב did not have much influence on the understanding of the passages.

Another example is the Talmudic Hebrew לבוד 'compact, solid', used of the building of walls; Syriac has the corresponding verb, meaning 'thicken, solidify'. Tur-Sinai believes that the Bible had this word. He reads Job 38. 30 as:

$$\text{כָּאֶבֶן מַיִם יִתְחַבָּאוּ וּפְנֵי תְהוֹם יִתְלַבָּדוּ:}$$

and translates:

'The waters are hidden as (behind) stone,
and the face of the sea sticketh together.'

He takes this to mean that there is no hole in the heavenly firmament. Since the MT is יתלכדו, the explanation assumes a consonantal corruption, as also at 41. 9 (but not at Isa. 5. 8). Since, however, לבוד was a technical term in Talmudic law, it is a little difficult to suppose that, if it was originally present in the text, it would fall out through misunderstanding. The evidence of late Hebrew is therefore somewhat unfavourable to the interpretation.

The rare word יקהה 'obedience' occurs only at Gen. 49. 10, Prov. 30. 17. The identification of this word is well established from comparative sources, e.g. both North and South Arabic. Late Hebrew and Jewish Aramaic on the other hand seem to show no trace of continued use. Translations such as LXX προσδοκία, Vulgate exspectatio, probably derive from the likeness to the common קוה 'hope' (Lam. 2. 16 προσδοκᾶν). The only faint association in late Hebrew is with קהה 'faint, long for' (Jastrow, p. 1322a). Yet the Targum with its ישתמעון עממיא וליה seems to indicate that the right sense was known. The complete disuse of a word, perhaps over many centuries, does not seem to have damaged the preservation of its form and sense; even the vocalization is in a credible form, and Rashi pointed out that the

---

[1] Brockelmann, Lexicon Syriacum, p. 100b.

formation is the same as in שִׂמְחַת. The absence of any other
obvious word with which confusion might have arisen may have
assisted its preservation.

We mentioned above[1] the identification by Driver at Jer. 12. 9
of a word צָבוּעַ 'hyena'. In favour of the identification of such a
word, and against the more normal construction as the passive
participle of the verb 'to dye, colour', one or two facts can be
quoted. There is not only the biblical place-name צְבֹעִים,
which has been construed as 'valley of hyenas';[2] there is also the
post-biblical noun צָבוּעַ, commonly taken to be a hyena, leopard,
or other beast.[3] Once again, however, this very fact, while it confirms the likelihood that a word צָבוּעַ for hyena existed in the
biblical period, also makes it harder to understand how the consciousness of this meaning at Jer. 12. 9 was lost if in fact this had
been the right meaning. Not only did the word צָבוּעַ exist, but
some discussion of the attributes of this strange animal is found in
the literature.[4] Moreover, the translation of עַיִט צָבוּעַ by
σπήλαιον ὑαίνης in the LXX here may itself be not a right diag-
nosis of the biblical sense, but a construction derived from awareness of the post-biblical צָבוּעַ.[5]

The possible influence of Aramaic is illustrated in the suggested
identification of a שׁדה 'pour out', with the noun שְׁדִי 'downpour,
outpouring'.

Ezek. 1. 24:   MT   קוֹל־שַׁדַּי   'the voice of the Almighty'
              read   קוֹל־שְׁדִי   'the sound of a downpour'
II Sam. 1. 21: MT שְׂדֵי תְרוּמֹת 'fields of offerings (?)'
              read שְׁדֵי תְהוֹמֹת 'outpourings of the depths'

But if this Hebrew word existed, it is unlikely that interpreters
would lose touch with it, because of the presence of the Aramaic
שׁדי, which is very common. The Aramaic אשׁד also means 'pour
out' e.g. Targ. Mic. 1. 4. In B. Ber. 54b the biblical noun אֶשֶׁד
(Num. 21. 15) is interpreted as 'poured out' (שׁפך); we can be sure
that this Aramaic verb was present in the minds of interpreters.
These considerations make it more difficult to accept the suggestion of a Hebrew שׁדה with the same sense.

---

[1] Cf. above, p. 128.   [2] See BDB, p. 840b.
[3] See Jastrow, p. 1257b.   [4] See references in Jastrow, ibid.
[5] Cf. the discussion below, pp. 260 ff.

We may conclude with the curious example of a word which, reconstructed for the biblical text, even achieved mention in a dictionary of modern Hebrew, and yet probably had no genuine history at all: the supposed עמלץ 'shark'. The MT of Ps. 74. 14 has:

$$\text{תִּתְּנֶ֫נּוּ מַאֲכָל לְעָם לְצִיִּים}$$

and a reorganization of this text as

$$\text{תתנ֫נו מאכל לְעַמְלְצֵי יָם}$$

'you gave it as food to the sharks of the sea'[1]

has received considerable recognition and acceptance. It came from I. Löw, and Koehler calls it 'simple and brilliant';[2] it is registered in KB, p. 715b.

The positing of a word עמלץ 'shark' seems intrinsically very attractive; in the end, however, one must doubt its correctness. Apart from Hebrew itself, it seems quite doubtful whether cognates of the supposed עמלץ have ever existed in any Semitic language as names for any kind of fish. The appeal made by Löw was to the Arabic m-l-ṣ. The change from an assumed אמלץ to עמלץ is not in itself very difficult. Greater difficulty lies in the meaning of the Arabic itself. The verb m-l-ṣ seems to mean 'be slippery'.[3] A form 'amlaṣ is actually cited with the sense of a 'smooth-headed man', and also of 'a thing that slips out of one's hand by reason of its smoothness'. But for 'a fish that slips from the hand by reason of its smoothness' the word is maliṣa. All senses quoted by Lane and relevant to fish are senses for fish which slip out of the hand. It is quite doubtful whether 'amlaṣ (or any other word from this root) is the name for a kind of fish.

Thus the comparative basis for the suggestion is not strong. When we turn to consider the evidence in extra-biblical Hebrew, the position is again doubtful. Has the word עַמְלָץ (or עַמְלָץ) ever been used in Hebrew? The dictionary of Grossmann, revised by Segal, indeed enters this word with the gloss 'shark', but marks it as a 'modern' word. I have not been able to find any previous history of usage. There is no entry in Ben-Jehuda. The suggestion

---

[1] Cf. the confusion of יָם 'sea' and the plural ending implied by a familiar reconstruction at Am. 6. 12.

[2] See Koehler, *DLz* NF ii (1925) 1055; *OTS* viii (1950) 151.

[3] See Lane, vii. 2736. Cf. also the consideration mentioned above, p. 165.

for Ps. 74. 14 is indeed mentioned in that *Thesaurus*, xi. 5459b; but even there it is treated only as a suggestion, and a doubtful one at that. This hardly suggests that the word had an authentic history; the entry עֲמָלֵץ in Grossmann-Segal seems itself to be a modern proposal made on the basis of Löw's suggestion for Ps. 74. 14! If so, it seems hardly to have succeeded, for the word actually used for 'shark' is כָּרִישׁ.[1]

Such then are some illustrations of the use of evidence from post-biblical Hebrew. Much more requires to be done to investigate the lexical relationships between the biblical and the post-biblical language. The more obvious similarities, we may expect, have long been observed; while modern investigation has tended to look rather towards the other cognate languages than towards late Hebrew. But even when suggestions have been inspired primarily by evidence from outside Hebrew, the post-biblical Hebrew evidence can do much to furnish a cross-check and to help us evaluate the probability of the suggestions.

---

[1] I now find that our strange word is a technical term for one species of shark in modern usage. This however does not alter the argument.

X

THE USE OF EVIDENCE FROM
THE VERSIONS

(1) *General*

THIS chapter will be devoted to a discussion of the way in which the early 'versions', i.e. the translations from the Hebrew Bible into Greek, Latin, Aramaic, and other languages, have been used in philological treatments.

In textual treatments the versions have commonly been evaluated as a separate witness to the original text. That is to say, a version like the LXX, in the absence of substantial variants in the Hebrew MSS., gives testimony to a text many centuries earlier than the MT, and thus enables us to get behind the MT and reconstruct an earlier form of the Hebrew text. This reconstruction fits with the context, explains how the LXX reading originated, and provides some reasonable possibility, under the accepted canons for probable scribal mistakes, of explaining also the origin of the present MT reading. Actually the procedure is considerably more complicated than this; but this statement will suffice for our purpose.

The essential thing is that, in this approach, the MT being considered difficult or doubtful, the LXX (or other version) is used as a source from which a Hebrew text different from MT is reconstructed. This implies retranslation from the version.[1] This is sometimes carelessly phrased by saying that the LXX 'read' such and such a Hebrew word.

The traditional term 'read' is ambiguous in this context. When scholars say that the LXX 'read' such and such a Hebrew word, this may mean that the Greek text, if retranslated into Hebrew, would provide such and such a Hebrew text; it may also mean that such and such were the actual signs on the manuscript from which the translation was made. We have no direct means of knowing what they 'read' in the latter of these senses, and all we can tell

---

[1] Goshen-Gottstein, in a penetrating recent study of methods in the use of the versions, uses the term 'retroversion'; see *Textus* iii (1963) 130–58.

directly is what they *wrote* in Greek (or, respectively, in another language). From what they wrote in Greek, taken in relation to other known characteristics of the version, we can form hypotheses about the Hebrew text from which the translators worked.

Knowledge of this Hebrew text, however, is indirect rather than direct. In the use of a version there are two steps to set against one in the transmission or quotation of a text in the same language. There are the signs seen in the original text, and there is the process of creating a new text in a new language. Since we have direct access only to the final product, i.e. the text produced in the new language, it is by a process of *indirect* decision that we determine how much of this new text is to be attributed to decisions of the translation process and how much is to be attributed to the signs of the original text.

This indirectness of the use of the versions is not mentioned in order to suggest that the versions are not reliable as a source of guidance; that the procedure is an indirect one is, in my opinion, a mere matter of fact, which has to be borne in mind in all our judgements about the relation of versions to the text from which they were translated.[1]

In any case the procedure of reconstruction of the original text by retroversion from the LXX or other translation is a very familiar one, perhaps the most familiar of all textual procedures with Old Testament texts at the present time. Many hundreds of suggestions in *BH*[3] follow this pattern.

This procedure is akin to, and often complementary with, the procedure of emendation. Since the version does not provide *direct* evidence of a different Hebrew text, there is a conjectural element in any textual suggestion, however probable, which depends on versional evidence, which would not be present if we were weighing different *Hebrew* manuscripts. Thus textual reconstruction on the basis of versions is easily allied with the more general practice of emendation, which may either have or lack versional support; and a very large number of emendations in fact make some sort of appeal to the versions. There is, however, a wide diversity in the degree to which emendations 'on the basis of LXX' (or similar

---

[1] My position is, I think, exactly the same as that taken by Goshen-Gottstein in the sample edition of Isaiah; e.g. p. 13, 'a reading inferred by retroversion, however plausible, is not the same as a reading in Hebrew, in black and white'; and p. 24: 'almost every assumption of a variant by means of retroversion is a matter of doubt'. See my review in *JSS* xii (1967) 113–22.

phrases) really rest on versional evidence (at one end of the scale) or (at the other end) merely quote the versions in connexion with a reconstruction which is logically almost entirely conjectural.

Philological treatments use the versions in a rather different way. They do not necessarily deny the approach which has just been outlined. But their main interest lies in another direction.

In philological treatments the versions have been evaluated primarily not as witnesses to a different *text*, but rather as witnesses which, while they follow from the *same text* (with room for altera-tions of vocalization as discussed above), provide confirmatory evidence for, or clues towards, a different *understanding* of it.[1] These understandings are taken to agree with the philological re-interpretation of the same text on the basis of cognate languages.

As with textual treatments the value of the clues provided by a version does not depend on the rightness of its translation. A rendering in a version is quite frequently taken to be valuable evidence of linguistic understanding even though at the point where it is found it is a wrong interpretation. The fact that the version could make *this particular error* is evaluated as evidence that the meaning in question, even if erroneously applied in trans-lating at this point, was nevertheless well known to the translators. Thus, it is argued, it furnishes evidence for their linguistic under-standing, and may be applied as confirmation at points where philologists have seen clues from cognate languages pointing in the same direction.

Thus the practice of philological treatments has often been to use the LXX or other version not as a direct corrective of MT but as evidence for the identification by comparative methods of Hebrew words or senses previously unknown. For the general approach we may quote Professor Winton Thomas:[2]

The Septuagint . . . frequently presupposes Hebrew words which are

---

[1] It should be added that there is a considerable difference of opinion about the value of the versions in relation to philological treatments. Driver has on the whole valued them highly. An opposite position is taken by Albright who, claiming that scores of passages in the Psalms have been cleared up on the basis of Ugaritic, writes (Peake's *Commentary*, p. 63): 'In virtually every case the LXX translators were just as ignorant of the true meaning as were the Massoretes.' Cf. recently Dahood, *Psalms*, p. xxiv. Albright and Dahood, however, actually use versional evidence, inconsistently, a good deal more than this would suggest. See my further remarks below, p. 268. It is Driver's approach that will mainly concern us here, since it at least makes the versions worth studying.

[2] In *Record and Revelation*, p. 396.

only explicable by reference to one or other of the Semitic languages, more particularly to Arabic. 'Arabisms' in the LXX have, of course, been suspected before now, and indeed some have already been recovered. Recently, however, the extent to which the Septuagint translators could 'Arabize' has gradually become more apparent.

Some examples are next given, and the passage continues:

How are these 'Arabizing' renderings to be explained? It is not to be supposed that the LXX translators had any knowledge of Arabic, any more than had Ben Sira's grandson, who frequently 'Arabizes' when translating his grandfather's work. On the contrary, it can only be assumed that these words originally belonged to the common stock of the Semitic languages, and that they formed at one time part of the Hebrew vocabulary, but that their meaning was generally lost, to be retained only by the Egyptian Jews, and traceable today only through the medium of Arabic. In the same way must be explained those renderings in the LXX which presuppose other Semitic languages.

A good first example is Ps. 47. 10 לֵאלֹהִים מָגִנֵּי־אֶרֶץ, literally apparently 'the shields of the earth'. The LXX (46. 10) has οἱ κραταιοὶ τῆς γῆς 'the powerful of the earth', cf. also Syriac *'whdnyh d'r'* 'the powers of the earth'.[1] The normal Hebrew sense 'shield' has been felt to be strange: are there 'shields of the earth' which belong to God? Emendations have been suggested which produce a sense like 'princes'; in these the versions are used as clues to construct a consonantal text different from MT. A philological treatment is offered by Driver, who says that the LXX here provides 'far the earliest evidence' for the root of Arabic *mājin* 'bold'.[2] Perhaps, then, there was a Hebrew מגן 'bold, insolent', preserved only through the versional evidence. KB, following Driver, registers this as a Hebrew word.

The textual and the philological treatments both result in roughly similar senses ('princes' or 'insolent ones', against the traditional 'shields'), but the mode by which this result is reached is different. In the one case it is reached by altering the text, in the other by offering a different explanation of the same text.

We do not need to decide now whether this philological explanation is the right one. In addition to these possibilities, one can also say that the meaning is 'shields' and that this is a figurative

---

[1] Brockelmann, *Lexicon Syriacum*, p. 12a.

[2] But what if the Arabic sense 'bold' is derived from the senses 'to joke, jest, jeer, make insolent jokes', etc.?

expression for the rulers or the mighty ones of the earth. This explanation through metaphor, if correct, also removes the original difficulty. It implies that the LXX were vague about the meaning and gave a general guess; or that in the translation they abandoned the metaphor and gave expression to that to which the figure referred, rather than reproduce the figure itself in Greek.[1]

Job 10. 22 has the phrase:

$$\text{אֶרֶץ עֵיפָתָה} \ldots \text{וְלֹא סְדָרִים}$$

Now the familiar Hebrew סֵדֶר means 'order'. It is not impossible to take the sentence in this way and understand as 'a land of darkness and chaos', but there are certain peculiarities. Firstly, a better figure might be absence of light rather than absence of order; secondly, the plural of סדר 'order' is unusual; thirdly, סדר 'order', though a very familiar late Hebrew word, is not found elsewhere in the Bible. Now the LXX rendering is:

εἰς γῆν σκότους αἰωνίου, οὗ οὐκ ἔστιν φέγγος

'into a land of eternal darkness, where there is no light'.

Using this as confirmation, Driver cites Arabic *sadira* 'be dazzled by glare', and thus identifies a sense of 'rays of light' for the Hebrew סְדָרִים.[2]

More important, because affecting a more frequent and more central word, is the case of שׁוּב. Driver has identified for certain passages a verb which is quite distinct from the familiar שׁוּב 'return'. The word 'return' is cognate with Arabic *ṯāba* (*w*), but the new word is cognate with Arabic *sāba* (*y*) 'run, wander at random', used especially of beasts.

At Jer. 8. 6 MT has (*K*) כֻּלֹּה שָׁב בְּמִרְצוֹתָם. Since the reference seems to be to the roaming or straying of animals, and 'return' does not seem to give good sense, Duhm emended to שָׁט 'go to and fro'. But Driver, retaining the MT and explaining it as 'wander at random', cites the LXX:

διέλιπεν ὁ τρέχων ἀπὸ τοῦ δρόμου αὐτοῦ

---

[1] Cf. further below, pp. 251 ff.

[2] He omits the words כמו אפל צלמות as a gloss. To that extent the treatment is textual; but presumably the gloss, if gloss it is, would have been an explanation of the strange word סדרים and thus would have been a textual gloss with a philological reason. In a completely different philological treatment, Tur-Sinai, *Job*, pp. 184 ff., takes סדרים as exorcistic 'arrangements' of words.

and claims that the Peshitta with its *mhlkyn* 'walking about' provides further support.[1]

One of the forms which shows substantial homonymy in Hebrew is עָנָה. This is further increased if we follow those scholars who have found yet another verb, cognate with Arabic *ǵaniya* 'stay in a place'. This has been identified at Mal. 2. 12 in the difficult phrase עֵר וְעֹנֶה, which is thus taken to mean 'gadabout and stay-at-home'; and also at Isa. 13. 22:

וְעָנָה אִיִּים בְּאַלְמְנוֹתָיו

where the sense would be:

'and jackals will dwell in its palaces'.

At this latter place the LXX renders in just this way:

καὶ ὀνοκένταυροι ἐκεῖ κατοικήσουσιν.

So it can be argued that the LXX were familiar with the verb in the sense already known for the Arabic cognate. At Mal. 2. 12, however, this is not so; the rendering ταπεινωθῇ depends on the more familiar verb עָנָה 'be humbled'. Thus the claim for recognition by LXX is modified by non-recognition on their part at another place.[2]

The procedure outlined above is not in any way confined to the LXX itself. It can be used in relation to the other ancient Greek versions, as preserved in the fragments of Origen's Hexapla and elsewhere, and also to versions in other languages, such as the Aramaic Targum.

Take the attractive case of the word עָשׁ, which is normally understood to mean 'moth'. At Hos. 5. 12, however, it occurs in

---

[1] One may doubt, however, whether the Syriac word when taken in context means this. The whole phrase is *klhwn mhlkyn bṣbynhwn* 'all of them walk in their own good pleasure', very close to the Targumic כולהון מסגן ברעות נפשהון; cf. also the Greek rendering of ὁ Σύρος. Probably במרצותם was diagnosed as a form from רצה, and this fact then led to the rendering of the verb as 'walking'; this produces the commonplace 'walking in one's own will or pleasure'. The Vulgate with its *omnes conuersi sunt ad cursum suum* agrees with the more traditional understanding.

[2] Cf. further below, p. 250. Non-recognition in Mal. 2. 12 is itself no insuperable objection. It is perfectly possible that the Isaiah translator knew a word which was unknown to the translator of the Dodecapropheton. In so far, however, as there is any force in the argument that a word is recognized by several translators, the converse must also be acknowledged, that it is proper to notice when recognition by more than one translator does *not* take place.

parallelism with רקב 'rottenness, pus'. Symmachus has εὐρώς, while Aquila has βρωστήρ. It is then possible to follow Driver and hold that there are more words עש than one. One of them, meaning 'moth', corresponds to Arabic *'utt*; another, meaning 'pus, rottenness', corresponds to Arabic *ǧatt*. Driver also identifies a third word עש meaning 'bird's nest', but for the sake of clarity we leave this aside for the present. We note simply that the evidence comes not from the LXX but from the later versions.[1]

Symmachus is not necessarily right in his rendering; he writes εὐρώς 'rot' at places where the meaning is certainly 'moth', such as Isa. 50. 9, Ps. 39. 12. But the erroneous rendering may still be good evidence. At Ps. 31. 11 we have similar renderings of the verb עשש (Symmachus εὐρωτίασαν). At Job 27. 18, where the MT has עש, the Targum has רקבוביתא.[2]

Thus, though the LXX will be the most frequently quoted, other versions may supply evidence equally well.

Erroneous renderings, as we have seen, may be taken as good evidence for the translators' knowledge of Hebrew; and under these circumstances, not surprisingly, arguments of some considerable subtlety can be found. Consider the following example.

Tobit 1. 13 reads:

καὶ ἔδωκεν [μοι S] ὁ ὕψιστος χάριν καὶ μορφὴν ἐνώπιον Ενεμεσσαρου.

Now Perles believed that there was a Hebrew word שכל meaning 'form', cognate with Arabic *šakl* 'form'. He thought that the original Hebrew of Tobit here was חן ושכל. In Tobit, however, in his opinion the word שכל actually meant 'sense, understanding', which is the normal meaning of this word in Hebrew. The translation thus rendered the (putative) Hebrew wrongly. Nevertheless Perles took the Greek text to be a reliable witness to the existence of a Hebrew שכל meaning 'form'. The other place where he found evidence is in I Sam. 25. 3, where we hear of the attractive Abigail:

וְהָאִשָּׁה טוֹבַת־שֶׂכֶל וִיפַת תֹּאַר

Perles took this to mean:

'fair of form and beautiful of appearance'.

---

[1] For further discussion of this example see below, pp. 252 n., 279.

[2] Since this word is found specifically of the decay caused by moths, however (Jastrow, p. 1496a), it is by no means clear evidence against an understanding of the original as 'moth'.

Here, however, the LXX said ἀγαθὴ συνέσει, 'good of under-standing'.

By this argument, then, the evidence for the existence of a שׂכל 'form' is a passage where the original Hebrew does not exist and where, according to the theory itself, the Greek translated wrongly; while, in the one place where the word (again according to the theory) actually occurred in the Bible, the Greek translated wrongly again. The argument is not an impossible one; but readers will grant that it is an exceedingly delicate one. This, however, is an extreme case.

With this, then, as a preliminary statement of the way in which the versions are used in philological treatments, we may now go on to discuss the problems involved in such use and to consider the criteria by which we may judge whether such use has been valid.

(2) *The Question of the Hebrew Text*

Firstly, we have to consider the possibility that the LXX may have been translated from a Hebrew text differing from that of the MT. This is, after all, the hypothesis upon which enormous labours of classical textual criticism have been performed. It is clear that this hypothesis, if overstressed or used uncritically, can be most unfortunate in its results. Where the Greek text gives a sense different from the Hebrew, the hypothesis that it was translated from a different Hebrew text is only one of a number of possibili-ties. It may have had the same text, but misread it; or been careless in handling it, or guessed at the sense, or paraphrased, or assimi-lated it to another passage; or, indeed, it may have sincerely trans-lated the same text in a way which we judge to be 'wrong' and which thus gives us the impression that the text was different. There are many possible relations between what the translators wrote down in Greek and what was on the page in Hebrew. Only when we eliminate a number of these possible relations are we entitled to translate back the Greek into a Hebrew text and say that the translators 'read' this text. It makes for a more sophisticated ap-proach if we consider the quite different possibility that the Greek may represent a different linguistic assessment of a Hebrew text close to MT or identical with it.

Nevertheless it is unlikely that any degree of such sophistication can eliminate the possibility that there is really a differing Hebrew

text behind the LXX translation. Scholars who have stressed the
value of the LXX for discovering new meanings for the Hebrew
words of MT have not really denied this. Just as, in spite of their
warnings against emendation, they have frequently emended, so
also, in spite of their use of the LXX as a clue to a different linguistic assessment of the same text, they have like other scholars
frequently continued to use the LXX as evidence of a varying text,
In particular the discovery at Qumran of new Hebrew texts
which agree with the LXX at points where it materially differs
from the MT, seems, if this evidence has been rightly assessed, to
prove conclusively that Hebrew texts differing from MT were
sometimes used for the Greek translation.[1]

What one has to inquire therefore is whether, at the points where
philological treatments have been offered, the question of a differing
text has been properly considered as a possible explanation for the
LXX rendering. Sometimes one wonders whether the attractive
prospect of a philological treatment does not lead scholars into an
over-confidence towards those texts which seem to support it—an
over-confidence which they do not consistently show towards the
interpretations of the Greek version.

For example, it has at times been argued that there is a verb
עשׂה which is not the familiar עשׂה 'do' but another verb עשׂה
cognate with Arabic ġašiya and meaning 'turn oneself, incline,
towards or away'. This can be well exemplified at I Kings 20. 40:

וַיְהִי עַבְדְּךָ עֹשֵׂה הֵנָּה וָהֵנָּה וְהוּא אֵינֶנּוּ

'Your servant turned in one direction and in another, but he was gone.'

The traditional sense 'do' is hard here, as was remarked by BDB,
p. 244b. Now it has sometimes been said that the argument was
clinched by the LXX of I Sam. 14. 32:

MT (*Kethibh*) ויעש העם אל־שלל

LXX καὶ ἐκλίθη ὁ λαὸς εἰς τὰ σκῦλα

which appears to coincide exactly with the interpretation of the
Hebrew as 'turn oneself, incline', as the philological treatment
maintained.

Here, however, there is a rather peculiar *Qere* ויעט. This word

---

[1] On such Qumran texts see, for instance, Cross, *Ancient Library of Qumran*,
e.g. pp. 133–45.

occurs elsewhere only in I Sam. 15. 19, where LXX has ὥρμησας 'rushed' (upon the spoil), and 25. 14, where we have:

MT וַיָּעַט בָּהֶם

LXX καὶ ἐξέκλινεν ἀπ᾽ αὐτῶν.

Thus, whatever the meaning of the strange word וַיָּעַט, and whatever the origin of its occurrence as a textual variant at I Sam. 14. 32, the translation at I Sam. 25. 14 makes it extremely probable that the LXX is a translation not of the present *Kethibh* at 14. 32 but of the present *Qere* וַיַּעַט. Thus the Greek translation, contrary to first appearance, does not show any sign of knowing a Hebrew עָשָׂה 'turn oneself, incline', although there is a reasonable case for the identification of this word on other grounds.

Driver argued that there is a word עַד meaning 'time'. Jer. 11. 12 has בְּעֵת רָעָתָם 'in the time of their trouble', and, a little later, in a continuation of the same passage, 11. 14 has בְעַד רָעָתָם. Here, however, some Hebrew manuscripts read בְּעֵת as in 11. 12, and editors commonly follow this easier reading. But, Driver points out, the LXX writes ἐν καιρῷ in both passages; the Vulgate has *in tempore*. Evidence can be found also at Isa. 30. 8, 64. 8, Ezek. 22. 4, 30. In this last, MT בְעַד הָאָרֶץ, LXX has ἐν καιρῷ τῆς γῆς, a rendering which means 'time' though there is no doubt that Ezekiel means 'on behalf of'.

There is reason to suppose, however, that some of the evidence is the product of assimilation and other textual processes. The LXX ἐν καιρῷ at Jer. 11. 14 is probably a translation from the assimilated reading בְּעֵת, or else an independent result of the same assimilation. At Isa. 30. 8 it is doubtful whether עַד is rendered by any form of καιρός, depending on textual variations in the Greek. Most of the versional evidence, in fact, can be accounted for through assimilation to other nearby phrases, along with the influence of other words like מוֹעֵד (frequently translated by καιρός) and Aramaic עִדָּן. Since none of the Hebrew contexts intrinsically favour the sense 'time', the suggestion therefore should probably not be accepted.

(3) *The Question of the Versional Text*

Secondly, we have to bear in mind the history of transmission of the Greek (or other) versional text and its possibilities of corruption, which may be quite independent of the Hebrew. Here again there is sometimes a danger that we may overvalue a particular form of the Greek text and set upon it a confidence which lies less in its own intrinsic merit than in the attractiveness of the philological treatment which it appears to confirm.

An important instance is גבול, normally taken to mean 'frontier', at Ps. 78. 54. Arabic has the familiar *jabal* 'mountain', and *gbl* 'mountain' has been identified in Ugaritic. Now in Ps. 78. 54 גבול is translated by ὄρος 'mountain':

ויביאם אל־גבול קדשו הר־זה קנתה ימינו : MT

LXX (77. 54) καὶ εἰσήγαγεν αὐτοὺς εἰς ὄρος ἁγιάσματος αὐτοῦ, ὄρος τοῦτο, ὃ ἐκτήσατο ἡ δεξιὰ αὐτοῦ.

This, not surprisingly, has been taken as evidence that גבול was known to mean 'mountain' by the LXX. But the Greek texts may be in error. The trouble may be caused by two facts: (a) the great similarity of the two Greek words, ὄρος 'mountain' and ὅρος (or ὅριον) 'frontier'; (2) the fact that ὄρος 'mountain' occurs (translating הר) in the second clause, a circumstance which could easily lead to an error in transcription. Grabe therefore suggested the emendation ὅριον, which is accepted by Rahlfs and printed as his text. A corruption would be even more understandable if the LXX had written ὅρος in the first place. Though they did not usually use ὅρος for 'frontier', they may have done so here precisely because of the juxtaposition with ὄρος 'mountain' in the same verse. All other cases of גבול in the Psalms are rendered by ὅριον.[1]

Thus the Greek evidence for a Hebrew גבול 'mountain' dissolves into an accident of the Greek text, caused by the remarkable similarity of the Greek words, along with the parallelism with 'mountain' in the text translated. We may add the absence of traces in other early versions or of survivals in later Hebrew.

Even more important than the history of the text, however, is the technique of translation used by the version, which may vary substantially from book to book and even between one part of a book and another. All claims that a version either presupposes a different text or shows a different linguistic understanding of the same text have to be tested by relating them to the general methods of the version in question. The sections which follow will illustrate

---

[1] Cf. also I Sam. 10. 2, and Wutz, *Onomastica Sacra*, p. 546.

some of the methods of translation which are important for this question.

(4) *Imprecise Methods of Translation*

At Ps. 84. 7:

גַּם־בְּרָכוֹת יַעְטֶה מוֹרֶה : MT

LXX καὶ γὰρ εὐλογίας δώσει ὁ νομοθετῶν

Rabin has suggested the presence of a Hebrew עטה 'give', cognate with the familiar Arabic 'a'ṭī. But in this Psalm the translator, who is normally a fairly sober and literal worker, has by the end of v. 6 (unlike the earlier part of the Psalm) got himself thoroughly lost. He missed מַעְיָן, which might have told him that the context was something about water; he thus fails to see that בְרֵכוֹת are 'pools', and takes them as the commoner homograph 'blessings'. With מוֹרֶה the sense 'rain' does not occur to him, though it is not uncommon in contexts clearly watery, as at Joel 2. 23 and (with יוֹרֶה) at Deut. 11. 14, Jer. 5. 24. He takes it as the much commoner word 'teacher, lawgiver'. Thus it turns out that the sentence is about a lawgiver who does something to blessings.

The verb is not a common one, and the translator varies his rendering according to the context. If there is a reference to clothing, he usually uses περιβάλλεσθαι or a similar word (LXX, 108. 19, 29), and so also, by a familiar metaphor, where the subject is shame (LXX, 70. 13). At 89 (88). 46, again of shame, he uses the metaphor not of clothing but of pouring upon. Given this degree of variability, he may well have written δώσει in our passage as a general rendering, which would give a passable sense, whatever the exact original metaphor might be.[1] The Gallican Psalter followed the LXX with *etenim benedictionem dabit legislator*, but the word 'give' disappears as soon as Jerome consults the Hebrew and writes *benedictione quoque amicietur doctor*. The Syriac, with its *w'p bwrkt' yt'ṭp s'm nmws'*, 'and he also who gives the law will be wrapped in blessing', agrees with the LXX in the interpretation of מוֹרֶה but not in the interpretation of the verb. This sense of מוֹרֶה was, of course, prominent at Qumran and elsewhere in late Hebrew.

---

[1] On this mode of translation in the Psalms see Flashar in *ZAW* xxxii (1912), *passim*.

It is quite improbable, therefore, that the passage is evidence of knowledge of a Hebrew word meaning 'give'.

Similar doubts are raised by the claim[1] that κατοικεῖν at Isa. 13. 22 is evidence of a word עָנָה 'stay in a place'. This would be plausible if the Isaiah translation were a precise one, carefully rendering each word with a close equivalent. We can test this in two ways: firstly, by looking at the way in which κατοικεῖν is used in the Greek Isaiah; secondly, by looking at the verses just before and after 13. 22 in order to see how closely the translator is following his text at that point.

The verb κατοικεῖν is used in Isaiah from time to time where it is not a close equivalent. At 9. 1 (8. 23) it is an expansion, and there is no Hebrew verb 'dwell'. 14. 23 is much the same. At 16. 7 it is used to translate the obscure word אֲשִׁישִׁים.[2] At 27. 10 it is hard to see what it is translating. At 62. 5 it is a general (rather than a close) rendering of בָּעַל 'live with', where the original reference is to marriage. Clearly, the use of κατοικεῖν in Isaiah does not necessarily suggest an exact equivalence to any Hebrew word.

Similarly, in the immediate context of Isa. 13. 22 a number of striking divergences (e.g. οὐδὲ μὴ εἰσέλθωσιν εἰς αὐτήν for MT וְלֹא תֵשֵׁב, and οὐδὲ μὴ διέλθωσιν αὐτήν for MT וְלֹא־יַהֵל) will show how far the translator is from attempting any precise rendering of the Hebrew text word for word.

As commonly in Isaiah, the translation includes wide divagations from an exact rendering. This is so even in words which were undoubtedly entirely familiar to the translator, such as שָׁכֵן. This verb, which ironically *does* mean κατοικεῖν, is twice given other and very imprecise renderings in the space of two verses. Words and phrases are missed out altogether, and there is a tendency to re-use a word which has just been used before, or one close to it (so εἰσελθεῖν, διελθεῖν, and ἀναπαύεσθαι). It is unlikely that the use of κατοικεῖν here for Hebrew עָנָה constitutes evidence of exact linguistic knowledge.

Sometimes a Greek text will agree with a possible philological treatment, but will leave us uncertain whether it does so by accident or on a basis of real knowledge. At I Sam. 1. 18:

MT וּפָנֶיהָ לֹא־הָיוּ־לָהּ עוֹד

LXX καὶ τὸ πρόσωπον αὐτῆς οὐ συνέπεσεν ἔτι

---

[1] See above, p. 243.　　[2] On this word cf. also below, p. 254.

we may adduce the sense 'fall', known for הוּא at Job 37. 6.
Against this, however, we may point out:

(a) Other versions do not support the LXX.

(b) The Greek locution may be an assimilation to a familiar
passage like Gen. 4. 6:

ἵνα τί συνέπεσεν τὸ πρόσωπόν σου;

(c) Even if 'fall' is a good gloss for Job 37. 6, it remains uncertain
whether the kind of 'falling' used in the phrase 'his face fell' could
be expressed with this verb. We should not be over-persuaded by
the fact that we use the same English gloss 'fall'. Senses known in
Hebrew apply only to snow, and (in the noun הַוָּה, הַוָּה) to
'disaster, calamity'.

(d) It is one thing to find a הוּא 'fall' in the peculiar vocabulary
of Job, another to find it in a prose section of Samuel, in which
היה in the common sense 'be' is very much more frequent than
in the poetic sections of Job.

The probability of a sense 'fall' for הָיוּ at I Sam. 1. 18 is thus
somewhat below 50 per cent.

(5) *The Use of Favourite Words*

The second point requiring attention in the use of the versions
is the fact that translators often have certain 'favourite' words. It
is a stylistic feature of the Greek Psalter to use one word freely for
a considerable number of different Hebrew words. Such an instance is the group κραταίωμα or κραταίωσις and the adjective
κραταιός.

The word סוֹד usually means 'secret; private council'. The
translation by κραταίωμα at Ps. 25 (24). 14 has been taken to point
to a Hebrew word cognate with the Arabic *sūd* 'chieftaincy'. Again,
we have seen how the מִגְנֵּי אֶרֶץ of Ps. 47 (46). 10 is translated by
οἱ κραταιοὶ τῆς γῆς, and this has been taken as evidence related
to Arabic words so as to give a sense 'bold, insolent'.[1]

But κραταίωμα (κραταίωσις) is clearly a word freely used in
the Greek Bible. We find it rendering סֶלַע 'rock' and מָעוֹז
'refuge'[2] as well as עַז 'strength' and מִשְׂגָב 'refuge'. The adjective

---

[1] See above, pp. 241 f.
[2] This rendering is an etymologizing one (the word is taken as from the root
of עַז 'strength').

κραταιός is used not only for obvious words like עֹז and עָצוּם but also for עָרִיץ and אַדִּיר.

An even more marked example in the Psalms is ταράσσω 'disturb'. This word is employed in numerous contexts, where a variety of meanings is found in Hebrew. We find it translating such various words as רעשׁ, חמר, שׁחח, סחר, רגז, עשׁשׁ,[1] חלל, צמת, פעם, שׁלל, נדד, להט, etc. Such a Greek translation can hardly be used as evidence for a philological reinterpretation of a Hebrew word. It seems rather that the idea of disturbance or non-disturbance appeals to the translator, and is used by him without concern for the way in which it obscures the difference between the Hebrew meanings in the verses translated.

Evidence for a Hebrew מיד, cognate with Arabic māda (y) 'be violently agitated', has been seen in Hab. 3. 6:

MT עמד וַיְמֹדֶד ארץ

LXX ἔστη, καὶ ἐσαλεύθη ἡ γῆ.

This solution avoids the emendation וַיְמֹעֶד.

But σαλεύεσθαι is a favourite LXX word; Hatch and Redpath register no fewer than twenty-three different Hebrew terms rendered with it. In the Dodecapropheton it is used also for נוע, מסס, מוג, and רעל, and it occurs in fact only a few verses earlier, at Hab. 2. 16 (σαλεύθητι or διασαλεύθητι, MT הערל, presumably reading as הרעל). The rendering is only an assimilation to a probable sense of the context and to the thought of passages like Ps. 18. 8, 46. 4, 68. 9, Nah. 1. 5; it is no sign of special linguistic knowledge.

To put it in another way, the 'shaking' of the earth can be treated as a stereotype of prophetic thought. The same is true of the idea of 'making firm' the creation, as at Isa. 51. 6:

MT כי־שׁמים כעשׁן נמלחו

LXX ὅτι ὁ οὐρανὸς ὡς καπνὸς ἐστερεώθη.

The Greek verb is not a clue to good linguistic knowledge of the sense of מלח; it is a stereotype of creation, found of 'heaven' at Ps. 33 (32). 6 (עשׂה), Isa. 45. 12 (נטה), 48. 13 (טפח), and of 'earth' at Isa. 42. 5, 44. 24 (רקע). The Targum, which construes Isa.

---

[1] This is of interest for the equivalence ὡς ταραχή = כעשׁ at Hos. 5. 12; cf. above, pp. 144, 243 f., and below, p. 279. Cf. also Index, no. 130.

51. 6 of the passing away of the heaven like smoke, is following a different stereotype.

Dahood, arguing that the verb formation with infixed /-t-/ remained alive through the biblical period, cites the translation of הִסְתִּיר פָּנָיו by ἀπέστρεψεν τὸ πρόσωπον αὐτοῦ and *auertit faciem suam*.[1] The form was thus taken by the translators to be from סוּר 'turn away'.

Even a brief study of the contexts shows, however, that this must have been a stylistic preference in Greek, and has nothing to do with the original Hebrew verb formation. Ἀποστρέφειν is a favourite LXX verb. The translation of הִסְתִּיר with it occurs almost only where the object is 'face'. (If we exclude cases where there is no LXX rendering, as sometimes in Job, there are forty-five cases where the object of סתר is not 'face', and forty-three of these are rendered with 'hide, shelter', etc., i.e. κρύπτω, ἀποκρύπτω, or σκεπάζω; the only partial exceptions are Isa. 57. 17, Ps. 89. 47.) The Vulgate, cited by Dahood, is not independent evidence, for this is the Gallican Psalter, translated from the LXX and therefore naturally agreeing with it. Where Jerome translated from the Hebrew, i.e. outside the Psalter, the rendering is almost always 'hide', and in the Psalter *iuxta Hebraeos* Jerome with complete regularity corrected from *auerto* with 'face' as object to *abscondo*.

The 'hiding' of the face is a quite genuine and an important aspect of Hebrew religious idiom. Dahood's interpretation destroys this, and his citation of the LXX is not evidence in favour of his interpretation, but only shows that they too, through some stylistic or theological preference, had lost, or were unable to reproduce, this insight.

(6) *Etymologizing*

Etymologizing is the procedure of interpreting a word by reference to the meaning of another (usually a better-known) Hebrew word which had a similarity to it and could, in more modern terminology, be taken as its root; or a word may be analysed into separate units from which it is taken to have been made up. More extreme still, a translator may strive, as Aquila sometimes did, to represent words of common root in Hebrew with words of common root in Greek. Though the etymologizing tendency is stronger in

---

[1] Dahood, *Psalms*, i. 64.

the later Greek translators, it appears sporadically also in the LXX.

Isa. 16. 7 has a rare word אֲשִׁישִׁים; Driver has argued that it means 'luxurious dwellers', after Arabic *'atta* 'be luxuriant, luxurious; live comfortably'. Whether this is so or not, it is not supported by the τοῖς εὐφραινομένοις of Symmachus; this is an etymologizing guess from the similarity to the familiar שׂישׂ 're- joice', so translated by him at Jer. 32 (39). 41, cf. LXX at Isa. 61. 10.

Etymologizing is also the probable explanation for the rendering of לְאֻמִּים by ἄρχοντες at Gen. 27. 29, Isa. 34. 1, 41. 1, 43. 4, 9, and by βασιλεῖς at Isa. 51. 4. At first sight, the frequency makes this identification very impressive. Driver writes: 'One cannot deny this sense, so frequently attested'; but he holds that this sense is never right at the places where the LXX find it; it is actually found at Ps. 148. 11, 7. 8. The former reads:

מַלְכֵי־אֶרֶץ וְכָל־לְאֻמִּים שָׂרִים וְכָל־שֹׁפְטֵי אָרֶץ׃

and would then mean:

> 'The kings of the earth and all rulers;
> ministers, and all the judges of the earth.'

The familiar sense 'peoples' seems at first sight to fit less well into the sequence. Ps. 7. 8 is a less clear case; an 'assembly of nations' is more likely to surround one than an 'assembly of rulers', and in 7. 9 the Lord judges 'nations' (עַמִּים).[1]

In later Hebrew לְאֹם was little used, and אֻמָּה was becoming more frequent. It is unlikely that the sense 'nation' came to be unknown, though it is possible that, when even this sense became infrequent, very occasional other senses (viz. that of 'ruler' in this case) came to be forgotten. Even in the biblical period לְאֹם was a somewhat traditional word. It was mainly used in the plural, was almost entirely poetical, and in parallelisms is almost always a 'B-word', i.e. a word taking second position in a parallel pair.[2]

That the LXX rendering is the result of etymologization can be seen from the רֵאשֵׁי אוּמִין which is a Targum of the tribal name לְאֻמִּים at Gen. 25. 3.[3] The word was analysed as אֻמָּה+ל.

---

[1] Cf. above, pp. 133, 172.
[2] See Boling in *JSS* v (1960) 221–55, and especially p. 233. In the Psalms Boling found only one exception out of nine occurrences.
[3] See *Gen. R.* ad loc. The same is the reading of the Neofiti text.

Jerome knew the same interpretation: *Laomim uero φυλάρχους, id est principes multarum tribuum atque populorum.*[1]

The rendering in LXX and Targum is probably affected also by stock parallelisms. All instances have לְאֻמִּים as the B-word; the A-word is usually 'nations' or the like, once 'man' (Isa. 43. 4). The Targum has מַלְכוּן 'kingdoms' at Gen. 27. 29, and similarly at Isa. 34. 1, 41. 1, 43. 4, 43. 9; the tendency to produce a parallelism of nations/kingdoms can be seen at 43. 4, where אָדָם is rendered by עַמְמַיָּא. The rendering of לְאֹם as 'ruler' never occurs in an independent sentence where the point would be substantially different if the sense were 'ruler' rather than 'people'.

Further arguments against this identification of 'ruler' are:

(*a*) This development is surely peculiar to Accadian, and even there the sense is not 'ruler' generally, but refers to the eponym of the year. The institutions are entirely Mesopotamian. In the Ugaritic phrase *ybmt l'imm*, the second word is usually taken to be 'peoples', rather than 'rulers' as Driver would have it.

(*b*) Even at Ps. 148. 11 in the Hebrew itself it is questionable whether the sense 'rulers' fits better. It would certainly do so if it were clear that lists of four items in a context of this type must always be homogeneous in order to give good sense. But the list may be one in which the liking for homogeneity is interfered with by the liking for supplementary parallelism, producing the very common parallelism of 'kings' and 'peoples'.[2] The verse then returns to continue the list of types of rulers. The pattern can be described as A-B-A-A.[3] This sense is not in any way a poor one. Since the sense 'peoples' for לְאֻמִּים was a very familiar one, there was no strain in passing from 'kings' to it and then back to other words for rulers. These considerations reduce the degree of difficulty in the accepted sense 'peoples', and thus reduce the original basis for the philological treatment.

(7) *Free Rewriting*

The fourth procedure on the part of the translators is that of very general paraphrasing. The rendering is a free rewriting of the passage, producing a sentiment which is really the translator's

---

[1] *Hebr. Quaest. in Gen.*, ad 25. 3.

[2] Cf. Ps. 72. 11 (with גּוֹיִם); 135. 10 (with גּוֹיִם first).

[3] Cf. Exod. 4. 11: dumb/deaf/clear-sighted/blind = A-A-B-A; Isa. 2. 12 (see below, pp. 280 f.): high/lofty/uplifted/low = A-A-A-B.

idea, connected here and there with the words of the original. This applies particularly to books like Proverbs and Job. These are books which contain many textual-philological difficulties and which for this reason have produced large numbers of philological treatments. They are also books in which the translators felt free to handle the text very loosely.[1] Painfully exact renderings may be succeeded in the next verse by examples of extreme freedom and complete rewriting.

Driver, arguing the existence of a Hebrew זר meaning 'enemy', says that the use of ἐχθρός to render זר in one passage where it is clearly wrong (Prov. 6. 1) proves its currency. The texts are:

MT   בְּנִי אִם־עָרַבְתָּ לְרֵעֶךָ תָּקַעְתָּ לַזָּר כַּפֶּיךָ

LXX   υἱέ, ἐὰν ἐγγυήσῃ σὸν φίλον,
παραδώσεις σὴν χεῖρα ἐχθρῷ.

Now the correspondence of one word to another is not decisive here; for the translator, while he has related himself to the text before him, has made quite a different thought out of it. In the original the whole verse is a conditional clause, stated in two parallel forms; the sequel does not come till the next verse. The sense is:

> 'My son, if you have become surety for your neighbour,
> or shaken hands in pledge for a stranger . . .'

The Greek rendering is:

> 'My son, if you pledge your friend,
> you will give over your hand to an enemy.'

Here the thought is already complete within the verse. Since he has seen the two parts of the sentence as a contrast, the translator has made it natural to see the זר of the second part as part of the total contrast in terms of friendship and enmity. The interpretation as 'enemy' may be no more than part of this understanding. It is doubtful whether it suggests any intrinsic linguistic knowledge that זר could mean 'enemy', and so it does not provide strong evidence for the identification of a זר meaning 'enemy' elsewhere. To say this is not to deny this identification, for which there is quite a good case on other grounds. But it does mean that we

---

[1] On these books see G. Gerleman, *Studies in the Septuagint* (Lund, 1946 and 1956).

cannot accept the simple equivalences of Hebrew and Greek words, as registered for instance in Hatch and Redpath, as evidence for new linguistic identifications without considering the way in which the whole context is handled by the translator. Moreover, (a) it was possible for the translator just to take 'strange' as equivalent to 'enemy' or 'evil' on quite non-linguistic grounds, as he does with the 'strange woman' of Prov. 5. 3 (Gk. φαύλῃ γυναικί, πόρνῃ); (b) he may have been influenced by צָר 'enemy'.

The wide separation between the ideas of the Hebrew text and those of the Greek rendering can be seen at Prov. 17. 14:

MT: פּוֹטֵר מַיִם רֵאשִׁית מָדוֹן וְלִפְנֵי הִתְגַּלַּע הָרִיב נְטוֹשׁ

'The start of strife is one who lets out water;
so let go before a dispute breaks out.'

LXX ἐξουσίαν δίδωσιν λόγοις ἀρχὴ δικαιοσύνης
προηγεῖται δὲ τῆς ἐνδείας στάσις καὶ μάχη.

'The beginning of righteousness gives authority to words;
but quarrelsomeness and fighting lead to poverty.'

The rendering στάσις καὶ μάχη does not help to identify a Hebrew נְטוֹשׁ 'clash of battle'. The translator has produced an admirable Hellenistic-Jewish sentiment of his own, which has occasional contacts with elements in the Hebrew, e.g. δικαιοσύνη for מָדוֹן, taken as from דִּין 'justice', and הִתְגַּלַּע, construed in the sense of 'litigation' (Jastrow, p. 250b).

If such a word נְטוֹשׁ is to be discovered, a better basis lies in the וַתִּטֹּשׁ הַמִּלְחָמָה of I Sam. 4. 2; but here no support can be found in the Greek.

In books where the translation is of free or paraphrastic type, such as Proverbs, quite a large proportion of the evidence is affected by this argument.

A few more examples may be of interest. At Prov. 23. 31:

MT: אַל־תֵּרֶא יַיִן כִּי יִתְאַדָּם

LXX μὴ μεθύσκεσθε οἴνῳ

the Greek is not really evidence in favour of the identification of a verb רָאָה = רוה 'drink', whatever evidence there may be for this from other sources; and Driver is over-literal in saying that 'there is no harm in looking on wine, whatever its colour be'.[1] The Greek version removed the subtlety of the Hebrew idiom, cutting out the indirectness of 'looking at' wine and going straight for the absolute moral issue of drunkenness. It is no evidence of linguistic knowledge.

A substantially stronger case, in my opinion, can be made for the identification of a verb חקר 'despise' at Prov. 28. 11:

MT: חָכָם בְּעֵינָיו אִישׁ עָשִׁיר וְדַל מֵבִין יַחְקְרֶנּוּ

LXX σοφὸς παρ᾽ ἑαυτῷ ἀνὴρ πλούσιος,
πένης δὲ νοήμων καταγνώσεται αὐτοῦ

Here Targum and Peshitta have renderings such as *bsr lh*, giving also the sense 'despise', though the Vulgate with its *pauper autem prudens scrutabitur eum* does not support them; and with Jerome there stand Aquila and Theodotion whose ἐξιχνιάσει follows the more normally recognized sense of this verb. It is not easy to maintain that the LXX reached their rendering at 28. 11 by mere guesswork from the context, and the philological suggestion (by Winton Thomas), while hardly absolutely certain, is well worth consideration. The חִקְרֵי־לֵב of Judges 5. 16 might then be thought of as 'scornings of the heart', which in the context would be a good sense. Another example occurs at Prov. 25. 27, but there the LXX is very remote from the Hebrew and probably offers no guidance.

Finally we may mention, for the sake of its intrinsic interest, the peculiar rendering of בארץ 'in the land' as μόλις 'scarcely' at Prov. 11. 31:

MT: הֵן צַדִּיק בָּאָרֶץ יְשֻׁלָּם אַף כִּי־רָשָׁע וְחוֹטֵא

LXX εἰ ὁ μὲν δίκαιος μόλις σῴζεται,
ὁ ἀσεβὴς καὶ ἁμαρτωλὸς ποῦ φανεῖται;

Driver may be right in attaching this to the influence of the Samaritan word cited by him as אֲרַץ 'compel, coerce'. The Peshitta agrees with the LXX in this rendering (*lmaḥsen*).

---

[1] See also Driver's recent intricate restatement of his interpretation in *JSS* ix (1964) 348 f. Whatever one thinks of the argument from the physics of wine in a cup, the LXX is not relevant evidence. The translators felt, just as Driver now argues, that drinking (or, rather, becoming drunk) is what matters, and they short-circuited the whole suggestive imagery of the verse.

These then show the variety which is to be found in the translation technique of books like Proverbs. As has been said, however, only very few of the examples sustain the weight of use as linguistic evidence in a philological treatment of the Hebrew.

(8) *Additional Points in the Use of the Versions*

Firstly, it is on the whole a support to a philological treatment if it rests on evidence from more than one version, or from versions in several languages. Take the instance of דְמִי, which has been identified as meaning 'half' (Driver, KB). The text for this is Isa. 38. 10: בִּדְמִי יָמַי אֵלֵכָה. LXX with its ἐν τῷ ὕψει seems to have taken this as ברום or בִרְמִי. But among the other Greek translations (though not Aquila, Symmachus, or Theodotion, who took the word to mean 'weakness' or 'silence') we have the annotation οἱ ἕτεροι· ἐν ἡμίσει τῶν ἡμερῶν μου, and this is supported by Peshitta *bplgwt*, Vulgate *in dimidio*. The argument that דְמִי could mean half is supported by the analogy of Accadian *mišlu*; the half is that which is 'like' the other half (is this convincing semantically?). Ezek. 1. 13 has the phrase ἐν μέσῳ where the Hebrew has וּדְמוּת, and Driver argues:

If there had been no such word as דְמִי or דְמוּת 'half', it would have been impossible for them so to translate דמות in a passage where the context did not suggest that meaning.

The claim that it would be 'impossible' to suggest a different explanation is certainly too strong; assimilation is not unlikely. Nevertheless the agreement of versions in several languages does appear to strengthen materially the case for this interpretation at Isa. 38. 10, and Driver may very well be right in his identification.

While, as I have said, it is on the whole a support to a philological treatment if it rests on evidence from several versions rather than one version, this is not true without some qualification and reservation. Firstly, there is the possibility of interdependence between versions in different languages: the LXX may, for instance, at places be influenced by an Aramaic Targum, while Peshitta and Vulgate may have followed the guidance of LXX. Secondly, even where one version has not been influenced by another, there remains a possibility that several versions have alike been guided by the same tradition of Jewish interpretation.

In spite of this qualification, it still remains generally true that the agreement of several versions in the interpretation of a Hebrew word is a sign of some positive value, and that where only one version can be quoted the chances of some idiosyncratic or accidental element in interpretation are the higher.

The evidence of the versions can also be related to our knowledge of late Hebrew and Jewish Aramaic. A particularly interesting case is that of חלק. Many scholars, struggling with the difficult phrase of Amos 7. 4, MT וְאָכְלָה אֶת־הַחֵלֶק, must have thought of the common Arabic ḥalaqa 'create' and wondered if the sense might be:

'It (i.e. the great fire) was eating up the creation'.

This was one of the first philological suggestions to occur to my own mind when I first learned Arabic; later I found it also in the work of scholars like Montgomery. I certainly did not wish to abandon so promising a lead.

Such a verb חלק appears to occur in the Hebrew of Sirach, where the Greek has κτίζω (about six cases). The same sense 'create' might also be applied to Job 38. 24:

MT: אֵי־זֶה הַדֶּרֶךְ יֵחָלֶק אוֹר

which could then mean something like:

'What is the way to where light is created?'

The suggestion is at first sight an extremely attractive one; yet important questions remain. Even if the late Hebrew of Sirach had חלק 'create', how did this insight not penetrate any of the versions at Amos 7. 4?[1] Does the fact that Sirach had this verb 'create' suffice to show that the Old Testament had a *noun* חֵלֶק meaning 'creatures, creation'? No such noun is found in Sirach.

Moreover, חלק in the Hebrew Sirach does not anywhere quite clearly cover the field of cosmic creation and thus coincide with the familiar ברא. The objects of the verb (or, if niphal, subjects) are in no case the familiar cosmic terms like 'heaven' or 'earth'. At 7. 15 the object is work, צבא מלאכה ועבדה, LXX γεωργία. At 34. 13 the reference is to the evil eye; LXX (numbered 31. 13) πονη-ρότερον ὀφθαλμοῦ τί ἔκτισται; At 34. 27 the subject is wine; LXX

---

[1] I do not imply that there is any intrinsic impossibility in the knowing of a word by Sirach and his translator which was unknown to the translator of the Minor Prophets. The question is still a valid one.

(31. 27) καὶ αὐτὸς ἔκτισται εἰς εὐφροσύνην ἀνθρώποις. At 38. 1 it is the doctor and his work. At 39. 25 it is 'good things', טוב; LXX ἀγαθὰ τοῖς ἀγαθοῖς ἔκτισται ἀπ' ἀρχῆς. At 40. 1 it is labour, עסק גדול, Greek ἀσχολία μεγάλη. At 44. 2 it is honour, כבוד, Greek δόξα.

The sense is always derivable from the familiar biblical sense of חלק 'allot, distribute, provide'. The range of meaning is not such that it can be extended with probability to the Amos passage. There is some proximity to a reference which could verge on creation, but the actual function of the word in Sirach is not 'create'. It is thus unlikely that we can conclude to a noun חלק meaning 'creation' as early as Amos, or, indeed, in Sirach himself. The noun actually found, i.e. מחלקת, seems to have a sense close to 'allotment'.[1] Thus after all the Hebrew Sirach does not give clear evidence of a word חלק 'create'; and this negative view is supported by the absence of such a word from other post-biblical Hebrew sources.

It may be thought that, even in passages where the Hebrew is lacking, the Greek κτίζω nevertheless suggests a sense which is strictly that of 'create'. But this in turn depends on the sense of the Greek word. Though it is used with a clear reference to cosmic creation, it is also well documented with a sense like 'make (somebody so and so, e.g., free)', and generally 'bring about (such and such a state)'. The Greek Sirach seems to use κτίζω in both ways. The full sense 'create' is clear in passages like 17. 1, κύριος ἔκτισεν ἐκ γῆς ἄνθρωπον and several others; but, from the evidence of the Hebrew fragments so far known, we may suspect that the Hebrew was ברא or יצר, or at any rate not חלק. The word is clearly a favourite one of the Greek Sirach, which has about twenty-three cases, as against about forty in all the rest of the Greek Old Testament. If we take the nouns for 'creation', i.e. κτίσις and κτίσμα, where these can be set clearly against the Hebrew fragments, the Hebrew words are בריה and מעשה. Thus the Greek evidence also does not vindicate the sense 'create' for חלק. The suggestion 'creation' for Amos 7. 4 has to rest on its own merits in the context of Amos, and not on the Hebrew or Greek evidence in Sirach.

[1] Smend, p. 68, gives *Verteilung* as the sense; at 42. 3 the Greek for this noun is δόσις; 41. 21 is not very clear. Our view has the support of Nöldeke in *ZAW* xx (1900) 85 f., who argues that the sense in Sirach shows at most a transitional meaning on the way that led to the Arabic sense 'create'.

If we can show that the rendering of a version reflects late Hebrew or Jewish Aramaic usage, this does not necessarily increase its evidential value. For the discovery of the original sense of a biblical passage it may be a point either of strength or of weakness. It may be a point of strength in that a late Hebrew usage may in fact have existed in biblical times. It may be a point of weakness in that the late usage may have displaced understanding of the biblical usage.

A verb to which some mystery attaches is דָּגַל. Ps. 20. 6 has בְּשֵׁם־אֱלֹהֵינוּ נִדְגֹּל. Symmachus here translates: τάγματα τάγματα διαστελοῦμεν. I would take this to mean 'we shall divide into separate companies', and this is surely related to the use of דגל now known from the War Scroll. The Targumic נְטַקֵס 'set soldiers in order' agrees in general with this. It is not quite correct to say that the AV 'set up banners' goes back to these translations;[1] rather, it goes back to an interpretation on the basis of the meaning 'flag' for דֶּגֶל; τάγμα is a standard and frequent LXX rendering for דגל. I think it likely that the philological interpretation of נדגל as 'wait upon' (related to Accadian *dagālu* 'wait for, look for, regard') or something similar is right; but the versions do not in fact provide support for it and do not suggest that any ancient translator knew of this meaning. LXX with its μεγαλυνθησόμεθα tried to render as if the consonants were *g-d-l*; the Vulgate followed with *magnificabimur*. Jerome in the *iuxta Hebraeos* wrote *ducemus choros*, which is taking them as if they were *d-l-g*. All this gives the impression that no one really knew the meaning.

(9) *Uncertainty about the Meaning of the Version*

Another point which should not be left out of consideration is that the *meaning* of a Greek text is not always clear and unambiguous. We should not suppose that, where a Hebrew text is obscure and uncertain, the consideration of a Greek rendering necessarily brings us out into the clear light of certainty.

In Lam. 4. 15 we read:

MT: כִּי נָצוּ גַּם־נָעוּ

LXX ὅτι ἀνήφθησαν καί γε ἐσαλεύθησαν

---

[1] Driver in *HTR* xxix (1936) 174 f.

This has been taken as evidence for a Hebrew verb cognate with the Arabic *naṣā* 'be joined' (cf. Freytag, iv. 290, V *'coniunctus fuit'*.)

Does ἀνάπτεσθαι, however, in this text mean 'be joined, touch, be attached'? In the LXX this is the usual sense of the simple verb ἅπτεσθαι (most commonly translating נגע). In close proximity to our verse, in 4. 14 and 4. 15, ἥψαντο ἐνδυμάτων αὐτῶν and ἀπόστητε μὴ ἅπτεσθε are both clear cases of a sense 'touch'. But the compound ἀνάπτεσθαι means not 'touch' but 'kindle' or 'light', whether this is the exact sense of the Hebrew (commonly יצת) or only its more general sense (e.g. יצא with fire as subject). In twenty-four cases listed by Hatch and Redpath I think there is no exception, and two are in Lamentations itself (2. 3, 4. 11), the latter only a few lines earlier. The Greek sense, then, is not 'be joined'. The sense is: 'do not touch them (i.e. the impure); for they are set on fire, they are shaken . . .'. The translator construed the word (*a*) as from יצת 'kindle', or (*b*) as from יצא 'burst out' (of fire), or (*c*)—in my opinion most likely—as from the root of נִיצוֹץ 'spark' and נִצְנֵץ 'be kindled', found in the Midrash in וּנִצְנְצָה בּוֹ רוּחַ הַקֹּדֶשׁ 'the Spirit of holiness was kindled in him'.[1]

Even within a familiar version like the LXX, then, the determination of the meanings of Greek words is not a simple matter; and at times the Greek support for a philological treatment has rested on a doubtful or erroneous understanding of the Greek.

This difficulty is even greater when highly special and artificial techniques of translation are used, as is most obvious with Aquila. Some of his words are *hapax legomena*, special coinages not used elsewhere in Greek; and some, though formally extant elsewhere in Greek, have in Aquila's work special senses intelligible only as renderings of Hebrew and thus different from normal meanings in Greek.

A word in an ancient translation, then, cannot be taken at its face value. Similar difficulties may arise in the Aramaic and Syriac versions, which may at times attempt to imitate the form of the Hebrew original.

Sometimes this can produce very difficult problems of meaning. This is particularly so if a word is not found, or is very rare, in Aramaic apart from the Targum itself. If the root is the same as

---

[1] *Cant. R.* 1. 12; Jastrow, p. 929b.

that of the Hebrew word translated, and if the Hebrew word itself is of uncertain meaning, there are two opposite possibilities: (*a*) the Targum may simply have produced a calque of the Hebrew word; (*b*) the Targumic rendering may be evidence which provides a right comparative philological lead to the sense of the Hebrew. Thus at I Sam. 7. 2,

וַיִּנָּהוּ כָּל־בֵּית יִשְׂרָאֵל אַחֲרֵי יהוה :MT

the verb וַיִּנָּהוּ has often been suspected and emended. The Targum has

ואתנהיאו כל בית ישראל בתר פלחנא דיוי

The opinion of S. R. Driver[1] was that the Targumic word was itself based on the Hebrew, i.e. my possibility (*a*) above. This might fit I Sam. 12. 14, where the same Aramaic renders ... וְהָיִתֶם אחר. But it is still not clear what the Aramaic word means. One tradition has it to mean 'be gathered',[2] (cf. the use to translate וְנִקְווּ at Jer. 3. 17); another has it to mean 'follow eagerly',[3] and cf. Stenning's 'by our devotion to his words' for בדנתנהי לפתגמוהי at Isa. 53. 5.

The view that the Aramaic word is chosen because it translates a similar Hebrew word is plausible at I Sam. 7. 2 and 12. 14, but does not explain the other passages, such as Jer. 3. 17, 30. 21 (MT ונגש), 31. 22 (remote from Heb.), 33. 13, Isa. 53. 5 (remote from Heb.), Hos. 2. 17 (MT וענתה), etc. Thus even if the Aramaic word received some kind of start in use as a rendering for Hebrew נהה or like forms, it seems to have gone beyond this and to have gained a currency of its own. I do not find examples in Aramaic outside the Targum.

On the whole, I am inclined to believe that the Targum has a right rendering of וַיִּנָּהוּ at I Sam. 7. 2; that its rendering was with a genuine cognate which gives a good explication of the difficult Hebrew word; and that this is one of those words which are found in the Aramaic of the Targums but not in other dialects such as Syriac. The sense would most likely be 'follow after, be devoted'. The sense 'follow' is known also in post-biblical Hebrew, e.g. Saadia writes לכל נוהיהם 'to all who follow them'.[4]

---

[1] *Notes on Samuel*, p. 62. [2] So Levy, ii. 94b.
[3] So Jastrow, p. 881b. [4] Cf. above, p. 231.

Another interpretation is found in KB,[1] following Driver,[2] giving a sense 'hold to' (KB says 'hold with', but means 'hold to, adhere to') on the basis of Arabic *nahā* (*y*) glossed as 'come'.

One of the difficulties of this solution is the semantics of the Arabic word itself. Though we do have evidence for senses like 'suivre le conseil de quelqu'un dans une affaire',[3] there is no doubt that the massive preponderance of meaning in Arabic lies in senses like 'prohibit, terminate'. The sense upon which this solution relies is probably remote from the chief or the earliest meaning of the Arabic word. This does not make the solution impossible, but must be noted as a factor in evaluating it. It may be that this consideration makes the Aramaic evidence just quoted more important and the Arabic evidence less so. The gloss 'come', offered by KB, certainly seriously over-simplifies the matter.

Similar problems may be found with the Syriac translation. Thus, though under *b't* we find a noun 'terror' and a verb 'terrify, rush in, invade, oppress', all cases registered by Brockelmann are in the Old Testament and almost all are at places where the Hebrew itself has בָּעַת. Some sense-borrowing from Hebrew may have taken place. Cf. also the interesting case at I Sam. 20. 13

MT: כִּי־יֵיטַב אֶל־אָבִי אֶת־הָרָעָה עָלֶיךָ

Pesh. *'n 'ṭb mn 'by byšt' d'lyk*

meaning 'if I learn from my father evil which is against you'.[4] The Syriac appears to have chosen a word similar in form to the Hebrew, which also produced a possible sense in the context, though that sense differed from the Hebrew sense.

(10) *The Versions and the Grammar of the Original*

One further point may be mentioned briefly. The versions will not generally give reliable guidance on the grammar of the original.[5] A philological treatment will at times depend on the assessing of a Hebrew form as originally, let us say, a noun or an adjective or a passive verb. Sometimes one finds the argument that a version took the Hebrew as such and such a part of speech,

---

[1] KB, p. 599a.　　　　　　　　　　　　[2] *JTS* xxxiv (1933) 377.

[3] Dozy, ii. 730, for *intahā fī l-shay 'ilā ra'y fulāni.*

[4] Cf. Brockelmann, *Lex. Syr.*, p. 265b. Cf. also above, p. 230 (חזה).

[5] See already above, pp. 209, 253.

because this was the part of speech used in the version. Such an argument is very precarious unless we know from samples of the version in this book that its technique included reproduction in the rendering of the same parts of speech, so far as is possible, which the original had. It will generally not be found that this is so, and especially where the text is an obscure one anyway.

Thus at Jer. 2. 31 MT has אֶרֶץ מַאְפֵּלְיָה but Ehrlich wants to read מַאְפִּילָה; and Driver supports this,[1] saying that 'all the versions support a participial or adjectival form'. This is more than can be asserted on the basis of the versions, which generally translate the sense and reference of the original without trying to reproduce its grammar. Similarly at Job 31. 23

$$\text{כִּי פַחַד אֵלַי אֵיד אֵל} : \text{MT}$$

LXX φόβος γὰρ κυρίου συνέσχεν με

it is very precarious to argue[2] that the συνέσχεν με 'indicates a verb for איד with pronominal object at the end of the clause'.

There are not, in fact, many instances in which philological treatments have tried to obtain from the versions guidance about the grammar and syntax of the original, and we need not give further space to the matter, providing that students will be warned against reliance on this kind of argument except where specific evidence for grammatical awareness on the part of the translators can be offered.

(11) Conclusions

The above discussion has taken account of the main factors and problems which may be met in the use of the versions as evidence for philological treatments. It remains to try to sum up the matter with a general evaluation of the use of versional evidence.

The first thing to realize is that many passages which are difficult for us today were difficult for the ancient translators also. In such a position of difficulty these translators had to make what they could out of the context and out of such indications as the text (i.e., primarily, the unpointed written text) had to offer. These indications might include 'etymological' similarities to other words,

---

[1] Driver in *JTS* xli (1940) 165 f.

[2] Driver in *AJSL* lii (1935-6) 165; cf., however, his somewhat different treatment in *Biblica* xxxii (1951) 182.

especially to words which were more familiar; they might occasionally include suggestions and influences from the vocabulary
of other languages known to the translators; and they quite
commonly included a practice in which the letters were taken in a
different sequence or otherwise jumbled, or arbitrary word-
divisions were implied.[1]

In taking guidance from the context the ancient translators
worked from the more familiar words to the more uncertain; and
they were influenced by parallelisms and the general tenor of the
passage, and by associations with words which accidentally had
occurred just before. Their procedure was not entirely different
from that of the modern philological interpreter, and so it is not
surprising if from time to time their results agree with or seem to
support those produced by philological treatments. Though many
other considerations of the modern interpreter were absent from
the mind of his ancient predecessor, the influence of context
worked in a similar way. When the two agree, it is often the
result not of knowledge of a rare word but of analogous divination
from the context.

My own study of past examples, where scholars have offered
versional evidence to support the identification of Hebrew words
not previously recognized, has led on the whole to an unfavourable
judgement. Out of well over one hundred examples closely studied,
using the criteria and considerations discussed in this chapter,
only a few seem to me to be certainly valid examples, while another
proportion of perhaps 15 per cent. may present some reasonable
probability. In a considerable majority of examples the versional
evidence can be explained more easily in some other way than as an
indication that unusual Hebrew words were exactly known to the
translators.

It should not be altogether surprising if this conclusion is
reached. Let us consider particularly the position of the LXX.
Philological treatments, as I have shown, often imply a very optimistic picture of the knowledge of Hebrew vocabulary on the
part of the Greek translators. But this optimistic picture is by no

---

[1] See examples like דגל, p. 262; שכבת, p. 137 n.; תשתע, p. 233 n.; להקת,
pp. 25 f., 231 f., 270 f. Similarly the rendering of the unusual verb נכר by
πέπρακεν at I Sam. 23. 7 is probably not evidence of knowledge of a rare verb
meaning 'sell'; faced with a puzzling form, the translators just guessed that it
belonged to מכר 'sell', which luckily enough gave good sense. Cf. above, p. 209;
Index, no. 214.

means that which the classical tradition of Septuagintal studies has maintained. Swete for instance writes:[1]

The majority of the translators had probably learnt the sacred language in Egypt from imperfectly instructed teachers, and had few opportunities of making themselves acquainted with the traditional interpretation of obscure words and contexts which guided the Palestinian Jew.

Thus philological opinion itself has traditionally been far from unanimous in its optimism about the guidance to be found in the versions. My own assessment of the versions is far from a negative one. It seems to me in general that the ancient translators did their task remarkably well, considering the circumstances.[2] Their grasp of Hebrew, however, was very often a grasp of that which is *average* and *customary* in Hebrew. Our concern, on the other hand, has been for abnormal or rare words or meanings. Rarity in the sense of quite out-of-the-way terms in subjects like architecture and tools did not necessarily leave the translators too much at a loss. Where it is a matter, however, of obscure words in *normal* contexts and of strange meanings for common words, there was a strong tendency towards the levelling of the vocabulary and the interpretation of that which was rare as if it was that which was more normal.

Sporadic aberrant renderings may then quite accidentally provide an apparent agreement with an unusual identification made by us today.

In the case of the LXX a significant point is its setting within the Egyptian Jewish community. The complete domination of Greek within this community rendered it particularly lacking in access to reliable knowledge of the sense of obscure Hebrew words. Thus, in so far as a translation was likely to depend on local sources

---

[1] Swete, *Introduction*, p. 319; and, for the opinion of a master in philology, see Nöldeke, *Die alttestamentliche Literatur* (Leipzig, 1868), p. 246. Cf. also above, p. 240 n.

[2] Terms like 'incompetence' have, however, been quite freely used; e.g. Katz, 'Septuagintal Studies', p. 200, summarizing and confirming the conclusions of earlier workers: 'The translator of Isaiah who worked at an early date was completely unequal to his task. Many Hebrew words were unknown to him . . .'. I differ, however, from workers like Dahood whose principle is that their philological identifications from Ugaritic are right and that the LXX, which does not recognize these, is therefore wrong. Against many of Dahood's interpretations I would consider that the absence of support from the LXX shows that the latter did know Hebrew quite well. Cf. p. 240, n. 1.

of knowledge of the original tongue, the setting in Egypt counts against a high expectancy of accuracy in the LXX.

This is particularly so, secondly, because the LXX bears the marks of an origin very early in the total history of Bible translating. Its translation is extremely uneven. Later the Jewish community, after growing experience of the trouble which could be caused by inaccurate translation, especially when it could be exploited in theological controversy, came to seek greater accuracy and uniformity; and so also did the Christians at a later time. The later Greek translations may on the whole be expected to have shown greater care and diligence in finding out what was really known of Hebrew idioms; but etymologizing and literalizing techniques may in return have obscured much of this diligence.

In general, then, the setting in the Egyptian community, and at so early a date, should tend to make us doubt any great claims for knowledge of rare lexical items on the part of the LXX. This does not mean that such unusual knowledge may not sporadically appear; but, to state the argument conversely, if we find that true instances of confirmation of philological solutions by LXX evidence are rare, then this would not conflict with our general knowledge of the origin of this version.

Another way in which the evidence of the versions may be tested is to consider cases in which the meaning, as discerned by philological treatments, has *not* been seen by the versions. Even those scholars who have most frequently maintained that the LXX or other version discerned rightly a sense which philology has now demonstrated to be correct have even more frequently had to say, or at least to imply, that the versions missed the sense entirely. Out of all the philological identifications which have been offered, the number which can reasonably claim some degree of right recognition by the ancient translators is not high—well below 25 per cent., I should say, even at a generous estimate, and perhaps something nearer to 10 per cent. Thus, while there is every reason to expect that versional evidence will *occasionally* show correct recognition of a word now known to us through comparative philology, the record of philological work itself does not lead us to expect that such correct recognition will be statistically very frequent.

Again, if we take not the total number of philological treatments but the number of those which seem to us to be highly successful, once more we find the relation of the versions to the right sense to be rather weak statistically. I would consider it to be a highly probable treatment when Ginsberg discovers a רֹבַע 'dust' in Num. 23. 10:

מי מנה עפר יעקב ומספר את רֹבַע ישראל

But if the word meant 'dust', this was unknown to LXX (τίς ἐξαρι-θμήσεται δήμους Ισραηλ;), to Jerome (nosse numerum stirpis Israel), to the Targum, which paraphrases on the basis of the sense 'four', as does Aquila (τοῦ τετάρτου Ισραηλ), or to the Peshitta (rwb'h 'the quarter').[1]

Again, the attractive explanation of מְכֵרֹתֵיהֶם at Gen. 49. 5 as 'counsels, plans' makes good sense and has good philological support.[2] The LXX rendering, ἐξ αἱρέσεως αὐτῶν, cannot be given a quite clear interpretation, but it seems rather probable that the ἐξ represents the מ of the Hebrew word, and that no root מכר was identified. Aquila with ἀνασκαφαί certainly saw here the verb כרה 'dig'. Other versions give either a distant paraphrase or the sense 'weapons', which, even if it should be right, does not indicate any exact understanding of the word מכרתיהם, since this sense would probably be deduced from the context, and especially from the preceding כלי, in any case. There is no evidence that any version had linguistic knowledge which would support any philological suggestion.

Again, I would consider that the identification of להקה at I Sam. 19. 20[3] is an attractive and probable treatment. The versional renderings, however, are more naturally interpreted as general surmises of the sense than as correct identifications of a rare word. LXX has ἐκκλησίαν, which could be taken to imply that their Hebrew manuscripts had קהלת (so the traditional textual treatment) but more probably is rather a construing of a written להקת as if it were קהלת. The Peshitta likewise has knš' 'assembly'. The Targum's סיעת 'company' is a very general rendering, and the cuneum of the Vulgate probably means simply a 'number' or 'quantity'.[4] The later Greek translators all have words simply

---

[1] Index, no. 294, cf. no. 295. Cf. also above, p. 11 n.

[2] See above, p. 57. A review of the evidence will be found in Skinner, Genesis (ICC), p. 516 n.　　　　[3] See above, pp. 25 f., 231 f., 267 n.

[4] Ducange provides an entry of the sense 'any number of men or things', and from Jerome's own writing one can cite adv. Iovin. 2. 8: quasi quidam pertur-bationum cunei ad arcem nostrae mentis intraverint; cf. also ep. 92. 3.

meaning 'group', 'gathering'—Aquila ὅμιλον, Theodotion σύστημα, Symmachus συστροφήν. No translator shows any sign of knowing the sense 'old man, old age', which is a component basic to the comparison with Ethiopic.[1]

Even when a versional rendering agrees with a philological identification, one may still have difficulty in deciding whether the agreement betokens precise and correct knowledge of the sense by the version, or whether on the other hand it may be a probable divination from the context and other factors. At Num. 16. 1 I consider the identification of a verb יָקַה 'be insolent'[2] to be highly attractive. Yet the agreement of the Greek ὑπερηφανεύθη may be the result of a good guess rather than a right knowledge of the sense of the word. We do not have much exact knowledge of the version known as ὁ Ἑβραῖος, but its tendency seems to have been one of paraphrastic remoteness rather than accurate adherence to the Hebrew.[3] Since many versions at Num. 16. 1 show wide diversity of understanding, along with considerable paraphrasing, the chances are on the whole that ὁ Ἑβραῖος should be classified in the same way. He was right, we may surmise, without knowing how or why he was right.

We repeat, then, that the considerable number of identifications which seem strong philologically but which have little support in the versions forms a further reason why we should not expect that versional evidence will support the philological treatment in a high proportion of cases.

To this we add another argument. Philological treatments, where they have appealed to versional evidence, have appealed much more often to the LXX than to other versions, such as the Aramaic Targums. But is this pre-eminence of the LXX not paradoxically an argument against the procedure? If there were rare words in biblical Hebrew, the knowledge of which was already dying out in ancient times, is it not much more likely that this knowledge survived among Aramaic-speaking Jews than among Greek-speaking? Yet I have found philological treatments to appeal relatively seldom to the Targums, in comparison with the number

---

[1] LXX γῆρας μητρός for לִיקֲהַת־אֵם at Prov. 30. 17 is surely a striking coincidence rather than sound evidence; cf. Greenfield, *HUCA* xxix (1958) 212 ff. [2] See above, p. 17 f.

[3] See Field, pp. lxxv–lxxvii, and especially the paraphrastic instances cited at the top of p. lxxvi.

of appeals to the LXX. May it not be the weaknesses rather than the strengths of the LXX translation techniques which have provided apparent evidence?

With this in mind we ought to reconsider the argument from mistaken renderings. As we noticed above, scholars have appealed to mistaken renderings by the LXX (or other versions) as evidence of real linguistic knowledge, even though the rendering was admittedly a wrong one at the point where it appeared. After consideration of the examples, one must judge that this argument, though a possible one, is not a probable one. Where a translator is wrong, there will often be other explanations more likely than the view that he has in mind some rare word known to him correctly (though not correctly for the passage in question) but generally unknown to scholars until now. The chances that he is confused, or is guessing, or is paraphrasing, or is rewriting altogether, are considerable. In the nature of the case most examples of alleged 'correct mistakes', if we may so call them, are extremely isolated, and great caution should be used before they are taken as evidence of real linguistic knowledge. Finally, something should surely be granted to the argument that a translator who is rendering wrongly is, just because he is wrong, displaying some degree of incompetence in handling language.

XI

SOME PARTICULAR LINGUISTIC, LITERARY, AND CULTURAL PROBLEMS

THIS chapter will gather together a number of other factors which may have an effect on our estimate of the probability of philological suggestions. Some are more directly linguistic in nature; others are more literary; and yet others belong to the springs of human motivation, ordinary or religious, which may underlie the words and passages investigated.

(1) *Onomatopoeia*

Professor Driver has laid some emphasis on the onomatopoetic origin of Semitic words, and this has been apparent especially in attempts to identify biblical birds and animals from their names. Thus:

Many of the names of birds will be found to be in Hebrew as in other languages onomatopoeic in origin; but no exact reproduction of a bird's cry must be expected. The onomatopoeon may represent a real attempt to reproduce the original sound or may be a mere echoing repetition of a single note to give the effect of a monotonous cry; and it may undergo every form of linguistic assimilation or dissimilation.[1]

The principle is then extended to all sorts of other words. Driver argues, for instance, that the element גע, as found in גּעשׁ, is a noise made in the abdomen when relaxing or in the bottom of the throat when vomiting; it is then applied to groaning or to disgust. When used of rivers and waters, it means 'rise up', and this explains וַתּגעשׁ at Ps. 18. 8.[2]

The principle is further extended so that it decides what is primary and what is secondary in meaning. The familiar גּוע 'expire, die' is related, by similar onomatopoetic formation, to

---

[1] *PEQ* April, 1955, p. 5; cf. *ZAW* lxv (1953) 255, 258; *JSS* vii (1962) 15 f.
[2] *ETL* xxvi (1950) 341; cf. Greenfield in *HUCA* xxix (1958) 205 f.

many words for throat or bowel sounds, and therefore must 'originally' have meant 'gasp for breath' and only secondarily 'die'. By the same token the state of death is 'properly' expressed by מות, originally 'be mute' (like many other words using /m/), and so 'be silent in death'.[1]

These reasonings, then, have an effect on the estimation of probabilities in linguistic history. In the question whether there is a verb כסף 'be pale', a start is made from the assertion that the biliteral base /g, k, q+z, s, ṣ/ expresses onomatopoetically the sound of cutting and tearing. Then, it is argued, there is an easy development from breaking to paleness, and *kaspu*, like Arabic *fiḍḍa*, will originally have described silver as 'broken stuff', since it was purified by breaking two or three times.

Thus the onomatopoetic theory is used to state the sequence of semantic development. The meanings of Hebrew words cannot be deduced from cognate languages without some view of general semantic probabilities. An onomatopoetic theory, because by its nature it attempts to state something extremely early in language formation, tends to dominate the assessment of developments in meaning. It therefore has considerable importance for our present subject.

Of this theory of onomatopoeia, it must be said that it has not approved itself to the majority of Semitic scholars, nor does it appear to have the support of modern general linguistics.[2] There has been a general abandonment of the attempt to find in onomatopoetic formation the origin for any substantial element in language. Even for the names of birds and the like such an origin is not widely found—for English, consider such names as *sparrow*, *thrush*, or *eagle*, alongside names like *cuckoo*, *peewit*. Even for sound-imitating words like *ding-dong*, it has long been noticed that these vary from language to language, and in each language fall into

---

[1] *JSS* vii (1962) 15 f.

[2] On this see for example Jespersen, *Language*, pp. 396–411; Bloomfield, *Language*, p. 156 f.; Hockett, *Course*, p. 298 f. Some of the words which look as if they were onomatopoetic can demonstrably be shown to have become so only through sound change; Saussure, *Course*, p. 69, cites French *fouet*, *fouetter* 'whip', derived from the Latin *fagus* 'beech-tree', which neither sounded like nor meant a whip. From a more philosophical point of view, Ziff, *Semantic Analysis*, p. 25, though himself using onomatopoeia as an argument against the complete conventionality of language, admits that 'onomatopoeia is of no great importance in language'. A particularly good discussion is in Ullmann, *Semantics*, pp. 82–96 and elsewhere.

the normal phonemic patterns of that language, although the natural sounds do not so vary at all. Even these words, therefore, have a strong element of the conventionality which characterizes language. The elements commonly called onomatopoetic may perhaps be better expressed as motivated terms, motivated 'as stylizations of acoustic impressions'.[1] It may be *felt* that the word is something like the natural sound; this is a sense or 'motivation' of the language user, but has nothing necessarily to do with origins.

This is not to say that there is no reality at all in the phenomenon of onomatopoeia. The principal weakness of the idea, as used in the philology of Semitic languages, is its application to the *origin* of words. Applied to their *function*, as for instance in the idea that certain words may be *felt* by their users to symbolize or represent actual sounds, rather more value can be granted to it. But the application of it to the origins of words, with the consequent establishment of a 'basic meaning' through onomatopoeia and the associated idea that language, though now conventional, was originally not so, is extremely precarious. This, we may add, is especially so with Semitic languages; their somewhat rigid restriction on possible formations leaves rather little room for suggestion through word-formation. For example, it has sometimes been thought that the vowel /i/ 'is admirably adapted to convey an idea of smallness';[2] but it is hard to see how this could work in Semitic languages, where the choice of vowels is generally dictated by the pattern in which words are cast.

Applied to Semitic the onomatopoetic theory is ultimately a very limited scheme according to which labial stops like /p/ indicate bursting open, dental stops like /d/ indicate cutting, nasals like /m/ indicate silence or low humming sounds, and so on; but this explains very little. There are indeed some Semitic words to which such explanations appear to fit; but such cases are of little importance, for they cannot be made to support a *general* theory except by arbitrary selection of meanings and precarious histories of semantic development.

The onomatopoetic theory therefore does not appear to have positive value in the present discussion, and arguments about semantic development which depend upon it are of no great weight. Much more importance attaches to the theory of biliteral

---

[1] Thieme, in Hymes, p. 586b.
[2] See Ullmann, *Semantics*, p. 87.

bases, which has often been associated with the idea of onomatopoeia; but the effects of this have already been discussed above.
The importance of the biliteral base does not depend on association
with onomatopoeia; indeed, on the contrary, the extremely limited
range of meanings attached to the bases as normally identified
could only imply a high degree of conventionality, and correspondingly a marked distance from the directness of
onomatopoeia, in the words developed from these bases.

(2) *Some linguistic-cultural relations*

There remain one or two conceptions about language in its
relation to thought and culture which may be mentioned briefly
because they have appeared in the context of philological treatments. One of these is the idea that the original sense of words was
always a 'concrete' one. Thus Eitan writes:

> It is a philological axiom that every word, whether noun or verb,
> had (or its root had) originally a concrete significance and that only by
> way of metaphor did it receive subsequently derived meanings, as need
> for them arose.[1]

One may doubt, however, whether this axiom has great validity,
and still more may one doubt the attempts to use it as a basis for
argument in particular cases. Eitan's own example is וַיַּחֲלֹשׁ at
Exod. 17. 13; the sense, he believes, is that Joshua 'carried off'
or 'snatched away' Amalek. So, he argues, the Palestinian Arabic
ḥalaša 'reap with a sickle' is merely a specialized shade of the more
general classical *ḥalasa* 'carry off, snatch away'.

Thus, he goes on:

> The Hebrews, a predominantly agricultural people, would naturally
> have derived from this general signification a more special one, 'to
> reap', i.e. to carry off with a sickle.

Eitan goes on to assert that this sense 'would have been' (*sic*)
preserved by Palestinian peasants up to the Islamic invasions (and
so passed from Hebrew into Palestinian Arabic).

I do not think that this particular type of argument has appeared
very frequently in philological treatments. I mention it here, however, because it illustrates how general conceptions of the relation
between language and culture may influence a scholar's picture of
a probable semantic history.

---

[1] Eitan, p. 35.

Occasionally solutions show some other kind of cultural preference. Of the interpretations offered by Hirschberg in a recent article,[1] for instance, a large proportion have a sexual reference. The notorious crux at Amos 5. 26 is interpreted by him through taking both the Ραιφαν of LXX (understood as a Hebrew רֵיפָה, cognate with Arabic *rayyif* 'fertile') and the כִּיּוּן as sexual objects or symbols.[2]

Philological procedures may at times be guided by particular lines of cultural assessment, and the student should be aware of this possibility if he is to evaluate philological arguments properly.

(3) *Parallelism*

Philological treatments frequently place a very heavy emphasis upon the phenomenon of parallelism. That parallelism is a marked feature of Hebrew poetry is a matter of common knowledge. But the importance of parallelism becomes even greater when the establishment of text or of meaning is in doubt. If we know the meanings, we notice and appreciate the parallelism, and the parallelism in turn sets the meanings in relief and forms them into a striking pattern. When we do not know the meanings, however, the parallelism becomes one of the principal guides by which we discover the meanings.[3] Among philological treatments of poetical texts, a large proportion make some considerable appeal to parallelism. Can so heavy a load be placed upon it?

Some sophisticated analyses of parallelism have been produced. These depend for the most part on the assumption that the meanings of the various Hebrew terms are known. When the study is rather an attempt to discover the meaning of a word, the situation is different. The question is not: given the meanings of two parts of a sentence, what is the nature of the parallelistic relation between them? It is rather: given a sentence which appears to be parallelistic, and given the meaning of one part, what chances are there that this will help us to know the meaning of the other part?

The obvious difficulties are:

(1) We do not know in the beginning whether the verse will be a synonymous parallelism or some other kind; we may not even have complete certainty that it is parallelistic at all.

---

[1] In *VT* xi (1961) 373–85. [2] Ibid., pp. 375 f.; cf. Index, no. 224.
[3] Cf. the saying of Menahem ben Sarūk, above, p. 62.

(2) Even where a verse is certainly parallelistic, we do not certainly know what effect this will have on a particular word within it. Two elements in a parallelism may be identical or synonymous within the sense of the customary definitions of these terms, and yet the words in one element may have quite considerable differences in meaning from the words in the other.

The former of these need, perhaps, not be illustrated with examples; for the second, a simple illustration in the English will suffice:

> Ps. 24. 3: 'Who shall ascend into the hill of the Lord?
> And who shall stand in his holy place?'

In this familiar sentence, let us suppose that one of the words in the second part is of unknown meaning. The parallelism helps us, but it helps us only a certain way. If the word 'place' were unknown, we might surmise from the parallelism that it meant 'temple' or 'house' or 'area' or 'ground'. If we really pressed the idea of synonymous or identical parallelism so as to make it apply to each word, we would guess that מָקוֹם is another Hebrew word meaning 'hill'. There are places where the parallelism of two words for 'hill' occurs, e.g. Isa. 10. 32:

ינפף ידו הר בית־ציון גבעת ירושלם

The same would be true if the meaning of קוּם 'stand' were uncertain. Parallelism might make us guess that it was another word for 'go up'.

This is a central problem in all use of parallelism as an interpretative key. The parallelism is a parallelism of the literary units; it does not guarantee that the lexical units used within each literary unit are synonyms.[1] One element in a parallelism may use 'walk', while another uses 'sit' (e.g. Isa. 9. 1; Ps. 1. 1 has 'walk', 'stand', and 'sit' as the three verbs).

Let us see how this works in a real instance of philological treatment. We have already looked at the interesting proposal to

---

[1] This is already recognized by earlier works, e.g. Driver in *JTS* xxxiii (1932) 43: 'parallel passages do not necessarily demand verbal identity' and 'close strophic parallelism is not so required' that words in parallelism 'must mean the same'.

identify a Hebrew עָשׁ 'rottenness' at Hos. 5. 12. The sentence as a whole is:

וַאֲנִי כָעָשׁ לְאֶפְרָיִם וְכָרָקָב לְבֵית יְהוּדָה׃

It is the close parallelism which gives strength to the suggestion that עָשׁ means 'rottenness', thus being identical with רָקָב, rather than meaning 'moth'. Both words then mean 'rottenness', giving an absolute parallelism. But when one looks at this a second time, one realizes that the absolute parallelism is not so great an advantage. Only if the parallelism is identical, not only in the two thoughts expressed in parallel, but also in each word used in each of the two thoughts, is the identification of two words both meaning 'rottenness' entirely satisfying.

Conversely, even if the relation is between 'moth' and 'rottenness', we still have a good parallelism. The two parallel phrases are both about forces of decay and corruption. If the total parallel sentence is an expression about decay or corruption in general, it is possible that the effect is strengthened, and not weakened, if we have words for two *different* corrupting agencies, i.e. moth and rot, rather than two words for rot. Thus, even if the interpretation of עָשׁ as 'rottenness' gives a more exact synonymy for רָקָב, the understanding of עָשׁ as 'moth' is actually perhaps more true to the general pattern of Hebrew parallelism. These considerations tell on the whole against the acceptance of this particular philological suggestion.

Parallelism, then, even when it seems to be of a 'synonymous' type, does not in itself provide any assurance that a particular *word* will be similarly parallel or synonymous with the corresponding word in the parallel clause. Or, to state the matter in another way, even when we know that there is a synonymous parallelism, we do not know in what aspects the two realities set in parallel will be compared. In the case just discussed, if 'rot' is specifically the point, then two words with this meaning will give a good effect; but if the point is a more general one of 'spoiling' or 'decay' or 'deterioration', then 'moth' and 'rot' provide a good parallelism even though they do not mean the same thing.

The argument from parallelism is rather stronger in Jer. 4. 31:

כִּי קוֹל כְּחוֹלָה שָׁמַעְתִּי צָרָה כְּמַבְכִּירָה

Though it is possible to take צָרָה as 'anguish', the parallelism with

קוֹל 'voice' was invoked by Driver in favour of an interpretation as 'shrill cry', implying another word צרה, cognate with Arabic ṣarra and ṣarīr, and homonymic (at least in the consonants) with צרה 'anguish'. The use of the verb 'hear' makes it a little more likely that the second object will be a sound rather than a state of distress. This argument, indeed, is not absolutely convincing. Firstly, in Hebrew one could probably speak of 'hearing' distress or anguish.[1] Secondly, one could say that a phrase 'anguish like (that of) one bearing her first child' is loosely attached to חולה, without implying logical dependence on שמעתי. Nevertheless the point has some considerable strength, and may be further confirmed by an appeal to the LXX:

ὅτι φωνὴν ὡς ὠδινούσης ἤκουσα, τοῦ στεναγμοῦ σου ὡς πρωτο-τοκούσης.

Further evaluation depends on consideration of the same explanation at Jer. 48. 5 (LXX 31. 5). At 4. 31 the fact that the same verb 'hear' seems to apply to both objects strengthens the case for a closely similar sense. At 48. 5 there is a parallelism with בְּכִי 'weeping'. On the whole I think that this example of philological treatment has been successful.

A still more striking example is Isa. 2. 16:

ועל כל־אניות תרשיש ועל כל־שכיות החמדה :MT

LXX: καὶ ἐπὶ πᾶν πλοῖον θαλάσσης καὶ ἐπὶ πᾶσαν θέαν πλοίων κάλλους.

Driver argues that sense and parallelism 'require' שכיות to be the name of a kind of boat and החמדה the name of a country. The identification of שכת is widely accepted; that of Arabia Felix as the country is less certain. 'Ships of Tarshish' is a set phrase; it is less likely that another phrase existed relating the name of ships of another region. The parallelism of cedars of Lebanon and oaks of Bashan, on the other hand, is stereotyped (cf. Zech. 11. 2; Ezek. 27. 5f.). The passage may go as follows:

All that is high and lofty	all that is uplifted and low
All cedars of Lebanon	all oaks of Bashan

---

[1] Cf. in Jer. 41. 11 (object רעה); 48. 29 (גאון מואב); 6. 7 (חמס ושד ישמע); Job 20. 3 (object מוסר כלמתי).

All the high hills   all the lofty mountains
Every high tower   every fortified wall
All the ships of Tarshish   all the lovely boats (views?)

'Low' (שׁפל) in the first line, if this is the right text and sense, implies that the parallelism is not absolute. In the LXX rendering, it may be θέαν that translates שׂכיות, and πλοίων may be an explanatory addition to fit the parallel of the first hemistich; or, since θαλάσσης is a midrashic-etymological rendering of תרשׁישׁ, πλοίων may be added to provide a complement.[1] No other translation perceives a word for 'ship' (cf. Aq., Sym. ὄψεις, θέας; Syr. *dawqe*).

Thus, though there is a strong case for the identification of שׂכת as the name of a boat, the argument from parallelism in itself is not entirely decisive.

A similar argument arises at Isa. 44. 24–28; a considerable chain of closely identical parallelisms may still leave uncertain the position in parallelism of a single term:

> He who says to Jerusalem, Thou shalt be inhabited
>   and to the cities of Judah, You will be built up;
>   and its ruins I shall set up again;
> He who says to the deep, Be dried up;
>   and its streams I shall dry up;
> He who says to Cyrus רֹעִי
>   and all my purpose he will complete;
> Saying to Jerusalem, Thou shalt be built,
>   and to the temple, Thou shalt be refounded.

What is the sense of רֹעִי? Traditionally it is taken as 'my shepherd', parallel with 'my anointed' in 45. 1. But the parallelism in 44. 28 is kept very close if we follow the LXX ὁ λέγων Κύρῳ φρονεῖν and interpret as in Syriac *r'ā*, *re'yānā*, etc., 'thought':

> He who tells to Cyrus my thought
>   and all my purpose he will complete.

The less rigid parallelism of 'my shepherd' and 'my anointed' is, however, more probable, and the LXX analysed as the same root which is found in רעיון (διαλογισμός Dan. 7. 28); cf. especially Ps. 139 (138). 2:

בַּנְתָּה לְרֵעִי   σὺ συνῆκας τοὺς διαλογισμούς μου.

---

[1] On this treatment of תרשׁישׁ see *BJRL* xxx (1967) 291 f. and *JSS* xii (1967) 117 f.

The designation of Cyrus as 'my shepherd' is in fact a good parallelism in thought, though not an exact one in form, with the completion of the purpose of the Lord.

In general it is a good rule to interpret by observation of the context. In the circumstances of our study, however, where one linguistic element is obscure, the following of context is not necessarily a good method. An unusual word may say just what one would *not* expect on the ground of context alone. It is by following context, where one linguistic element is uncertain, that interpreters and translators are led to harmonizations and assimilations. Parallelism may make clear the general bearing of a passage without determining the exact information furnished by particular words. There are different kinds of parallelism, and sometimes a passage may turn out to be not parallelistic at all. It cannot be invoked as a straightforward guide to the meaning of uncertain words. It remains, however, a very important factor, which the scholar cannot neglect. Finally, where Ugaritic words are used for the elucidation of Hebrew, it should be remembered that the meanings of many of these depend in the first place on parallelisms in Ugaritic, and the same caution has to be used in any reliance on these Ugaritic meanings.

(4) *Religious Factors*

The problems discussed in this book do not belong directly to theology or the study of religion, and we have worked almost entirely on a textual and linguistic level. There are, however, ways in which judgements of a religious or theological nature may affect our estimate of probabilities in a philological or a textual treatment. These would seem to fall into two main categories:

(*a*) Judgements of fact about the religious situation of a particular time, which may affect our discernment of what a text may be saying, and

(*b*) Judgements of style and taste, of religious logic and theological consistency, which may help us to know whether a given utterance 'makes sense', whether it is credible that a person of a given period could find it meaningful.

Turning to the first of these two categories, we should give some particular mention to Nyberg. His discussion of the text of Hosea was accompanied by the development of some rather original

views of the religious history of Palestine, and these views in turn
reacted on his textual and philological discussion. The combination of these two was characteristic of his method.

At the difficult place Hos. 7. 5:

יֹום מַלְכֵּנוּ הֶחֱלוּ שָׂרִים חֲמַת מִיָּיִן מָשַׁךְ יָדֹו אֶת־לֹצְצִים :

Nyberg[1] took מַלְכֵּנוּ to refer to the god Melek and שָׂרִים to refer to
his heavenly court; while of the words מֹשֵׁךְ יָדֹו he pronounced that
their meaning was unknown, but that they seemed to refer to
some ritual action, in which the god Melek was subject.

A similar element in Nyberg's thought is the prominence of the
divine name 'Al. Nyberg identifies this at several points in Hosea,
and its presence enables him to avoid emendation. Thus at Hos.
11. 7 (usually dealt with by emendation):

וְאֶל־עַל יִקְרָאֻהוּ

Nyberg changes only the word-division and reads the text as

וְאֶל־עָל יִקְרָא

'and therefore to 'Al they cry'.[2]

The identification of the divine name 'Al, this time in the form
עֵלוֹ (cf. Ugar. *'lw*), has been particularly well received at I Sam.
2. 10: עָלָו בַּשָּׁמַיִם יַרְעֵם. If the first word is taken as the divine
name עֵלוֹ, we have good parallelism with the other half-verse, and
there is no need for the textual emendation to עֶלְיֹון, proposed by
BH[3], which gives us semantically the same result.

Such then are some examples of the possibility that information
about religious thought in the Near East may enable us to see
meaning in a biblical passage where it has formerly eluded us, and
thereby avoid emendation of the text.

Less frequently discussed and more subtle in nature is the
question of whether a given religious utterance 'makes sense' or
not.

There is a familiar verse in Proverbs:

Prov. 29. 18 בְּאֵין חָזֹון יִפָּרַע עָם

AV 'Where there is no vision the people perish'.

---

[1] Nyberg, *Hoseabuch*, p. 50. Cf. Hos. 8. 10, מלך שרים, Nyberg, *ZAW*, p. 251.
[2] Nyberg, op. cit., p. 89; for his chief argument about 'Al see p. 58; and for
the divine name 'Am cf. p. 27.

RSV 'Where there is no prophecy the people cast off restraint'.

Driver's comment is: 'Vision can hardly be said to restrain a people from excesses.' This conviction leads him to seek another explanation; and, guided by the ἐξηγητής of LXX, οὐ μὴ ὑπάρξῃ ἐξηγητὴς ἔθνει παρανόμῳ, he considers a word חָזוֹן meaning 'magistrate' and cognate with Accadian and Aramaic words. This interpretation is weak, however, for two reasons. Firstly, it fails to take into account the high originality of the Proverbs translator. It is possible that his ἐξηγητής, meaning vaguely a guide or interpreter of the divine will, is only his interpretation of חזון 'vision'. He may also have seen a reference to the familiar synagogue term חַזָּן. The Hebrew word in any case is to him only the source of his literary inspiration.

Secondly, in the context of Hebrew religion, with the importance attached by it to prophetic 'vision', it is an entirely credible sentiment that 'vision' should keep a people from excesses or from disaster. The original doubt about the meaningfulness of the text if the word was understood as 'vision' is thus misplaced.

The גילו ברעדה of MT at Ps. 2. 11 f. raises the same kind of question. Is it indeed an improbable conjunction to construe as 'rejoice with trembling'? Would the psychology of religion find this lacking in congruity? The sense that some other meaning must be required was present already in the Middle Ages, when interpreters were already discussing the possibility of a גיל meaning 'tremble' or the like. Reider thought that the sense was 'worship', and compared Ps. 43. 4 שמחת גילי, understood as 'the joy of my worship'; Driver identified a word meaning 'be affrighted' (see Index, nos. 76–77). Is not the textual reorganization ברעדה נשקו ברגליו still the most convincing suggestion?[1]

Another interesting example is found in the Qumran Isaiah text 1QIsA at 52. 14. Here the MT reading is:

$$\text{כֵּן־מִשְׁחַת מֵאִישׁ מַרְאֵהוּ}$$

This has commonly been taken (with vocalization as מָשְׁחָת) to mean:

'His appearance was so marred, beyond human semblance.'

---

[1] Cf. above, pp. 5, 175.

This is, of course, from the verb שָׁחַת 'mar, spoil, destroy'. Now the reading of the scroll is:

כן משחתי מאיש מראהו

Guillaume, discussing this, says that the verb cannot have been the מָשַׁח 'anoint', which is 'inconceivable without Christian ideas'. He believes nevertheless that this is a verb מָשַׁח; it must be one different from the familiar מָשַׁח 'anoint'. Once again philological treatment produces a new homonym. The true cognate in Arabic is not *masaha* 'smear' but *masaha*, which 'in its primitive sense' meant 'to gall the back of a camel and exhaust it', and is also used of the fraying of thread and of the transforming of men into animals. The Arabic form *masīh* is, according to the Qāmūs, 'of ugly form and without comeliness'. The meaning of the Isaiah passage is thus probably 'so did I mar his appearance'.

We do not need to go into the complicated series of considerations which are needed to evaluate this suggestion. The point for the present is that we should note the starting-point in the assurance that in this context the idea of anointing is impossible.

Such then are some examples of the way in which judgements of theology and of religious history may enter into the determination of probabilities in textual and philological matters.

(5) *The Argument from Actuality*

It may seem quaint that one should take a title such as this, since purists might demand that all arguments should be based on some kind of actuality. What I mean here is to notice comprehensively all sorts of information which is not itself primarily linguistic or literary in nature but which may affect our judgement of the possible sense of linguistic items. Archaeology, the study of the geography of the ancient world, the knowledge of social customs and technological development may all by their increase help to explain and clarify, and thereby justify, linguistic terms which were formerly obscure, or may give suggestions for semantic connexions and developments which were a cause of trouble. Such arguments from actuality may thus form the start of a dissatisfaction with the received meaning of a text, and so lead to the search for new meaning through textual or philological treatment. We have already mentioned how archaeological discovery has validated the text of I Sam. 13. 21 and given us clear evidence for the weight 'pim' or 'payim'. There is nothing new in the kind of argumentation we are describing here; it is one of the oldest forms of exegetical thinking. All I want to do is to illustrate it for modern philological treatments.

Pregnancy is esteemed as a great blessing by Oriental women. Yet the speech of God to Eve in Gen. 3. 16 is, by the usual interpretation, a statement which represents pregnancy as something punitive or disastrous. Through this observation, Rabin is moved to seek a different meaning for the word הֵרֹנֵךְ. He is influenced also by the parallelism with תְּשׁוּקָה 'desire', and he finds the meaning to be probably 'sexual desire', and possibly 'whining', with reference to Ugaritic and Arabic cognates.

The actuality observed may be a piece of fact known from outside the story, or it may be the congruity of the story itself. At Judges 19. 2 Driver cleverly notices that the words וַתִּזְנֶה עָלָיו פִּילַגְשׁוֹ should not mean 'she prostituted herself', as the customary understanding of the verb זנה would suggest. There is no hint of such an element elsewhere in the story of the Levite's concubine. Indeed, the tragedy is substantially heightened if the woman had been chaste right up to the time of the evil deed at Gibeah. Moreover, several of the versions appear to agree in avoiding the stain on the poor woman. The Targum has ובסרת עלוהי 'she despised him'; Jerome writes *reliquit eum*; LXX has καὶ ὠργίσθη αὐτῷ (A text) 'she was angry at him', or ἐπορεύθη ἀπ' αὐτοῦ 'she departed from him' (B text). This is of interest because the normal meaning of the verb זנה must have been sufficiently familiar to these translators. The cognate Accadian *zenū* 'be angry' may thus give a solution, incidentally adding another homonym to Hebrew.

Place-names are another possible setting for this kind of problem; and especially so when, as sometimes happens, a form can be construed either as a place-name or as some other kind of word. We saw above[1] the possible place-name Izalla at Ezek. 27. 19, which (if correct) serves to remove an enigmatic participial form from the lists of exceptions in our grammars and lexica. Philological treatments can cause place-names to disappear as well as to come into existence. Some interpreters have removed Ophir from the text of Isa. 13. 12:

אוֹקִיר אֱנוֹשׁ מִפָּז וְאָדָם מִכֶּתֶם אוֹפִיר

[1] See p. 189.

arguing that it means:

> 'I shall value a man more than gold;
> more than fine gold shall I esteem a man.'

The word אוֹפִיר is then supposed to be from a verb יָפַר, cognate with Arabic *wafara* 'be plentiful', Ugaritic *ypr* 'make to abound'. If this is right, one presumably has to argue that the other two cases of the collocation כֶּתֶם אוֹפִיר (Job 28. 16; Ps. 45. 10), plus the other significant associations of Ophir with gold, have produced an assimilation of the sense at Isa. 13. 12 and caused the verb to be mistaken for the place-name. I myself think that 'gold of Ophir' is a much more likely sense for Isa. 13. 12 also.

XII

SUMMING-UP

WE have sought in this study to work out the criteria by which we may judge a suggested philological treatment to be successful or unsuccessful. These criteria are not rules the simple observation of which will certainly lead to a right result. They themselves are probable rather than absolute; and sometimes they may seem capable of working in either direction—as we have seen, a philological suggestion may be confirmed by the fact that a parallel exists in post-biblical Hebrew, but may also be weakened thereby. There may always be extreme cases which defy the probabilities which generally apply; but it would be unfortunate if some such extreme cases were to be taken as the rule and thereby allowed to justify a long series of others equally extreme. Thus, though we cannot set out rules which can be mechanically followed, the following is a summary of the points which should normally come into consideration when a philological treatment is suggested:

(1) How far the word in question lies within the normal phonological correspondences with a cognate word considered for its elucidation, and what are the long-range consequences for comparative studies if this is ignored or treated lightly.

(2) How far the meaning given for the cognate word is a real meaning, stated with adequate precision, and known with reasonable probability as one which may go back to such time that a cognate with a meaning semantically relatable may have survived in Hebrew also.

(3) A critical consideration of the semantic connections presumed in the identification, in relation to acknowledged examples and with a developed awareness of the difference between theoretical constructions and historically controlled evidence.

(4) An awareness of the possibility that words are adoptions from non-Semitic languages, or have been influenced in their history by such adoptions; or that the information given about them in dictionaries has been confused through contamination with such adoptions.

(5) A consideration of the possibility of a textual error, i.e. that the form in the text has arisen by an accident of the graphic transmission.

(6) If the new identification produces a new homonym in Hebrew, some consideration of how this is statistically related to other homonyms and to the total extent of homonymy in Hebrew and in Semitic languages generally.

(7) If the new identification produces a new synonym or near-synonym in Hebrew, or, to put it another way, if it comes very close to the semantic field of words already known, some consideration of the change of balance this causes in the lexical stock.

(8) Some consideration of the statistical probabilities for the assumption that a word in another Semitic language will be likely to lead to the identification of a cognate in Hebrew.

(9) If the identification relies on versional evidence, a full consideration of the versional reading for (a) the possibility that the version had a different Hebrew text, (b) the style and translation techniques of the translator of this book, (c) possible vicissitudes in the graphic transmission of the version itself, and, in general, (d) the possibility that the rendering rests not upon exact knowledge of the Hebrew word but upon other influences, such as theological interpretation, paraphrasing, etymologizing, and divination from parallelisms or from the general context.

(10) A consideration of post-biblical usage, including Jewish Aramaic; and including also the possible effects of midrashic expositions upon the history of understanding; and also, finally, the views of the medieval Jewish lexicographers.

(11) If the new identification involves an abandonment of the Massoretic vocalization, a consideration of how the Massoretic vocalization arose and what it means, and of how our abandonment of it, seen in the long run, would affect (a) our view of the history and nature of Massoretic activity, (b) our total knowledge of the Hebrew language and meanings in it.

(12) Finally, it goes without saying that all new identifications, even if all these requirements have been taken into account, have still to be weighed for probability against the more traditional or accepted meanings for the Hebrew words in question.

Of these various criteria, the one which deserves some further elaboration at this point is the semantic one. As was noted earlier,[1]

---

[1] Above, pp. 88 ff.

the semantic side in traditional philology was often naïve, hasty, and thoughtless. The following points are offered as suggestions which may assist the student:

(1) The approach to the study of meaning must be strictly linguistic, rather than logical, in character. It may seem strange to insist on this: readers may ask whether, during the long reign of philological method, this has not always been so. The answer is that it has not. The older historical and comparative philology, lacking an adequate approach to questions of meaning (especially because of its concentration on the separate tracing of atomic elements in their development), in its semantic notions very often fell a prey to conceptions of a logical rather than of a linguistic nature. This can be plentifully illustrated from the traditional Semitic philology. Take a statement (admittedly, a fairly extreme example) about נתר. This verb is supposed to mean 'tear'; but the piel is used of insects which hop. In Arabic we have *tarra* 'be severed', *tarr* 'prancing, trotting'; thus, Driver writes:[1]

> There can be no objection to connecting *n-t-r* as applied to locusts with *tarr* as applied to light horses; and the underlying idea by which verbs of rending or tearing asunder are linked to verbs denoting trotting quickly or prancing or hopping seems to be that of separation from the ground, whereby the beast appears to be now touching the earth and now suspended in mid-air.

Though it is an extreme case, this passage typifies the way in which many semantic relations were set up in the older philology. The investigator, taking a series of forms which seem to be cognate and of which the senses are known, works by thinking out a common factor attaching to them all, so that a more or less direct relation from this common factor to the meaning of each form in each of several languages can be seen. The procedure is logical rather than linguistic in type, because it works by consideration of common features in the referents rather than by working out a process of meaning transfer within stages of linguistic usage. It is true that Driver frequently detects 'secondary' elements in these groups of meanings; but this is hardly enough to alter the basic character of the method. The method is fundamentally one of association of actual features of groups of referents. It is difficult

---

[1] In the Robinson Festschrift (1946), pp. 70 ff.

to find any way of relating such an approach to that of modern semantic studies.[1]

Linguistic history would seem to suggest rather that the meanings of groups of cognates, collected across the lines of temporal differences and from different languages, will tend to be haphazard in their relation to common features of any group of referents designated. Meanings are not derived from one basic idea, or directly from a class of referents, but from the meanings of forms already found. Form x, let us say, designates the referent p; and in association with form x we find the forms y and z, which appear to be cognate with x. It may be expected that, if *all* the history of development is known, their meanings may be seen to have *some* relation to that obtaining between x and its referent p; but we do not know which of the many aspects of this relation may be relevant for the senses of y and z, nor do we know that the aspect relevant for y will also be relevant for z. Semantic transfers will not generally flow smoothly from a basic general idea, but may arise from features which are quite minor, and which are thus logically accidental and unpredictable, in relation to the meaning of a form taken as original, or in relation to a previous change of meaning.

This criticism of a 'logical' approach does not mean that logic is irrelevant, or that semantic work can be done without some foundation of general theory. The logic implied in the process we have just criticized would seem to be one of simple relations between things and names, the names attaching to evident qualities of the things.[2] A more sophisticated logic of linguistic usage may not necessarily have this damaging effect.

(2) Students may find it helpful to use the distinction between reference and information.[3] By 'reference' I mean that to which a word refers, the actual or thought entity which is its referent.

[1] As exemplified, for instance, in recent treatises such as the works of Ullmann.

[2] Such a logic seems to be implied in the very important 'as' of the traditional Hebrew dictionary, e.g. when it is explained that חנית 'spear' is so called 'as' flexible etc.; so BDB, p. 333b, though this explanation is not necessarily accepted by BDB. The logic of this 'as' is all-pervasive in BDB; and no difference is made by the simple observation that for this or that word a different derivation can be suggested.

[3] Already mentioned above, p. 118. The terms of the distinction were suggested to me by that between 'meaning' and 'reference' in Quine, *From a Logical Point of View*, e.g. pp. 9, 21 f., 47, etc. I have used 'information' because it has now become fairly technical for the effect of choices within a recognized sign system.

By 'information' I mean the difference which is conveyed, within a known and recognized sign system (a language like Hebrew or Arabic), by the fact that it is *this* sign and not another that is used. The major linguistic interest, it would seem to me, lies in the latter. Many arguments in which biblical scholars adduce linguistic evidence appear to me, however, to involve some confusion between the former and the latter.

For instance, there are certainly places where Canaanite and Aramaic inscriptions use a word cognate with Hebrew מָקוֹם, and where the reference is to a place of burial. It does not follow that this word communicates the specific *information* 'tomb, grave, place of burial'. Rather, the writers, *referring to* a tomb or the area around it, called it a 'place'. While it is interesting to note that the word is used of a tomb, this fact does not entitle us to suppose that 'tomb' (as information of a distinction from any other place) is the meaning of this word, and then to transfer it, as Dahood wants to do, to Hebrew passages like Job 16. 18, Qoh. 8. 10 (where it does not improve the sense anyway).[1] Though the place referred to in some inscriptions is in fact a tomb, this does not make 'tomb' the information specified by the choice of this word and thereby transferable to other contexts.

(3) An increased emphasis should be laid upon the statement of meaning in one language only. A Hebrew word has its meaning only in Hebrew, an Arabic word only in Arabic. We have to overcome the heritage of that supposedly comparative approach (actually anti-comparative in its effects) which defines a Hebrew word by thinking about what 'it means' in another language. The resources used in philological treatments (for example, the meaning of an Arabic word) are meanings in that language, while the results to be reached are meanings in Hebrew. Meaning in Hebrew is independent of meaning in Arabic, and depends on choices within the Hebrew lexical stock of a given time. This is an argument for, and not against, the comparative study of Semitic languages; it is a source of confusion when scholars quote Arabic or other meanings as if it were somehow 'natural' that they would also be the meanings in Hebrew, and part of sophistication in comparative philology is the learning to avoid this kind of confusion.[2]

---

[1] Index, no. 280.
[2] One example out of many: Gray, *Kings*, p. 306, mentioning a quite normal

This point is also confirmed by the emphasis on 'information' which we have just discussed. The communication of meaning in Hebrew was not determined at all by what the words meant in Arabic, and was not primarily determined by what they meant in proto-Semitic; it was primarily determined by the choice between the words available in Hebrew. Because words operate in relation to one another within Hebrew, all philological solutions to particular difficulties have to be considered not only in themselves, for the satisfaction they give in a particular difficult context, but also in their more general implications, for the effect they have on the total balance of the available series of choices in Hebrew.

(4) One may on the whole expect that the results of our semantic work, in the conditions which call for the use of philological treatment from the cognate languages, will be probabilistic and approximative rather than decisive and exact. This is not because some philological suggestions are right and others wrong; rather, it is something that is likely to attach to the method intrinsically even if it can be substantially improved and refined. Only occasionally will solutions achieve such certainty that they can become *given* realities of the Hebrew lexical stock in the same way as familiar and well-attested words with numerous known contexts are given realities.

For one thing, our knowledge of the semantic developments which have led to the various meanings of cognates in the ancient Semitic languages is generally hypothetical and indirect; and, for another, even if we can be sure of the rightness of a suggestion inspired by a cognate word, it is unlikely that this will provide us with an *exact* knowledge of the sense in Hebrew. Such a suggestion is more likely to assure us of the rightness of the Hebrew text and of the general field of meaning in which the word may lie; this being done, the further determination of meaning will depend mainly on the context. Precise references, nuances, and overtones, even when suggested within a philological treatment, will generally be decided not by the evidence of cognates but by the Hebrew context itself.

occurrence of דבש 'honey', tells us that it 'might indicate Arabic *dibs*' (a liquid preparation from grape-juice), and then goes on to agree that it probably means honey (from bees). The repeated casual dragging in of the Arabic meanings, as if they had some natural probability, is a source of confusion, and not of enlightenment.

For instance, the identification of בְּצִקְלֹן on the basis of Ugaritic *bṣql* is as certain and successful a philological treatment as can ever be expected.[1] Yet it does not give us the exact sense in Hebrew. We know that in Ugaritic *bṣql* is a kind of vegetation, the growth of which is highly esteemed and desired, and that it is of value for food. Applied to the Hebrew example, this information is enough to give certain negative precisions: it excludes the possibility that the initial בּ is the preposition 'in', and so it excludes all exegesis in senses like 'in his bag'. We are thus sure that some kind of grain or vegetable is meant (or the plot in which such was grown); but this was already clear as the general sense of the passage in any case, and the uncertainty was its relation to this word. We cannot be sure that there was a Hebrew בצקל which meant exactly the same plant as was meant at Ugarit. There are ample instances of words for animals, foods, commodities, and so on, where different objects are designated by words formally cognate.[2] Thus even a very successful philological treatment can give a good deal of negative discrimination but does not necessarily furnish a clear and positive precision of meaning.

These then are some ways in which we may expect the semantic side of the assessment of philological treatments to develop.

Some further explanation should be added about the emphasis just made on meaning within one language. The point is that the meaning of words can be stated as the difference made by their choice as against other words in the same language at the same time; and negatively this implies that senses cannot be indiscriminately imported from other languages just because words are cognate. This does not mean, however, that the cognate languages can be merely neglected, or that intra-Hebraic etymologizing is to be encouraged. The latter has, indeed, historically been the source of much trouble, from which the use of cognate languages has done much to liberate us.

That אַל־תִּשְׁתָּע at Isa. 41. 10 had the general sense of 'do not fear' was perhaps always fairly clear; but it was the discovery of Phoenician שתע and the Ugaritic cognate which made it clear that

---

[1] See above, p. 26.

[2] Cf. *dibs*/ דבשׁ, above, p. 292 n.; Hebrew לֶחֶם is 'bread' or 'food' generally, but Arabic *laḥm* is 'meat' (Hebrew בשׂר) and Socotri *leḥem* is 'fish'; ארי is 'lion' in Hebrew, but Geez *'arwe* 'wild animal' generally, Tigrinya *'arawit* 'serpent' (see Leslau, *Harari*, p. 31), and also Accadian *erū* 'eagle', etc.; see Ullendorff in *VT* vi (1956) 192.

this was indeed the sense, and so overcame the necessity for a dubious derivation within Hebrew through שׁעה in a sense like 'gaze about (in fear)'. Similarly, we have seen in the case of חֹזֶה how the sense 'agreement' was known long ago, but this understanding came to be confused and darkened by attempts to derive from the verb חזה 'see'. In such cases the philological treatment validates the form and meaning as Hebrew, where the tendency to derive from other extant Hebrew words has obscured or confused the morphological interpretation and the semantic tradition.

Again, it has been a common tendency to take the Hebrew מָהִיר in a phrase like סוֹפֵר מָהִיר (Ps. 45. 2) as meaning 'quick', because the verb מהר is 'hasten'; but comparison with the Ethiopic sense 'train, teach' and other cognate senses may suggest that the sense is rather 'skilled'. Similarly, in Isa. 16. 5 מְהַר צֶדֶק may be 'skilled in justice' rather than 'swift in justice'. 'Skilled' is in fact given as a gloss in the standard dictionaries; but in KB it is the second gloss given, while in BDB it is the fourth. The effect of the comparative information is to restore primacy to a sense which the Hebrew context itself favours, but which has been somewhat obscured by the attempt to show derivation from the sense of the actual verb in Hebrew. Such an attempt, we may add, is favoured by the tendency to look for a common root-meaning and to identify it if possible with the sense of the verb.

When we talk of meaning within Hebrew, then, this is the meaning of units as seen within the collocations in which they occur and within the semantic fields of agreement and opposition in which they function. Attempts to state meaning derivationally cannot be intra-Hebraic in many cases, because the forms and senses extant in biblical Hebrew may not be those through which the derivation actually took place. One of the values of the comparative approach has been that it has set free senses, which are likely in the Hebrew context, from domination by derivations reached from within Hebrew alone.

Our arguments here have some effect on priorities in education for biblical scholarship. The strong influence of comparative philological method may have produced an unfortunate over-emphasis on comparative study in the training of students. The prestige and fashionableness of the philological approach often cause students to study a larger number of Semitic languages than they can master. These languages are not mastered properly and all the effort does not lead to a thorough knowledge of the texts. This in turn leads to the cheapness and poor quality which we have sometimes seen reason to deplore in philological treatments of the Hebrew Bible, and especially to the phenomenon of dictionary-searching.[1] To observe this, unfortunately, is not enough to put a stop to the tendency. The intellectual prestige of the philological approach is reinforced by the apparent social prestige of linguistic polymathy. It continues to be widely supposed that study of a large *number* of Semitic languages is the gateway to competence in biblical studies.[2]

All this would not matter if the effect of learning many languages were accompanied by the acquisition of a thorough knowledge of Hebrew. This, however, is not always so. Students may sometimes be found to begin with Hebrew but, before they have really gained wide experience in this language, to be directed to other languages, on which their more developed and mature talents are then spent. Thus the comparative emphasis, though intended for the elucidation of the Hebrew Bible, in educational practice has sometimes weighted the balance against a thorough knowledge of Hebrew.

Moreover, in the comparative approach there has been a certain tendency to treat Hebrew as the distinctively unknown language, while the other Semitic languages (with some exception for Ugaritic, in which, as we have remarked, comparative insights are particularly the basis of knowledge) tend to be treated as known quantities, used as sources from which Hebrew can be elucidated.[3] Thus the student, starting out to learn Hebrew, has to learn a series of languages which are to serve as sources for the elucidation of Hebrew. Within the study of these other languages, however,

---

[1] Cf. the similar argument of Driver in *VTS* iv (1957) 5 etc.

[2] I have sometimes advised students not to over-extend their mental energies by attempting too many languages, and thus for example to avoid the effort of learning Arabic when they had no intention of reading Arabic texts on any scale; yet have been told that it would be a real disadvantage to them in an academic career if they had only a small *number* of Semitic languages registered on their records.

[3] An occasional exception will prove this rule: Driver, discussing Ps. 22. 30 כל־דשני־ארץ, says that the clue is in the Syriac rendering *kpnh d'r''*; this does not mean *famelici terrae* (Walton), but 'those who are wrapped up' in the earth. This sense of *k-p-n* is not in the dictionaries but is suggested by cognate words such as Hebrew כפן 'be involved, intricate'. Note the parallelism with כל־יורדי עפר. Thus the Hebrew is used as part of the evidence to explain the Syriac, and the Syriac, once so explained, is used to explain the Hebrew. This **type of argument is, however, very exceptional in my experience.**

he does not find to anything like the same degree a spirit of expectancy that problems will have to be solved by going outside of
the language being studied: Arabic is not taught as a language
which has to be elucidated through reference to Hebrew. Moreover, Arabic is now increasingly taught as a spoken language, and
this enhances its familiarity; sometimes it is the only Semitic
language known to the biblical student as a living mode of communication.

Thus the proliferation of the comparative philological approach
has created a practical problem in the teaching of Hebrew. One
might expect the logical sequence to be: first learn Hebrew; then
gain experience in the reading of Hebrew literature; finally, progress
to a study of cognate languages and their literatures. This sequence
was already made more difficult by the rise of textual emendation,
which greatly limited the ease with which biblical texts could be
used for the simple gaining of experience in reading. Now philological treatments appear to make it doubtful whether there
exists an agreed body of 'Hebrew' in the sense in which there is an
agreed body of 'Greek' or of 'French', and to suggest that there is
no stable basis until 'Hebrew' has first been reconstructed from
cognate sources. If such is the case, then the task of teaching is
indeed difficult.

Perhaps, indeed, there is no help for this, and biblical Hebrew
is simply a more corrupt and obscure entity than the other classical and Semitic languages. In its degree of being a consistent and
knowable linguistic entity, suitable for study in itself, Hebrew
may perhaps be more like Ugaritic than like Arabic or Syriac,
more like Sogdian or Tocharian than like Latin or Greek. I am
not sure, however, that this unhappy conclusion should be drawn,
and one doubts whether it has been meant even by those philologists who have most devotedly added to the content of Hebrew
from cognate sources.

In spite of the multitude of difficulties and obscurities which have
provoked the recourse to philological treatment, it must be emphasized that Hebrew is a knowable and manageable linguistic corpus,
with a rich though diverse transmission of meaning from ancient
times on. The gaining of substantial experience within this corpus
is one of the most important ways in which the information yielded
by cognate sources can be controlled; and failure to study and
utilize the tradition of meaning has been one of the ways in which

the philological approach has tended to impoverish scholarship.[1] In spite of our debt to comparative philology, Hebrew does remain a teachable subject in its own right; and, while the student must now always be aware of the contributions of cognate languages, he will, unless he is ready to study these languages thoroughly, be best employed not in gaining a smattering of them but in learning how to evaluate, in relation to his Hebrew knowledge, the suggestions made on the basis of them. This means that eventually adequate modes of communication and co-operation have to be built up between two kinds of scholar: (a) those who really know the cognate languages or some of them (can any now really know them all?) and (b) those who only assimilate this knowledge within their own grasp of Hebrew. But we can at least do something to depreciate the false prestige which has attached to the polyglot ideal, and rebuild the picture of the Hebraist. The polyglot ideal, we may remind ourselves, by no means obtains in the Indo-European field; no one supposes that to appreciate Greek literature one must study all the Indo-European languages.

It would, on the other hand, be a hopelessly retrograde step if one were to imagine that work within Hebrew might once again proceed as if the pressure of comparative insights and methods merely did not exist. This pressure is no new thing, but has been acting upon biblical study for centuries; only lately, however, has its presence begun to cause a kind of crisis in understanding. The discussion of the comparative philological approach reveals many new ways in which Hebrew requires to be studied, and makes it impossible for us to contemplate a return to a traditionalist Hebrew study, divorced from the framework of general linguistic study (a framework even wider than that of Semitic comparative philology).

We may now pass on to mention some particular practical tasks in which our discussion may have some effect.

(1) Our discussion should have some effect on the work of biblical translation, which is constantly going on. Sometimes the production of philological suggestions has been connected with a plea for the production of an absolutely accurate translation of the Hebrew Bible. The approximative character of the information

---

[1] In this respect philology, by going behind the tradition of meaning, has an aspect similar to archaeology when the latter goes straight to the ancient sites and cuts behind the literary historical traditions.

yielded by comparative approaches, however, means that this is by
no means easy to achieve. Translations have often been conceived
with the aim of furnishing the 'right' meaning. Where the philological information provides the exclusion of some impossibilities,
plus a range of relative probabilities, this is likely to force a
premature choice. Unless several alternative translations are
furnished, therefore, the act of translation is likely at times to give
a poor rather than an adequate representation of the result of
philological work.

This, we may add, is one main reason why the biblical student
has to study the original languages. It is sometimes argued that
improved modern translations are making linguistic study less
necessary than it used to be. Quite the contrary is true. Increased
modern philological knowledge, while it has enabled us to overcome certain difficulties which the older translations had, has
also made the assessment of meaning more approximative in
character, has multiplied the factors which may bear upon it, and
may thus have made the production of definitive translations
more remote.

(2) Our discussion has shown the importance of certain
statistical information, such as comparative counts of homonyms
and of the percentages of words having cognates in groups of
related languages. The procedures used in this book for these
questions are extremely crude; the refinement of techniques for
this sort of problem should be undertaken in the years ahead.

(3) The desirability of an etymological dictionary of the Semitic
languages has often been asserted. Our discussion has shown that
such a work should not only register the existence of a word in a
certain language, but also negatively its non-existence. Registration of the non-occurrence of cognates is essential if we are to
assess the percentage of cognates normally found. Similarly, it has
to register the cases where a language has a certain root, but only
in a word-class or part of speech different from that of the other
languages; or, likewise, where it exists only in one or two particular
fixed forms, and is no longer free or productive.

(4) Dictionaries of Hebrew should be designed in such a way
as to distinguish those statements of meaning which are based
upon the actual collocations in Hebrew from those statements
which are based upon cognates and etymological information.
One might consider that a dictionary, instead of beginning with the

mention of cognates, might restrict itself to stating meaning within Hebrew, leaving etymological discussion to a separate dictionary, as is done with modern languages like English; or it might place the citation of cognates after the discussion of the Hebrew contexts, so as to avoid the possibility that the statement of meaning in Hebrew is distorted in order to show a plausible line of development from the preferred etymology; again, typographical devices might be used in order to distinguish the different kinds of source. The advantage of a separate etymological dictionary would be that it could give full discussion instead of only the brief citation of preferred examples.

If dictionaries were produced which gave less prominence to comparative material than has lately been the custom, they might give more space to contextual factors which indicate meaning, such as parallelism (this is a most important indication, even though we have shown that it is far from a simple or infallible one), and to the oppositions or contrasts with other items which might be expected to enter the same semantic field.

(5) The study of biblical Hebrew cannot be deemed complete without a satisfactory follow-up into post-biblical Hebrew. The present biblical dictionaries make only limited excursions as far as Sirach and Qumran. It would not be an impossible undertaking to construct in one volume a dictionary of the post-biblical interpretation of biblical Hebrew words, in which would be discussed the treatment of words implied in the early Greek and other versions, used in halachic and midrashic interpretation, and stated in the Jewish lexicographers and commentators, up to about A.D. 1300 or 1400. Such a work would be far from providing the 'right' interpretation of biblical words; but it would provide the setting within which linguistic meaning was transmitted and might thus help us to assess ways in which such meaning had been either preserved or distorted.

(6) Another practical problem is the design of a critical edition of the Hebrew Bible. Classically, an edition has been conceived as a representation of the *textual* evidence. But the significance of this evidence depends on linguistic considerations. How can space be found in a critical apparatus, however, for linguistic as well as textual evidence? Yet to print only textual evidence, without linguistic discussion, is to invite retrograde and conservative constructions of it from many readers. Versional evidence in

particular cannot be printed without some linguistic evaluation. Perhaps no means other than compromise and good sense can be found to solve this problem.[1]

It is clear that philological treatments have now come to occupy the centre of interest which in the scholarship of the nineteenth and early twentieth centuries was held by the practice of emendation. Amid the general loss of confidence in these emendations today, it is easy to forget that in their time they may have served a significant purpose. They were an attempt to rationalize the study of the text, in that they insisted that scholarly solutions must make sense within the recognized body of knowledge of the Hebrew language: arbitrary exceptions to this could not be made, and the artificial interpretative tricks of earlier periods were to be rejected. Simply because this was tried so hard, and because emendation explored and exhausted its own possibilities, emendation in due course provided a certain important stimulus to the new rise of philological treatments.

Nevertheless emendation produced in the end a deep depression and scepticism, for the impression given was that the interpreter in many cases was rewriting the text rather than explaining what was written. The most serious criticism was both for arbitrariness and for banality. The confidence that the grammar and lexicon of Hebrew were already well known, a confidence which is part of the rationalizing tendency just mentioned, had the result that many emendations presented a much more familiar-looking Hebrew than the existing text displayed. Emendations which result in an easier text, however, break the familiar rule of *difficilior lectio potior* (a rule which, indeed, is not universally and absolutely valid). The process implied that an easier text was corrupted into a more difficult, a corruption which is far from satisfactorily explained by an appeal to the irrational stupidity and incompetence of scribes.

The philological treatment displays a different and a better approach in these regards. It is just to claim with Winton Thomas that it ventures out into the unknown; in a puzzling text it has the chance of discovering something new, not a scrambled version of familiar Hebrew but words and phrases which hitherto were not known to be Hebrew at all. Such an expectation of expansion

---

[1] On these problems see in particular my review of the sample edition of Isaiah in *JSS* xii (1967) 113–22, and especially pp. 119 ff.

was only right in an era when the knowledge of Semitic languages, and particularly those of the environment of the Old Testament, was being greatly enlarged.

Nevertheless there is some danger that the present pursuit of the philological treatment will end by being regarded with the same deep scepticism which has been the fate of the fashion for textual emendation. Firstly, many of the followers of the philological approach have also from time to time used drastic emendation of the consonantal text. As for the vowel text, the low opinion of it has been so widespread, and the rewriting of it so drastic, as to create an even worse impression of arbitrariness than was produced by the older emendations of the consonantal text. Emendation had generally treated the existing signs, i.e. the written letters of the MT, as evidence which serves as a clue towards the discovery of the true text, or which at least must be explained when the discovery is made; but philological treatments have often held themselves free to alter the vocalization without giving an account of it, and have not accepted the existing vocalization signs as presumptive evidence. Thus the treatment of the vocalization in the philological approach has often been more arbitrary than straight emendation of the consonantal text has been.

Secondly, and perhaps more fundamental, there is the sense that philological treatments are often a semantic rewriting of the text: just as emendation abandoned the graphic tradition of the text in order to create a new or reconstructed writing, so philological treatments abandon the semantic tradition of meaning in Hebrew in order to create a determination of meaning from elsewhere. For these reasons philological treatments are not quite so far removed from textual emendation as some claims would suggest, and the danger of an ultimate scepticism hangs over them both alike if their procedures are pressed too recklessly and too uncritically. The bewildering number and variety of philological treatments, and their lack of considered comprehensive theory hitherto, are likely to make the student eventually feel that not all of these suggestions can be right.

Such a judgement can by no means be attributed to an antecedent hostility to the philological approach; for it is one which may be confirmed also to some considerable extent by the judgements of those who have themselves been foremost within it. Even where scholars have committed themselves whole-heartedly to the comparative philological approach, this fact in itself has not necessarily led to any considerable measure of agreement among them. Of the very numerous suggestions which have come from Tur-Sinai, for instance, how many have received wide acceptance even among devotees of the philological approach? Again, many of the critical analyses used on philological treatments in this book are represented also in Driver's very strong strictures on Dahood.[1] Once we allow for considerable crudity and extravagance in the application of the method by Dahood, we must ask whether the method strictly as a method is not only that which Driver himself, and the movement for philological treatments in general, has implied throughout. In other words, these strong criticisms of Dahood, while striking at a lack of judgement in the application of a method, do not appear to provide us with adequate means to discriminate between a satisfactory philological method and one which is not satisfactory.[2] Thus, to sum up this point, philological treatments have not as yet, in spite of a general agreement in method, succeeded in presenting a very wide body of agreed results; while, on the other hand, in discussing the method as a whole we can claim to be doing no more than drawing out the implications of types of critical evaluation which philological scholars are already tacitly applying to their own and their colleagues' work. Our investigation is thus not a criticism of the method of philological treatments, but a making explicit of the criteria implicit in the method.

It would, in my judgement, be a great misfortune if the movement for philological treatments were to be received in the end with unthinking scepticism. Faulty it has been in a number of regards. It has prided itself on freedom from the faults of textual conjecture, when it has in fact shared these faults and has also obscured the fact that textual emendation is not at all an impossible or invalid approach. Many suggestions have been offered over-confidently, and the exultation of knowledge about

[1] In *JSS* x (1965) 112–17; this review appeared when the argument of the present book was already complete.

[2] Cf. the judgement of D. N. Freedman in Hyatt, *The Bible in Modern Scholarship*, p. 303. While far from committing himself to the rightness of Dahood's interpretations (he gives the cautious qualification 'even if only a fraction stand the test of scholarly criticism') he maintains that Dahood's work is 'only a logical extension of the pioneering effort of other Ugaritic specialists'. Quite so; but some may judge that such an extension proves that there is something wrong with the logic.

new-found materials like Ugaritic has often encouraged extravagant over-assertiveness and the ignoring of problems which are quite plain to common sense. As I have argued several times, there has been a failure to face the cumulative consequences which follow when a method, quite valid in the single case, is applied over many hundreds or even thousands of examples. There has been a failure to consider the problem systematically and to give equal considera-tion to all the criteria which are relevant.

If this has been so in the past, however, it does not mean that it need be so in the future. If an adequate awareness of the wider aspects of the problems, and especially of the relevant criteria, is fostered, there is every reason to expect that the better solutions will be well received and the poorer sifted out. The basic assump-tion, that study of the relations between the Semitic languages may further the understanding of the Hebrew Bible, is incon-trovertible. The trouble has not lain in comparative scholarship, but in poor judgement in its application, and in failure to see and follow out some of the general linguistic questions which are already implied in the primary use of comparative method. Though it is not true that the comparative method is any longer the major way to the understanding of language, and though it has in the past sometimes shown an undesirable imperialism, it remains highly desirable that its interests should be followed up. This book is therefore consecrated to the deeper and fuller study of that linguistic world in which the Hebrew Bible is set, and against the background of which our future growth in under-standing of its language must take place.

The time is past, however, when the primary creative and positive contribution of comparative study was the production of in-dividual philological solutions. That this was tried, and to some extent accomplished, is entirely understandable, just as, at an earlier stage of scholarship, it is understandable that every effort was made to exploit the method of conjectural emendation. We have now reached the stage, however, at which mere productivity in philological suggestions has become negative and confusing in effect, and the positive task is the exploration of the method in itself. This present book is, I believe, the first to be wholly devoted to this purpose.

APPENDIX

SYRIAC VERBS AS IN BROCKELMANN,
SET AGAINST HEBREW VERBS AS IN BDB
(SLIGHTLY MODIFIED)

(*see above, pp. 162 f.*)

Verb	Sense	A Hebrew, with close sense	B Hebrew, sense remote	C Hebrew, but not verb	D not Hebrew
b'š	be evil	x			
bgh	be delayed				x
bgl	be talkative				x
bgn	cry, seek				x
bgr	close, hold in				x[1]
	escape (?)				x
bd	mix		x		
	be poured out				x
	be disturbed (*etbadbad*)				x
bd'	pretend		x		
	be talkative			x (?)	
bdl	be mad		x[2]		
bdq	scatter				x
	examine				x
	disclose				x
bdq II	(denom.) repair	x			
bdr	disperse	x[3]			
bhbh	be anxious				x[4]
bhl	be quiet		x		
bhq	shine			x	
bhr	be glorious			x	
bht	be ashamed	x			
b(w)d	perish				x
b(w)q	rot			x[5]	
bwr	be uncultivated				x
bwt	pass the night				x
bz	spoil	x			
bzh	scorn				x
bz'	cleave				x
bzq	scatter				x

[1] Cf. MH בגר ‘be of age’.

[2] Hebrew sense = ‘divide’.

[3] בזר rare, usually פזר.

[4] Unless cogn. Hebrew בֹּהוּ ‘vanity’.

[5] Or perhaps column *D*.

X

Verb	Sense	A Hebrew, with close sense	B Hebrew, sense remote	C Hebrew, but not verb	D not Hebrew
bḥn	examine	x			
	show		x		
bḥr	examine		x (?)		
	choose (?)	x			
	repair (?)		x		
bḥš	move, excite				x
bṭl	cease	x¹			
bṭn	(denom.) conceive			x	
byʾ	console		x²		
byn	understand	x			
byʿ	cease, delay				x
byt	(denom.) make familiar			x	
bkʾ	weep	x			
bkr	be ripe	x			
bl	mix	x			
blʾ	wear out	x			
blm	silence, bind mouth	x³			
blʿ	be struck		x		
blṣ	flower				x
blq	appear, be directed		x		
blš	spoil				x
bnʾ	build	x			
bsʾ	despise	x⁴			
bsm	smell good, enjoy			x	
bsr	despise, refute				x
bsr	(denom.) be incarnate			x	
bʿʾ	desire	x			
bʿd	depart			x	
bʿṭ	kick	x			
bʿk	tread to dust				x
bʿl	marry; begin to ripen	x			
bʿq	strike				x
bʿr	seek out, glean		x		
bʿt	oppress	x			
bʿt II	rouse				x⁵
bṣ	(denom.) become thin				x
bṣʾ	examine				x
bṣr	be lacking, diminish	x (or B)			

¹ Qoh. only.   ² Cogn. בּיּ?   ³ Hap. leg.
⁴ But Hebr. /z/; cf. Grundriß, i. 153.   ⁵ = בעשׁ if Brockelmann is right.

Verb	Sense	A Hebrew, with close sense	B Hebrew, sense remote	C Hebrew, but not verb	D not Hebrew
bq	rot		x		
bq'	examine, decree				x[1]
bqr	examine	x			
br'	create	x			
brḥ	make clear		x		
brk	kneel, swear	x			
brm	consume				x
brṣ	penetrate, reveal				x
brq	flash	x			
bšl	ripen, cook	x			

----

[1] Unless in personal name.

ABBREVIATIONS

ABR	*Australian Biblical Review*
AJSL	*American Journal of Semitic Languages*
AnOr	Analecta Orientalia
AO	*Archiv Orientálni*
ASTI	*Annual of the Swedish Theological Institute*
BASOR	*Bulletin of the American Schools for Oriental Research*
BDB	Brown, Driver, and Briggs, *Hebrew Lexicon*
BH³	*Biblia Hebraica* (Kittel), 3rd or later edition
BJRL	*Bulletin of the John Rylands Library*
BO	*Bibliotheca Orientalis*
BSOAS	*Bulletin of the School of Oriental and African Studies*
BWANT	Beiträge zur Wissenschaft des Alten und Neuen Testaments
BWAT	Beiträge zur Wissenschaft vom Alten Testament
BZAW	Beiträge zur *Zeitschrift für die Alttestamentliche Wissenschaft*
CBQ	*Catholic Biblical Quarterly*
CC	*Corpus Christianorum*
CML	*Canaanite Myths and Legends* (Driver)
DLZ	*Deutsche Literaturzeitung*
ESA	Epigraphic South Arabian
ET	*Expository Times*
ETL	*Ephemerides Theologicae Lovanienses*
GB	Gesenius, *Handwörterbuch über das Alte Testament* (17th ed. by Buhl, 1915)
GK	Gesenius' *Hebrew Grammar*, ed. Kautzsch, 2nd English ed. by A. E. Cowley (Oxford, 1910)
HTR	*Harvard Theological Review*
HUCA	*Hebrew Union College Annual*
ICC	International Critical Commentary
IDB	*Interpreter's Bible Dictionary*
IEJ	*Israel Exploration Journal*
IJAL	*International Journal of American Linguistics*
JAOS	*Journal of the American Oriental Society*
JBL	*Journal of Biblical Literature*
JJS	*Journal of Jewish Studies*
JNES	*Journal of Near Eastern Studies*
JPOS	*Journal of the Palestine Oriental Society*
JQR	*Jewish Quarterly Review*
JRAS	*Journal of the Royal Asiatic Society*
JSS	*Journal of Semitic Studies*
JTS	*Journal of Theological Studies*
KB	L. Koehler and W. Baumgartner, *Lexicon in Veteris Testamenti Libros* (Leiden, 1953)

LSJ	Liddell and Scott, *Greek–English Lexicon* (rev. ed. by H. Stuart Jones and R. Mackenzie, Oxford, 1940)
MH	Middle Hebrew, Mishnaic Hebrew
MT	Massoretic Text
OBL	*Orientalia et Biblica Lovaniensia* (ed. G. Ryckmans, Louvain. 1957)
OED	*Oxford English Dictionary*
OLZ	*Orientalistische Literaturzeitung*
Or Suec	*Orientalia Suecana*
OTMS	*The Old Testament and Modern Study* (ed. H. H. Rowley, Oxford, 1951).*
OTS	*Oudtestamentische Studiën*
PEQ	*Palestine Exploration Fund Quarterly*
PL	*Patrologia Latina* (Migne)
RB	*Revue biblique*
ScrH	*Scripta Hierosolymitana*
SJT	*Scottish Journal of Theology*
TLS	*The Times Literary Supplement*
UH	*Ugaritic Handbook* (by C. H. Gordon, AnOr xxv, Rome, 1947)
VD	*Verbum Domini*
VT	*Vetus Testamentum*
VTS	*Vetus Testamentum Supplements*
WO	*Die Welt des Orients*
ZA	*Zeitschrift für die Assyriologie*
ZAW	*Zeitschrift für die Alttestamentliche Wissenschaft*
ZDMG	*Zeitschrift der deutschen Morgenländischen Gesellschaft*
ZNW	*Zeitschrift für die Neutestamentliche Wissenschaft*

BIBLIOGRAPHY

This bibliography lists works mentioned in the text and some others which are relevant for the general questions discussed. It does not, however, provide individual listing for periodical articles in which philological treatments have appeared; for these the reader is referred to the Index of Examples.

AISTLEITNER, J., *Wörterbuch der ugaritischen Sprache* (Berlin, 1963).

BACHER, W., 'Die hebräische Sprachwissenschaft vom 10. bis zum 16. Jahrhundert', in Winter, J., and Wünsche, A., *Die jüdische Literatur seit dem Abschluß des Kanons*, ii. 135–235 (Trier, 1894).

——, 'Die Anfänge der hebräischen Grammatik', *ZDMG* xlix (1895) 1–62, 335–92.

BARR, J., *The Semantics of Biblical Language* (Oxford, 1961).

——, *Biblical Words for Time* (London, 1962).

——, *Old and New in Interpretation* (London, 1966).

——, 'St. Jerome's Appreciation of Hebrew', *BJRL* xlix (1966–7) 281–302.

——, 'St. Jerome and the Sounds of Hebrew', *JSS* xii (1967) 1–36.

——, 'Vocalization and the Analysis of Hebrew among the ancient Translators', in the Baumgartner Festschrift (Leiden, 1967), pp. 1–11.

BARTH, J., *Etymologische Studien* (Leipzig, 1893).

BAUER, H., and LEANDER, P., *Historische Grammatik der hebräischen Sprache des alten Testaments* (Halle, 1922).

BEESTON, A. F. L., *A Descriptive Grammar of Epigraphic South Arabian* (London, 1962).

BEN-JEHUDA, E., *Thesaurus totius hebraitatis et veteris et recentioris* (Berlin, later Jerusalem, 1908–59).

BERGSTRÄSSER, G., *Einführung in die semitischen Sprachen* (Munich, 1928).

Bertholet Festschrift: *Festschrift für Alfred Bertholet* (Tübingen, 1950).

BIRKELAND, H., *The Language of Jesus* (Oslo, 1954).

BLAU, J., 'Etymologische Untersuchungen auf Grund des palästinischen Arabisch', *VT* v (1955) 337–44.

——, 'Über homonyme und angeblich homonyme Wurzeln', *VT* vi (1956) 242–8.

BLOOMFIELD, L., *Language* (London, 1935).

BLUMENTHAL, D. R., 'A Play on Words in the Nineteenth Chapter of Job', *VT* xvi (1966) 497–501.

BIBLIOGRAPHY 311

BOLING, R. G., ' "Synonymous" Parallelism in the Psalms', *JSS* v (1960) 221–55.

BORGEN, P., *Bread from Heaven* (Leiden, 1965).

BOTTERWECK, G. J., *Der Triliterismus im Semitischen* (Bonner Biblische Beiträge iii, Bonn, 1952).

BROCKELMANN, C., *Grundriß der vergleichenden Grammatik der semitischen Sprachen* (2 vols., Berlin, 1908–13).

——, *Lexicon Syriacum* (2nd edition, Halle, 1928).

——, *Hebräische Syntax* (Neukirchen, 1956).

BRÜLL, A., *Fremdsprachliche Redensarten und ausdrücklich als fremdsprachlich bezeichnete Wörter in den Talmuden und Midraschim* (Leipzig, 1869).

BUCK, C. D., *A Dictionary of Selected Synonyms in the Principal Indo-European Languages* (Chicago, 1949).

BUXTORF, J., *Tiberias sive commentarius masorethicus triplex* (Basiliae, 1620).

CAPPELLUS, L., *Arcanum punctationis revelatum sive de punctorum vocalium et accentuum apud Hebraeos vera et germana antiquitate* (Leiden, 1624).

Casey, R. P. Festschrift: *Biblical and Patristic Studies* in memory of R. P. Casey (ed. BIRDSALL, J. N., and THOMSON, R. W., Freiburg, 1963).

CASKEL, W., *Die Bedeutung der Beduinen in der Geschichte der Araber* (Köln, 1953).

——, 'Zur Beduinisierung Arabiens', *ZDMG* ciii (1953) *28–36.

——, 'The Bedouinization of Arabia', American Anthropological Society Memoir no. 76 (1954).

CASTELL, E., *Lexicon Heptaglotton* (London, 1669).

Chicago, Oriental Institute of the University, *The Assyrian Dictionary*, (Chicago, from 1956).

CROSS, F. M., and FREEDMAN, D. N., *Early Hebrew Orthography* (New Haven, 1952).

——, *The Ancient Library of Qumran* (London, 1958).

DAHOOD, M., 'The Value of Ugaritic for Textual Criticism', *Biblica* xl (1959) 160–70.

——, 'Qoheleth and Northwest Semitic Philology', *Biblica* xliii (1962) 349–65.

——, 'Northwest Semitic Philology and Job', in McKenzie, J. L., *The Bible in Current Catholic Thought* (New York, 1962), pp. 55–74.

——, 'Hebrew–Ugaritic Lexicography', *Biblica* xliv (1963) 289–303, xlv (1964) 393–412, xlvi (1965) 311–32, xlvii (1966) 403–19, xlviii (1967) 421–38.

——, *Proverbs and Northwest Semitic Philology* (Rome, 1963).

DAHOOD, M., *Psalms 1–50* (Anchor Bible, New York, 1966).

——, *Ugaritic–Hebrew Philology*, (Rome, 1965).

DELITZSCH, FRIEDRICH, *Prolegomena eines neuen hebräisch-aramäischen Wörterbuches zum Alten Testament* (Leipzig, 1886).

DHORME, P., *Le Livre de Job* (Paris, 1926).

DILLMANN, A., *Lexicon linguae aethiopicae* (Leipzig, 1865).

——, *Ethiopic Grammar* (E.T., London, 1907).

DOZY, R. P. A., *Supplément aux dictionnaires arabes* (2 vols., Leiden, 1881).

DRIVER, G. R.: for a full bibliography, including much material relevant to this study, see the Driver Festschrift (below), pp. 191–206.

——, *Problems of the Hebrew Verbal System* (Edinburgh, 1936).

——, 'Hebrew Poetic Diction', *VTS* i (1953) 26–39.

——, *Canaanite Myths and Legends* (Edinburgh, 1956).

——, *Aramaic Documents of the Fifth Century* B.C. (abridged and revised edition, Oxford, 1957).

——, *The Judaean Scrolls* (Oxford, 1965).

Driver Festschrift: *Hebrew and Semitic Studies presented to G. R. Driver* (ed. D. WINTON THOMAS and W. D. McHARDY, Oxford, 1963).

DRIVER, S. R., *Notes on the Hebrew Text and Topography of the Books of Samuel* (2nd ed., Oxford, 1913).

EFROS, I. I., *Maimonides' Treatise on Logic* (Proceedings of the American Academy of Jewish Research, viii, New York, 1938).

EHRLICH, A. B., *Randglossen zur hebräischen Bibel* (7 vols., Leipzig, 1908–14).

EISSFELDT, O., *The Old Testament: an Introduction* (Oxford, 1965).

Eissfeldt Festschrift: *Von Ugarit nach Qumran* (ed. HEMPEL, J., and ROST, L., BZAW lxxvii, Berlin, 1958).

EITAN, I., *A Contribution to Biblical Lexicography* (New York, 1924).

ELLENBOGEN, M., *Foreign Words in the Old Testament: their origin and etymology* (London, 1962).

EMERTON, J. A., 'The Purpose of the Second Column of the Hexapla', *JTS* N.S. vii (1956) 79–87.

——, 'Did Jesus speak Hebrew?', *JTS* N.S. xii (1961) 189–202.

EPPENSTEIN, S., *Übersicht über die hebr.-arabische Sprachvergleichung bei den jüdischen Autoren des Mittelalters* (Frankfurt a. M., 1905).

FIELD, F., *Origenis hexaplorum quae supersunt* (2 vols., Oxford, 1875).

FITZMYER, J. A., *The Genesis Apocryphon from Qumran* (Rome, 1966).

FLASHAR, M., 'Exegetische Studien zum Septuagintapsalter', *ZAW* xxxii (1912) 81–116, 161–89, 241–68.

FRAENKEL, S., *Die aramäischen Fremdwörter im Arabischen* (Leiden, 1886).

FREEDMAN, D. N., 'The Biblical Languages' in Hyatt, *The Bible in Modern Scholarship*, pp. 294–312.

FREYTAG, G. W., *Lexicon Arabico-Latinum* (Halle, 1830–7).

FÜCK, J., *Die arabischen Studien in Europa* (Leipzig, 1955).

GEMSER, B., *Sprüche Salomos* (2nd ed., Tübingen, 1963).

GERLEMAN, G., *Studies in the Septuagint*: I. *The Book of Job* (Lund, 1946); III. *Proverbs* (Lund, 1956).

GLEASON, H. A., *An Introduction to Descriptive Linguistics* (revised ed., New York, 1961).

GOLIUS, J., *Lexicon Arabico-Latinum* (Leiden, 1653).

GONDA, J., 'The Etymologies in the Ancient Indian Brāhmaṇas', *Lingua* v (1955–6) 61–85.

GORDIS, R., *The Biblical Text in the Making* (Philadelphia, 1937).

—— *Koheleth—the Man and his World* (New York, 1955).

GORDON, C. H., *Ugaritic Handbook* (AnOr xxv, Rome, 1947).

GOSHEN-GOTTSTEIN, M. H., 'Linguistic Structure and Tradition in the Qumran Documents', *ScrH* iv (1958) 101–37.

——, *Text and Language in Bible and Qumran* (Jerusalem, 1960).

——, 'The Tiberian Bible Text', in *Biblical and other Studies* (ed. Altmann, Harvard, 1963), pp. 79–122.

—— (ed.), *The Book of Isaiah: Sample Edition with Introduction* (Jerusalem, 1965); review by Barr in *JSS* xii (1967) 113–22.

GRAY, G. B., *Isaiah i–xxvii* (ICC, Edinburgh, 1912).

GRAY, JOHN, *I & II Kings* (London, 1964).

——, *The Legacy of Canaan* (*VTS* v, Leiden, 1957; 2nd edition, Leiden, 1965).

GREENBERG, J. H., 'The Patterning of Root Morphemes in Semitic', *Word* vi (1950) 162–81.

GROSSMANN, R., and SACHS, H., *Compendious Hebrew–English Dictionary* (revised edition by M. H. Segal, Tel-Aviv, 1949).

GUDSCHINSKY, S. C., 'The ABC's of Lexicostatistics (Glottochronology)', *Word* xii (1956) 175–210; reprinted in shorter form in Hymes, *Language in Culture and Society*, pp. 612–22.

GUILLAUME, A., 'A Contribution to Hebrew Lexicography', *BSOAS* xvi (1954) 1–12.

—— 'The Arabic Background of the Book of Job', Hooke Festschrift (Edinburgh, 1963), pp. 106–27.

——, 'Paronomasia in the Old Testament', *JSS* ix (1964) 282–90.

——, *Hebrew and Arabic Lexicography* (= *Abr-Nahrain* i. 3–35; ii. 5–35; iii. 1–10; iv. 1–18), Leiden, 1965.

HALKIN, A. S., 'The Mediaeval Jewish Attitude toward Hebrew', in *Biblical and Other Studies* (ed. Altmann, Harvard, 1963), pp. 233–48.

HALPERIN, H., *Rashi and the Christian Scholars* (Pittsburgh, 1964).

HAMORI, A., 'Paronomasia in Abu Tammām's Style', *JSS* xii (1967) 83–90.

HARRIS, Z. S., *The Development of the Canaanite Dialects* (New Haven, 1939).

HATCH, E., and REDPATH, H. A., *A Concordance to the Septuagint* (2 vols., Oxford, 1897).

HAYWOOD, J. A., *Arabic Lexicography* (Leiden, 1960).

HOCKETT, C. F., *A Course in Modern Linguistics* (New York, 1958).

HOENIGSWALD, H. M., *Language Change and Linguistic Reconstruction* (Chicago, 1960).

Hooke Festschrift: *Promise and Fulfilment* (ed. by F. F. BRUCE, Edinburgh, 1963).

HUFFMON, H. B., *Amorite Personal Names in the Mari Texts* (Baltimore, 1965).

HYATT, J. P., ed., *The Bible in Modern Scholarship* (Nashville, 1965).

HYMES, D., 'Rate of Morpheme Decay in Arabic', *IJAL* xxv (1959) 267–9.

——, ed., *Language in Culture and Society* (New York, 1964).

IBN KHALDŪN, *Muqaddimah* (ed. F. Rosenthal, 3 vols., New York, 1958).

JACOB, B., 'Das hebräische Sprachgut im Christlich-Palästinischen', *ZAW* xxii (1902) 83–113.

JASTROW, M., *A Dictionary of the Targumim, the Talmud Babli and Yerushalmi, and the Midrashic Literature* (London, 1903).

JEFFERY, A., *The Foreign Vocabulary of the Qur'ān* (Baroda, 1938).

——, 'Hebrew Language', in *IDB* ii. 553–60.

JESPERSEN, O., *Language* (London, 1922).

KAHLE, P., *The Cairo Geniza* (2nd ed., Oxford, 1959).

KATZ, P., 'Septuagintal Studies in the Mid-Century', in *The Background of the New Testament and its Eschatology: Studies in Honour of C. H. Dodd* (ed. W. D. Davies and D. Daube, Cambridge, 1964), pp. 176–208.

KAUTZSCH, E. F., *Die Aramäismen im Alten Testament* (Halle, 1902).

KOEHLER, L., 'Vom hebräischen Lexikon', *OTS* viii (1950) 137–55.

KOPF, L., 'Religious Influences on Mediaeval Arabic Philology', *Studia Islamica* v (1956) 33–59.

——, 'Das arabische Wörterbuch als Hilfsmittel für die hebräische Lexicographie', *VT* vi (1956) 286–302.

——, 'The Treatment of Foreign Words in Mediaeval Arabic Lexicology', *ScrH* ix (1961) 191–205.

BIBLIOGRAPHY 315

KOSKINEN, K., 'Kompatibilität in den dreikonsonantigen hebräischen Wurzeln', *ZDMG* cxiv (1964) 16–58.

KRAUS, H.-J., *Geschichte der historisch-kritischen Erforschung des Alten Testaments* (Neukirchen, 1956).

——, *Psalmen* (Biblischer Kommentar, Neukirchen, 2 vols., 1961).

KRAUSS, S., 'Talmudische Nachrichten über Arabien', *ZDMG* lxx (1916) 321–53.

KUTSCHER, E. Y., הלשון והרקע הלשוני של מגילת ישעיהו השלמה ממגילות ים המלח (Jerusalem, 1959).

——, 'Contemporary Studies in North-western Semitic', *JSS* x (1965) 21–51.

——, 'Yemenite Hebrew and Ancient Pronunciation', *JSS* xi (1966) 217–25.

LAMBTON, A. K. S., *Persian Vocabulary* (Cambridge, 1954).

LANDAU, E., *Die gegensinnigen Wörter im Alt- und Neuhebräischen* (Berlin, 1896).

LANE, E. W., *Arabic–English Lexicon* (8 vols., London, 1863–93).

LEHMANN, W. P., *Historical Linguistics: an Introduction* (New York, 1963).

LESLAU, W., *Ethiopic and South Arabic Contributions to the Hebrew Lexicon* (Berkeley, 1958).

——, *Etymological Dictionary of Harari* (Berkeley, 1963).

Levi della Vida Festschrift: *Studi orientalistici in onore di Giorgio Levi della Vida* (2 vols., Rome, 1956).

LEVY, J., *Chaldäisches Wörterbuch über die Targumim und einen grossen Theil des rabbinischen Schriftthums* (3rd ed., Leipzig, n.d.—1867?).

LÖW, I., 'Aramäische Fischnamen', in *Orientalische Studien Th. Nöldeke . . . gewidmet* (Giessen, 1906), pp. 549–70.

MAIMON, MOSES BEN, *Treatise on Logic* (ed. I. I. Efros, American Academy for Jewish Research, New York, 1938).

MENNER, R. J., 'Conflict of homonyms in English', *Language* xii (1936) 229–44.

METZGER, B. M., *The Text of the New Testament* (New York, 1964).

MIRSKY, A., 'Biblical Variants in Medieval Hebrew Poetry', *Textus* iii (1963) 159–63.

MONTGOMERY, J. A., *Kings* (ed. H. S. Gehman, ICC, Edinburgh, 1951).

MOORE, G. F., *Judges* (ICC, Edinburgh, 1895).

MORAG, S., *The Vocalization Systems of Arabic, Hebrew and Aramaic* (The Hague, 1962).

——, העברית שבפי יהודי תימן (Jerusalem, 1963) (for an English review, see under Kutscher).

MORAN, W. L., 'Gen. 49. 10 and its Use in Ezek. 21. 32', *Biblica* xxxix (1958) 405–25.

MOSCATI, S., *The Semites in Ancient History* (Cardiff, 1959).

——, ed., *An Introduction to the Comparative Grammar of the Semitic Languages* (Wiesbaden, 1964).

MOWINCKEL, S., *Han Som Kommer* (Copenhagen, 1951); English, *He That Cometh* (Oxford, 1956).

NEUBAUER, A. (ed.), *Book of Hebrew Roots* by Marwān b. Janāḥ (Oxford, 1875).

NIDA, E. A., *Toward a Science of Translating* (Leiden, 1964).

NÖLDEKE, T., 'Wörter mit Gegensinn (Aḍdad)' in his *Neue Beiträge zur semitischen Sprachwissenschaft* (Strassburg, 1910), pp. 67–108.

Nötscher Festschrift: *Alttestamentliche Studien* (ed. Junker, H., and Botterweck, J., Bonner Biblische Beiträge, i, Bonn, 1950).

NOTH, M., *Die israelitischen Personennamen* (BWANT, iii Folge, 10, Stuttgart, 1928).

NYBERG, H. S., *Hilfsbuch des Pehlevi* (Uppsala, 2 vols., 1928 and 1931).

——, 'Das textkritische Problem des Alten Testaments am Hoseabuche demonstriert', *ZAW* lii (1934) 241–54.

——, *Studien zum Hoseabuche* (Uppsala, 1935).

PALACHE, J. L., *Semantic Notes on the Hebrew Lexicon* (Leiden, 1959).

PAYNE, D. F., 'Ambiguity in Old Testament Exegesis', *ASTI*, forthcoming.

PEAKE, A. S., ed., *The People and the Book* (Oxford, 1925).

Peake's *Commentary on the Bible* (2nd ed. by M. BLACK and H. H. ROWLEY, London, 1962).

PERLES, F., *Analekten zur Textkritik des Alten Testaments* (Munich, 1st series 1895, 2nd series 1922).

POPE, M. H., *El in the Ugaritic Texts* (*VTS* ii, Leiden, 1955).

——, *Job* (Anchor Bible, New York, 1965).

——, 'Marginalia to M. Dahood's *Ugaritic–Hebrew Philology*', *JBL* lxxxv (1966) 455–66.

QUINE, W. V. O., *From a Logical Point of View* (New York, 1963).

RABIN, C., *Ancient West-Arabian* (London, 1951).

——, *Qumran Studies* (Oxford, 1957).

✓ ——, 'The Historical Background of Qumran Hebrew', *ScrH* iv (1958) 144–61.

——, 'The Origin of the Subdivisions of Semitic', in *Hebrew and Semitic Studies presented to G. R. Driver* (Oxford, 1963), pp. 104–15.

——, 'Hittite Words in Hebrew', *Orientalia* xxxii (1963) pp. 113–39.

——, מלים בודדות, in *Encyclopaedia Miqrait.*

RANKIN, O. S., *Jewish Religious Polemic* (Edinburgh, 1956).

Record and Revelation (Essays by members of the Society for Old Testament Study, ed. ROBINSON, H. W., Oxford, 1938).

REICHELT, H., *Awestisches Elementarbuch* (Heidelberg, 1909).

RICHTER, E., 'Über Homonymie', Kretschmer Festschrift (Vienna, 1926), pp. 167–201.

ROBERTS, B. J., *The Old Testament Text and Versions* (Cardiff, 1951).

ROBINS, R. H., *General Linguistics: An Introductory Survey* (London, 1964).

Robinson Festschrift: *Studies in Old Testament Prophecy* (ed. ROWLEY, H. H., Edinburgh, 1950).

ROBINSON, H. W. (ed.), *Record and Revelation* (Oxford, 1938).

ROSENTHAL, E. I. J., 'Medieval Jewish Exegesis: Its Character and Significance', *JSS* ix (1964) 265–81.

ROSENTHAL, F., *A History of Muslim Historiography* (Leiden, 1952).

ROSENZWEIG, A., 'Die Al-Tikri Deutungen', in *Festschrift zu I. Lewys 70. Geburtstag* (Breslau, 1911).

ROSSINI, C. C., *Chrestomathia arabica meridionalis epigraphica* (Rome, 1931).

ROWLEY, H. H., ed., *The Old Testament and Modern Study* (Oxford, 1951).

RUDOLPH, W., *Jeremia* (Tübingen, 1947).

——, *Esra und Nehemia* (Tübingen, 1949).

RŮŽIČKA, R., 'Ueber die Existenz des ġ im Hebräischen', *ZA* xxi (1908) 293–340.

——, 'La Question de l'existence du ġ dans les langues sémitiques', *AO* xxii (1954) 176–237.

Saadia: Siddur R. Saadja Gaon, *Kitāb Ǧāmiʿ Aṣ-Ṣalawāt wat-Tasābīḥ* (ed. DAVIDSON, I., ASSAF, S., and JOEL, B. I., Jerusalem, 1941).

SAUSSURE, F. DE, *Course in General Linguistics* (E. T., New York, 1959).

SCHINDLER, B., and MARMORSTEIN, A., *Occident and Orient ...: Gaster Anniversary Volume* (London, 1936).

SCHULTENS, A., 'Dissertatio theologica–philologica de utilitate linguae arabicae in interpretanda sacra lingua', in his *Opera Minora* (Leiden, 1769), pp. 487–510.

SCHULTHESS, F., *Homonyme Wurzeln im Syrischen* (Berlin, 1900) (cf. review by Nöldeke in *ZDMG* liv [1900] 152–64).

——, *Lexicon Syropalaestinum* (Berlin, 1903).

318 BIBLIOGRAPHY

SEELIGMANN, I. L., *The Septuagint Version of Isaiah: a discussion of its problems* (Leiden, 1948).

SEGAL, J. B., *The Hebrew Passover* (London, 1963).

SEGAL, M. H., 'Mishnaic Hebrew and its Relation to Biblical Hebrew and to Aramaic', *JQR* xx (1908) pp. 647–737.

——, *A Grammar of Mishnaic Hebrew* (Oxford, 1927).

SIDDIQI, A., *Studien über die persischen Fremdwörter im klassischen Arabisch* (Göttingen, 1919).

SKINNER, J., *Genesis* (ICC, Edinburgh, 2nd ed., 1930).

SMEND, R., *Die Weisheit des Jesus Sirach* (Berlin, 1906).

SODEN, W. VON, *Akkadisches Handwörterbuch* (Wiesbaden, from 1959).

SPERBER, A., 'Hebrew based upon Greek and Latin Transliterations', *HUCA* xii–xiii (1937–8) 103–274.

STENNING, J. F., *The Targum of Isaiah* (Oxford, 1949).

SUTCLIFFE, E. F., 'St. Jerome's Pronunciation of Hebrew', *Biblica* xxix (1948) 112–25.

SWETE, H. B., *An Introduction to the Old Testament in Greek* (Cambridge, 1900).

THIEME, P., 'The Comparative Method for Reconstruction in Linguistics', in Hymes, *Language in Culture and Society*, pp. 585–97.

THUMB, A., *Handbook of the Modern Greek Vernacular* (Edinburgh, 1912).

TORCZYNER, H., 'Al Tikre', *Encyclopaedia Judaica*, ii, pp. 74–87 (Berlin, 1928).

TORREY, C. C., *The Second Isaiah* (Edinburgh, 1928).

TUR-SINAI, N. H., הלשון והספר (2 vols., Jerusalem, 1954–5).

——, *The Book of Job* (Jerusalem, 1957).

ULLENDORFF, E., 'The Contribution of South Semitics to Hebrew Lexicography', *VT* vi (1956) 190–98.

——, 'The Knowledge of Languages in the Old Testament', *BJRL* xliv (1962) 455–65.

ULLMANN, S., *Semantics* (Oxford, 1962).

VERMES, G., *Scripture and Tradition in Judaism: Haggadic Studies* (Studia Post-Biblica, iv, Leiden, 1961).

VOLLERS, K., 'Das Dodekapropheton der Alexandriner', *ZAW* iii (1883) 219–72.

WAGNER, M., *Die lexikalischen und grammatikalischen Aramaismen im alttestamentlichen Hebräisch* (BZAW xcvi, Berlin, 1966).

WALLENSTEIN, M., *Some Unpublished Piyyuṭim from the Cairo Genizah* (Manchester, 1956).

WECHTER, P., *Ibn Barūn's Arabic Works on Hebrew Grammar and Lexicography* (Philadelphia, 1964).

WEHR, H., *A Dictionary of Modern Written Arabic* (ed. J. M. Cowan, Cornell, 1961).

WEIL, G., ''Aḍdād', in *The Encyclopaedia of Islam* (2nd edition, London and Leiden, 1960, i, pp. 184–6).

WEIL, G. E., 'La nouvelle édition de la Massorah (BHK iv) et l'histoire de la Massorah', *VTS* ix (1963) 266–84.

——, *Élie Lévita* (Leiden, 1963).

WEINREICH, U., *Languages in Contact* (New York, 1953).

WEISS, A. VON, *Hauptprobleme der Zweisprachigkeit* (Heidelberg, 1959).

WELLHAUSEN, J., *Der Text der Bücher Samuelis* (Göttingen, 1871).

——, *Die Kleinen Propheten* (Berlin, 1898).

WERNBERG-MØLLER, P., *The Manual of Discipline* (Leiden, 1957).

WILD, S., *Das Kitāb al-'Ain und die arabische Lexikographie* (Wiesbaden, 1965).

WRIGHT, G. E., (ed.), *The Bible and the Ancient Near East* (New York, 1961).

WÜRTHWEIN, E., *The Text of the Old Testament* (Oxford, 1957).

WUTZ, F. X., 'Die Transkriptionen von der Septuaginta bis zu Hieronymus' (BWAT, ii Reihe, 9, Stuttgart, 1933).

——, *Onomastica Sacra* (Texte und Untersuchungen, xli. 1–2, Leipzig, 1914–15).

YAHUDA, A. S., *The Language of the Pentateuch in its Relation to Egyptian* (London, 1933).

YASIN, IZZ AD-DIN AL-, *The Lexical Relation between Ugaritic and Arabic* (New York, 1952).

ZIFF, P., *Semantic Analysis* (Ithaca, 1960).

ZIMMERMANN, F., 'Folk Etymology of Biblical Names', *VTS* xv (1966) 311–26.

INDEX OF EXAMPLES

THIS Index includes only a selection from the total number of philological treatments known to me. Almost all those referred to in the text of this book are included, along with others which provide a representative collection.

Information is presented in a very compressed form. In order to understand the arguments advanced, readers should consult the source itself. Where a suggestion has been applied to several different passages, I generally cite only the more striking instances.

The order of presentation is as follows:

(1) Examples are listed in alphabetical order of roots, except in a few cases, in which the familiar form is listed and a cross-reference given.

(2) The Hebrew meaning alleged by the suggestion.

(3) The chief language or languages used for cognate evidence, and, if necessary, the form or sense therein. A question mark is added where the existence or the sense of the cognate form cited seems to be seriously doubtful in that language.

(4) One or more of the biblical passages concerned.

(5) In parenthesis, relevant details such as parallelisms or versional readings.

(6) A cross-reference, if the example has been discussed in the text of this book.

(7) The source of the suggestion, not necessarily in its earliest form, but in one which states the argument adequately and is reasonably accessible (see p. 11).

This Index is not intended as a glossary of Hebrew; it is for use in conjunction with the discussion in this book. Inclusion of entries does not imply that I consider the data or conclusions to be correct. I have not, however, intentionally included anything which seems likely to mislead, provided that the arguments of this book have been studied. Obvious misprints and minor errors in the sources have been corrected.

1. אבחה A. 'slaughter', Accad. *abāḫu* (?). Ezek. 21. 20 (σφάγια). Delitzsch, pp. 74 f. (but later abandoned?).

2. אבחה B. 'brightness', Ar. *'ubbahā*. Ezek. 21. 20. Reider, *HUCA* ii (1925) 95.

3. אבך 'carry away', Accad. *abāku*. Isa. 9. 17. Driver, *JTS* xxix (1928) 390.

4. אבל 'be dry', Accad. Jer. 12. 4 (|| יבש), etc. Driver in Schindler, p. 73.

5. אפן '(moon) disc'. Ct. 7. 3. See text, p. 107. Reider, *HUCA* ii (1925) 94.

6. אדב 'bind, oppress', Accad. (?). I Sam. 2. 33. Driver, *JTS* xxiii (1922) 70.

7. אדם A. 'earth', as אֲדָמָה. Prov. 30. 14 (|| אֶרֶץ), etc. Dahood, *Proverbs*, pp. 57 f.

8. אדם B. 'delightful', Eth. Prov. 12. 27, see text, pp. 28 f. Eitan, p. 28. Cf. Ullendorff, *VT* vi (1956) 191 f.

9. אדם C. 'skin', Ar. Hos. 11. 4, see text, p. 154. Driver, *JTS* xxxix (1938) 161.

10. אדן 'father', Ugar. Prov. 27. 18. Dahood, *Proverbs*, p. 55.

11. אהבה 'leather', Ar. Hos. 11. 4, see text, pp. 144, 154. Driver, *CML*, p. 133; *JTS* xxxix (1938) 161; Hirschberg, *VT* xi (1961) 373.

12. אהבו הבו (הוב) 'become guilty', MH חוב, Ar. ḥāba and cf. CDC 3. 10. Hos. 4. 18. Rabin, *ScrH* viii (1961) 389. Cf. no. 103.

13. אהל A. 'have grazing rights', Ar. Gen. 13. 12, 18. Rabin, *ScrH* viii (1961) 384.

14. אהל B. 'count worthy', Ar. Job 25. 5. Driver, *AJSL* lii (1935–6) 161 f., following Ehrlich.

15. אוד 'be grievous, burdensome', Ar. *'āda*. II Sam. 13. 16 (MT עַל־ אוֹדת). Cf. Job 31. 23. See text, p. 266. Driver, in Nötscher, p. 48.

16. איד 'one burdened', participle of above. Prov. 17. 5 (|| רָשׁ; ἀπολλυμένῳ). Driver, *Biblica* xxxii (1951) 182, cf. Dahood, *Proverbs*, p. 38.

17. מאד 'grief', noun from no. 15. Ps. 31. 12; point מָאֹד. Driver, *JTS* xxxii (1931) 256.

18. תאוה A. 'lament, plaint', Ar. (?— '-w-y 'feel pity' or ta'awwaha 'moan, complain', Lane, pp. 130b, 129c?). Ps. 38. 10 (|| אנחתי), 10. 17. Driver, *JTS* xliii (1942) 153; Leveen, ibid. xlv (1944) 19.

19. תאוה B. 'ease, inactivity', Ar. *'awā* 'turn aside, lodge'. Prov. 21. 25 etc. Dahood, *Proverbs*, p. 41 f., after Reider, no. 20.

20. אוה 'dwell', as above. Num. 34. 7. Reider, *VT* ii (1952) 113.

21. תאוה C. 'abode', as above. Gen. 49. 26. Reider, ibid.

22. אול 'freeman', Accad. *awīlum*. II Kings 24. 15 (*Kethibh*). Driver, *JTS* xxxiv (1933) 33 f.; *JQR* xxviii (1937–8) 116.

23. אור 'rain, dew', Ar. *'ary*. Isa. 18. 4, cf. צח, no. 268; Job 37. 11 and medievals. Eitan, *HUCA* xii–xiii (1938) 65 f.

24. אוש 'gift', Ugar. *'šn*, Ar. *'ws*. Prov. 8. 21 (MT יֵשׁ); see text, p. 181. Dahood, *Biblica*, xxxiii (1952) 33 n.

25. אזן 'equipment' ESA *'dn*. Deut. 23. 14. Rabin, *ScrH* viii (1961) 387.

26. אחר A. 'substitute', MH אחראיות. Gen. 22. 13. Rabin, *ScrH* viii (1961) 387.

27. אחר B. 'with', not 'after', Ugar. *'aḫr* || *'mn*. Qoh. 12. 2. Scott, *JTS* l (1949) 178; Dahood, *Biblica* xliii (1962) 363.

28. אמם 'walk forward', Ar. *'mm*. Isa. 60. 4, read תָּאַמְנָה (MT תֵּאָמַנָה).
   Eitan, *HUCA* xii–xiii (1938) 83 f.

29. אמר A. 'lift up, be high', cf. Accad. *Amurru*. Job 22. 28–9. Tur-Sinai,
   Job, p. 349.

30. אמר B. 'refuse, retract', Talm. Aram. Job 3. 3. Tur-Sinai, *Job*, p. 50.

31. אמר C. 'see', Accad. Ps. 71. 10 ('my foes are on the look-out for me').
   Dahood, *Biblica* xliv (1963) 295 f.; cf. 'see' as 'original' Hebrew
   sense in Albright, *JAOS* lxxiv (1954) 229 n. 47.

32. אסר A. 'clinch, close', not 'begin' ('according to etymology'). I Kings
   20. 14. Gray, *Kings*, p. 377.

33. אסר B. 'totality', Ar. Hos. 10. 10. See text, p. 74. Nyberg, *Hosea*,
   p. 79.

34. אפונה 'to the uttermost', Accad. *appūna* (= 'moreover', von Soden,
   p. 60). Ps. 88. 16. Delitzsch, pp. 135–7.

35. אפל 'be late', Aram., Accad. *uppulu*. Jer. 2. 31, here '(land) becoming
   parched late in season' (|| מדבר; κεχερσωμένη). See text, p. 266.
   Driver, *JTS* xli (1940) 165 f.

36. אֶפֶס 'ocean' as ultimate sense, Accad. *apsu*, non-Semitic. Pope, *El*,
   p. 72.

37. אראל 'herald', Accad. *urullu*. Isa. 33. 7 (MT אֶרְאֶלָּם). Oesterley,
   Record and Revelation, p. 419.

38. ארב 'sexual desire', Arab. *'irba*. Hos. 7. 6. Nyberg, *Hosea*, pp. 52 f.

39. ארג 'smoke, smell', Ar. *'arija*. Job 7. 6. Tur-Sinai, *Job*, pp. 137 f.

40. ארץ 'vermin', Ar. *'araḍ*. Job 12. 8, Gen. 1. 26. Tur-Sinai, *Job*,
   p. 210.

41. אשד 'warriors', ESA *'sd*, cf. Ar. *'asad* 'lion'. Deut. 33. 2 (MT
   אֶשְׁדָּת; ἄγγελοι). Beeston, *JTS* N.S. ii (1951) 30 f.; Miller,
   HTR lvii (1964) 241 ff.

42. אשר 'strong, strengthen', Aram. Isa. 1. 17 etc. (cf. Isa. 47. 15 βοήθεια
   for אֲשֶׁר). Driver, *WO* i. 234, *JTS* xxxviii (1937) 37, *Biblica*
   xxxv (1954) 300.

43. אשש A. 'be luxurious', Ar. *'atta*. Isa. 16. 7, see text, pp. 250, 254.
   Driver, in Eissfeldt Festschr., p. 43; Bertholet Festschr., p. 144.

44. אשש B. 'be strong', Accad. *ašišu* (?). 1Qp Hab. 6. 11. Mansoor, *VTS*
   ix (1963) 320 f.

45. אתנן 'effigy', Ar. *tinn, tanīn* (Lane, p. 318). Mic. 1. 7. See text, p. 145.
   Halper, *AJSL* xxxiv (1907–8) 366–8; Driver, *VT* iv (1954) 242.

46. בג 'share, lot', scribal error for בז, suggested by בג, Aram. from Iran.
   baga-. Ezek. 25. 7. Perles, *JQR* xviii (1906) 384. Cf. Driver,
   Aramaic Documents, p. 40 n.

47. בד 'diviner', Accad. (Mari) *baddum*. Isa. 44. 25 (Vg. *divinorum*) etc.
   Driver, *WO* ii. 19.

48. בּוֹךְ (בּוֹךְ) 'source', Ugar. *mbk, npk*. Prov. 8. 24 (MT נִכְבַּדִּי). Albright, *VTS* iii (1955) 8. Job 28. 11, 38. 16. Driver, *CML*, p. 162 n.

49. בּוֹךְ 'squeeze, distress' (not 'wander'), Ar. *bāka*. Ex. 14. 3. Rabin, *ScrH* viii (1961) 388.

50. בּוֹץ 'run ahead', Ar. *bāṣa*. Ezek. 30. 9 (read בְּצִים; σπεύδοντες). Driver, *Biblica* xxxv (1954) 300.

51. בּחר 'join', Ugar. *pḥr*. Qoh. 9. 4, I Sam. 20. 30. Dahood, *Biblica* xliii (1962) 361.

52. בטח 'fall, lie'. Jer. 12. 5, Job 40. 23; see text, pp. 90 f. Driver, Robinson Festschr., pp. 59 f.; *ETL* xxvi (1950) 341 f.; Kopf, *VT* viii (1958) 165 ff.

53. בּיה 'remember', Ar. *bāha* (?—see text, p. 166). Ps. 68. 5 (read as בַּיָּה). Guillaume, *JTS* N.S. xiii (1962) 322 f.

54. בִּין 'region', Ar. *bīn* (not *bayn*). Isa. 44. 4 ('field of grass') etc. See text, p. 165. Guillaume, *JTS* N.S. xiii (1962) 109 ff.

55. בְּלִי? 'rottenness', Syr. *bly*. Isa. 38. 17. Driver, *JTS* xxxviii (1937) 47.

56. בלע 'reach, slander', Ar. *blġ*. Ps. 52. 6, Isa. 28. 7. Driver, *JTS* xxxiii (1932) 40; *ZAW* lii (1934) 52.

57. במה 'beast', after relation of במה/בהמה by Albright, *VTS* iv (1957) 255 f. Isa. 2. 22 (במה נחשב הוא) 'must be considered a beast'). Dahood, *Biblica* xliv (1963) 302.

58. בעד 'price', cf. Ar. *b'd* '(far) behind'. Prov. 6. 26 (τιμή, *pretium*). Driver, *VT* iv (1954) 243 ff.

59. בעי 'beggar', Syr. *ba'āyā*. Job 30. 24 (1 בְּעָי). Driver, *AJSL* lii (1935–6) 164.

60. בעל 'do, make', Ugar. Qoh. 8. 8 etc. See text, pp. 100 f. Dahood, *Biblica* xliii (1962) 361 f.

61. בצקלן 'fresh vegetation', Ugar. II Kings 4. 42; see text, pp. 26, 294. Driver, *CML*, p. 164 n.

62. בקע 'go away', Ar. *baqa'a* (?; see text, p. 166). Isa. 7. 6 ('make it go over to', ἀποστρέψομεν). Eitan, *HUCA* xii–xiii (1938) 58.

63. בקש 'magnify', Accad. *baqāšu* (= *rabū*, synon. list). Prov. 29. 10. Driver, *Biblica* xxxii (1951) 194, *JSS* xii (1967) 108.

64. ברד 'be cool', Ar. *bārid*. Isa. 32. 19. Reider, *HUCA* xxiv (1952–3) 88 f.

65. ברית 'splendour', Accad. *barāru* 'shine'. Isa. 42. 6 (|| אוֹר). See text, p. 144. Tur-Sinai, *JPOS* xiv (1936) 7.

66. ברח 'wound', Ar. *baraḥa* 'bruise'. Job 20. 24. Driver, *VTS* iii (1955) 81.

67. בריח 'primeval', Ar. *bāriḥ* 'past (of time)', cf. Eg. *b'ḥ*. Ug. *bṭn brḥ*, || Is. 27. 1, Job 26. 13. Albright, *BASOR* lxxxiii (1941) 39 f., n. 5.

109. הרוּן 'sexual desire', Ugar. *hrr*. Gen. 3. 16; see text, p. 286. Rabin, *ScrH* viii (1961) 390.

110. הרן 'pledge', Ar. *rahana*, cf. MH. Job 34. 32 (1 הַרְגִי). See text, p. 166. Tur-Sinai, *Job*, pp. 486 f.

111. הר 'stony tract', Ar. *ḥarrat*. Amos 1. 13. Reider, *VT* iv (1954) 279.

112. זבול A. 'princely estate', Ugar. Ps. 49. 15 (δόξα). Driver, *CML*, p. 149.

113. זבול B. 'throne-platform', Ugar. Albright, Robinson Festschr., p. 16.

114. זר (√זור) 'enemy', Accad. Ezek. 7. 21; Prov. 6. 1 ἐχθρῷ, see text, pp. 256 f. Driver, *Biblica* xxxv (1954) 148 f.

115. זמר 'protect', Ar. *ḍamara*. Exod. 15. 2; see text, pp. 29 f., 182. Winton Thomas, *ET* xlviii (1936–7) 478; *Record and Revelation*, pp. 395 f.

116. זנה 'be angry', Accad. *zenū*. Jud. 19. 2; see text, p. 286. Driver, *ETL* xxvi (1950) 348.

117. חבב 'pure ones', Accad. *ebēbum* 'be pure'. Deut. 33. 3, cf. no. 41. Miller, *HTR* lvii (1964) 241 ff.

118. חבר A. 'connect, inform', Ar. *ḥabar* (but 'companion' = *ḥbr*). Job 16. 4. Rosenthal, *Historiography*, p. 10 n. 2. Cf. no. 119.

119. חבר B. 'heap up', Ugar. *bt ḥbr* 'store-house'. Job 16. 4. Tur-Sinai, *Job*, pp. 262 f. Cf. no. 118.

חגר see no. 140.

120. חדל 'be plump', Ar. *ḥadula*. I Sam. 2. 5. Winton Thomas, *VTS* iv (1957) 14 f.

121. חוק 'gather', Accad. *ḥiāqum* 'mingle'. Prov. 8. 29. Driver, *Biblica* xxxii (1951) 178.

122. חוש 'worry', Accad. etc. Qoh. 2. 25. Ellermaier, *ZAW* lxxv (1963) 197–217.

123. חזה, חזות 'agreement', ESA *ḥdyt*. Isa. 28. 15, 18; see text, p. 230. Driver, *JTS* xxxviii (1937) 44. Also verb, cf. Ar. *ḥḏ*, Job 8. 17, *JTS* xl (1939) 391.

124. חזן 'magistrate', Accad. *ḥazannu*. Prov. 29. 18; see text, pp. 283 f. Driver, *WO* i. 235.

125. חטאת A. 'step, walk', Ar. *ḥaṭwa*. Job 14. 16; see text, pp. 142 n., 144. Eitan, pp. 38–42.

126. חטאת B. 'penury', Eth. *ḥāṭi'at*. Prov. 10. 16. See text, pp. 144, 166. Winton Thomas, *JTS* N.S. xv (1964) 295 f.

127. חלה A. 'be sorry, think', Eth. *ḥäläyä*. I Sam. 22. 8 (πονῶν); Jer. 5. 3. Driver, *JTS* xxix (1928) 392, *JQR* xxviii (1937–8) 101. Eitan, *HUCA* xii–xiii (1937–8) 82 f.

128. חלה B. 'be alone', Ar. *ḥalā*. Qoh. 5. 12 ('a singular evil'). Eitan, ibid., p. 62.

129. חלה C. 'adorn', Ar. ḥalā. Prov. 3. 35 (MT יְנַחֲלוּ), 14. 18 (MT נְחֲלוּ). Driver, Biblica xxxii (1951) 177.

130. חלל, חיל 'be troubled'. Ps. 55. 5, 109. 22, alternative forms, different semantic fields, both LXX ταράσσω; cf. text, p. 252. Kaddary, VT xiii (1963) 486–9.

131. חלם 'be healthy', Aram. ḥlm. Ps. 126. 1, so Tg. Strugnell, JTS N.S. vii (1956) 239–43.

132. חלק A. 'create', Ar. ḥlq. Am. 7. 4; see text, pp. 69, 260 f. Montgomery, JBL xxiii (1904) 95 f.; Driver, VTS iii (1955) 91.

133. חלק B. 'die, perish', Ugar. ḥlq. Ps. 5. 10, 12. 4. Dahood, Psalms, pp. 35, 73.

134. חלש 'reap', Pal. Ar. ḥalaša. Isa. 14. 12; see text, p. 276. Eitan, pp. 42–6.

135. מחנה 'protective siege-work' (not 'camp'), cf. MH חֲנוּת. Ezek. 4. 2. Driver, Biblica xxxv (1954) 148.

136. חפץ 'make straight, stretch'. Job 40. 17, Ps. 37. 23. Perles, Analekten, p. 76.

137. חקר 'despise', Ar. ḥaqara. Prov. 28. 11 (καταγνώσεται, bsr), 25. 27; see text, p. 258. Winton Thomas, JTS xxxviii (1937) 402 f., after Perles; Eitan, p. 7 n.

138. חרב 'deceitfulness, vain speech', Ar. ḥaraba (Dozy, i. 356). Ps. 59. 8; Jer. 25. 9 (ὀνειδισμός). See text, p. 116. Driver, JTS xxxiii (1932) 42 f.

139. חרבה 'palace', ESA mḥrb 'castle', Ar. miḥrāb 'pavilion' (contrast root ḥrb 'ruin'). Job 3. 14 etc. Daiches, JQR xx (1908) 637 ff.; Driver, ETL xxvi (1950) 349; but cf. Pope, Job, p. 31.

140. חרג (חגר) 'fear', Aram. חרגתא, Ps. 18. 46. But versions 'limp', read ויחגרו, as II Sam. 22. 46 = Aram., Syr. 'limp'. Gunkel, Psalmen, p. 73; Driver, HTR xxix (1936) 174.

141. חרה 'be angry', Ar. waḥar (so not from 'burn'). Rabin, ScrH viii (1961) 390 f.

142. חרם 'cut off', Accad. ḥarāmu. Isa. 11. 15; see text, p. 119. Driver, JTS xxxii (1931) 251.

143. חתא 'shatter', Ugar. ḥt'. Hab. 3. 6–7; see text, p. 190. Albright, BASOR lxxxii (1941) 47 n. 27; Robinson Festschr., pp. 11 f., 15.

144. טאטא 'pound (mud floor); annihilate', Ar. waṭi'a. Isa. 14. 23; see text, p. 56. Kopf, VT viii (1958) 174 f.

145. טבב 'know, announce', Syr., Ar., Eth. Prov. 15. 2; see text, pp. 171 f. Driver, Biblica xxxii (1951) 181.

146. טוב A. 'speech'. Hos. 14. 3 etc.; see text, pp. 16 f. Gordis, VT v (1955) 88–90.

330 INDEX OF EXAMPLES

188. לבשׁ A. 'linger', Ar. *labiṭa*. Isa. 14. 19. Eitan, *HUCA* xii–xiii (1938) 63.

189. לבשׁ B. 'draw near', Ar. *labisa* 'join closely'. Judges 6. 34 etc. Reider, *JJS* iii (1952) 79.

190. לג 'waves', Ar. *lujj* 'depth of sea'. Job 12. 23 (MT לַגּוֹיִם). Tur-Sinai, *Job*, p. 219.

191. להקה A. 'elder-company', Eth. *lhq*. I Sam. 19. 20, see text, pp. 25 f., 231 f., 267 n., 270 f. Driver, *JTS* xxix (1928) 394; Ullendorff, *VT* vi (1956) 194; Winton Thomas, *JTS* xlii (1941) 154 (Prov. 30. 17).

192. להקה B. 'company', Ar. *'ilḥāq* 'affiliation', with criticism of no. 191. Greenfield, *HUCA* xxix (1958) 212 ff.

193. לְמָדִים 'strings', MH (?). Isa. 8. 16. Tur-Sinai, *Job*, p. 240.

194. מגן 'powerful', Ar. *mājin* 'bold'. Ps. 47. 10; see text, pp. 241, 251. Driver, *JTS* xxxiii (1932) 44. Cf. Albright, *VTS* iii (1955) 10 ('beggar').

195. מֶדֶר 'wet clay', Eth. *mədr* 'earth'. Job 37. 17 (MT מִדְּרוֹם); see text, p. 190. Tur-Sinai, *Job*, p. 515.

196. מהיר 'skilled', Eth. *mähärä* 'teach'. Ps. 45. 2, Isa. 16. 5. See text, p. 295. Ullendorff, *VT* vi (1956) 195.

197. מחץ 'dip', Accad. *maḥāṣu*. Ps. 68. 24; see text, p. 192. Delitzsch, *Proleg.*, pp. 69 ff. Cf. no. 205.

198. מָטוּ 'war, campaign', ESA *mṭw*. Hab. 3. 9, 14. Albright, Robinson Festschr., p. 15.

199. מיד, מודד 'be shaken', Ar. *māda*. Hab. 3. 6 (ἐσαλεύθη); see text, p. 252. Driver, *ZAW* lii (1934) 54 f.

200. מכר 'counsel', Eth. Gen. 49. 5; see text, pp. 57, 270. Winton Thomas, *JTS* xxxvii (1936) 388 f.; Ullendorff, *VT* vi (1956) 194.

201. מלח 'be dark', Ar. *maliḥa* 'be grey'. Isa. 51. 6; see text, p. 252. Driver, *ETL* xxvi (1950) 349 f.

202. מלך A. 'advise', Aram. Hos. 8. 4; see text, pp. 188 f. Driver, Nötscher Festschr., p. 50. Cf. no. 306.

203. מלך B. 'take possession', Ar. Neh. 5. 7; see text, p. 188. Kopf, *VT* ix (1959) 261 f.

204. מעה 'multitude', Ar. *ma'iyya* 'company'. Isa. 48. 19. Gray, *Legacy*, p. 192.

205. מצח 'tread', Ugar. *mṣḥ*. Ps. 68. 24 (l תמצח; MT תמחץ is graphic error caused by ימחץ in v. 22). Reider, *HUCA* xxiv (1952–3) 101. Cf. no. 197.

206. משׁח A. 'measure, extend', MH. Ezek. 28. 14. Driver, *JTS* xli (1940) 169 f.

207. משׁח B. 'mar', Ar. *masaḥa, masīḥ* 'ugly'. Isa. 52. 14 Qumran; see text, p. 285. Guillaume, *JBL* lxxvi (1957) 41 f.

208. מֹתֶן 'strength', MH and Ar. *matuna*. Qoh. 7. 7. (MT מַתְנָה, εὐτονία, *robur*); see text, p. 91 n. Driver, *VT* iv (1954) 229 f.

209. נגד 'blow', Aram. Job 10. 17. Tur-Sinai, *Job*, pp. 181 f.

210. נד 'fire', Eth. *näddä*. Isa. 17. 11. Eitan, *HUCA* xii–xiii (1938) 65. Cf. no. 212.

211. נחל 'sift', Ar. *naḥala*, Accad., Syr. Ps. 82. 8. Driver, *HTR* xxix (1936) 187.

212. נחלה 'destruction', Eth. *nəhlä* 'collapse'. Isa. 17. 11. Eitan, cf. no. 210.

213. נטוש 'clash (in battle)', Ar. *waṭasa*, *waṭīs*. Prov. 17. 14 (μάχη), I Sam. 4. 2; see text, p. 257. Driver, *Biblica* xxxii (1951) 182.

214. נכר 'acquire, sell', Ugar. *nkr*. I Sam. 23. 7 (πέπρακεν); see text, p. 267 n. Hos. 3. 2. Gray, *Legacy*, p. 190.

215. נמה 'bring tidings', Ar. *namā*. Isa. 41. 27; see text, pp. 182, 193. Guillaume, *JBL* lxxvi (1957) 40 f.

216. נסג 'forge', Ar. *nasaja*. Mic. 2. 6; see text, p. 15. Reider, *VT* iv (1954) 280.

217. נער 'sparrow', Ar. *nuġar*. Job 40. 29. Winton Thomas, *VT* xiv (1964) 114 ff.; cf. Gordis, ibid., 491–4.

218. נצה 'be joined', Ar. *naṣā*. Lam. 4. 15 (ἀνήφθησαν); see text, pp. 262 f. Driver, *ZAW* lii (1934) 308; Winton Thomas, *Record and Revelation*, p. 396.

219. נשא 'utter, pronounce', Accad. *našū* 'take oath'. Isa. 42. 2, 11, and מָשָׂא. Tsevat, *HUCA* xxix (1958) 119.

220. נָשָׁר, נַשָּׁר 'herald', Ar. *naššār*. Hos. 8. 1, Job 39. 25; see text, pp. 26 f. Tur-Sinai, *Job*, p. 551.

221. נתר 'tear; hop, leap'. Accad. *nutturu*. Hab. 3. 6 etc. Driver, Robinson Festschr., pp. 70 ff., *VT* iv (1954) 241; and full discussion in Emerton, *ZAW* lxxvi (1964) 191 ff. See text, p. 290.

222. סדר 'rays of light', Ar. *sadira*. Job 10. 22 (φέγγος); see text, p. 242. Driver, *VTS* iii (1955) 76 f.

223. סוד 'chieftaincy', Ar. *sūd*. Ps. 25. 14; see text, p. 251. Driver, *JBL* lv (1936) 102, *ETL* xxvi (1950) 345.

224. סכות 'pole' (cultic symbol), Talm. סכתא. Am. 5. 26; see text, p. 277. Hirschberg, *VT* xi (1961) 375.

225. סכן 'care for', not Accad. *šaknu* 'governor' but rel. Ar. *zakina* 'be familiar', MH סַכָּנָה 'danger'. I Kings 1. 4, Qoh. 10. 9. Rabin, *ScrH* viii (1961) 395.

226. ספסג 'glaze', Ugar., Hittite. Prov. 26. 23 (MT כסף סיגים); see text, pp. 219 f. Ginsberg, *BASOR* xcviii (1945) 21.

227. מספר 'limit, boundary', Ar., Aram. סְפַר. Deut. 32. 8 (‖ גבלת). Zimmermann, *JQR* N.S. xxix (1938–9) 241 f.

228. עַד 'time'. καιρός at Jer. 11. 14, Isa. 30. 8, 64. 8, Ezek. 22. 4, 30; see text, p. 247. Driver, *WO* i. 412; *CML*, p. 140.

229. עדה A. 'hostility', Ar. *ʿdw*. Job 10. 17 (MT עֶדְיֵךְ). Pope, *Job*, p. 79, following Ehrlich.

230. עדה B. 'prime', Ar. *ġdw* 'morning, early'. Ps. 103. 5 (|| נעורייכי). Driver, *JTS* xxxvi (1935) 155.

231. עוד 'go round', Eth. *ʿodä*. Job 25. 5 (point עָד). Driver, *AJSL* lii (1935–6) 161.

232. עזב A. 'help', Eth. *ʿäzzäbä*. Jer. 49. 25; see text, p. 140. Driver, *JQR* xxviii (1937–8) 126.

233. עזב B. 'be agreeable', Ar. *ʿaduba*. Job 9. 27; see text, p. 141. Driver, *VTS* iii (1955) 76.

234. עזי 'patience', Ar. *ʿazā* (*ʿazw*). Ex. 15. 2; see text, pp. 29 f. Rabin, *ScrH* viii (1961) 387. Or 'warrior', Ar. *ġazi*; Gaster and Winton Thomas, *ET* xlviii (1936–7) 45, 478; xlix (1937–8) 189.

235. עזר A. 'be valiant', Ugar. *ġzr*. I Chr. 12. 1; see text, pp. 139 f. Driver, *CML*, p. 142.

236. עזר B. 'justify', Ar. *ʿadara* 'excuse'. Isa. 50. 7, 9 (|| מצדיק); see text, pp. 139 f. Eitan, *HUCA* xii–xiii (1938) 81.

237. עזר C. 'hinder', Ar. *ʿazara* 'rebuke'. Job 30. 13; see text, p. 139. Driver, *AJSL* lii (1935–6) 163.

238. עזר D. 'be copious', Ar. *ġazura*. Zech. 1. 15; see text, p. 140. Eitan, p. 8.

239. עטה 'give', Ar. *ʾaʿṭī*. Ps. 84. 7 (δώσει); see text, p. 249. Rabin, *West-Arabian*, p. 40, n. 5 and p. 32.

240. עיט 'den', Ar. *ġayiṭ*. Jer. 12. 9; see text, pp. 128 f., 153, 235. Driver, *PEQ*, Apr. 1955, 139. Cf. no. 266.

241. עין, עון 'company, group'. Hos. 10. 10; see text, p. 226. Wernberg-Møller, p. 59; Driver, *Judaean Scrolls*, p. 435.

242. עיר A. 'revile', Eth. *täʿäyyärä*. Job 3. 8; see text, p. 125. Driver, *VTS* iii (1955) 72.

243. עיר B. 'invasion', Ar. *ġāra*. Jer. 15. 8; see text, p. 125. Driver, *JQR* xxviii (1937–8) 113.

244. עיר C. 'fire', Ar. *waġara* 'be hot'. Hos. 7. 4; see text, p. 126. Wutz, p. 312. Cf. Nyberg, *Hosea*, p. 52.

245. עיר D. 'inmost recesses', Ugar. *ġr*. II Kings 10. 25; see text, p. 126. Gray, *Kings*, p. 507.

246. עיר (עַרִים) E. 'protectors, gods', Ugar. *ġyr*. Mic. 5. 13 etc.; see text, pp. 126, 153 n. Dahood, *Psalms*, pp. 55 f. Cf. no. 253.

247. עיר F. 'bore', Ar. *ġāra* 'sink deep', *ġawr* 'depth'. Isa. 50. 4; see text, p. 126. Driver, *JTS* xli (1940) 164.

266. צבוע 'hyena', Ar. *ḍabuʿ*. Jer. 12. 9 (ὑαίνης); see text, pp. 128, 235. Driver, *PEQ*, Apr. 1955, p. 139. Cf. no. 240.

267. צור 'midst', Accad. *ṣurru* 'heart'. Ezek. 21. 25 (ἐν μέσῳ αὐτῆς). Driver, *JTS* xli (1940) 169. Cf. Jer. 49. 13 (LXX 30. 7).

268. צח 'sun'. Ar. *ḍiḥḥ*, Eth. *ḍäḥay*. Isa. 18. 4. Eitan, *HUCA* xii–xiii (1937–8) 65 f. Cf. no. 23.

269. ציץ 'salt', Accad., Ugar. gloss *ṣi-ṣu-ma*. Jer. 48. 9. Moran, *Biblica* xxxix (1958) 69 ff.

270. צלצל 'boat', Aram. צלצלא. Isa. 18. 1 (|| כלי גמא); Job 40. 31 (θ' πλοίοις). Driver, Robinson Festschr., p. 56.

271. צפה 'arrange', Ar. *ṣaffa*. Isa. 21. 5. Eitan, *HUCA* xii–xiii (1937–8) 67. Cf. no. 272.

272. צפית 'guest', Ar. *ḍayf*. Isa. 21. 5, cf. no. 271. Eitan, as no. 271.

273. צפון A. 'island', cf. צוף 'float', Ugar. Land floats over void. Job 26. 7. Tur-Sinai, *Job*, pp. 380 f.

274. צפון B. 'hiding-place'. Job 37. 22. Tur-Sinai, *Job*, p. 517.

275. צרה 'shrill cry', Ar. *ṣarra*, *ṣarīr*. Jer. 4. 31 (|| קול; στεναγμός), 48. 5 (LXX 31. 5); see text, pp. 279 f. Driver, *JBL* lv (1936) 105, *JQR* xxviii (1937–8) 123.

276. קבוץ 'fixing; statue', Syr. *qbāʿā*. Isa. 57. 13; see text, p. 122. Driver, *JTS* xxxvi (1935) 294.

277. קהל 'forget', Ar. *jahila* 'be ignorant', Amarna *qālu* 'withdraw, neglect'. Job 11. 10; see text, p. 162. Tur-Sinai, *Job*, p. 194.

278. קו, קי 'infant' (קיא 'vomit'). Job 22. 20 (קי מגו l), cf. Isa. 28. 10. Tur-Sinai, *Job*, p. 345.

279. מקום A. 'opposition', Ar. *maqāma* 'combat'. Nah. 1. 8. Driver, *JTS* xxxvi (1935) 300 f.

280. מקום B. 'grave', Phoen. *mqm*. Qoh. 8. 10; see text, p. 292. Dahood, *Biblica* xliii (1962) 360.

281. קור 'dig', Ar. *qāra* 'cut a round hole'. Prov. 12. 27; see text, pp. 28 f. Eitan, pp. 25 ff.

282. קטן 'household', Ar. *qaṭana* 'reside'. Isa. 22. 24. Eitan, *HUCA* xii–xiii (1938) 68 f.

283. קלע 'uproot', Ar. *qalaʿa*. Jer. 10. 18; see text, p. 108. Driver, *JQR* xxviii (1937–8) 107.

284. קן 'strength', Eg. *qny* 'strong', *qnt* 'strength'. Job 29. 18. Driver, *VTS* iii (1955) 85.

285. קנה 'shoulder-joint', Ugar. *qn*. Job 31. 22. Driver, *CML*, p. 144.

286. קצף 'be sad, vexed', Syr. *qṣap*. II Kings 3. 27; see text, p. 122. Driver, *JTS* xxxvi (1935) 293.

287. קְרָא 'follow', Ar. qarā (qrw). Isa. 41. 25 (‖ אָתָה). Eitan, HUCA xii–xiii (1938) 77.

288. קרה 'hold feast, invite to feast', Ugar. qry. Exod. 3. 18; see text, pp. 102 f. Cf. no. 180.

289. ראה 'drink' (= רוה). Prov. 23. 31 etc.; see text, pp. 257 f. Driver, Biblica xxxii (1951) 187.

290. רב A. 'showers', Ugar. rb, rbb. Job 36. 28. Driver, CML, p. 155.

291. רב B. 'arrow' (רבה 'shoot'). Am. 7. 4 (l לְרָבֵי אֵשׁ). Cf. Job 16. 13 רַבָּיו, λόγχαις. Driver, JTS xli (1940) 171 f.

292. רב C. 'weak, afraid', Ar. rwb. Job 4. 3; see text, pp. 134 f. Tur-Sinai, Job, pp. 76 f.

293. יריב 'great', Syr. yaributā 'size'. Hos. 5. 13; see text, p. 123. Driver, JTS xxxvi (1935) 295.

294. רְבַע 'dust', Accad. turbu'u 'dust spiral'. Num. 23. 10; see text, pp. 11 n., 270. Ginsberg, ZAW li (1933) 309.

295. תרבעת 'dust cloud', Accad. As no. 294. Albright, JBL lxiii (1944) 213.

296. רזיל 'wickedness', Ar. raḏīl 'base'. Isa. 24. 16. Rabin, ScrH viii (1961) 386.

297. ריב 'trembling', Accad. rību. Job 33. 19. Dhorme, Job, p. 454.

298. רכב 'gather', cf. MH 'graft, join, connect'. Ps. 68. 5, cf. νεφεληγερέτα. Ullendorff, VT vi (1956) 194 f.

299. תָּרְמָה 'treachery', Accad. turmum. Judges 9. 31; see text, p. 216. Dossin, OBL, i (1957) 163–7, but cf. Gevirtz, JNES xvii (1958) 59 f. (√תרם).

300. רמם 'rebuild, repair', Ugar. trmm. Ezr. 9. 9, Prov. 11. 11. Driver, CML, p. 153.

301. רעב 'be bewitched, fear', Ar. ra'aba (cf. רעב 'hunger' = Ar. raġiba 'desire'). Job 18. 12. Driver, ZAW lxv (1958) 260.

302. רעה 'thought', Syr. r'ā. Isa. 44. 28; see text, pp. 281 f. Driver, JTS xxxvi (1935) 82.

303. רשע 'rich', Ar. rassaġa, rasīġ (Lane, p. 1080 c). Job 24. 6; see text, p. 145. Guillaume, Hooke Festschr., p. 116.

304. שאה 'wish', Ar. šā'a. Gen. 4. 7 (MT שְׁאָת). Rabin, ScrH viii (1961) 399.

305. משׁה 'place for sheep', analogy of Ar. mas'ada 'place to expect lions' etc. Exod. 12. 4. Rabin, ScrH viii (1961) 394.

306. שׁוּר, הֵשִׁיר 'obtain advice', Ar. šwr, 'ašāra. Hos. 8. 4; see text, pp. 165, 188 f. Source as no. 202.

307. שׂחה 'wash, flood' (not 'swim'), Syr. Ps. 6. 7. Driver, JTS xxxvi (1935) 147. Am. 4. 13 (l וּמַגִּיר לָאֲדָמָה מֵי שָׂחוּ 'pours on the earth the flood waters', Tur-Sinai, Lashon, ii. 403 f.

308. שׂכל 'form, beauty', Ar. šakl. I Sam. 25. 3; see text, pp. 244 f. Perles, *JQR* N.S. xvii (1926–7) 233.

309. שׂפק 'abound', MH. Isa. 2. 6 (‖ מלא); see text, pp. 232 f. Winton Thomas, *ZAW* lxxv (1963) 88 ff.

310. שׂפת 'decree, ordain', denom. from שׂפה 'lip'. Ps. 22. 16, Isa. 26. 12; see text, p. 85. Beeston, *VT* viii (1958) 216 f.; cf. Ullendorff, *VT* vi (1956) 196 f.

311. שׂבם 'muzzle', Ar. šabama, Ugar. šbm. Ps. 68. 23 (‖ אֶשָּׁבֵּם מְצוּלֹת יָם). Dahood, *JBL* lxxx (1961) 270 f.; Miller, *HTR* lvii (1964) 240.

312. שׂבר A. 'attend to', Ar. ṯabara 'apply oneself with zeal'. Neh. 2. 13, 15 (συντρίβων). MT שׂבר. Driver, *JTS* xxxv (1934) 382 f.

313. שׂבר B. 'measure by the span', Ar. šabara. Job 38. 10. Guillaume, Hooke Festschr., p. 123.

314. שׂדד 'expel', Eth. sädädä. Prov. 19. 26. Winton Thomas, *VTS* iii (1955) 289.

315. שׂדי, שׂדה 'pour out, downpour', Aram. Ezek. 1. 24, II Sam. 1. 21; see text, p. 235. Gordis, *JTS* xli (1940) 34 ff.; Driver, ibid., 168, and *VT* iv (1954) 239 f.

316. שׂיב 'run about', Ar. sāba (y); cf. שׂוב 'return' = ṯāba (w). Jer. 8. 6; see text, pp. 242 f. Driver, *JQR* xxviii (1937–8) 105.

317. שׂיל 'governor, prince'. Gen. 49. 10; see text, pp. 120 f. Moran, *Biblica* xxxix (1958) 405–25, has full discussion.

318. שׂיר 'travel', Syr. šyartā 'caravan', Ar. sāra. Ps. 138. 5; Ezek. 27. 25. Driver, *JTS* xxxv (1934) 388.

319. שׂכב 'pour', Ar. sakaba. Job 38. 37; see text, p. 137. Orlinsky, *JBL* lxiii (1944) 19–44.

320. שׂכח A. 'be paralysed', Ar. kasiḥa by metathesis. Ps. 137. 5; see text, pp. 48, 152. Eitan, *JBL* xlvii (1928) 193 ff.

321. שׂכח B. 'droop, wilt', Ugar. ṯkḥ. Ps. 137. 5; cf. no. 320. Driver, *CML*, p. 151; but cf. Pope, *JSS* xi (1966) 240.

322. שׂכת 'ship', Ugar. ṯkt, Eg. škti. Isa. 2. 16; see text, pp. 280 f. Driver, Robinson Festschr., pp. 52 f.

323. שׂלג 'soapwort', MH אשׂלג. Job 9. 30; see text, p. 110. Pope, *Job*, p. 72.

324. שׂמח 'be kind, clement', Ar. samuḥa. Hos. 7. 3. Nyberg, *Hosea*, p. 46.

325. שׂמר A. 'cultivate'. Hos. 4. 10 f.

326. שׂמר B. 'rage', Accad. šamāru. Am. 1. 11.

327. שׂמר C. 'cast out, reject', Syr. šmr. Ps. 37. 28.
For 325–7 see text, pp. 119 f., 141 f. Driver, *JTS* xxxv (1934) 384 ff. For 327, also Tur-Sinai, *Job*, p. 240.

328. שׂנה 'be eminent, of high rank', Ar. *sny, sanā*'. Prov. 24. 21 etc.
Eitan, pp. 10 f.; Winton Thomas, *ZAW* lii (1934) 236 ff., *VTS*
iii (1955) 286.

329. משׁנה 'equivalent', Accad. *mištannu* (not 'twice as much'). Deut. 15.
18; Jer. 16. 18. Tsevat, *HUCA* xxix (1958) 125 f.

330. שׂעה 'betake oneself', Ar. *saʿā* 'move quickly'. I Sam. 14. 32 (MT
(וישע)); see text, p. 98. Reider, *HUCA* xxiv (1952–3) 85.

331. שׁרשׂ 'be angry', Ar. *šarisa* 'be vicious'. Job 5. 3. Tur-Sinai, *Job*,
p. 94.

332. שׁתע 'fear', Phoen., Ugar. *ṯtʿ*. Isa. 41. 10; see text, pp. 180, 233 n.,
294 f. Greenfield, *HUCA* xxix (1958) 226–8.

333. תָּהֳלָה 'folly', Eth. *tätäḥälä* 'wander', Dillmann, col. 552. Job 4. 18.
Pope, *Job*, p. 37.

334. תוה 'wander in mind', Ar. *tāha*. Isa. 44. 9, read as verb. Eitan,
HUCA xii–xiii (1938) 78.

תנן see no. 45.

INDEX OF BIBLICAL PASSAGES

Ordering and numbering are as in the Hebrew text. Arabic figures refer to pages of the text; italic figures to numbers of the Index of Examples.

Z 2

INDEX OF SUBJECTS

Arabic figures refer to pages of the text; italic figures to numbers of the Index of Examples.

PRINTED IN GREAT BRITAIN
AT THE UNIVERSITY PRESS, OXFORD
BY VIVIAN RIDLER
PRINTER TO THE UNIVERSITY